INTRODUCTION

It is estimated that over 60,000 words are included in the pattern words which comprise the pattern words included in this book.

All words have been carefully selected from the English language. Not only do the pattern words include virtually every common pattern word in English up to eight-letters in length, but thousands of words infrequently and rarely used are also included.

Without the use of a computer this compilation would have been impossible. Every word has been checked against its pattern and every pattern has been alphabetized.

Many days and countless hours have been spent in collecting, checking, and double checking the words in this book. If this book assists you in solving even one cryptogram, my time and efforts will have been worthwhile.

Sheila Carlisle

PATTERN WORDS

THREE-LETTERS TO EIGHT-LETTERS IN LENGTH

ISBN: 0-89412-135-9   (soft cover)
ISBN: 0-89412-136-7   (library bound)

AEGEAN PARK PRESS
P.O. Box 2837
Laguna Hills, California 92654
(714) 586-8811

Manufactured in the United States of America

Pattern words are words which contain repeated letters. The pattern of a word is obtained by replacing the letters of the word with successive letters of the alphabet, repeating when necessary those letters which occur more than once in the word. For example, the word BOOK is a pattern word because it contains the repeated letter O. Its pattern is ABBC. Likewise, the word SUCCESS is a pattern word because it contains not only the letter S which occurs three times, but the letter C which occurs twice. Its pattern is ABCCDAA.

In the compilation of pattern words that follows, patterns are sorted first by length and then by pattern. Knowing a pattern, all words which fit into that pattern can easily be found by searching alphabetically for the desired pattern.

THREE-LETTER PATTERN WORDS

AAB EEG EEK EEL

ABA AHA AKA AMA ASA AVA BAB BIB BOB BUB DAD DID DUD EKE EVE EWE EYE GAG GIG GOG
HUH MUM NUN OHO OXO PAP PEP PIP POP PUP SIS SOS SYS TAT TIT TOT TUT WOW

ABB ADD ALL ASS BEE BOO COO EBB EGG ELL ERR FEE GEE GOO ILL INN LEE LOO MOO NEE
ODD OFF PEE POO ROO SEE TEE TOO VEE WEE WOO ZEE ZOO

FOUR-LETTER PATTERN WORDS

AABC EELS EENY OOPS OOZE OOZY   **ABAA** DODD LOLL LULL SASS

ABAB COCO DODO ISIS LULU MAMA MIMI MUMU NANA PAPA TETE TUTU YOYO

ABAC ADAM AFAR AGAR AJAR AJAX ALAN ALAS AMAH AMAN ANAL ARAB ATAP AWAY AYAH BABE
BABS BABY BIBS BOBS BUBS COCK DADO DADS DUDE DUDS EDEN EKED EKER EKES EVEN EVER
EVES EWES EXEC EXES EYED EYES FIFE GAGE GAGS GIGS GOGS IBID IBIS IRIS LILA LILT
LILY LOLA MEMO MIME MOMS MUMS PAPS PEPS PIPE PIPS POPE POPS PUPS RARE RORY SASH
TATE TATS TITS TOTE TOTS TUTS VIVA VIVE VIVO WOWS

ABBA ANNA BOOB DEED ELLE NOON POOP SEES TOOT

ABBC ABBE ABBY ADDS ALLY AMMO ANNE ANNO BEEF BEEN BEEP BEER BEES BEET BOOK BOOM
BOON BOOR BOOS BOOT COOK COOL COON COOP COOS COOT DEEM DEEP DEER DEES DOOM DOOR
EBBS EBBY EDDY EGGS EGGY ELLA ELLS EMMA ERRS FEED FEEL FEES FEET FOOD FOOL FOOT
GEES GEEZ GOOD GOOF GOOK GOON GOOP HEED HEEL HOOD HOOF HOOK HOOP HOOT IFFY ILLS
INNS JEEP JEER KEEL KEEN KEEP KOOP LAAP LEEK LEER LEES LOOK LOOM LOON LOOP LOOT
MEEK MEET MOOD MOON MOOR MOOS MOOT NEED NOOK ODDS PEED PEEK PEEL PEER PEES POOF
POOH POOL POOR REED REEF REEK REEL ROOF ROOK ROOM ROOS ROOT SEED SEEK SEEM SEEN
SEEP SEER SOOK SOON SOOT TEED TEEM TEEN TEES TOOK TOOL VEER VEES WEED WEEK WEEP
WOOD WOOF WOOL WOOS ZEES ZOOM ZOOS

ABCA AGRA AGUA AIDA ALMA AQUA AREA ARIA ASIA AURA BARB BLAB BLEB BLOB BLUB BOMB
BULB CHIC CROC DEAD DIED DOWD DYAD DYED EASE EAVE EDGE EIRE ELSE ELVE ERIE EYRE
FIEF GANG GLUG GONG GREG GROG HASH HATH HIGH HUSH KICK KINK KIRK KONK MAIM NEON
NOUN OHIO OLEO OLIO OSLO PALP PIMP PLOP POMP PREP PROP PULP PUMP REAR ROAR SAGS
SANS SAPS SAWS SAYS SEAS SETS SEWS SHES SINS SIPS SIRS SITS SKIS SOBS SODS SONS
SOTS SOUS SOWS SPAS SUBS SUDS SUES SUMS SUNS SUPS TACT TAFT TART TEAT TENT TEST
TEXT THAT TIFT TILT TINT TORT TOUT TROT TUFT TWIT URDU WHEW

ABCB AGOG ANON ASKS ASPS BOLO BOYO BOZO CASA CEDE CERE COHO DATA DENE ENON FETE
FIJI GAZA GENE GURU HERE HOBO HOMO JAVA KIWI KUDU LAMA LAVA LOBO LOCO LOGO LOTO
LUAU MAJA MANA MAYA MERE METE MIDI MONO NAPA NISI ONAN PARA PELE PETE POGO POLO
RAGA RAJA RAMA SAGA SALA SARA SHAH SOHO SOLO STET TAPA TARA TELE TIKI USES WERE
ZAMA ZULU

ABCC AGEE BALL BANN BASS BATT BELL BESS BILL BOLL BONN BOSS BUFF BULL BUSS BUTT
BUZZ CALL CELL CESS COBB CUFF CULL CUSS DELL DILL DOLL DUFF DULL FALL FELL FILL
FIZZ FLEE FREE FULL FUSS FUZZ GAFF GALL GHEE GILL GLEE GUFF GULL HALL HELL HILL

HISS HUFF HULL JAZZ JEFF JELL JESS JIFF JILL KILL KISS KNEE LAPP LASS LESS LOSS
LYNN MALL MASS MESS MIFF MILL MISS MITT MOLL MOSS MUFF MULL MUSS MUTT NELL NESS
NULL PALL PASS PILL PISS POLL PUFF PULL PURR PUSS PUTT RAZZ RIFF RILL ROLL ROSS
RUFF RUSS SELL SHOO SILL TALL TASS TELL THEE TIFF TILL TOFF TOLL TOSS TREE TYEE
WALL WATT WEBB WELL WHEE WILL YEGG YELL

FIVE-LETTER PATTERN WORDS

AABAC EELED EELER   **AABCA** EERIE   **AABCB** LLAMA

AABCD AARON OOMPH OOZED OOZES   **ABAAB** MAMMA NANNA

ABAAC BOBBY BUBBY DADDY LOLLS LOLLY LULLS LULLY MAMMY MOMMA MOMMY MUMMY NANNY
NINNY NONNY PAPPY PEPPY PIPPY POPPA POPPY PUPPY SASSY SISSY TATTY TITTY TUTTI

ABABC CACAO COCOA DODOS JUJUB LILIS LULUS MAMAS MIMIC PAPAL PAPAS TATAR TETES
TUTUS VIVID

ABACA RARER   **ABACB** MAMBA PAPUA   **ABACC** AMASS TATOO

ABACD ABACK ABAFT ABASE ABASH ABASK ABATE ADAGE ADAMS ADAPT AGAIN AGAPE AGARS
AGASP AGAST AGATE AGAZE ALACK ALAMO ALARM AMAHS AMANI AMAZE ANALS APACE APART
ARABS AVAIL AVAST AWAFT AWAIT AWAKE AWARD AWARE AWARP AWASH AWAVE AWAYS AYAHS
BABEL BABES BABIE BEBOP BIBLE CACHE CACTI CECIL CICAD COCKS COCKY CYCAD CYCLE
DADOS DIDOS DIDST DODGE DODGY DUDES EDEMA EJECT ELECT ELEGY ENEMA ENEMY ERECT
EVENS EVENT EVERY EXERT EYERS FIFED FIFER FIFES FIFTH FIFTY GAGED GAGER GAGES
GAGLE IBIDS ICIER ICILY ICING IDIOM IDIOT ILIAC ILIAD ILIUM IRISH IVIES LILAC
LILAS LILTS MAMBO MAMIE MEMOS MIMED MIMEO MIMER MIMES MUMPS NANCY NANDI NINES
NINTH OBOES ODORS ODOUR OVOID OZONE PAPER PAPES PIPED PIPER PIPES PIPET PIPEY
POPES PUPAE PUPAL PUPAS PUPIL REROW RERUB RERUN RURAL SASHY SISAL SUSAN TATER
TETCH TETON TETRA TITAN TITHE TITLE TITRE TITUS TOTAL TOTED TOTEM TOTER TOTES
TUTOR UNUSE USUAL USURE USURP USURY VIVRE WOWED

ABBAC ALLAH ALLAN ALLAY AMMAN ANNAS ARRAY ASSAM ASSAY ATTAP ATTAR BOOBS BOOBY
DEEDS DEEDY EBBED EGGED EGGER ELLEN ELLES EMMET ERRED ESSEX NOONS ORROW OTTOS
PEEPS PEEPY POOPS TEETH TOOTH TOOTS

ABBCA EMMIE HOOCH SEEDS SEEKS SEEMS SEEPS SEETS SOOKS SOOTS

ABBCB ADDED ASSES BEEVE ERROR GEESE   **ABBCC** COOEE

ABBCD ABBES ABBEY ABBOT ADDER ADDLE AFFIX ALLEY ALLOT ALLOW ALLOY AMMOS ANNEX
ANNOY ANNUL APPLE APPLY ARROW ASSET ATTIC BEECH BEEFS BEEFY BEEPS BEERS BEERY
BEETS BEETY BOOED BOOKS BOOKY BOOMS BOOMY BOONE BOONS BOORS BOOST BOOTH BOOTS
BOOTY BOOZE BOOZY COOED COOER COOEY COOKS COOKY COOLS COOLY COOMB COONS COOPS
COOTS DEEMS DEEPS DEERS DOOMS DOORS DOOZY EMMAS EMMYS ENNUI ESSAY FEELS FOODS
FOOLS FOOTS FOOTY GOODS GOODY GOOEY GOOFS GOOFY GOOKS GOONS GOONY GOOSE HEEDS
HEELS HOODS HOODY HOOED HOOFS HOOKS HOOKY HOOPS HOOTS HOOVE INNED INNER ISSUE
JEEPS JEERS KEELS KEEPS LAAPS LEECH LEEDS LEEKS LEEKY LEERS LEERY LOOFA LOOKS
LOOKY LOOMS LOONS LOONY LOOPS LOOPY LOOSE LOOTS MEETS MOOCH MOODS MOODY MOOED

MOONS MOONY MOORS MOOSE MOOTS NEEDS NEEDY NOOKS NOOKY NOOSE OCCUR ODDER ODDLY
OFFAL OFFEN OFFER ORRIS OTTER PEEKS PEEKY PEELS PEERS POOCH POOLS POORS REEDS
REEDY REEFS REEFY REEKS REEKY REELS ROOFS ROOFY ROOKS ROOKY ROOMS ROOMY ROOST
ROOTS ROOTY SEEDY SEEPY SOOTH SOOTY TEEMS TEENS TEENY TOOLS UDDER UPPED UPPER
UTTER VEERS WEEDS WEEDY WEEKS WEENY WEEPS WEEPY WOODS WOODY WOOED WOOER WOOES
WOOFS WOOLS WOOLY WOOPS WOOSH WOOZY ZOOMS

ABCAA EMCEE SWISS   **ABCAB** ALGAL EDGED MIAMI ONION SENSE SHUSH VALVA VERVE

ABCAC EASES ENDED TESTS

ABCAD ABEAM AHEAD ALGAE ALIAS ALMAS ALTAR ANZAC APIAN AQUAS AREAS ARIAS ARYAN
ASIAN ASWAY ATLAS AURAL AURAS AVIAN AXIAL BARBS BIMBO BLABS BLEBS BLOBS BOMBE
BOMBS BRIBE BULBS BULBY CATCH CHECK CHICK CHICO CHICS CHOCK CHUCK CINCH CIRCA
CLACK CLICK CLOCK CLUCK COACH COACT CONCH COUCH CRACK CRICK CROCK CROCS CUZCO
CZECH DANDY DAWDY DEADS DILDO DIODE DOWDY DYADS EAGER EARED EASED EASEL EASER
EATEN EATER EAVED EAVES EDGER EDGES EGRET EIDER EISEL ELDER ELVEN ELVES EMBED
EMBER ENDER ENTER ERMES ESTER ETHEL ETHER EXCEL EXPEL EYRES FIEFS GANGS GAUGE
GLUGS GONGS GORGE GOUGE GROGS GUNGE HIGHS HIGHT IMPIS INDIA INDIO IONIC KHAKI
KICKY KINKS KINKY KIRKS KONKS KYAKS LADLE LAXLY LISLE LOWLY MAIMS MARMS MYOMA
NEONS NOUNS ORION OXBOW PALPS PIMPS PLOPS POMPS PREPS PROPS PULPS PULPY PUMPS
REARM REARS REDRY RETRY ROARS SHIST SLASH SLOSH SLUSH SMASH SOUSE SPASM SQUSH
STASH SUDSY SWASH SWISH TACTS TARTS TASTE TASTY TEATS TENTH TENTS TESTY TEXTS
THATS THETA TILTH TILTS TILTY TINTS TINTY TOITY TORTE TORTS TOUTS TRITE TROTH
TROTS TRUTH TUFTS TUFTY TWITS UNCUT UNDUE UNDUG UNGUM UNPUT UPCUT URDUS VALVE
VULVA WHEWS

ABCBA CIVIC DEWED KAYAK LEVEL MADAM RADAR REFER ROTOR SAGAS SARAS SEXES SHAHS
SOHOS SOLOS TENET

ABCBB LEVEE MELEE PEWEE SETEE TEPEE

ABCBC CASAS CEDED QUEUE SALAL SLYLY YESES

ABCBD ACOCK BAHAI BANAL BASAL BEGEM BEGET BERET BESET BEVEL BEZEL BOLOS BORON
BOSOM BOSON BOZOS CABAL CANAL CARAT CEDER CEDES CERES CIVIL COHOE COHOS COLON
COLOR COMOX CUTUP DALAI DATAL DEFER DESEX DETER DIGIT DIXIE DONOR DRURY FARAD
FATAL FAVAS FECES FETED FETES FEVER FEWER FIJIS FINIS GALAH GENES GURUS HEMES
HERES HEWED HEWER HEXED HEXER HEXES HOBOS HONOR HUMUS INANE JAPAN JAVAS JEWEL
KARAT KEYED KEYER KILIM KIWIS KUDUS LAMAS LANAI LAVAS LEGER LEPER LEVEN LEVER
LICIT LIMIT LIPID LIVID LOGOS LOTOS LUPUS MACAO MACAW MADAN MALAY MASAI MAYAN
MAYAS MEGER METED METER METES MEWED MEWER MEWES MONOS MORON MOTOR MUCUS NASAL
NATAL NAVAL NAWAB NEVER NEWEL NEWER PAEAN PAGAN PALAY PELES PETER PETES PIXIE
PIXIS POGOS POLOI POLOS RAGAS RAJAH RAJAS RAMAS RANAS REBEL REGET RENEG RENEW
REPEL RESET RESEW RESEX REVEL REWED REWET RIGID ROBOT RUFUS SALAD SARAH SATAN
SEDER SEMEN SEVEN SEVER SEWED SEWER SEXED SEXER SIPID SODOM SOLON STATE SUNUP
TAPAS TARAS TASAR TIBIA TIMID VEXED VEXER VEXES VIGIL VINIA VINIC VISIT VIZIR
WEBER YEMEN ZULUS

ABCCA SELLS SHOOS SILLS SKIIS TWEET YAPPY YUMMY

- 3 -

ABCCB BELLE FEMME FREER GAMMA GYPPY HANNA JESSE KAPPA LOTTO MANNA MISSI MOTTO
SOTTO ZORRO

ABCCD AFOOT ALOOF BAGGY BALLS BALLY BANNS BARRE BARRY BASSO BATTS BATTY BELLS
BELLY BENNY BERRI BERRY BESSY BIDDY BIFFY BILLS BILLY BITTY BLEED BLOOD BLOOM
BLOOP BOGGY BOLLE BOLLS BONNY BOSSY BREED BROOD BROOK BROOM BUDDY BUFFO BUFFS
BUFFY BUGGY BULLS BULLY BUNNY BURRO BURRS BURRY BUTTE BUTTS BUTTY BUZZY CABBY
CADDY CALLS CANNY CARRY CATTY CELLO CELLS CHEEK CHEER CHOOK CISSY CIVVY COBBS
COBBY COMMA COMMY CONNY CORRY CREED CREEK CREEL CREEP CROOK CROON CUBBY CUDDY
CUFFS CUFFY CULLS CUPPY CURRY CUTTY DABBY DAFFY DALLY DEBBY DERRY DILLS DILLY
DIPPY DITTO DITTY DIVVY DIZZY DOBBY DOFFS DOGGY DOLLS DOLLY DONNA DOTTY DROOL
DROOP DUBBY DUFFS DUFFY DULLS DULLY DUMMY DUNNY EQUUS FADDY FALLS FANNY FATTY
FELLS FELLY FENNY FERRY FIGGY FILLS FILLY FINNY FIZZY FLEER FLEES FLEET FLOOD
FLOOR FOGGY FOLLY FOPPY FREED FUGGY FULLS FULLY FUNNY FURRY FUSSY FUZZY GABBY
GAFFS GALLS GAMMY GARRY GASSY GELLS GEMMA GEMMY GESSO GIDDY GILLS GILLY GINNY
GIPPO GIPPY GLOOM GOLLY GOTTA GREED GREEK GREEN GREET GROOM GUFFS GULLS GULLY
GUMMY GUNNY GUPPY GYPPO HALLO HALLS HAMMY HAPPY HARRY HATTY HELLO HELLS HELLY
HENNA HENNY HILLS HILLY HIPPO HIPPY HISSY HOBBY HOLLY HOPPY HUBBY HUFFS HUFFY
HULLO HULLS HURRY HUSSY JAGGS JAGGY JAMMY JAZZY JEFFS JELLS JELLY JEMMY JENNA
JENNY JERRY JETTY JIBBY JIFFS JIFFY JILLS JIMMY JINNY JOLLY JOTTY JUTTY KELLY
KERRY KIDDO KILLS KISSY KITTY KNEED KNEEL KNEES KRAAL KREEL LAPPS LARRY LASSO
LEGGY LEMMA LIPPY LOBBY LORRY LYNNS MALLS MANNY MAPPY MARRY MATTE MATTS MATTY
MECCA MERRY MESSY MEZZO MIDDY MIFFS MIFFY MILLE MILLS MILLY MINNE MISSY MITTS
MITTY MOLLS MOLLY MOSSY MUDDY MUFFS MUGGS MUGGY MURRY MUSSY MUTTS MUZZY MYRRH
NAPPY NATTY NAVVY NELLS NELLY NETTY NIPPY NITTY NOBBY NUBBY NULLS NUTTY PADDY
PALLS PARRY PASSE PATTY PEGGY PENNY PERRY PETTY PIGGY PILLS PIZZA POLLS POLLY
POMME POMMY POSSE POSSY POTTY PREEN PROOF PUFFS PUFFY PUGGY PUKKA PULLS PULLY
PUNNY PURRY PUSSY PUTTS PUTTY QUEEN QUEER RABBI RAGGY RALLY RATTY RIBBY RILLS
RILLY ROLLS RUDDY RUFFS RUFFY RUGGY RUMMY RUNNY RUTTY SAGGY SALLY SAMMY SAPPY
SAVVY SCOOP SCOOT SHEEN SHEEP SHEER SHEET SHOOK SHOOT SILLY SIPPY SKEET SKOOT
SLEEK SLEEP SLEET SLOOP SNEER SNOOD SNOOK SNOOP SNOOT SOBBY SODDY SOGGY SONNY
SOPPY SORRY SPEED SPEEL SPOOF SPOOK SPOOL SPOON SPOOR STEED STEEL STEEP STEER
STOOD STOOK STOOL STOOP SULLY SUNNY SURRY SWEEP SWEET SWOON SWOOP TABBY TAFFY
TAGGY TALLS TALLY TAMMY TANNY TARRY TEDDY TELLS TELLY TERRA TERRY THEED TIBBY
TIDDY TIFFS TIFFY TILLS TILLY TINNY TIPPY TIZZY TODDY TOFFS TOFFY TOLLS TOLLY
TOMMY TONNE TOPPY TOSSY TREED TREES TROOP TUBBY TULLE TULLY TUMMY TWEED TWEEN
TYEES VILLA WADDY WALLS WALLY WATTS WEBBY WELLS WELLY WHEEL WHEES WHOOF WHOOP
WHOOS WIGGY WILLS WILLY WINNE WITTY WORRY YELLS YUCCA ZIPPY

ABCDA ALOHA ALPHA AMIGA ANIMA AORTA APNEA ARECA ARENA AROMA ATRIA BLURB CETIC
COLIC COMIC CONIC COSEC CUBIC CUNIC CYNIC DARED DATED DAZED DICED DIKED DINED
DIVED DOLED DOMED DOPED DOSED DOTED DOVED DOWED DOZED DREAD DRIED DRUID DRYAD
DUPED EAGLE ECOLE ELATE ELITE ELOPE ELUDE EMOTE ENSUE ENURE ERADE ERASE ERODE
ETUDE EVADE EVOKE EXILE EXUDE EYRIE GOING HARSH HATCH HEATH HITCH HUMPH HUNCH
HUTCH IRANI IRAQI KAPOK KIOSK KLICK KLINK KLUNK KNACK KNICK KNOCK KODAK KOPEK
KULAK LABEL LAPEL LEGAL LIBEL LOBAL LOCAL LOYAL MAXIM MIASM NYLON OGLIO ORTHO
OUTDO OUTGO PINUP PLUMP POLYP PRIMP RACER RAGER RAKER RAPER RATER RAVER RAWER
RAYER RAZER RAZOR RECUR RICER RIDER RIGOR RIPER RISER RIVER ROBER ROPER ROVER
ROWER RUDER RULER RUMOR SACKS SAFES SAGES SAILS SAKES SALES SALTS SANDS SARIS
SATES SAVES SAXES SCABS SCADS SCAMS SCANS SCARS SCATS SCOTS SCOWS SCUDS SCUMS
SEALS SEAMS SEARS SEATS SECTS SELFS SEMIS SENDS SERBS SERFS SHAGS SHAMS SHAWS

SHEDS SHIES SHIMS SHINS SHIPS SHIVS SHODS SHOES SHOPS SHOTS SHOWS SHUGS SHULS
SHUNS SHUTS SIDES SIFTS SIGHS SIGNS SIKHS SILKS SILOS SILTS SINES SINGS SINKS
SINUS SIRES SITES SIXES SIZES SKATS SKEDS SKEWS SKIDS SKIES SKIMS SKINS SKIPS
SKITS SLABS SLAGS SLAMS SLAPS SLATS SLAVS SLAWS SLAYS SLEDS SLEWS SLIMS SLIPS
SLITS SLOBS SLOGS SLOPS SLOTS SLOWS SLUBS SLUGS SLUMS SLURS SLUTS SMOGS SMUTS
SNAGS SNAPS SNIPS SNITS SNOBS SNOTS SNOWS SNUBS SNUGS SOAKS SOAPS SOARS SOCKS
SODAS SOFAS SOILS SOLES SONGS SORES SORTS SOULS SOUPS SOURS SPAES SPANS SPARS
SPATS SPAYS SPEWS SPIES SPINS SPITS SPOTS SPUDS SPURS STABS STAGS STARS STAYS
STEMS STEPS STEWS STIES STIRS STOPS STOWS STUBS STUDS STUNS SUCKS SUITS SULKS
SUMAS SUMPS SURFS SWABS SWAGS SWANS SWAPS SWATS SWAYS SWIGS SWIMS SWOTS SYNCS
TACIT TAINT TAPIT TAROT TAUNT TEMPT THEFT TIBET TIGHT TOAST TRACT TRAIT TREAT
TRENT TROUT TRUST TRYST TWIST TWIXT WIDOW XEROX YAWNY YOLKY YUCKY

ABCDB ADZED AERIE AGING ALKYL ARBOR ARDOR ARMER ARMOR ASHES ATILT BALSA BARCA
BEIGE BELIE BERNE BRIAR BRIER BYWAY CEASE COMBO CONGO CORSO CRYER DACHA DEICE
DELVE DENSE DEUCE DREAR DRIER DRYER FACIA FAUNA FENCE FLAIL FOLIO FORGO FRIAR
FRIER FRYER GENIE GENRE GEODE GYPSY HAIDA HAIFA HALVA HEAVE HEDGE HENCE HINDI
IDLED ISLES KARMA KASHA KEDGE KNOWN LABIA LAMBA LARVA LAURA LEASE LEAVE LEDGE
MAFIA MALTA MANIA MARIA MAZDA MERGE METRE MYOPY NERVE NISEI ORDER PADUA PANDA
PARKA PARMA PASHA PASTA PEACE PEKOE PENCE PENSE PERLE POLIO PORTO PRIOR PYGMY
REDYE REHOE REICE RETIE REUSE REVUE RODEO ROMEO RONDO SABRA SAMBA SANTA SAUNA
SEDGE SEGUE SEINE SEIZE SERGE SERVE SKULK SKUNK SMARM START STILT STINT STOAT
STOUT STRUT STUNT TAIGA TAMPA TEASE TENSE TERSE THIGH TOKYO TORSO TRIER TRUER
TSARS UNION UNMAN UNPEN UNPIN UNTIN UNWON URGER USERS VARIA VELDE VENGE VENUE
VERDE VERGE VERSE WEAVE WEDGE WHICH WRIER WRYER

ABCDC AIDED AIRER ALIBI APSIS BARER BASES BASIS BESTS BLINI BODED BORER BOSES
BRAMA BROMO BUSES BUSKS BUSTS CABOB CANON CARER CASES CASTS CHILI CLEVE CODED
CORER COSTS COYLY CREPE CRETE CREWE CURER CUSPS CYSTS DARER DESKS DIANA DISCS
DISKS DOSES DRAMA DRYLY DUSKS DUSTS EASTS FADED FARER FASTS FISTS FLYBY FUROR
FUSES GASES GASPS GAYLY GHANA GISTS GLEBE GORER GREBE GUANA GUAVA GUSTS HAITI
HASPS HIRER HOSES HOSTS HUSKS ILAMA IRENE JADED JESTS JUROR JUSTS KABOB KEBAB
KOALA KYOTO LASTS LHASA LIANA LIEGE LINEN LISPS LISTS LOSES LURER LUSTS LYSIS
MASKS MASTS MISES MISTS MOSES MOSTS MUSES MUSKS MUSTS NABOB NESTS NIECE NODED
NOSES NUDED OASES OASIS OBESE OCTET OMAHA OSAKA OUSTS PARER PASTS PESOS PESTS
PETIT PHOTO PIECE PLAYA PLAZA PLEBE PORER POSES POSTS PROVO PURER RASPS REDID
RESTS RISES RISKS ROSES RUSES RUSKS RUSTS SCENE SHYLY SIDED SIEGE SIEVE SKENE
SORER SPECE STELE SUEDE SURER SWEDE TASKS TENON THEME THERE THESE TIARA TIDED
TIRER TRAMA TUSKS UNDID UNGAG VASES VESTS VISAS VISES WADED WASPS WESTS WHERE
WIRER WISES WISPS WISTS WRYLY ZESTS

ABCDD ABUZZ ABYSS AGREE AMISS ASCII ATOLL BALOO BLESS BLISS BLUFF BRASS BRIGG
BRILL CHAFF CHESS CHILL CHUBB CHUFF CLASS CLIFF CRASS CRESS CROSS DRESS DRILL
DROLL DROSS DWELL FLOSS FRILL FRIZZ FUSEE GAUSS GENII GLASS GLOSS GRASS GRILL
GROSS GRUFF GUESS IDYLL IGLOO KAZOO KNELL KNOLL KRILL KVASS LYCEE MUSEE PAYEE
POUFF PRESS PUREE QUAFF QUELL QUILL RANEE RUPEE SAREE SCOFF SCOTT SCREE SCUFF
SCULL SHALL SHELL SHILL SHREE SKIFF SKILL SKOFF SKULL SLUFF SMALL SMELL SNELL
SNIFF SNUFF SPALL SPELL SPIFF SPILL SPREE STAFF STALL STIFF STILL STUFF SUTEE
SWELL SWILL TABOO THREE TOPEE TRESS TRILL TROLL TRUSS TWILL WHIFF WHIRR WHIZZ
YAHOO YAZOO

SIX-LETTER PATTERN WORDS

AABACD EELERS EELERY OOLONG   **AABCAB** EERIER   **AABCAD** EELIER

AABCBD LLAMAS   **AABCDE** EELING LLOYDS OOCYST OOCYTE OODLES OOMPAH OOZIER

ABAABC MAMMAL MAMMAS PAPPAS PEPPED PEPPER PIPPIN   **ABAACA** SASSES

ABAACC TATTOO

ABAACD BABBLE BABBLY BIBBED BIBBER BOBBED BOBBER BOBBIE BOBBIN BOBBLE BUBBLE
BUBBLY COCCYX DIDDLE DODDER DODDLE GAGGED GAGGER GAGGLE GIGGLE GIGGLY GOGGLE
LOLLED LOLLER LULLED LULLER MAMMON MUMMED MUMMER PIPPED PIPPEN PIPPER POPPED
POPPER POPPET PUPPET SASSED SUSSEX TATTED TATTER TATTIE TATTLE TITTER TOTTED
TOTTER TUTTED

ABABBC COCOON REREEL   **ABABCA** ACACIA   **ABABCB** PAPAYA

ABABCD COCOAS DODOES FIFING ICICLE JOJOBA JUJUBE MIMICS MIMING PAPACY PAPAIN
PIPING REREAD TATARS TITIAL VIVIFY

ABACAC ILICIC   **ABACAD** ARAWAK AVATAR ELEVEN EVENED EVENER EYELET IRIDIC

ABACBD GAGMAN MAMBAS MEMBER MEMOED NONCOM SASHAY TETHER UNURNS

ABACCD ANALLY BABOON REROOF REROOT TATOOS

ABACDA ACADIA ALASKA ATAXIA AZALEA CYCLIC DODGED EMERGE EMERSE ENERVE GAGING
SASHES SUSANS

ABACDB DEDUCE ODORED RERAKE RERATE REROBE SESAME USURPS

ABACDC ABASES ALASES CICADA IBISES IRISES PEPSIS POPEYE USURER

ABACDD CUCKOO REROLL

ABACDE ABACUS ABASED ABASER ABATED ABATES ACAJOU ACANTH ADAGIO ADAPTS AGATES
ALAMOS ALARMS ALARUM AMAZED AMAZES AMAZON ANALOG ANARCH APACHE APATHY ARABIC
ARABLE ARAGON AVAILS AWAITS AWAKED AWAKEN AWAKES BABIED BABIES BIBLED BIBLER
BIBLES BOBCAT BYBLIS BYBLOW CACHES CACHET CACKLE CACTUS CECILS COCAIN COCKED
COCKIE COCKLE COCKUP CYCADS CYCLED CYCLER CYCLES DEDUCT DODGER DODGES DUDLEY
EDEMAS EDEMIC EJECTS ELECTS EMETIC ENEMAS ENERGY ERECTS EVENLY EVENTS EVERTS
EXEMPT EXERTS EYEFUL EYEING EYELID FIFTHS ICIEST ICINGS IDIOCY IDIOMS IDIOTS
ILIADS ILIUMS IRISHY LILACS LILTED MAMBOS MEMBRA MEMOIR MEMORY MIMEOS MIMERS
MIMOSA MOMENT MUMBLE NINETY NINTHS NONFAT NONTAX NONUSE ODOURS OVOIDS OZONED
OZONER OZONES OZONIC PAPERS PAPERY PAPIER PAPISH PAPISM PAPIST PAPYRI PEPSIN
PEPTIC PEPTID PIPERS PIPERY POPERY POPGUN POPING POPISH POPLAR POPLIN PUPATE
PUPILS RAREFY RARELY RAREST RARIFY RARING RARISH RARITY RERUNS SASHED SESQUI
SISTER SYSTEM TATIES TATLER TETCHY TETONS TETRAS TETRIC TETRIX TITANS TITHED
TITHER TITHES TITLED TITLER TITLES TITRES TOTALS TOTEMS TOTERS TOTING TUTORS
UNUSED USURED VIVANT WOWING

ABBABA DEEDED   **ABBABB** MUUMUU   **ABBABC** INNING PEEPED PEEPER TEETER

ABBACA DOODAD EFFETE   **ABBACB** ASSAYS   **ABBACC** APPALL

ABBACD AFFAIR ALLAYS ANNALS ARRANT ARRAYS ASSAIL ATTACH ATTACK ATTAIN ATTARS
DOODAH DOODLE EFFECT EGGERS EGGERY EMMESH GEEGAW HEEHAW IFFIER ILLIAD ILLIUM
OPPOSE PEEPUL POOPED SEESAW TOOTED TOOTER TOOTHS TOOTHY TOOTLE TOOTSY

ABBCAB ARREAR EDDIED

ABBCAD ANNUAL APPEAL APPEAR APPIAN ATTRAP ECCLES EDDIES EDDOES

ABBCBA DEEMED REEFER REEKER REELER

ABBCBB ASSESS BOOHOO HOODOO PEEWEE TEEPEE VOODOO WOOHOO

ABBCBC HEEDED JEERER NEEDED REEDED SEEDED WEEDED

ABBCBD ASSIST BEEFED BEEFER BEEMEN BEEPED BEEPER BEEVES DEEMER DEEPEN DEEPER
ERRORS FEEDER FEELER GEEZER HEEDER HEELED HEELER JEERED KEELED KEELER KEENER
KEEPER LEERED LEEVES MEEKER PEEKED PEELED PEELER PEEVED PEEVER PEEVES PEEVEY
REEFED REEKED REELED REEVES SEEDER SEEKER SEEMED SEEPED TEEMED TEEMER VEERED
WEEDER WEENED WEEPED WEEPER WEEZED

ABBCCD COOEES COOLLY WOOLLY

ABBCDA ATTILA DOOMED DOORED EFFACE EFFUME EFFUSE HOOKAH HOOTCH ROOFER ROOMER
ROOTER SOOTHS

ABBCDB ADDEND ADDLED ASSETS ATTEST BEETLE EGGING EGGNOG ESSAYS FEEBLE ISSUES
NEEDLE SEETHE WEENIE

ABBCDC ALLEGE ANNEXE ARROYO BOOSTS ERRATA GOOSES HOODED LOOSES NOOSES OTTAWA
POORER ROOSTS WOODED

ABBCDD ABBESS ACCESS BOOTEE COOLEE LOOKEE

ABBCDE ABBEYS ABBOTS ACCEND ACCENT ACCEPT ACCORD ACCOST ACCOYS ACCRUE ACCUSE
ADDERS ADDICT ADDING ADDLES ADDUCE ADDUCT AFFECT AFFINE AFFIRM AFFLUE AFFLUX
AFFORD ALLEYS ALLIED ALLIES ALLIUM ALLOTS ALLOWS ALLOYS ALLUDE ALLURE AMMINE
AMMINO ANNETS ANNOYS ANNULS APPEND APPETS APPLED APPLES APPOSE ARREST ARRIDE
ARRIVE ARROWS ASSENT ASSERT ASSIFY ASSIGN ASSIZE ASSORT ASSUME ASSURE ATTEND
ATTICS ATTIRE ATTONE ATTUNE BEECHY BEESOM BOOGIE BOOING BOOKED BOOKER BOOKIE
BOOKSY BOOMED BOOMER BOOTED BOOTER BOOTHS BOOTIE BOOZED BOOZER BOOZES COOERS
COOEYS COOING COOKED COOKER COOKIE COOLED COOLER COOLIE COOMBE COOMBS COOPED
COOPER DEEJAY DEEPLY EBBING EFFIGY EFFLUX EFFORT EGGBOX EGGCUP ERRAND ERRANT
ERRING FEEBLY FOOLED FOOLER FOOTED FOOTER FOOTIE GOOBER GOODLY GOOFED GOOFER
GOOIER GOONEY GOONIE GOOSED GOOSEY HOOFED HOOFER HOOKAS HOOKED HOOKER HOOKEY
HOOKUM HOOKUP HOOPED HOOPER HOOPLA HOORAY HOOTED HOOTER HOOVED HOOVEN HOOVES
IMMESH IMMUNE IMMURE IMMUTE INNAMS INNARD INNATE INNERS ISSUED ISSUER IZZARD
IZZATS KEENLY LEEWAY LOOFAH LOOKED LOOKER LOOMED LOOMER LOONEY LOOPED LOOPER

LOOSED LOOSEN LOOSER LOOTED LOOTER MCCOYS MEEKLY MOOCHA MOOING MOONED MOONER
MOONEY MOONIE MOORED NOODLE NOOKED NOOSED NOOSER NOOTKA OCCULT OCCUPY OCCURS
ODDEST ODDISH ODDITY ODDMAN ODDMEN OFFALS OFFCUT OFFEND OFFERS OFFICE OFFING
OFFISH OFFLET OFFSET ORRICE OSSIAN OSSIFY OSSING OTTERS PEEVIT PEEWIT POODLE
POOHED POOLED POOLER POORED POORLY REEBOK ROOFED ROOKED ROOKIE ROOMED ROOMIE
ROOTED ROOVED ROOVES SEEING SEEMLY SOONER SOOTED SOOTER SOOTHE TEEING TEENSY
TOOLED TOOLER UDDERS UNNAME UPPARD UPPERS UPPING UPPISH UPPITY UTTERS VEEING
WEEKLY WEENSY WEEPLY WEEVIL WOODEN WOODLY WOODSY WOOERS WOOFED WOOFER WOOING
WOOLED WOOLEN WOOLER WOOLIE WOOZLE ZOOFUL ZOOMED ZOOMER

ABCAAD BLOBBY EMCEED EMCEES ESTEEM EXCEED FLUFFS FLUFFY GROGGY OCTOON ONLOOK
SUISSE TROTTY TWITTY

ABCABA DEADED REARER SENSES   **ABCABB** RETREE TESTEE

ABCABC BONBON BYEBYE CANCAN CHICHI DUMDUM MURMUR PALPAL POMPOM TARTAR TESTES
TOMTOM TSETSE VALVAL VERVER

ABCABD ALKALI BULBUS DEADEN DEADER DIADIC ENDENT GEIGER GORGON INKING INTINE
MADMAN MERMEN MORMON NEONED ONIONS ONIONY OSMOSE PAMPAS POMPON REARED REBRED
REBREW RECREW REDREW REGRET REGREW SENSED SENSER TARTAN TENTED TENTER TESTED
TESTER TEXTED UNHUNG UNRUNG UNSUNG UNSUNK UNTUNE VALVAE VELVET VERVET

ABCACA BOABAB   **ABCACD** CAUCUS IMBIBE INSIST IODIDE

ABCADA ALPACA ANKARA ARMADA CALCIC EOCENE EUGENE ROARER SOUSES SPASMS STASIS
SUDSES TOMTIT

ABCADB AERATE ASIANS ASRAMS BALBOA BRIBER CONCHO ESTERS INDIAN OSMOUS PEOPLE
PROPER RETRUE THATCH UNTURN

ABCADC BARBER CRECHE DREDGE EASELS EASERS EXTENT GEWGAW GORGER HASHES HUSHES
IONIAN LADLED LISLES MICMAC SHASTA SUDSED TACTIC TARTER TASTES TIPTOP VULVAL
WIGWAG ZIGZAG

ABCADD BAMBOO DUNDEE EGRESS EXCESS INFILL UNFULL UNHULL

ABCADE ABLATE ABLAZE ABOARD ABRAID ABRASE ACUATE AFEARD AFLAME AFLARE AFRAID
AGHAST AGLARE ALBANY ALTARS ALWAYS ANZACS APIARY AQUAKE ARCADE ARCADY ARCANE
AREADY ARIANS ARMAGH ARYANS ASHAME ASLANT ASPACE ASWARM AUDACE AVIARY AVIATE
BARBED BAUBLE BEDBUG BIMBOS BLABER BOMBAY BOMBED BOMBER BRIBED BRIBES BULBED
BUMBLE BURBLE BURBLY BUSBOY CANCEL CANCER CATCHY CHECKS CHECKY CHICKS CHICKY
CHICLE CHOCKS CHUCKS CIRCAS CIRCLE CIRCLY CIRCUM CIRCUS CLACKS CLICHE CLICKS
CLICKY CLOCHE CLOCKS CLUCKS COACTS CONCHA CONCHS CONCHY CONCUR COUCHE CRACKS
CRACKY CROCKS CROCUS CZECHS DANDER DANDLE DAWDLE DEADLY DIADEM DILDOS DIODES
DISDAR DREDGY DRUDGE DYADIC EATERS EATERY EAVERS ECZEMA EDGERS EGRETS ELDERS
ELDEST EMBEDS EMBERS ENDEAR ENDERS ENMESH ENTERS EQUERY ETHELS ETHERS EXCELS
EXCEPT EXPECT EXPELS EXPEND EXPERT EXTEND FITFUL GADGET GANGED GANGES GANGLY
GARGLE GAUGED GAUGER GAUGES GINGER GONGED GORGED GORGES GOUGED GOUGER GOUGES
GURGLE GURGLY HASHED HASHER HIGHER HIGHLY HITHER HUSHED HUSHER HYPHEN IDLING
IGNITE IMPISH INCISE INCITE INDIAS INDICE INDICT INDIES INDIGO INDIOS INFIRM

INGIRD INKIER INKISH INSIDE INVITE IODINE IODIZE IONICS IONISM IONIST IONIZE
IVYING KICKED KICKER KICKUP KINKED KINKER LADLER LADLES MADMEN MAIMED MAIMER
MARMOT MATMEN MERMAN MNEMIC NUANCE OBLONG OCTOID OCTOPI ONLOAD ORIOLE ORIONS
ORMOLU OXFORD OXHORN PALPED PAMPER PAUPER PIGPEN PIMPED PIMPLE PIMPLY POMPED
POMPEY POTPIE PREPAY PROPEL PROPYL PULPED PULPER PULPIT PUMPED PUMPER PURPLE
PURPLY RAMROD REARMS REDRAW REGRIP REGROW RETRIM REWRAP ROARED RUBRIC SEASON
SENSOR SIESTA SLASHY SLOSHY SLUSHY SOUSED SOUSER SUBSEA SUBSET SUNSET SWISHY
TACTOR TARTED TARTLY TASTED TASTER TAUTEN TAUTER TAUTLY TENTHS TERTIA TESTOR
TILTED TILTER TINTED TINTER TIPTOE TORTES TOUTED TOUTER TOUTES TRITON TROTHS
TRUTHS TUFTED TUFTER TURTLE TWITCH TWITED UNCURB UNCURD UNCURL UNDULY UNFURL
UNGUMS UNHURT UNHUST UNJUST UNPURE UNRULY UNRUST UNSURE UNTUCK UNTURF UPCURL
UPFURL UPTUCK UPTURN URSULA VALVED VALVES VULVAR VULVAS WIGWAM

ABCBAB DECEDE REVERE   **ABCBAC** LYSYLS

ABCBAD AEGEAN CIVICS DIVIDE GARAGE KAYAKS LEVELS MADAME MADAMS RADARS REFERS
REVERB REVERT ROTORS TENETS

ABCBBA DESEED   **ABCBBC** CANAAN REDEED

ABCBBD BAZAAR JEREED LEVEED LEVEES MELEES REDEEM REFEED RESEED TEPEES VENEER

ABCBCA SALALS TENENT   **ABCBCB** BANANA

ABCBCD DINING FINING KABABS LINING MINING OILILY PINING QUEUED QUEUER TINING
VINING WILILY

ABCBDA DEFEND DEPEND GIVING REBEAR REGEAR REHEAR REWEAR SALADS SAPANS SARAHS
SATANS SEVENS SEVERS SEWERS SEXERS SODOMS SOLONS STATES STATUS SUNUPS

ABCBDB BAHAMA BIKINI BIMINI CABALA CABANA CANADA CASABA CASAVA CELEBE DELETE
MALAGA MALAYA PAJAMA PANAMA RAMADA RECEDE REDEYE RENEGE SAHARA SECEDE SERENE
SEVERE

ABCBDC AIRIER BASALS BESETS BOSOMS DETECT DETENT DETEST FILIAL MINION MIRIER
NASALS PINION RESETS RESEWS RETEST SUBURB TIDIED VISITS WIRIER

ABCBDD BEFELL HARASS JEWESS RESELL RETELL

ABCBDE AEGEUS AENEID AIDING AILING AIMING AIRILY AIRING AIRISH ANONYM AUBURN
AUGURE AUGURS AUGURY AUGUST AUTUMN BAHAIS BASALT BEDECK BEGETS BEHEAD BEHELD
BEHEST BEMEAN BEREFT BERETS BETELS BEVELS BEZELS BIDING BIKING BITING BOGOTA
BOLOED BORONS BOSOMY BOVOID CABALS CAJANS CALAIS CANALS CANAPE CANARD CANARY
CARAFE CASATE CEDENT CEDERS CELERY CELEST CEMENT CEREAL CILIUM CITIED CITIES
CITIFY CITING CIVILS CIVISM COHOES COHOLS COHORT COJOIN COLONS COLONY COLORS
COLORY COLOUR CONOID CORONA COYOTE CUMULI CUPULA CUTUPS DAMAGE DAMASK DECEIT
DECENT DECERN DEFEAT DEFECT DEFERS DEGERM DEJECT DEMEAN DEMENT DESERT DETERS
DEVEST DEWERS DICING DIEING DIGITS DIKING DIMITY DIVINE DIVING DIXIES DOLOUR
DONORS DRYROT DRYRUB DULUTH EUNUCH FACADE FARADS FEVERS FEVERY FEWEST FEYEST
FIJIAN FILING FINIAL FINISH FINITE FINITY FIRING FIXING FIXITY FUGUES FUTURE
GALAHS GALANT GALAXY GENERA GENEVA GODOWN HAZARD HELENA HEREAT HEREBY HEREIN

HEREOF HEREON HERESY HERETO HETERA HETERO HEWERS HEXERS HIDING HIKING HIRING
HOBOED HOBOES HONORS HONOUR ICECAP IODOUS IODOXY JAPANS JEWELS JEWELY JIBING
JIMINY JIVING JOCOSE JOYOUS KARAIT KARATE KARATS KEYERS KIBITZ KILIMS KITING
KITISH LANARK LAVAGE LAVANT LAVASH LAXATE LEGEND LEPERS LEVERS LIAISE LIBIDO
LIKING LIKINS LIMING LIMITS LIPIDE LIPIDS LIVING LOCOED LUXURY MACANS MACAOS
MACAWS MADANS MALADY MALAYS MANAGE MAWALI MAYANS MERELY MEREST MESELF METELS
METEOR METERS MEWERS MIKING MILIEU MIRING MIXING MIXITE MONOID MORONS MOROSE
MOTORS MOTORY MUTUAL NAPALM NATALS NAVAJO NAWABS NEREID NEWELS NEWEST NIHILS
NOBODY NOTORY OARAGE OEDEMA OILIER OILING OILISH PAEANS PAGANS PAGANY PALACE
PALAIS PALATE PALAYS PARADE PAVANE PAVANS PAYANS PETERS PICINE PIKING PILING
PIRIES PIRITE PITIED PITIER PITIES PIXIES POGOED POMONA POROUS RAFAEL RAJAHS
RAMAGE RAVAGE REBELS REBEND REBENT RECENT REDEAL REDECK REFECT REFELT REGENT
REHEAD REHEAL REHEAP REHEAT REHELM REJECT RELEAD RELEAP RELEND RELENT RELETS
RELEVY REMEDY REMELT REMEND RENEST RENEWS REPEAL REPEAT REPEGS REPELS REPENS
REPENT RESEAL RESEAM RESEAT RESECT RESEDA RESELF RESEND RESENT RESEWN REVEAL
REVEIL REVELS REVENT REVEST REWEDS REWELD REWETS RICING RIDING RIGIDS RIMING
RIPING RISING ROBOTS SAFARI SALAME SALAMI SALARY SARAPE SAVAGE SAVANT SELECT
SENECA SERENA SEWERY SIDING SILICA SIMIAL SIMIAN SIMILE SIPING SIRING SITING
SIZIER SIZING SLALOM SODOMY SOJOUR SOLOED SONOMA SONORA STATED STATER STATIC
STATUE STITCH SUTURE TABARD TAMALE TERESA TIBIAE TIBIAL TIBIAS TIDIER TIDIES
TIDILY TIDING TIEING TILING TIMING TINIER TINIES TINILY TIRING TOXOID TOXONS
UNKNIT UNKNOT UNKNOW UNSNAP VACANT VACATE VAGANT VAGARY VEXERS VIGILS VIKING
VILIFY VIRIAL VIRILE VISIER VISION VIZIER VIZIRS WIDING WIDISH WIFING WIFISH
WIKIUP WILING WIPING WIRILY WIRING WISING WIVING YEMENI

ABCCAD LITTLE SNOOSE SWOOSH TWEETS   **ABCCBA** DENNED REDDER

ABCCBB LESSEE SETTEE

ABCCBC BEDDED BOWWOW HORROR HUBBUB MESSES POWWOW RATTAT REDDED WEDDED YESSES

ABCCBD BALLAD BEDDER BEGGED BELLED BETTER BIDDIE BORROW BOTTOM CALLAS CELLED
CELLER COMMON COTTON DALLAS DOLLOP FELLED FELLER FENNEL FERRET FETTER FEZZES
FOLLOW GALLAH GAMMAS GELLED GEMMED GETTER HELLER HEMMED HEMMER HOLLOW JELLED
JETTED JETTER KENNEL KIDDIE LEGGED LESSEN LESSER LETTED LETTER LIZZIE LOTTOS
MESSED MESSER MINNIE MORROW MOTTOS NASSAU NETTED NETTER PEGGED PEGGER PELLET
PENNED PENNER PETTED PETTER POLLOI RATTAN REDDEN RENNET REVVED SELLER SETTER
SORROW TELLER VASSAL VASSAR VESSEL VETTED WALLAH WEBBED WEBBER WELLED WETTED
WETTER WILLIE WINNIE YELLED YELLER YESSED

ABCCDA DABBED DAMMED DILLED DIMMED DINNED DIPPED DOFFED DOGGED DOLLED DONNED
DOTTED DUBBED DULLED DUNNED HURRAH HUZZAH NISSAN NOGGIN RAMMER RAPPER RATTER
RIBBER RIDDER RIGGER RIMMER RIPPER ROBBER ROLLER ROTTER RUBBER RUDDER RUFFER
RUGGER RUNNER RUTTER SCOOPS SCOOTS SHEEPS SHEERS SHEETS SHOOTS SKEETS SLEEPS
SLEETS SLOOPS SNEERS SNOODS SNOOPS SNOOTS SPEEDS SPOOFS SPOOKS SPOOLS SPOONS
SPOORS STEEDS STEELS STEEPS STEERS STOOLS STOOPS SWEEPS SWEETS SWOONS SWOOPS
TAPPET TAPPIT TURRET WALLOW WILLOW WINNOW

ABCCDB FETTLE JENNIE JESSIE KETTLE MEDDLE MERRIE METTLE MYRRHY NETTLE PEBBLE
PEDDLE SETTLE WHOOSH

ABCCDC BARRER BASSES BOSSES BREEZE BUDDED BURRER BUSSES CANNON CHEESE CUDDED
CUSSES FINNAN FLEECE FREEZE FUSSES GADDED GASSES GREECE HISSES JOSSES KIDDED
KISSES LASSES LIDDED LOSSES MARRER MASSES MESSRS MIRROR MISSES MISSUS MOSSES
MUDDED MUSSES NODDED PADDED PASSES PODDED PURRER PUSSES RIDDED RODDED SLEEVE
SNEEZE SODDED TANNIN TARRER TERROR TOSSES TWEEZE WADDED WARRER WHEEZE

ABCCDD COFFEE HALLOO LASSOO PUTTEE SUTTEE TOFFEE YIPPEE

ABCCDE AUSSIE BADDER BAFFLE BAGGED BAGGER BAGGIE BALLED BALLER BALLET BALLOT
BANNED BANNER BARRED BARREL BARREN BARRIO BARROW BASSET BATTED BATTEN BATTER
BATTLE BEGGAR BELLOW BETTOR BIDDEN BIDDER BIGGER BILLED BILLER BILLET BILLOW
BINNED BITTEN BITTER BLEEDS BLEERY BLOODS BLOODY BLOOMS BLOOMY BLOOPS BOFFIN
BOGGED BOGGLE BOLLED BONNET BONNIE BOPPED BOPPER BOSSED BOSSER BOTTLE BREECH
BREEDS BREEZY BROOCH BROODS BROODY BROOKS BROOKY BROOMS BUDDAH BUDDHA BUFFED
BUFFER BUFFET BUGGED BUGGER BULLET BUMMED BUMMER BURRED BURROS BURROW BUSSED
BUSSER BUTTAL BUTTED BUTTER BUTTON BUZZED BUZZER BUZZES CABBED CADDIE CALLED
CALLER CALLOW CAMMED CANNED CANNER CAPPED CAPPER CARRIE CARROT CATTLE CELLAR
CELLOS CHEEKS CHEEKY CHEEPS CHEEPY CHEERS CHEERY CHEESY CHOOSE CHOOSY COBBED
COBBER COBBLE COBBLY CODDLE COFFER COFFIN COGGED COGGER COGGLE COLLAR COLLIE
COMMAS COMMIE COMMIT COMMIX CONNED CONNER CONNIE COPPED COPPER CORRAL COSSET
COTTER CREEDS CREEKS CREEKY CREELS CREEPS CREEPY CROOKS CROONS CUDDLE CUDDLY
CUFFED CULLED CULLER CUMMIN CUPPED CUPPER CURRAN CUSSED CUSSER CUTTER CUTTLE
DABBER DABBLE DAGGER DAMMER DAPPER DAPPLE DAZZLE DIFFER DIGGER DIMMER DINNER
DIPPER DITTOS DOBBIN DOGGER DOGGIE DOLLAR DOTTER DROOLS DROOLY DROOPS DROOPY
DUBBER DUBBIN DUFFEL DUFFER DUFFLE DULLER DUNNER FADDLE FAGGED FAGGER FAGGOT
FALLEN FALLER FALLOW FANNED FANNER FARROW FATTED FATTEN FATTER FELLOW FERRIS
FIBBED FIBBER FIDDLE FILLED FILLER FILLET FINNED FITTED FITTER FIZZED FIZZER
FIZZES FIZZLE FLEECY FLEETS FLOODS FLOODY FLOORS FLOOZY FOBBED FODDER FOGGED
FOGGER FOPPED FOSSIL FREELY FUDDLE FULLED FULLER FUNNEL FURRED FURROW FUSSED
FUSSER FUZZED FUZZES GABBED GABBER GABBLE GADDER GAFFED GAFFER GAFFES GALLED
GALLER GALLEY GALLIC GALLON GALLOP GALLOW GAMMON GARRET GASSED GASSER GIBBED
GIBBER GIBBET GIBBON GIDDAP GILLED GILLER GINNED GINNER GLOOMY GOBBED GOBBER
GOBBLE GOSSIP GOTTEN GREEDS GREEDY GREEKS GREENS GREENY GREETS GROOMS GROOVE
GROOVY GUFFAW GULLET GULLEY GUMMED GUMMER GUNNED GUNNEL GUNNER GUSSET GUTTED
GUTTER GUZZLE GYPPED GYPPER GYPPOS HAGGIS HAGGLE HAGGLY HALLOW HAMMED HAMMER
HAPPEN HARRIS HARROW HASSID HASSLE HATTED HATTER HELLOS HENNAS HICCUP HIDDEN
HILLED HIPPED HIPPOS HISSED HISSER HITTER HOBBED HOBBER HOBBIT HOBBLE HOBBLY
HOGGED HOGGER HOLLER HOPPED HOPPER HORRID HOTTED HOTTEN HOTTER HUBBED HUBBER
HUDDLE HUFFED HUFFER HUGGED HUGGER HULLED HULLER HUMMED HUMMER HURRAY HUSSAR
HUSSEY HUTTED JABBED JABBER JAGGED JAMMED JAMMER JARRED JAZZED JAZZES JIBBED
JIBBER JIGGED JIGGER JIGGLE JIGGLY JITTER JOBBED JOBBER JOGGED JOGGER JOGGLE
JOSSED JOSSER JOTTED JOTTER JUGGED JUGGLE JUTTED KAFFIR KELLYS KIBBLE KIDDER
KIDDOS KILLED KILLER KIPPED KIPPER KISSED KISSER KITTED KITTEN KNEELS KRAALS
KUMMEL LADDER LADDIE LAGGED LAGGER LAPPED LAPPER LASSIE LATTER LESSON LESSOR
LIBBER LIDDER LIGGET LINNET LIPPED LISSOM LITTER LOBBED LOBBER LOGGED LOGGER
LOGGIA LOPPED LOPPER LOTTED LOTTER LUBBER LUFFED LUFFER LUGGED LUGGER LUMMOX
MADDEN MADDER MAGGOT MALLED MALLET MALLOW MANNED MANNER MAPPED MAPPER MARRED
MARROW MASSED MASSIF MATTED MATTER MELLON MELLOW MERROW MEZZOS MIDDAY MIDDEN
MIDDLE MIFFED MILLED MILLER MILLET MINNOW MISSAL MISSED MITTEN MIZZEN MOBBED
MOBBER MOLLIE MOPPED MOPPER MOPPET MORRIS MOSSED MOTTLE MOZZIE MUDDLE MUFFED
MUFFIN MUFFLE MUGGED MUGGER MULLAH MULLED MULLER MURRAY MUSSED MUSSEL MUTTER

MUTTON MUZZLE MYRRHS NABBED NABBER NAGGED NAGGER NAPPED NAPPER NAPPIE NARROW
NATTER NETTLY NIBBED NIBBER NIBBLE NIGGLE NIGGLY NIPPED NIPPER NIPPLE NOBBLY
NODDER NOGGED NOTTED NOZZLE NUBBED NUBBLY NUGGET NULLED NUTTED NUTTER NUZZLE
PADDER PADDLE PALLED PALLET PALLID PALLOR PANNED PANNER PARROT PASSED PASSEL
PASSER PATTED PATTER PEBBLY PHOOED PHOOEY PIDDLE PIFFLE PIGGED PILLAR PILLED
PILLER PILLOW PINNED PINNER PITTED PITTER PIZZAS PODDER POLLED POLLEN POLLER
POLLET POMMEL POMMIE POSSIE POSSUM POTTED POTTER PREENS PROOFS PUDDLE PUDDLY
PUFFED PUFFER PUFFIN PUGGED PULLED PULLER PULLET PULLEY PUNNED PUNNER PURRED
PUTTED PUTTER PUZZLE QUEENS QUEERS RABBIS RABBIT RABBLE RAFFLE RAGGED RAMMED
RAPPED RATTED RATTLE RATTLY RAZZED RAZZES RAZZLE RIBBED RIBBON RIDDEN RIDDLE
RIFFED RIGGED RILLED RIMMED RIPPED RIPPLE RIPPLY ROBBED ROLLED ROTTED ROTTEN
RUBBED RUBBLE RUBBLY RUFFED RUFFLE RUGGED RUNNEL RUSSEL RUSSET RUSSIA RUSSKI
RUSSKY RUTTED SADDEN SADDER SADDLE SAGGED SAGGER SALLOW SAPPED SAPPER SAPPHO
SAVVEY SHIITE SHOOED SILLED SIMMER SINNED SINNER SIPPED SIPPER SITTAR SITTER
SIZZLE SKIIER SKIING SLEEPY SLEETY SLEEZY SMOOCH SMOOTH SNEERY SNEEZY SNOOPY
SNOOTY SNOOZE SNOOZY SOBBED SOBBER SOCCER SODDEN SODDER SOFFIT SONNET SOPPED
SOPPER SORREL SOTTED SPEECH SPEEDY SPOOKY SPOONY STEELY STOOGE SUBBED SUCCOR
SUDDEN SUFFER SUFFIT SUFFIX SULLED SULLEN SUMMED SUMMER SUMMIT SUMMON SUNNED
SUPPED SUPPER SUPPLE SUPPLY SURREY SUTTLE SWEETY SWOONY TABBED TABBER TAGGED
TAGGER TALLER TALLOW TANNED TANNER TAPPED TAPPEN TAPPER TARRED TASSEL TENNIS
TIDDLY TIFFED TIGGER TILLED TILLER TINNED TINNER TIPPED TIPPER TIPPLE TIPPLY
TISSUE TODDLE TOGGED TOGGLE TOLLED TOLLER TOPPED TOPPER TOPPLE TORRID TOSSED
TOSSER TOSSUP TROOPS TUBBED TUBBER TUGGED TUGGER TUNNEL TUSSAH TUSSLE TWEEDS
TWEEDY VALLEY VELLUM VILLAN VILLAS VITTLE VOLLEY WADDER WADDIE WADDLE WADDLY
WAFFLE WAFFLY WAGGED WAGGER WAGGLE WAGGLY WALLED WALLER WALLET WALLOP WARRED
WARREN WATTLE WHEELS WHEELY WHEEZY WHOOPS WIGGED WIGGER WIGGLE WIGGLY WILLED
WILLER WINNER WIPPED WITTAL WITTED WOBBLE WOBBLY YABBER YAKKED YAKKER YAPPED
YAPPER YARROW YELLOW YIPPED YUCCAS ZAGGED ZIGGED ZIPPED ZIPPER

ABCDAA ENTREE LOWELL SCHUSS STRESS

ABCDAB ANDEAN CHURCH DECADE DECIDE DECODE DELUDE DEMODE DENUDE DERIDE DORADO
EDITED EMBLEM ERASER ESPIES GEORGE ICENIC ICONIC INVEIN MAXIMA ORATOR REBORE
REFIRE REHIRE RETIRE REWIRE ROMERO SHYISH TOMATO UNSPUN

ABCDAC ANYWAY COERCE EARNER EASIES ENSUES INTUIT MIASMA PRIAPI RETORT RISERS

ABCDAD ELIDED ELUDED ENODED ERASES ERODED EVADED EXUDED KIOSKS MIASMS NOVENE
TAHITI TOASTS TRUSTS TRYSTS TWISTS

ABCDAE ABORAL ABROAD ACETAL ACTUAL ADRIAN ADULAR AERIAL AERIAN AFGHAN AFLOAT
AGLEAM AIRMAN AIRWAY ALOHAS ALPHAS AMEBAS AMNIAC AMORAL AMULAE ANIMAL ANODAL
ANORAK AORTAE AORTAL AORTAS APNEAS ARECAS ARENAS AROMAL AROMAS ASHCAN ASHMAN
ASHPAN ASQUAT ASTRAL ASTRAY ATONAL ATRIAL AUREAL AVOCAT AVOWAL AXEMAN AXONAL
BLURBS BRUMBY CALICO CANUCK CHANCE CHANCY CHOICE CHOICY CLENCH CLINCH CLUTCH
COLICS COMICS CONICS COTICE CROTCH CROUCH CRUNCH CRUTCH CUBICS CURACY CYNICS
DIPODE DIPODY DIRNDL DREADS DROUDS DRUIDS DRYADS EAGLED EAGLES EAGLET EAGRES
EARNED EASIER EASTED EASTER ECHOED ECHOER ECHOES EDGIER EDUCES EITHER ELATED
ELATER ELATES ELITES ELOPED ELOPER ELOPES ELUDER ELUDES ELUTED EMOTED EMOTER
EMOTES ENAMEL ENSUED ENSUER ENURED ENURES ENVIED ENVIER ENVIES ERADES ERASED
ERODES ESCHEW ESPIED ESPIER ETCHED ETCHER ETCHES ETUDES EVADER EVADES EVILER

EVOKED EVOKER EVOKES EXILED EXILER EXILES EXITED EXITES EXONER EXUDES GOINGS
GRANGE GRINGO GRUDGE HEATHS HEATHY HEIGHT IAMBIC IBERIA IBERIC IMPAIR INLAID
INSTIL IRANIS IRAQIS IRONIC ISCHIA ITALIC KAPOKS KLINKS KLUNKS KNACKS KNACKY
KNICKS KNOCKS KODAKS KOPEKS KULAKS LABELS LABILE LACILY LAIDLY LAMELY LANKLY
LAPELS LASTLY LATELY LAZILY LAZULI LEANLY LEGALS LEWDLY LIABLE LIBELS LIKELY
LIMPLY LIONLY LIVELY LOCALE LOCALS LOCULE LOCULI LOFTLY LONELY LONGLY LORDLY
LORELS LOTHLY LOUDLY LOVELY LOYALS LUSHLY LUSTLY MAXIMS NAMING NOMINA NOSING
NOTING NOVENA NUDING NYLONS OAKBOY OCELOT ONFLOW OPTION OREGON OUTROW OWLDOM
PINUPS PLUMPS PLUMPY POLYPS PRIAPE PRIMPS PROMPT RACERS RAKERS RAPERS RATERS
RAVERS RAYERS RAZERS RAZORS REBORN REBURN REBURY RECORD RECORK RECURL RECURS
REDARN REFORD REFORM REFURL REGARD REMARK REMORA REPORT RESORT RETARD RETURF
RETURN REWARD REWARM REWARN REWORD REWORK RICERS RIDERS RIGORS RIMERS RIVERS
ROBERS ROPERS ROSARY ROSERY ROTARY ROVERS ROWERS RULERS RUMORS SADISM SADIST
SAFEST SAGEST SALISH SAMISH SANEST SCHISM SCHIST SHYEST SIWASH SKYISH SLYEST
SLYISH SOFIST SOREST SPARSE SPLASH SPLOSH SPOUSE SQUASH SQUISH SUREST TAINTE
TAINTS TAPETS TAROTS TAUNTS TEMPTS THEFTS THIRTY TIGHTS TINCTS TOASTY TONITE
TOXITY TRACTS TRAITS TREATS TREATY TROUTS TROUTY TRUSTY TWENTY TWISTY UMLAUT
UNFOUL UNGLUE UNIQUE UNPLUG UNSOUR UNTRUE URANUS URNFUL USEFUL UTERUS VOTIVE
WIDOWS WIDOWY

ABCDBA ANGINA CISTIC CITRIC DEBTED DECKED DEFIED DEICED DELVED DENIED DENTED
DESKED DEUCED DIAMID DIOXID ENGINE EVOLVE HALVAH LABIAL LARVAL MUSEUM NEATEN
NIACIN NOTION READER REAMER REAPER RELIER RENDER RENTER RUMOUR SABRAS SAMBAS
SANTAS SAUNAS SEGUES SEINES SEIZES SELVES SERGES SERIES SERVES SKULKS SKUNKS
SMARMS STARTS STILTS STINTS STOATS STOUTS STRUTS STUNTS TIDBIT TILSIT WARSAW

ABCDBB DEBTEE DECREE DEGREE FEUDEE LENDEE SEABEE SENDEE VENDEE

ABCDBC BANYAN BEDOED BIGWIG COSMOS CUTOUT DENSEN FANTAN HEDGED HERDER HEYDEY
HOBNOB INTENT JERKER KASHAS KEDGED KERNER KOWTOW LEDGED LONDON MAYDAY MERGER
MESHES MUKLUK NAYSAY NITWIT OUTJUT OUTPUT PASTAS PAYDAY PENMEN PICNIC RAGBAG
RAGTAG RANDAN RESUES SANPAN SERGER SERVER TERSER TORPOR UNKINK VERGER VERSER
WAYLAY WEDGED

ABCDBD BAGDAD BALSAS BEADED BEARER BENDED BIOSIS CEASES DEARER FEARER FENDED
FEUDED GELDED HEADED HEARER HERDED KANSAS LEADED LEASES LENSES MELDED MENDED
MENSES NEARER PENSES RENDED REUSES SEARER SEPTET SEXTET STRATA TEARER TEASES
TENDED TENSES TERSES TORSOS VENDED VERSES WEARER WELDED WENDED

ABCDBE AERIED AERIES AINOID ALKYLS ANOINT ANYONE ARBERS ARBORS ARBORY ARDERS
ARDORS ARMERS ARMORS ARMORY ARTERY BADMAN BAGMAN BALKAN BALSAM BANTAM BANZAI
BARMAN BASHAW BASIAL BATEAU BATMAN BAYMAN BEADER BEAKED BEAKER BEAMED BEAMER
BEANED BEARED BEATEN BEATER BEAVER BEIGES BELIED BELIEF BELIER BELIES BELTED
BELTER BENDER BESPEW BESTED BESTER BETHEL BIACID BIGLIP BIOPIC BIOTIC BIOTIN
BIOXID BIRDIE BLUELY BONGOS BORZOI BOSTON BOYDOM BRIARY BRIERS BRIERY BUGOUT
BULGUR BURNUP BYWAYS CABMAN CADEAU CAESAR CAFTAN CANVAS CAPMAN CAPRAS CAPUAN
CARIAN CARMAN CARNAL CARPAL CASBAH CASUAL CATHAY CATNAP CAUSAL CAVEAT CAVIAR
CAYMAN CEASED CEILED CEILER CENSED CENTER COMBOS COMPOT CONDOM CONDOR CONSOL
CONVOY CORDON COUPON COWBOY CRIERS CRYERS CUPFUL CURIUM DACHAS DAYMAN DEAFEN
DEAFER DEALER DECKER DECREW DEFIER DEFIES DEFLEA DEFLEX DEFTER DEICER DEICES
DELVER DELVES DENIER DENIES DENSER DENTER DENVER DEUCES DEWIER DEXTER DIAPIR

```
DIETIC DIMWIT DISTIL DOBSON DOCTOR DREARS DREARY DRIERS DUGOUT DUSTUP EARCAP
EARLAP EARWAX ENDING ENFANT ENLINK FABIAN FACIAL FACIAS FAECAL FAUNAE FAUNAL
FAUNAS FEARED FELTED FELTER FENCED FENCER FENCES FENDER FERNED FESTER FIBRIL
FIBRIN FIRKIN FLAILS FLATLY FLIPLY FOLIOS FOLSOM FORGOT FRIARS FRIARY FRIERS
FRYERS FUMOUS FUNDUS FUNGUS GALWAY GASMAN GATEAU GEARED GELDER GENDER GENIES
GENRES GEODES GERMED GESTED GESTER GEYSER GILPIN GIRLIE GLADLY GLIBLY GLUILY
GLUMLY HABEAS HAIDAN HAIDAS HALVAS HANGAR HEADER HEALED HEALER HEAPED HEAPER
HEATED HEATER HEAVED HEAVEN HEAVER HEAVES HEBREW HEDGER HEDGES HEFTED HEFTER
HEIFER HELMED HELMET HELPED HELPER HERIES HERMES HEROED HEROES HERPES HINDIS
HOTBOX HOTDOG HUMBUG HUMOUR HUMOUS INBENT INBOND INCANS INCANT INCEND INDENT
INFANT INLAND INSANE INSUNK INTEND INTONE INVENT JACKAL JAGUAR JERKED JERSEY
JESTED JESTER JUGFUL KAFTAN KANGAS KARMAS KASBAH KASHAN KASPAR KEDGER KEDGES
KENTED KERNED KERNEL KEYMEN KILTIE KNOWNS LANDAU LARIAT LARVAE LARVAS LASCAR
LAURAS LAWMAN LAYMAN LEADEN LEADER LEAFED LEAFEN LEAFER LEAKED LEAKER LEANED
LEANER LEAPED LEAPER LEASED LEASER LEAVED LEAVEN LEAVER LEAVES LECHER LECHES
LEDGER LEDGES LEFTER LEGMEN LENDER LENSED LEVIED LEVIER LEVIES LEWDER LICHIS
LIMBIC LIMNIC LIMPID LIMPIN LIPOIC LIPOID LIQUID LITHIA LITHIC LOTION LOWBOY
MACKAW MADCAP MADRAS MAFIAS MAGYAR MANGAR MANIAC MANIAS MANUAL MARIAN MARIAS
MAYHAP MAZDAS MEAGER MEANED MEANER MEDLEY MELDER MELTED MELTER MENDER MEOWED
MERGED MERGES MESHED METHES METIER METRES MEWLED MEWLER MIDAIR MIDPIT MIOTIC
MISFIT MISHIT MONGOL MOSCOW MOTION MOUTON MUCOUS MUGFUL NARWAL NEARED NEATED
NEATER NECKED NECKER NEPHEW NERVED NERVES NESTED NESTER NETHER NEUTER NICKIE
NITRIC OAHUAN OARMAN OASEAN OCRACY OCTICS ORDERS ORDURE ORNERY OUTBUY OUTGUN
OUTRUN PADUAN PALMAE PANDAS PARIAH PARIAL PARKAS PARLAY PASCAL PATHAN PAUSAL
PEAHEN PEAKED PEAKER PEALED PEALER PEATED PECKED PECKER PEDLER PEGMEN PEKOES
PELTED PELTER PEONES PERGED PERGES PERKED PERMED PESTER PETREL PEWTER PIDGIN
PIDJIN PINKIE PISTIA PISTIL POGROM POISON POLIOS PORION POTBOY POTHOS POTION
PREARM PREDRY PRETRY PRIERS PRIORS PRIORY PURSUE QUORUM RACIAL RADIAL RADIAN
RADMAN RAGLAN RAGMAN RAIYAT RASCAL RATBAG REAMED REAPED RECHEW REFLEW REFLEX
REFUEL REHOED REHOES REINED RELIED RELIEF RELIES RENGED RENTED RENTES REOPEN
RESKEW RESLEW RESPEW RESTED RESTEM RESTEP RESUED RETIED RETIES REUSED REVIEW
REVUES RHYTHM RODEOS ROMEOS ROSCOE ROSTOV RUCKUS RUEFUL RUFOUS RUMPUS RUNOUT
SACRAL SAMOAN SAMPAN SANDAL SATRAP SAWMAN SCARCE SCONCE SCORCH SCOTCH SEABED
SEALED SEALER SEAMED SEAMEN SEAMER SEARED SEATED SEATER SECRET SEGUED SEINED
SEINER SEIZED SEIZER SENDER SEQUEL SERGED SERVED SEXIER SILKIE SILVIA SKUNKY
SLIMLY SLOWLY SMARMY STILTY STINTY STOUTY STUNTY SUBDUE SULFUR TAGMAN TAIGAS
TAIPAN TAIWAN TAPMAN TARMAC TARMAN TARSAL TARZAN TAXMAN TEAMED TEAMER TEARED
TEASED TEASER TEMPER TEMPES TENDER TENSED TENSER TERCEL TERMED THIGHS TIGRIS
TOMBOY TONSOR TOYDOM TRIARY TRIERS TUBFUL TUMOUR TURNUP UNBEND UNBENT UNBIND
UNBONE UNDONE UNHAND UNHANG UNIONS UNKIND UNLINE UNLINK UNPENS UNPENT UNPINS
UNRING UNSENT UNWIND UNWONT URGERS VACUAL VANDAL VARIAD VARSAL VEILED VEILER
VEINED VEINER VENDER VENTED VENTER VENUES VERDET VERGED VERGES VERSED VERTEX
VESPER VESTED VESTER VETOED VETOER VETOES VICTIM VIOLIN VIRGIN VITRIC WAXMAN
WAYMAN WEAKEN WEAKER WEALED WEANED WEANER WEASEL WEAVED WEAVER WEAVES WEDGER
WEDGES WEFTED WEIRED WELDER WELTED WELTER WESTED WESTER WETHER WITHIE WITHIN
YELPED YELPER YEOMEN ZEALED ZEROED ZEROES ZESTED
```

ABCDCA AURORA CLINIC CRITIC DIETED DUELED DUOPOD ENGAGE ESTATE PHILIP RIEVER
SCENES SIEGES SIEVES SUEDES SWEDES TENANT TRILIT TWILIT

ABCDCB ACIDIC BREWER GLYCYL GREYER OSIRIS PETITE POTATO PREFER PREYER REVIVE
UNEVEN

ABCDCC OBSESS   **ABCDCD** CRISIS SUEDED THESES TIERER WHEYEY ZENANA

ABCDCE ALEGER ALIBIS AMINIC ANILIC APEXED APEXES ASTUTE AURORE AWNING AXEMEN
BALDLY BASEST BIAXAL BLINIS BOLDLY BONING BORERS BREMEN BREVET BREWED BRIGIT
BROMOS BRUTUS CABOBS CALMLY CANINE CANING CANONS CARERS CHEWED CHEWER CLEVER
CLINIA COAXAL COLDLY CONANT CONING CORERS CRAVAT CREPED CREPES CREPEY CRETES
CREWEL CUEMEN CURARE CURERS DARERS DECOCT DEIFIC DESIST DIESEL DIETER DISUSE
DRAMAS DUELER DUOMOS ELICIT ELIXIR ENTITY FAECES FARERS FIRERS FLEAED FLEWED
FLEXED FLEXES FLEYED FLYBYS FRACAS FRIGID FUELED FUELER FURORE FURORS GLEBES
GORERS GRAHAM GREBES GREYED GUANAS GUAVAS HIATAL HIRERS HOLILY HONING IBEXES
ICEMEN ILAMAS INGAGE IRENES ISOLOG ISOPOD ISOPOR ITEMED JURORS KABOBS KEBABS
KEBOBS KOALAS LIANAS LIEDER LIEFER LIEGER LIEGES LINENS LINENY LURERS MILDLY
MISUSE MOANAS MOTETS MUTATE NABOBS NAEVES NIECES NOTATE OBEYED OBEYER OCTETS
OCULUS OMELET OMENED OPENED OPENER ORIGIN OVERED OVULUM OWNING OXIDIC PALELY
PANING PARERS PENANG PETITS PHASAL PHILIA PHOTON PHOTOS PIECED PIECER PIECES
PIEMEN PIERED PINONS PLANAR PLAZAS PLEAED PLEBES PORERS PRECES PREMED PRESET
PREYED PROLOG PROTON PROVOS PRUNUS QUEBEC RAISIN RECOCK RESIST RIATAS ROTATE
SALTLY SCARAB SCENED SEABAG SEAMAN SEAWAY SHAMAN SHEKEL SHOLOM SHTETL SIEGED
SIEGER SIEVED SIEVER SKEWED SKEWER SKIVIE SLEWED SOEVER SOLELY SONANT SPEWED
SPEWER SPIRIT SPUTUM STALAG STEREO STEVEN STEWED STOLON SWEDEN TAURUS TEAMAN
TENONS THEMED THEMER THEMES THERES THORON TIARAS TIERED TIPUPS TIRERS TONING
TRIFID TRIVIA TUNING UNCOCK UNGAGS UNIFIC UNIOID UNSASH UPCOCK URNING VIEWED
VIEWER VILELY WANING WHERES WHEYED WIENER WILDLY WILELY WIRERS WISEST XENONS
XYLOLS ZONING

ABCDDA SCOFFS SCOTTS SCREES SCUFFS SCULLS SHELLS SHILLS SHIRRS SHMOOS SKIFFS
SKILLS SKULLS SLUFFS SMALLS SMELLS SNIFFS SNUFFS SPELLS SPIFFS SPILLS SPREES
STAFFS STALLS STIFFS STILLS STUFFS SWELLS

ABCDDB PAELLA STREET UNSEEN UPKEEP

ABCDDC APOLLO BOPEEP CAREER DIEPPE FUSEES GROTTO INDEED PIAZZA PIERRE STEPPE

ABCDDE ABLOOM AGREED AGREES ASLEEP ASWOON ATOLLS BETOOK BLOTTY BLUFFS BLUFFY
BLURRY BRAGGY BRASSY BRATTY BRIGGS BROLLY CAHOOT CAREEN CAROON CHAFFS CHAFFY
CHAPPY CHARRY CHATTY CHERRY CHEVVY CHILLS CHILLY CHIPPY CHITTY CHIVVY CHOPPY
CHUBBY CHUFFS CHUFFY CHUKKA CHUMMY CLAMMY CLASSY CLIFFS CLIFFY CLODDY CLOGGY
CLOPPY CLOTTY CLUBBY CRABBY CRAGGY CRANNY CRAPPY CRUDDY CRUMMY DEWOOL DRABBY
DRAGGY DREGGY DRESSY DRILLS DRIPPY DROPPY DRUGGY DRUMMY DUALLY DUENNA DWELLS
EVILLY EXMOOR FAILLE FLABBY FLAGGY FLAPPY FLITTY FLOPPY FLOSSY FLURRY FOULLY
FRAPPE FRETTY FRILLS FRILLY FRIZZY FROGGY GABOON GALOOT GHETTO GLARRY GLASSY
GLOBBY GLOSSY GLUMMY GLUTTY GNATTY GOUTTY GRABBY GRAMMY GRANNY GRASSY GRILLS
GRILLY GRINNY GRIPPE GRIPPY GRITTY GRUBBY GRUFFY HUZOOR IDYLLS IGLOOS INDOOR
INROOM JOHNNY KAZOOS KNELLS KNOBBY KNOLLS KNOLLY KNOTTY KNUBBY KRILLS LAGOON
LATEEN LYCEES MAILLE MAROON MOUSSE ODESSA ORALLY OVALLY PAYEES PHALLI PLATTY
PLOTTY PLUGGY PLUMMY POTEEN POUFFS PRETTY PRISSY PSYLLA PUREED PUREES QUAFFS
QUARRY QUELLS QUERRY QUILLS QUILLY QUIPPY QUIZZY RACOON RANEES REALLY REBOOK
RECOOK RECOOL REHOOD REHOOK REHOOP RETOOK RETOOL RUPEES SALOON SATEEN SCABBY
SCARRY SCATTY SCHOOL SCOTTY SCREEN SCUDDY SCUFFY SCUMMY SCURRY SCYLLA SHABBY
SHAGGY SHAMMY SHELLY SHERRY SHILLY SHIMMY SHINNY SHNOOK SHODDY SHOPPE SHOPPY
SIENNA SIERRA SKIDDY SKINNY SKIPPY SKITTY SKIVVY SKULLY SLABBY SLAGGY SLAPPY

```
SLIPPY SLITTY SLOBBY SLOPPY SLUBBY SLUMMY SLURRY SLUTTY SMELLY SMOGGY SMUTTY
SNAGGY SNAPPY SNAZZY SNIFFY SNIPPY SNOBBY SNOTTY SNUBBY SPARRY SPIFFY SPINNY
SPLEEN SPOTTY STAGGY STARRY STROOP STUBBY STUCCO STUFFY SWAGGY SWELLY TABOOS
THREES TOPEES TRAPPY TRESSY TRILLS TROLLS TROLLY TUREEN TWIGGY TWILLS TWILLY
TYCOON UMTEEN UNBOOT UNCOOP UNFEEL UNHEED UNHOOD UNHOOK UNHOOP UNLOOP UNPEEL
UNREEL UNROOF UNROOT UNSOOT UPROOT VACUUM VIENNA WHAMMO WHAMMY WHERRY WHIFFS
WHIFFY WHINNY WHIPPY WHIRRS WHIRRY WHOLLY YAHOOS YAZOOS
```

```
ABCDEA AFRICA AGENDA ALTHEA ALUMNA AMELIA AMOEBA ANEMIA ANGOLA ANGORA ANOMIA
ANOXIA AREOLA ARNICA ASTHMA ATHENA BENUMB CELIAC CELTIC CHOLIC CLERIC CLONIC
COGNAC CONIAC COPTIC COSMIC CRANIC CULTIC CYANIC CYSTIC DAMNED DAMPED DANCED
DANGED DARNED DARTED DASHED DAUBED DAWNED DAYBED DEMAND DESAND DEVOID DIALED
DINGED DINTED DIRGED DISBUD DISHED DISKED DOCKED DORMED DOUSED DOWNED DOWSED
DRAPED DRAWED DRAYED DRONED DUCKED DUCTED DULCED DUMPED DUNCED DUNKED DURNED
DUSKED DUSTED DUTIED EDIBLE ELAINE ELAPSE EMBOLE EMIGRE EMPALE EMPIRE ENABLE
ENCAGE ENCAKE ENCASE ENCODE ENCORE ENDIVE ENDURE ENLIVE ENRAGE ENSURE ENTICE
ENTIRE ENZYME EPOCHE EQUATE EQUINE ERMINE ESCAPE ETHANE EUCHRE EUNICE EUROPE
EVALUE EVINCE EXCISE EXCITE EXCUSE EXHALE EXHUME EXPIRE EXPOSE GAMING GAPING
GATING GAZING GLUING GORING GYPING HAUNCH HEALTH HEARTH HOWDAH INCUBI ISMALI
KODIAK KOPECK LACTYL LAPFUL LAUREL LAWFUL LENTIL LETHAL LIMBAL LINEAL LINTEL
LIONEL LUMBAL LUTEAL MAGNUM MANISM MAYHEM MEDIUM MEGRIM MOSLEM MUSLEM MUSLIM
NAPKIN NATION NELSON NEURON NEWTON NORMAN NUBIAN OCTAVO OSWEGO OVERDO OVERGO
PREAMP PRECAP RACIER RACKER RAFTER RAIDER RAILER RAINER RAISER RAMPER RANCOR
RANGER RANKER RANTER RAPIER RAPTER RAPTOR RASHER RASPER RASTER RATHER RECTOR
REPAIR REPOUR RESTIR RHYMER RICHER RIDGER RIFLER RIFTER RIGOUR RINGER RINKER
RINSER RIOTER RISKER ROAMER ROCKER ROMPER ROPIER ROSIER ROSTER ROUSER ROUTER
RUINER RUSHER SABLES SABOTS SABRES SAHIBS SAINTS SAITES SALONS SALVES SALVOS
SANDYS SARGES SATINS SATYRS SAUCES SAUDIS SAUTES SAVERS SAVORS SAVOYS SAWERS
SAXONS SAYERS SCALDS SCALES SCALPS SCAMPS SCARES SCARFS SCATHS SCAUDS SCENTS
SCIONS SCOLDS SCONES SCOPES SCORES SCORNS SCOURS SCOUTS SCOWLS SCRAMS SCRAPS
SCREWS SCRIMS SCRIPS SCRUBS SCUBAS SCYTHS SEBUMS SEDANS SEPIAS SEPOYS SERIFS
SERUMS SERVOS SETUPS SEXTUS SHACKS SHADES SHAFTS SHAKES SHALES SHAMES SHANKS
SHAPES SHARDS SHARES SHARKS SHARPS SHAULS SHAVES SHAWLS SHEAFS SHEARS SHEIKS
SHIFTS SHINES SHIRES SHIRKS SHIRTS SHOALS SHOATS SHOCKS SHORES SHORNS SHORTS
SHOUTS SHOVES SHREDS SHREWS SHRUBS SHRUGS SHUCKS SHUNTS SICLES SIDERS SIDLES
SIENAS SIGHTS SINEWS SINGES SIRENS SIROPS SIRUPS SITARS SITHES SIXERS SIXTES
SIXTHS SIZERS SKATES SKEINS SKIERS SKIRLS SKIRTS SKITES SLACKS SLADES SLAKES
SLANGS SLANTS SLATES SLAVES SLICES SLICKS SLIDES SLIMES SLINGS SLINKS SLOPES
SLOTHS SLUMPS SLUNKS SLURPS SMACKS SMARTS SMEARS SMELTS SMILES SMIRKS SMITES
SMITHS SMOCKS SMOKES SNACKS SNAFUS SNAILS SNAKES SNARES SNARLS SNEAKS SNIPES
SNORES SNORTS SNOUTS SOBERS SOLARS SOLERS SOLIDS SOLVES SONARS SONICS SOUNDS
SOUTHS SOWERS SPACES SPADES SPAINS SPANKS SPARES SPARKS SPATES SPAWNS SPEAKS
SPEARS SPENDS SPERMS SPICES SPIELS SPIERS SPIKES SPINES SPIRES SPITES SPLAYS
SPLITS SPOILS SPOKES SPORES SPORTS SPOUTS SPRATS SPRAYS SPRIGS SPUMES SPURNS
SPURTS SPYERS SQUABS SQUADS SQUATS SQUAWS SQUIDS STACKS STAGES STAINS STAIRS
STAKES STALES STALKS STAMPS STANDS STAPHS STARES STARKS STAVES STEADS STEAKS
STEALS STEAMS STEINS STENOS STERNS STICKS STILES STINGS STINKS STOCKS STOICS
STOKES STOLES STOMAS STOMPS STONES STORES STORKS STORMS STOVES STRAPS STRAWS
STRAYS STREWS STRIPS STROPS STRUMS STUMPS STYLES STYLOS STYLUS SUDANS SUGARS
SUINGS SUITES SULFAS SUMACS SUPERS SURGES SUTRAS SWAINS SWAMIS SWAMPS SWANKS
SWARDS SWARMS SWATHS SWEARS SWEATS SWIFTS SWINGS SWIPES SWIRLS SWORDS SWORLS
```

SYLPHS SYLVAS SYNCHS SYNODS SYRUPS TABLET TALENT TAMEST TANIST TAOIST TAPIST
TAPLET TARGET TARPOT TAUGHT TEAPOT THEIST THIRST THREAT THRIFT THROAT THRUST
THWART TICKET TIPLET TOILET TOMCAT TRIACT TRICOT TRIVET TRUANT TRYOUT TUNIST
TURBOT TYPIST TYRANT WINDOW WINROW YACHTY YEARLY YEASTY YIELDY YOUTHY

ABCDEB ABSORB ACETIC ADORED AGEING ALPHYL ANDRON ARBOUR ARCHER ARDOUR ARGUER
ARMOUR ARTIER ASCOTS ASIDES ASKERS ASPENS ASPICS ASPIES ASTERS ATWIST ATWIXT
BALUGA BEADLE BEAGLE BEANIE BECAME BECOME BEDAZE BEFAME BEFORE BEGONE BEHAVE
BEHOVE BELATE BELTIE BEMUSE BENOTE BERATE BERIDE BERIME BESIDE BETAKE BETIDE
BEWARE BILOXI BOLERO BONITO BORNEO BRACER BRAKER BRAVER BRAYER BRINER BROKER
BUREAU BYPLAY CAMERA CAPITA CARDIA CAYUGA CENTRE CERISE CERULE CHETAH CLAVEL
CLINAL CLONAL COMEDO CRATER CRAVER CROWER CRUDER DACOTA DAHLIA DAKOTA DATURA
DEARIE DEBASE DEBATE DECATE DECIME DECISE DECKLE DECORE DEFACE DEFAME DEFILE
DEFINE DEFUSE DELIME DELINE DELUGE DELUXE DEMISE DEMOTE DEMURE DENOTE DEPOSE
DERATE DERIVE DESIRE DESIZE DETUNE DEVICE DEVISE DEVOTE DOMINO DRAPER DRAWER
DRIVER DRONER DROVER EDWARD EMBALM ENJOIN ENSIGN ESTRUS FARINA FASCIA FATIMA
FELINE FEMALE FEMINE FERINE FLORAL FOREGO FRAMER FRASER GENTLE GLOBAL GLYCOL
GRACER GRADER GRATER GRAVER GRAYER GRAZER GRIPER GROCER GROPER GROWER HECATE
HECKLE HEKATE HEXODE HEXOSE IMBALM INBORN INKMAN INKMEN INTERN INTURN IRONER
ISLAMS ISLAYS ISLETS KELPIE KERITE KETONE KETOSE KEWPIE KRONER LAGUNA LAMBDA
LAMINA LEAGUE LEGATE LEGUME LYMPHY MANILA MANTRA MARINA MEAGRE MEALIE MEANIE
MEASLE MENACE MENAGE MENTHE MODULO MONACO MORPHO NAPTHA NAUSEA NEGATE NESTLE
NEWFIE OGLING ORBIER OSCARS PAGODA PATINA PATRIA PAYOLA PEDULE PENILE PERSUE
PERUSE PESTLE PETRIE PEYOTE PLURAL PRAYER PREWAR PRICER PRIMER PRIZER PROBER
PROVER PRUNER PSALMS PSYCHS REBAKE REBALE REBASE REBATE REBUKE RECAGE RECASE
RECIPE RECITE RECODE REDATE REDIVE REDONE REDUCE REFACE REFILE REFINE REFUGE
REFUSE REFUTE REGALE REGIME REGIVE REGLUE REHALE REHIDE RELATE RELIME RELINE
RELIVE REMADE REMAKE REMISE REMOTE REMOVE RENAME REPACE REPAGE REPAVE REPINE
REPOSE REPUTE RESALE RESCUE RESHOE RESIDE RESITE RESIZE RESOLE RESUME RETAKE
RETAME RETAPE RETILE RETUNE RETYPE REVILE REVISE REVOKE REVOTE REWAKE REWAVE
REWOKE REWOVE REZONE ROADEO ROMANO SABINA SALIVA SALVIA SANDRA SCENIC SEANCE
SECURE SEDATE SEDUCE SEMITE SEMPLE SENATE SENILE SERAPE SEWAGE SHEATH SHEIKH
SHILOH STRAIT STREIT STRICT STUART STYLET SWATOW SYDNEY SYLPHY SYNODY SYRUPY
TABULA TACOMA TANICA TARSIA TEMPLE TENDRE TENURE THOUGH THRASH THRESH THRUSH
TIVOLI TOLEDO TOREDO TRACER TRADER TREMOR TYPIFY UNBORN UNGOWN UNHEWN UNISON
UNJOIN UNLEAN UNMOWN UNOPEN UNPAWN UNPLAN UNREIN UNSAWN UNSEWN UNSKIN UNSOWN
UNSPAN UNSPIN UNTORN UNTOWN UNWORN USAGES USHERS USINGS UTMOST VAGINA VENICE
WEARIE WRITER YAKIMA

ABCDEC AISLES AMNION APTEST ARCTIC AREOLE ARSONS ARTIST AVENGE AVENUE AVERSE
BADGED BARGER BARKER BARTER BASHES BASICS BASILS BASINS BENIGN BESOMS BESOTS
BIRDER BISONS BODIED BORDER BRAHMA BRONCO BRYONY BUDGED BUNION BUNSEN BURGER
BURIER BURLER BURNER BURSAR BUSHES BUSIES CADGED CAGING CANTON CANYON CARDER
CARPER CARTER CARVER CASERS CASHES CATGUT CHEQUE CHERIE CHEVRE CLEAVE COBWEB
CORDER CORKER CORNER COSIES CRANIA CREASE CREATE CREOLE CURBER CURLER CURSER
CURSOR CURTER CURVER CUSHES CUTEST CUTLET CYSTIS DARKER DARNER DARTER DASHES
DELTAL DHARMA DISCUS DISHES DOGLEG DORMER DOSERS DRACMA DURBAR EDGING EXTANT
EXTORT FAERIE FARMER FENIAN FERVOR FIERCE FIRMER FISCUS FISHES FLYBOY FOLIAL
FORCER FORGER FORKER FORMER FUDGED FURLER FUSILS GARNER GARTER GASHES GAYETY
GIRDER GISMOS GORIER GRAMPA GREASE GUNMAN GUNMEN GUSHES GUSTOS HARBOR HARDER
HARIER HARMER HARPER HASIDS HECTIC HEYDAY HORNER HORSER HOSTAS HURLER HURTER

HYDRID INSETS INTACT INTEXT JAHWEH JOSEFS JOSHES JOSIES JUDGED KENYAN LACTIC
LARDER LARGER LARKER LASERS LASHES LATENT LATEST LAYBOY LAYERY LINDEN LINGEN
LINGON LINTEN LODGED LOSERS LURKER LUSHES LUTIST LYNDEN LYSINS MADRID MARKER
MARTYR MASERS MASHES MASONS MAYFLY MESONS MINCAN MISERS MORTAR MUNION MUNTIN
MURDER MUSERS MUSHES MUSICS MUTANT MUTEST MUTIST NOTIST NUDGED NURSER NUTLET
OCTANT OFTEST ONSETS OUTACT OUTEAT OUTFIT OUTHIT OUTJET OUTLET OUTSET OUTSIT
OUTWIT OVARIA PAGING PARKER PARLOR PARSER PARTER PASTES PATENT PECTIC PENMAN
PHASMA PIERCE PINKEN PINMAN PINMEN PINYON PISCES PLAGIA PLASMA PLEASE PLEDGE
POESIE PORKER PORTER POSERS POSEYS POSIES POTENT PREMIE PREVUE PRONTO PURGER
PURLER PURSER PUSHES QUADRA QUALIA QUANTA RAGING RASHES RASTUS REDBUD REHASH
RENOWN REPUMP RESAWS RESINS RESODS RESOWS RIDGED RINCON ROSIES ROTGUT RUANDA
RUSHES SCABIA SCENAE SETOUT SHEAVE SHELVE SIDLED SIECLE SLEDGE SORCER SORTER
SPATIA SPECIE SPENCE SPRIER SPRYER STANZA STELAE SUNKEN SUNTAN SURFER SVELTE
SWERVE TARIER TENDON TENPIN TENSON THENCE THYMEY TINMAN TINMEN TOPCAP TRAUMA
TREBLE TURNER TUSHES TWELVE UGANDA UNBARB UNDEAD UNDYED UNEASE UNEDGE UNPROP
UNSETS UNSEWS UNTILT UPROAR UPSETS UPTILT URANIA URGING VARIER VIRGER VISERS
VISORS VISTAS WAGING WAMPUM WANTON WARDER WARMER WARNER WARPER WASHES WASTES
WHENCE WIDEND WILFUL WISENS WISERS WISHES WORDER WORKER WORMER YAHWEH YARDER
YARNER

ABCDED ABIDED ABODED ABUSES ABYSMS ADHERE ADORER AMPERE AMUSES ANISES APIECE
ARISES ATHENE AURENE BALDED BANDED BAWDED BEASTS BIASES BIGEYE BIRDED BLADED
BLASTS BOASTS BOLSAS BONDED BOWSES BRIDED BRISKS BUGEYE BURSAS BURSES BURSTS
CANDID CARDED CAUSES CENSUS CHASES CHASMS CHESTS CHIDED CHOSES CHROMO CLASPS
CLOSES COASTS COHERE COPSES CORDED CRESTS CRISES CRISPS CRUSTS CUPOLO CURDED
CURETE CURSES DEISTS DOCETE DOMINI DOUSES DOWSES DULSES EARBOB EIGHTH EXISTS
FAIRER FALSES FEASTS FIRSTS FLARER FLASKS FLISKS FOISTS FOLDED FORDED FRIEZE
FRISKS FROSTS FUHRER FUNDED GAMETE GEMINI GHOSTS GILDED GIRDED GLIDED GLYCIC
GOADED GOLDED GORSES GRADED GRASPS GRIDED GRIEVE GRISTS GUESTS GUIDED GUISES
HANDED HAWSES HEISTS HOISTS HORSES HOUSES IGUANA IMPALA IMPEDE IPECAC ITHACA
JICAMA JOISTS JOUSTS KIMONO LANDED LAPSES LARDED LAUDED LEASTS LIASES LOADED
LORDED LOUSES MANSES MEDICI MENSAS MIASES MIDSTS MIGNON MINDED MIOSES MITRER
MOISTS MOLDED MOUSES MYOSES MYOSIS NOISES NORSES NURSES OCEANA OCTENE OLEANA
OPUSES OUTDID PAIRER PARSES PARSIS PAUSES PHASES PHLEME PHOEBE PHOSIS PICENE
PIRANA PIRENE PLASMS PLASTS PLUSES POISES PONDED POURER PRIDED PRISES PRISMS
PROSES PULSES PURSES PYJAMA PYRENE QUADED QUESTS RAIDED RAISES RHESUS RINDED
RINSES ROADED ROASTS ROUSES ROUSTS SANDED SCARER SCHEME SCORER SHADED SHARER
SHORER SIRENE SLIDED SLIPUP SNARER SNORER SOARER SONATA SORDID SOURER SPADED
SPARER SPHERE SPRYLY STARER STORER THESIS THIEVE TOADED TOURER TRADED UROSIS
VERSTS VERSUS VIOLAL VOIDED WAISTS WANDED WAPITI WARDED WHISKS WHISPS WHISTS
WHORER WINDED WORDED WORSTS WRESTS WRISTS YARDED YEASTS

ABCDEE ACROSS APOGEE ASWELL AVOWEE BEFALL BRULEE BURGEE BYPASS CARESS CONGEE
COULEE CUTOFF DEBURR DEHULL DHOTEE DRAWEE DURESS EMBOSS ENMASS ENROLL EXTOLL
GOATEE HOAXEE JAYCEE JILTEE KAROSS KUMISS LAYOFF LICHEE LOANEE LYCHEE MISADD
MORASS PARSEE PAWNEE PAYOFF PONGEE QUOTEE REBILL REBUFF RECALL REFALL REFILL
REMILL REMISS REPASS REPUFF RETILL RETOSS REWALL RUNOFF SARCEE SCROLL SCRUFF
SETOFF SHRILL SKIDOO SOIREE SQUALL STROLL TARIFF THRALL THRILL TOUPEE UNFILL
UNFREE UNLESS UNROLL UNWELL UPHILL UPNESS UPROLL UPWELL WRITEE YANKEE

SEVEN-LETTER PATTERN WORDS

AABACDE OOLOGIC OOLONGS   **AABBCDA** EELLIKE

AABCADE EELIEST EERIEST OOSPORE   **AABCDED** OOCYSTS

AABCDEF EELBOAT EELFISH EELPOTS EELSHOP EELSKIN OOCYTES OOZIEST

ABAABCA SISSIES

ABAABCD LOLLOPS LOLLOPY MAMMALS MAMMARY MAMMATE NINNIES PEPPERS PEPPERY PIPPIER
PIPPING PIPPINS SISSIER SISSIFY TITTIES

ABAACBD PEPPIER   **ABAACCD** TATTOOS

ABAACDA DIDDLED DODDARD DODDLED GAGGING

ABAACDE BABBLED BABBLER BABBLES BOBBERS BOBBIES BOBBING BOBBINS BOBBLED BOBBLES
BUBBLED BUBBLER BUBBLES DADDIES DODDERS DODDERY DODDLES GAGGERS GAGGLED GAGGLER
GAGGLES GIGGLED GIGGLER GIGGLES GOGGLED GOGGLER GOGGLES LOLLERS LOLLERY LOLLIES
LOLLING LULLABY LULLERS LULLING MAMMIES MAMMOTH MOMMIES MUMMERS MUMMERY MUMMIED
MUMMIES MUMMIFY MUMMING NUNNERY NUNNISH PAPPIES PEPPILY PEPPING PEPPINS POPPERS
POPPETS POPPIED POPPIES POPPING POPPISH PUPPETS PUPPIED PUPPIES PUPPILY SASSIER
SASSING SESSION TATTERS TATTERY TATTIED TATTIES TATTING TATTLED TATTLER TATTLES
TITTERS TITTERY TITTLED TITTLER TOTTERS TOTTERY TOTTLED TOTTLES TUTTING

ABABBCD COCOONS REREELS   **ABABCAD** ACACIAN ACACIAS COCOACH

ABABCBD CACARAS PAPAYAS REREBEL VIVIFIC   **ABABCCA** SUSURRS

ABABCDE COCONUT DADAISM DADAIST ICICLED ICICLES JOJOBAS JUJUBES MIMICAL MIMICRY
PAPABLE PAPAINS PIPIEST PIPINGS POPOVER PUPULOS REREADS REREIGN REREMIT RERENTS
TATAMIS TITIANS ULULANT ULULATE VIVIDER VIVIDLY

ABABDBA REREFER   **ABACADA** ALABAMA   **ABACADD** EVERETT EYELESS

ABACADE ADAMANT ARAMAIC ARAPAHO ARAWAKS AVATARS ELEMENT ELEVENS EVENERS EVENEST
EVEREST EYELETS EYEWEAR INITIAL ODOROUS OZONOUS UNUSUAL URUGUAY

ABACBBD NONBOOK NONFOOD   **ABACBDA** SASHAYS TITLIST

ABACBDE FIFTIES GIGLIOS LILTING MEMBERS NONCOMS NONFORM NONGODS NONGOLD NONPOET
NONPORT PAPUANS POPCORN SISTINE TETHERS TETHERY TITHING TITLIKE TITMICE UNURNED

ABACCDC AMASSES

ABACCDE ADAZZLE ALADDIN AMASSED AMASSER ASADDLE BABOONS OPOSSUM PAPOOSE REROOFS
REROOTS TATOOER

ABACDAA ELECTEE   **ABACDAB** AMALGAM ERECTER USUROUS

ABACDAC ALASKAS EXERTER   **ABACDAD** EMENDED EMERSES EVERSES

ABACDAE ACADIAN ALASKAN ANAGRAM ARABIAN AZALEAS CYCLICS EGESTED EJECTED ELECTED
ELEGIES EMENDER EMERGED EMERGES EMERSED ENEMIED ENEMIES ENERVED ENERVES ERECTED
EVENTED EVERTED EXERTED IDIOTIC NANKING NONBANK NONSANE NONSINE NONSYNC TITRATE

ABACDBA DEDUCED NINEPIN SESAMES   **ABACDBB** USURESS   **ABACDBD** RERISES

ABACDBE DEDUCES NONEGOS NONPROS NONSTOP OZONIZE PAPULAE POPEDOM RERAGES RERAKED
RERAKES RERATED RERATES RERISEN RERIVET REROBED REROBES REROPED REROPES REROWED
TETCHED TITANIC

ABACDCB USURERS   **ABACDCD** PAPERER UKULELE

ABACDCE CECILIA CICADAE CICADAS EVENING GIGOLOS IMITATE PAPERED PIPEMEN POPEYED
POPEYES USURARY

ABACDDC PIPETTE SUSANNA

ABACDDE CUCKOOS FIFTEEN REROLLS RURALLY TOTALLY USUALLY

ABACDEA ACANTHA ANAEMIA ANALGIA ARABICA DIDUCED ELEGIZE ELEVATE EMETINE EPERGNE
EVETIDE EXECUTE EYELIKE EYELINE EYESORE MEMBRUM SISTERS SYSTEMS TETRACT TITRANT

ABACDEB ADAPTED ATAVIST CYCLOPY ERECTOR IRISHER JUJITSU MOMENTO NONHERO NONZERO
ODOURED PAPRIKA PEPSINE PEPTIDE PEPTIZE RERAISE REROUTE UNURBAN USURIES

ABACDEC ABANDON ABASERS ABASHES AWARDER DODGING IMITANT IRISHES PEPSINS PIPEAGE
USURPER WOWSERS

ABACDED ACADEME AWARDED COCKEYE CYCLENE MIMOSAS NONUSES OBOISTS PAPISTS SASHIMI
TUTORER

ABACDEE AWARDEE EYEBALL ICINESS KOKANEE PAPLESS

ABACDEF ABALONE ABASHED ABASING ABASURE ABATERS ABATING ACADEMY ADAGIOS ADAMITE
ADAPTER ADAPTLY ADAPTOR AGAINST ALAMODE ALARMED ALARUMS AMATEUR AMATORY AMAZING
AMAZONS ANALGIC ANALITY ANALOGS ANALOGY ANALYSE ANALYST ANALYZE ANAPEST ANARCHS
ANARCHY ANATHEM ANATOMY APACHES APARTED APATHIC ARABICS ARABISM ARABIST ARABITE
ARABIZE ARABLES ATANGLE ATAVISM AVAILED AVARICE AVARISH AVAROUS AWAITED AWAITER
AWAKENS AWAKING BABYDOM BABYING BABYISH BABYLON BIBELOT BOBCATS BOBSLED BOBTAIL
BUBONIC CACHETS CACHING CACKLED CACKLER CACKLES CACTOID COCAINE COCHINS COCHLEA
COCKADE COCKERS COCKIER COCKIES COCKILY COCKING COCKISH COCKLED COCKLER COCKLES
COCKNEY COCKPIT COCKUPS CUCKOLD CYCLERS CYCLIAN CYCLING CYCLISM CYCLIST CYCLIZE
CYCLOID CYCLONE CYCLOPS DEDUCTS DIDACTS DODGERS DODGERY DODGIER DODGILY DUDGEON
DUDLEYS EJECTOR ELECTOR ELECTRA ELECTRO ELEGANT ELEGIAC ELEGIST EMERALD EMETICS
ENERGIC ERECTLY EREWHON ESEXUAL ETERNAL EVESONG EXEDIFY EXEDING EXEMPLY EXEMPTS
EYEBROW EYECUPS EYEDROP EYEFLAP EYEFULS EYELASH EYELIDS EYEPITS EYEWASH FIFTHLY
GAGSTER IDIOTCY IDIOTRY IRIDATE IRISHLY ITINERA LALIQUE MAMBOED MEMBRAL MEMOING
MEMOIRS MEMORIA MEMPHIS MOMENTA MOMENTS MUMBLED MUMBLER MUMBLES NINTHLY NONACID
NONACTS NONAGED NONBASE NONCASH NONEPIC NONEVIL NONFACT NONFARM NONGAME NONGRAY

NONGREY NONJURY NONLIFE NONPAID NONPEAK NONPLUS NONSALE NONSELF NONSKID NONSLIP
NONSUCH NONSUIT NONTERM NONUSER NUNCIOS NUNLIKE OBOEIST ODONTIA ODONTIC ODORANT
ODORATE ODORFUL ODORIZE OVOCYTE OVOIDAL OZONATE OZONERS OZONIFY PAPULES PAPYRUS
PEPINOS PEPLUMS PEPTALK PEPTICS PEPTIDS PIPEFUL PIPEMAN POPEISM POPETRY POPGUNS
POPLARS POPLINS POPULAR PUPATED PUPATES PUPELOS PUPILAR PUPILED RAREBIT RARIETY
RERACKS RERAILS RERANKS RERINGS SASHING SISTERN SISTRUM SUSCEPT SUSPECT SUSPEND
SUSTAIN SYSTOLE TETANUS TETRADS TETRAZO TETRYLS TITHERS TITLERS TITULAR TITULED
TOTABLE TOTABLY TOTALED TOTEMIC TOTINGS TUTORED TUTORLY UNUPSET UNURGED UNUSAGE
USURING USURPED UVULARS VIVANTS

ABBABBC MUUMUUS   **ABBABCD** INNINGS PEEPERS REERECT TEETERS TEETERY

ABBACAD ARRAYAL ASSAGAI DOODADS ENNEWED ILLICIT

ABBACBD DEEDIER PEEPIER TEETHED TEETHER TEETHES

ABBACDA DOODLED ENNERVE ESSENCE SEESAWS   **ABBACDB** ARRAYER ASSAILS ATTAINT

ABBACDC OPPOSES

ABBACDE ADDABLE AFFABLE AFFABLY AFFAIRS ALLAYED ALLAYER APPAREL ARRAIGN ARRANGE
ARRAYED ASSAULT ASSAYED ASSAYER ATTACHE ATTACKS ATTAINS DEEDBOX DEEDFUL DEEDILY
DEEDING DOODLER DOODLES EFFECTS EFFENDI EGGEDLY HEEHAWS IFFIEST ILLIUMS IMMIXED
IMMIXES NOONDAY OPPOSAL OPPOSED OPPOSER OTTOMAN PEEPING POOPING TOOTERS TOOTHED
TOOTHER TOOTING TOOTLED TOOTLER TOOTLES TOOTSIE

ABBCABD ARREARS BOOTBOY   **ABBCADB** ATTRACT OSSEOUS   **ABBCADC** APPEASE

ABBCADD EGGLESS

ABBCADE ACCLAIM AFFIANT AFFLATE AFFRAYS AGGRADE AGGRATE ALLIANT ANNEALS ANNUALS
ANNUARY APPEALS APPEARS APPLAUD ASSUADE ASSUAGE EGGHEAD HOOCHES INNUITS ISSUING
LOOPLET REEARNS UPPLUCK WOODWAX

ABBCBAA SEERESS   **ABBCBAD** REEDERS REEFERS REEKERS REELERS REEXERT

ABBCBBD BOOHOOS HOODOOS PEEWEES TEEPEES VOODOOS   **ABBCBCD** JEERERS

ABBCBDA SEEDERS SEEKERS SEEMERS   **ABBCBDB** ASSISTS

ABBCBDD FEELESS PEERESS

ABBCBDE COOKOUT DEEMERS DEENERS DEEPENS DEEPEST FEEDERS FEELERS GEEZERS HEEDERS
HEELERS JEEPERS KEELERS KEENERS KEENEST KEEPERS LOOKOUT MEEKENS MEEKEST MEETERS
NEEDERS PEELERS PEEVEYS REEJECT REELECT TEEMERS WEEDERS WEEKEND WEEPERS ZOOLOGY

ABBCCDE ADDEEMS REESSAY UNNEEDY WOOLLED WOOLLEN

ABBCDAD EFFUDED EFFUSES OFFEROR

ABBCDAE ACCRUAL ACCUSAL AMMONAL ANNULAR APPOSAL ARRIVAL ARROYAS ASSEGAI EFFACED

EFFACER EFFACES EFFUMED EFFUMES EFFUSED ESSAYED ESSAYER HOOKAHS ILLOGIC ILLUVIA
LEERILY LOOSELY NEEDING NOOKING NOOSING REENTRY ROOKERS ROOKERY ROOMERS ROOTERS
ROOTERY SOONEST SOONISH SOOTISH

ABBCDBA ADDENDA REEDIER REEFIER REEKIER REENTER SEETHES WOODROW

ABBCDBB LEECHEE   **ABBCDBC** BEERIER LEERIER NEEDLED PEERIER SEEDBED

ABBCDBD ATTESTS

ABBCDBE ADDENDS ANNOINT ANNUENT ATTRITE BEECHES BEEFIER BEETIER BEETLED BEETLER
BEETLES BOOKDOM DOORBOY EGGNOGS FEEBLED FEEBLER FEEBLES HOOSGOW KEELMEN KEESTER
NEEDIER NEEDLER NEEDLES REEMBED REEXPEL ROOFTOP SEEDIER SEEDLET SEEDMEN SEEPIER
SEETHED SEETHER TOOLBOX WEEDIER WEENIES WEEPIER WOODBOX WOODLOT

ABBCDCB UDDERED   **ABBCDCC** OFFEREE

ABBCDCD ACCEDED OFFERER OTTERER UTTERER

ABBCDCE ACCEDER ACCEDES ALLEGED ALLEGER ALLEGES ALLITIC AMMETER ANNEXED ANNEXER
ANNEXES ARROYOS COOEYED COONING KEENING LOOSEST LOOSISH MOONING OFFERED OSSIFIC
OTTAWAN OTTAWAS OTTERED UTTERED WEENING

ABBCDDE BOOTEES COOKEES

ABBCDEA AMMONIA ECCRINE EFFABLE EFFLUVE EFFULGE EGGLIKE ELLIPSE ENNICHE ENNOBLE
GOOFING GOOPING GOOSING HOOFISH HOOKISH LOOPFUL ROOKIER ROOMIER ROOSTER ROOTIER
SEEINGS SOONERS SOOTERS SOOTHES SOOTIES

ABBCDEB ADDUCED ARRIVER ASSENTS ASSERTS ASSIGNS ASSIZES ASSORTS ASSUMES ASSURES
ATTEMPT BEEHIVE BEELINE FEEABLE ILLEGAL ISSUERS KEELAGE PEERAGE REEVADE SEEABLE
SEEDAGE SEEPAGE TEENAGE

ABBCDEC ACCRUER ALLEDGE ASSEIZE ASSERVE IMMENSE IMMERGE IMMERSE INNERVE LOOSENS
LOOSERS NOODLED NOOSERS OFFENCE OFFENSE OFFSETS POODLED ROOTLET SEEDPOD UNNERVE
WOOSHES

ABBCDED ACCOSTS ACCRETE ACCUSES AFFUSES ALLUDED ALLURER ARRESTS ARRIDED ARRISES
ARRODED ASSIEGE ASSURER ASSUROR ATTIRER ILLUDED UNNESTS

ABBCDEE ADDRESS AGGRESS ALLNESS ALLOTEE ELLIOTT ILLNESS INNLESS ODDBALL ODDNESS
OPPRESS

ABBCDEF ABBOTCY ACCENDS ACCENTS ACCEPTS ACCOILS ACCORDS ACCOUNT ACCRUED ACCRUES
ACCURSE ACCUSED ACCUSER ADDIBLE ADDICTS ADDUCER ADDUCES ADDUCTS AFFECTS AFFICHE
AFFIRMS AFFIXER AFFIXES AFFLICT AFFORDS AFFRONT ALLEGRO ALLERGY ALLOVER ALLOWED
ALLOYED ALLUDES ALLURED ALLURES ALLUVIO ALLYING AMMINES AMMONIC ANNELID ANNOYED
ANNOYER ANNUITY APPENDS APPLIED APPLIER APPLIES APPOINT APPOSED APPRISE APPRIZE
ARRIDES ARRIVED ARRIVES ARRODES ARROWED ASSLIKE ASSUMED ASSUMER ASSURED ATTENDS
ATTIRED ATTIRES ATTUNED ATTUNES BEEFILY BEEFING BEEFISH BEEPING BEERILY BEERISH
BEESWAX BOODLES BOOGIES BOOJUMS BOOKEND BOOKERS BOOKERY BOOKFUL BOOKIER BOOKIES

```
BOOKING BOOKISH BOOKLET BOOLIAN BOOMERS BOOMIER BOOMING BOORISH BOOSTED BOOSTER
BOOTERS BOOTERY BOOTIED BOOTIES BOOTING BOOTLEG BOOTMAN BOOTMEN BOOZERS BOOZIER
BOOZILY BOOZING COOKERS COOKERY COOKIES COOKING COOLANT COOLERS COOLEST COOLIES
COOLING COOLISH COONERS COOPERS COOPERY COOPING DEEJAYS DEEMING DEEPISH DEERFLY
DOOMERS DOOMFUL DOOMING DOORMAN DOORMAT DOORMEN DOORWAY DOOZERS DOOZIES EDDYING
EFFORTS EFFRONT EGGCUPS EGGFISH ELLAGIC ELLFISH ERRANCY ERRANDS ERRANTS ERRATIC
ERRATUM FEEDBIN FEEDBOX FEEDING FEEDLOT FEEDMAN FEELING FOOLERS FOOLERY FOOLING
FOOLISH FOOTAGE FOOTERS FOOTING FOOTMAN FOOTMEN FOOTPAD FOOTSIE FOOTWAY FOOYUNG
GOOBERS GOODHAP GOODIES GOODISH GOODMAN GOODMEN GOOFERS GOOFIER GOOFILY GOOIEST
GOONEYS GOONIES GOOSIER HEEDFUL HEEDILY HEEDING HEELING HEELTAP HOODCAP HOODLUM
HOOFERS HOOFING HOOKERS HOOKEYS HOOKIER HOOKIES HOOKING HOOKUPS HOOPERS HOOPING
HOOPLAS HOOSIER HOOTERS HOOTING ILLUMES IMMORAL IMMUNED IMMUNES IMMURED IMMURES
IMMUTED IMMUTES INNARDS INNATED INNERLY INNYARD ISSUANT JEERING KEELING KEELMAN
KEEPING LEERING LEERISH LEEWARD LEEWAYS LOOFAHS LOOKERS LOOKING LOOMERY LOOMING
LOONERY LOONEYS LOONIER LOONIES LOOPERS LOOPIER LOOPING LOOPIST LOOSING LOOTERS
LOOTING MCCARTY MEETING MOOCHED MOOCHER MOOCHES MOODIER MOODILY MOODISH MOOINGS
MOONERS MOONIER MOONIES MOONILY MOONISH MOONLIT MOONSET MOORAGE MOORHEN MOORING
MOORISH MOOTERS MOOTING NEEDFUL NEEDHAM NEEDILY NOODLES NOOKERY NOOKIER NOOKIES
OCCIPUT OCCLUDE OCCLUSE OCCULTS OCCURSE ODDLING ODDMENT OFFBEAT OFFCAST OFFCUTS
OFFENDS OFFHAND OFFICED OFFICER OFFICES OFFINGS OFFLETS OFFSIDE OFFSPIN OFFTAKE
OFFTYPE OFFWARD OSSUARY PEEKING PEELING PEERDOM PEERING PEEVING PEEVISH PEEWITS
POOCHES POODLES POOLERS POOLIER POOLING POOREST POORISH REEBOKS REEDILY REEDING
REEDISH REEDMAN REEFING REEKING REELING REEMPTY REENACT REENDOW REENJOY REEQUIP
REEXALT REEXIST ROOFAGE ROOFING ROOFMAN ROOFMEN ROOKIES ROOKING ROOKISH ROOKLET
ROOMFUL ROOMIES ROOMILY ROOMING ROOSTED ROOTING ROOVING SEEDBOX SEEDFUL SEEDILY
SEEDING SEEDMAN SEEKING SEEMING SEEPING SOOTHED SOOTHER SOOTIED SOOTIER SOOTILY
SOOTING TEEMING TOOLERS TOOLING TOOLMAN TOOLMEN UNNAILS UNNAKED UNNAMED UNNAMES
UNNOBLE UNNOBLY UNNOTED UNNOVEL UPPINGS UPPOINT UTTERLY VEERING WEEDFUL WEEDING
WEEDISH WEEKDAY WEEPFUL WEEPING WEEVILS WEEVILY WEEZING WOOABLE WOODBIN WOODCUT
WOODENS WOODENY WOODERS WOODIER WOODING WOODISH WOODMAN WOODMEN WOOFERS WOOFING
WOOLENS WOOLERS WOOLIER WOOLIES WOOLING WOOLMAN WOOLMEN WOOLSEY WOOZILY ZOOCYST
ZOOFULS ZOOLITE ZOOLITH ZOOMING
```

ABCAACD BLEBBED PREPPED REARRAY   **ABCAADB** ESTEEMS PROPPER TROTTER

ABCAADE BLABBED BLOBBED BLOBBER BLUBBED BLUBBER EXCEEDS FLUFFED FLUFFER OCTOONS
ONLOOKS PLOPPED PROPPED SCISSOR TROTTED TWATTLE TWITTED TWITTER

ABCABAD CONCOCT REARERS   **ABCABBC** TESTEES

ABCABBD REBREED REGREEN REGREET RETREES UNFUNNY UNSUNNY

ABCABCA ALFALFA ENTENTE   **ABCABCB** BARBARA TSETSES

ABCABCD BARBARY BERBERS BERBERY BONBONS CANCANS CHICHIS DUMDUMS KINKING MURMURS
POMPOMS TARTARE TARTARS TARTARY TINTING

ABCABDA ASPASIA ASTASIA HIGHISH SENSERS SHUSHES TINTIST

ABCABDB CASCARA DEADEYE OSMOSES OSMOSIS OSTOSIS   **ABCABDC** RETREAT TESTERS

ABCABDD CARCASS CATCALL LEGLESS NEWNESS REDRESS REGRESS REPRESS

ABCABEF ALKALIC ALKALIS CARCASE CASCADE CONCORD COXCOMB DEADENS DEADERS DEADEST
DIADICS ENVENOM FANFARE GEIGERS GORGONS INRINGS INSINEW INWINDS KICKIER KICKING
KICKISH KINKIER KINKILY LAPLAND LEGLETS LIPLIKE MORMONS ONIONED OSMOSED PALPATE
PAMPANO PIMPING PIMPISH POMPONS POMPOUS REBREWS RECREWS REDREAM REFRESH REGRETS
RETREAD SAPSAGO SAUSAGE SHUSHED SHUSHER SUBSUME SUNSUIT TAGTAIL TARTANS TENTERS
THITHER TILTING TILTISH UNBUNGS UNGUNAL UNLUNAR UNTUNED UNTUNES VALVATE VELVETS
VELVETY VERVETS WAYWARD WOEWORN

ABCACBD PROPORT   **ABCACDC** INSISTS

ABCACDE ASTATIC BRIBING BULBLET IMBIBED IMBIBER IMBIBES INTITLE IODIDES MAIMING
PROPOSE PUMPMAN PUMPMEN TUITION TUITIVE UNRURAL

ABCADAB ENLEVEN TESTATE   **ABCADAC** ENDEWED INCIVIC

ABCADAD EAGERER ENTERER

ABCADAE ABRAXAS ALMANAC ALPACAS ARCANAL ARMADAS EAGERED EASELED EDGEMEN ENJEWEL
ENTERED EOCENES ETHENES ETHERED EXPEDES INDICIA INHIBIT INSIPID OCTOPOD PANPIPE
ROARERS SUBSIST TACTITE TOMTITS

ABCADBA ATLANTA REDRIER REORDER   **ABCADBC** GANGMAN ONGOING PREPARE REDRIED

ABCADBD INDIANA

ABCADBE AERATED AERATES BRIBERS BRIBERY BULBOUS CIRCUIT COACTOR CONCHOS DEADMEN
DISDAIN ELDERLY GANGWAY GREGORY HUSHFUL INDIANS INDIGNS KOLKHOZ PEOPLED PEOPLER
PEOPLES PERPLEX PREPART PROPERS PULPOUS REARMED REDRIES REPRIED REPRIES RETRIED
RETRIES RETRUED RETRUES REURGED REURGES TACTUAL TESTIER THATCHY UNBURNT UNGUENT
UNTURNS

ABCADCA DREDGED GANGING GONGING HASHISH SHASTAS   **ABCADCB** DREDGER REBRIBE

ABCADCC FULFILL

ABCADCE AFEARED ASIANIC ASIATIC AVIATIC BARBERS BARBERY BULBELS CALCULI CHECKED
CHECKER CRECHES DEADMAN DEADPAN DREDGES EXTENTS GORGERS MICMACS PULPILY PURPORT
RETROTS SEISMIC SENSING TACTICS TENTING TIPTOPS TORTURE WIGWAGS ZIGZAGS

ABCADDE AURALLY AXIALLY BAMBOOS EQUERRY INFILLS KICKEES REPROOF UNFULLY UNFUSSY
UNHULLS UNPUFFS

ABCADEA ACUARIA ALBANIA APHASIA APLASIA AQUARIA ARCADIA ATHALIA DANDIED DANDLED
DAWDLED DRUDGED ENWEAVE EXPENSE GORGING GOUGING SARSENS SEASONS SENSORS SIESTAS
SLASHES SLOSHES SLUSHES SMASHES SOUSERS STASHES SUBSETS SUNSETS SWISHES TARTEST
TARTLET TAUTEST TRITEST

ABCADEB ASHAMES CRACKER CROCKER DRUDGER GANGLIA INDIGEN INVIRON LEGLIKE NEONATE
POMPANO REARGUE REARISE REAROSE REBRACE RECRATE REDRAPE REDRIVE REDROVE REFRAME

REGRADE REGRATE REPRICE REPRIME REPRISE REPRIVE REPROVE REPRUNE RETRACE RETRADE
RETRUDE RETRUSE REWRITE REWROTE SEASIDE SENSATE SENSILE SENSURE SPYSHIP TEATIME
TESTONE TEXTILE TEXTURE TOSTADO UNHUMAN

ABCADEC ABRASER AERATOR AGEABLE ARCADIC BURBLER BUSBOYS CIRCLER CONCERN ENSEALS
ENSEAMS ENSEATS GARGLER HASHERS HUSHERS INDITED INSIDES IODIZED PREPAVE PURPLER
RETRACT RETRUST TASTERS TASTIES TESTORS TURTLER UNCUBIC UNDUPED

ABCADED ABRADED ABRASES ALIASES ARCADED ATLASES CONCEDE DUODENE EMPEROR INCIDED
INCISES INLISTS IONISMS IONISTS TOSTADA UNDUSTS UNHUSKS UNRUSTS

ABCADEE COACHEE COACTEE CONCUSS COUCHEE INVITEE KICKOFF LAWLESS LIDLESS LIPLESS
POMPEII RECROSS REDRILL

ABCADEF ABLATED ABLATES ABRADES ABRASED ACUATED ACUATED ADVANCE AIDABLE ALGATES
ALTARED AMIABLE AMIABLY ANTACID APHASIC AQUAFER AQUATES AQUATIC ARCADES ASCARED
ASHAMED ASKABLE ASKANCE ATHALIE AUTARCH AVIATED AVIATES AVIATOR BARBING BAUBLES
BOMBARD BOMBAST BOMBAZE BOMBERS BOMBING BUGBEAR BULBIER BULBING BULBOSE BUMBLED
BUMBLER BUMBLES BURBANK BURBLED BURBLES CALCIFY CALCINE CALCITE CALCIUM CANCELS
CANCERS CATCHER CATCHES CATCHUP CHECKUP CHICAGO CHICANE CHICKEN CHICKER CHICLES
CHICORY CHOCKED CHOCKER CHOCTAW CHUCKED CHUCKER CHUCKLE CINCHED CINCHER CINCHES
CIRCLED CIRCLES CIRCLET CIRCUSY CLACKED CLACKER CLICHED CLICHES CLICKED CLICKER
CLOCKED CLOCKER CLUCKED COACHED COACHER COACHES COACTED CONCAVE CONCEAL CONCEIT
CONCEPT CONCERT CONCHAL CONCHED CONCHER CONCHES CONCISE CONCURS COUCHED COUCHES
CRACKED CRACKEY CRACKLE CRACKLY CRICKET CROCEUS CROCHET CROCKED CRUCIAL CRUCIFY
CUPCAKE DANDERS DANDIER DANDIES DANDIFY DANDILY DANDLER DANDLES DAWDLER DAWDLES
DEADISH DENDRIC DEWDROP DIADEMS DOLDRUM DOWDIER DOWDIES DOWDILY DRUDGES DUODENA
DYADICS EAGERLY EASEFUL ECHELON ECZEMAS EDGEMAN ELBERTA EMPERIL ENDEARS ENDEMIC
ENTERIC ENVELOP ETHERIC EUGENIA EUGENIC EXCEPTS EXCERPT EXPECTS EXPENDS EXPERTS
EXTENDS FANFOLD FIEFDOM FORFEIT FORFEND FOXFISH FUNFEST GADGETS GADGETY GARGLED
GARGLED GARGOLS GINGERS GINGERY GINGHAM GOUGERS GURGLED GURGLES HASHIER HASHING
HIGHBOY HIGHERS HIGHEST HIGHLOW HIGHTOP HIGHWAY HOGHEAD HOTHEAD HUSHING HYPHENS
ICKIEST IDLINGS IGNITED IGNITER IGNITES IMPIETY IMPINGE IMPIOUS INCISAL INCISED
INCISOR INCITED INCITER INCITES INDICES INDICTS INDIGOS INDITER INDITES INFIDEL
INFIELD INFIRMS INFIXED INFIXES INKIEST INSIDER INSIGHT INTICED INVIGOR INVITED
INVITER INVITES IODINES IODITES IODIZER IODIZES IONICAL IONIZED IONIZES IOTIZED
IOTIZES KHAKIED KICKERS KICKOUT KICKUPS KINKERS LADLERS LADLING LAWLIKE LEYLAND
LOWLAND LOWLIED LOWLIER LOWLIES LOWLIFE MAIMERS MALMSEY MARMITE MARMOTS MERMAID
MIDMORN MIDMOST MISMADE MISMATE MISMOVE NUANCED NUANCES OBLONGS OCTOBER OCTODES
OCTONAL OCTOPAL OCTOPED OCTOPUS OHIOANS ONLOADS ORIOLES ORMOLUS OSMOTIC OXFORDS
OXHORNS OXHOUSE OXWORTS PAMPERS PAUPERS PEAPODS PIEPANS PIGPENS PIMPLED PIMPLES
POMPIER POMPING PREPACK PREPAID PREPAYS PREPLAN PREPLOT PREPOST PROPANE PROPELS
PROPHET PROPJET PROPMAN PROPMEN PROPYLS PULPERS PULPIER PULPIFY PULPING PULPITS
PUMPERS PUMPING PUMPKIN PURPLED PURPLES PURPOSE RAMRODS REARING REBRAID REBRAND
REBRICK REBROWN REBRUSH RECRAMP RECRANK RECROWN RECRUIT RECRUSH REDRAFT REDRAGS
REDRAWN REDRAWS REFRACT REFRAIN REFRONT REGRAFT REGRASP REGRIND REGRIPS REGROUP
REGROWN REGROWS REPRINT RETRACK RETRAIN RETRAMP RETRAYS RETRIAL RETRIMS RETRIPS
REWRAPS RIMROCK ROARING RUBRICS SALSIFY SEASICK SEISMAL SENSORY SENSUAL SHUSWAP
SHYSTER SKYSAIL SLASHED SLASHER SLOSHED SLOSHER SLUSHED SLUSHER SMASHED SMASHER
SMASHUP SOUSING SPASMED SPASMIC SPASTIC STASHED SUASION SUASIVE SUBSECT SUBSIDE
SUBSIDY SUBSIGN SUBSIZE SUBSOIL SUDSIER SUDSING SUNSPOT SWISHED SWISHER TACTFUL

```
TACTILE TACTIVE TANTRUM TARTING TARTISH TASTIER TASTILY TASTING TAUTENS TECTRIX
TENTFUL TENTHLY TENTILY TERTIAL TERTIAN TERTIAS TERTIUS TESTACY TESTIFY TESTILY
TESTING TEUTONS TEXTUAL THETICS THETINS TILTERS TILTUPS TINTERS TINTYPE TIPTOED
TIPTOES TORTUGA TORTULA TOUTERS TOUTING TRITELY TRITYLS TROTHED TUFTERS TUFTIER
TUFTILY TUFTING TURTLED TURTLES TWITCHY UNBUILD UNBUILT UNBULKY UNBURST UNBUXOM
UNCULAR UNCURBS UNCURDS UNCURED UNCURLS UNCURSE UNDULAR UNFURLS UNFUSED UNGUARD
UNGUYED UNHUMID UNJUDGE UNJUICY UNLUCID UNLUCKY UNLUSTY UNMUTED UNPURSE UNQUICK
UNQUIET UNQUOTE UNRULED UNRULES UNSULKY UNTUCKS UNTURFS UPBUILT UPCURLS UPCURVE
UPSURGE UPTURNS VALVING VULVATE WARWICK WAXWING WAXWORK WIGWAMS
```

ABCBAAD LEVELLY   **ABCBABA** DECEDED REVERER   **ABCBABB** REFEREE REVEREE

ABCBABD CARACAS DECEDES LEVELED LEVELER REVERED REVERES

ABCBADA DIVIDED MINIMUM

ABCBADB REMERGE RENERVE RESERVE REVERIE REVERSE SENESCE

ABCBADE AWKWARD DIVIDER DIVIDES GARAGED GARAGES INANITY KAYAKED KAYAKER MADAMES
MINIMAL PARAPET REJERKS REVERBS REVERTS STETSON UPSPURT

ABCBBAC DESEEDS   **ABCBBCD** REDEEDS   **ABCBBDA** SALAAMS

ABCBBDC RESEEDS RESEEKS

ABCBBDE BAZAARS BESEECH REDEEMS REFEEDS REFEELS REHEELS REMEETS STUTTER UNANNEX
VENEERS

ABCBCAD TENENTS   **ABCBCBD** BANANAS ROCOCOS   **ABCBCDB** STATANT

ABCBCDD ONENESS

ABCBCDE DININGS FININGS LININGS MININGS PININGS PRERENT QUEUERS TININGS

ABCBDAB MAHATMA STATIST TORONTO

ABCBDAE DEFENDS DEPENDS GIVINGS LICITLY LIVIDLY REBEARS REGEARS REHEARD REHEARS
RELEARN REVELRY REWEARS RIVIERA ROBOTRY SIZIEST SOLOIST STATISM TUMULTS UPSPOUT

ABCBDBA DELETED DESEXED MACADAM RECEDER REDEFER RENEGER RENEWER RESEVER REVELER
SAHARAS SALADAS SECEDES SERENES

ABCBDBB KEGEREE   **ABCBDBC** BEDEWED CASABAS LAYAWAY RELEVEL RESEXES SERENER

ABCBDBD HAVANAN LEVERER METERER RECEDED SECEDED SEVERER

ABCBDBE BAHAMAS BEJEWEL BEVELED BEVELER BEZELED BIKINIS CABALAS CABANAS CANADAS
CARAVAN CARAWAY CATALAN CUMULUS DELETES DEMETER FARADAY FARAWAY FEVERED GALAHAD
HOMOLOG HUMULUS JEWELED JEWELER JEZEBEL LEVERED MALAYAN METERED MILITIA MOLOTOV
MONOLOG PAJAMAS PANAMAS PETERED RAMADAN RAMADAS REBESET RECEDES RENEGED RENEGES
RENEWED RESEWED RESEXED SECEDER SEVENED SEVENER SEVERED SEWERED SOLOMON STATUTE
```
```

TAMARAC TUMULUS

ABCBDCA SUBURBS   **ABCBDCB** DETENTE   **ABCBDCD** DETESTS RETESTS UNENDED

ABCBDCE CEREBRA DECENCY DETECTS DETENTS FILIALS MINIONS MORONRY MUTUATE PAEANED
PINIONS RECENCY RETENTS VACANCY VITIATE

ABCBDDB MALACCA MOROCCO SAVANNA   **ABCBDDC** RESELLS

ABCBDDE BANALLY BASALLY BERETTA CATARRH CIVILLY COLOSSI COROLLA FATALLY JEWELLY
NASALLY REBECCA RETELLS REVELLY UPSPEED

ABCBDEA APEPSIA AUGUSTA COLONIC DAMAGED DIVINED EARACHE EATABLE ELFLIKE ENDNOTE
ENSNARE FLYLEAF LIMINAL RAVAGER SAFARIS SALAMIS SARAPES SAVAGES SAVANTS SELECTS
SENECAS SERENAS SIDINGS SILICAS SIMIANS SIMILES SIRINGS SIZINGS SLALOMS SOJOURS
STATERS STATICS STATORS STATUES SUTURES TABARET TIDIEST TINIEST

ABCBDEB ACYCLIC BATAVIA BELEAVE BEREAVE CANASTA CATALPA CELESTE COLOMBO DECEASE
DECEIVE DEFENCE DEFENSE DEMERGE DESERVE DETENUE GALATEA JAKARTA JAMAICA LASAGNA
MALARIA MANAGUA MARATHA PANACEA PARAZOA RECEIVE REFENCE REHEDGE RELEASE RESEIZE
RETENUE REVENGE REVENUE REWEAVE UNKNOWN

ABCBDEC COLONEL CORONER DESERTS HOMONYM KITIMAT MITIEST PARADER PAYABLY PESETAS
POGOING RESEALS RESEAMS RESEATS RESECTS RESENDS RESENTS RETEMPT RISINGS SAYABLY
SONORAN UNSNAPS UPSPINS VISIONS

ABCBDED AUGURER AUGUSTS BEHESTS COLORER DAMASKS DEVESTS FACADED GENESIS HONORER
LIAISES MUCUSES PARADED POROSIS PRORATA REGESTS RENESTS REVESTS TRIREME VIBISTS

ABCBDEE FLYLESS HONOREE MANAGEE VISITEE

ABCBDEF AIRIEST AIRINGS ANONYMS APEPTIC APOPLEX ARMREST AUBURNS AUDUBON AUGURED
AUTUMNS BALANCE BEDEVIL BEHEADS BEHEARS BEMEANS BENEATH BENEFIC BENEFIT BENELUX
BEPELTS BEVEILS BIDINGS BILIARY BILIATE BILIOUS BITINGS BOGOTAS BOLOGNA BOLONEY
BORONIC BOROUGH BOSOMED BOSOMER CABARET CADAVER CALABUR CANALED CANALER CANAPES
CANARDS CAPABLE CAPABLY CARAMEL CASAQUE CATALOG CAVALRY CEDENTS CEMENTS CEREALS
CILIATE CILIUMS CITIZEN COBOURG COHORTS COJOINS COLOGNE COLORED COLOURS COLOURY
CONOIDS CORONAS CORONET COYOTED COYOTES CUMULAR CUPULOS DAMAGER DAMAGES DATABLE
DATABLY DECEITS DECERNS DEFEATS DEFECTS DEJECTS DEMEANS DEMENTS DEMERIT DETENUS
DEVELOP DICINGS DIGITAL DIGITUS DIRIGES DIVINER DIVINES DIVISOR DOLOURS DOROTHY
ENSNARL EUNUCHS FACADES FANATIC FEDERAL FIJIANS FILIATE FILINGS FINIALS FINICKY
FINITED FINITES FIRINGS FIXINGS FUTURAL FUTURED FUTURES FUTURIC GENERAL GENERIC
GENETIC GENEVAS GODOWNS HAZARDS HEGEMON HEREOUT HERETIC HIDINGS HIJINKS HIRINGS
HOBOING HOBOISM HOMOGEN HONORED HONORIA HONOURS ICECAPS INANELY INSNARE INSNARL
JEWELRY JUGULAR KARATES LARAMIE LASAGNE LAVAGED LAVAGES LAXATED LAXATES LAZARUS
LEGENDS LIAISED LIAISON LIBIDOS LIKINGS LIMIEST LIMITED LIMITER LINIEST LIPIDES
LIVINGS MACABER MACABRE MALAISE MALARKY MANACLE MANAGED MANAGER MANAGES MARAUDS
MATADOR METEORS MILIEUS MILIEUX MINIBUS MINICAR MIRIEST MIXIBLE MIXIBLY MIXINGS
MIXITES MONOCLE MONODIC MONOFIL MONOIDS MORONCY MORONIC MOTOCAR MOTORED MUTUELS
NAMABLE NAMABLY NAPALMS NAVAHOS NAVAJOS NEREIDS OARAGES OILIEST PAGANIC PAGANLY
PAGANRY PALACED PALACES PALADIN PALATED PALATES PALAVER PANACHE PARABLE PARADES

PARADOX PARAGON PARASOL PAVANES PAYABLE PELERIN PICINAE PILINGS PINIEST PIRITES
PITIERS PITIFUL POLOIST POTOMAC PRORATE QUEUING RATABLE RATABLY RAVAGED RAVAGES
REBEATS REBEGAN REBEGIN REBEGUN REBEKAH REBENDS RECEIPT REDEALS REDEALT REDEBIT
REDECKS REDEIFY REDELAY REFECTS REFEIGN REFETCH REGENCY REGENTS REHEADS REHEALS
REHEAPS REHEATS REHELMS REJECTS RELEADS RELEAPS RELEAPT RELENDS RELENTS REMELTS
REMENDS REMETAL RENEWAL REPEALS REPEATS REPENTS RETEACH REVEALS REVEILS REVENTS
REWEIGH REWELDS REWENDS RIDINGS RIGIDLY RIMIEST RISIBLE SABAYON SARACEN SATANIC
SAVAGED SAVAGER SAYABLE SELENIC SENECAL SENEGAL SEVENTH SEVENTY SEVERAL SILICON
SIMILAR SIMILED SOJOURN SOLOING SOLONIC STATELY STATING STATION STATIVE STATIZE
STATUED STATURE SUBUNIT SUTURAL SUTURED TABARDS TABASCO TAMABLE TAMABLY TAMALES
TARAGON TAXABLE TAXABLY TEHERAN TIDINGS TILINGS TIMIDER TIMIDLY TIMINGS TIRINGS
TOXOIDS TUBULAR TUBULES TUMULAR UNANGRY UNINKED UNKNITS UNKNOTS UNSNAKY UNSNARE
UNSNARL UPSPEAK VACANTS VACATED VACATES VALANCE VEGETAL VENERAL VETERAN VEXEDLY
VICIOUS VIGILED VIKINGS VIRILES VISIBLE VISIBLY VISITED VISITER VISITOR VIZIERS
WASATCH WAVABLE WAVABLY WILIEST WINIEST WIRIEST WIRINGS YEMENIS ZULUDOM

ABCCABD RATTRAP   **ABCCACC** TREETEE   **ABCCACD** TWEETED

ABCCADE BELLBOY LITTLED LITTLER LITTLES MILLMAN MILLMEN OUTTOPS TREETOP

ABCCBAD NIPPING REDDERS SUFFUSE   **ABCCBBA** SETTEES   **ABCCBBC** LESSEES

ABCCBBD BELLEEK   **ABCCBCA** GINNING

ABCCBCD BAGGAGE BINNING DINNING FINNING HORRORS HUBBUBS LINNING MISSISH PINNING
POWWOWS SILLILY SINNING TINNING WINNING

ABCCBDA DIVVIED DIZZIED GILLING RIBBIER SELLERS SETTERS SILLIES SORROWS

ABCCBDB HELLENE

ABCCBDC DIGGING FIGGING FITTIST GIDDIED JIGGING KIDDIED LESSENS MESSERS NASSAUS
PIGGING RIGGING VASSALS VESSELS WETTEST WIGGING

ABCCBDE BALLADS BALLAST BARRACK BARRAGE BETTERS BIDDIES BIDDING BIFFIES BIGGISH
BILLIES BILLING BORROWS BOTTOMS BOTTONY CABBAGE CABBAGY CALLAIS CATTAIL CIVVIES
COMMODE COMMONS CONNOTE CORRODE CORRODY COTTONS COTTONY DESSERT DIBBING DILLIES
DILLING DIMMING DIMMISH DIPPIER DIPPING DIVVIES DIZZIER DIZZIES DIZZILY DOGGONE
DOLLOPS FALLACY FELLERS FENNELS FERRETS FERRETY FETTERS FIBBING FILLIES FILLING
FILLIPS FINNIER FINNISH FISSION FITTIER FITTING FIZZIER FIZZING GALLANT GEMMERS
GETTERS GIDDIER GIDDIES GIDDILY GIMMICK GINNIER HAGGARD HELLERS HEMMERS HILLIER
HIPPIER HISSING HITTING HOLLOWS JETTERS JIBBING JIFFIES JIGGIER JIGGISH JIMMIED
JIMMIES JIMMINY JINNIES KENNELS KENNERS KIDDIER KIDDIES KIDDING KIDDISH KILLING
KISSING KITTIES KITTING LAGGARD LEGGERS LETTERS LIPPIER LIPPIES LIPPING LIZZIES
MALLARD MASSAGE MIDDIES MILLIES MILLING MINNIES MISSILE MISSING MISSION MISSIVE
MORROWS MOTTOED MOTTOES NARRATE NETTERS NIPPIER NIPPILY OILLIKE OUTTURN PASSAGE
PEGGERS PELLETS PELLETY PENNERS PETTERS PIGGIER PIGGIES PIGGISH PILLING PILLION
PITTING POLLOCK RATTAIL RATTANS RATTANY REDDEST RIBBING RIDDING RIGGISH RIMMING
RIPPING SABBATH SILLIER SILLING SIPPING SITTING SKOOKUM SORROWY SUCCUBI SUCCUMB
TAMMANY TANNAIC TELLERS TENNERS TIFFINS TILLIES TILLING TINNIER TINNILY TIPPIER
TIPPING TIZZIES VILLIFY WALLABY WARRANT WASSAIL WATTAGE WEBBERS WIGGIER WIGGISH

WILLIAM WILLIES WILLING WINNIES WITTIER WITTILY YELLERS YIDDISH YIPPING ZINNIAS
ZIPPIER ZIPPING

ABCCDAA SUCCESS   **ABCCDAB** DERRIDE TAFFETA

ABCCDAC NAGGING NISSANS OUTTROT

ABCCDAE COLLECT CONNECT COPPICE CORRECT COSSACK COTTICE HURRAHS HUZZAHS NABBING
NAGGINS NAPPING NODDING NOGGINS NUBBING NULLING NUTTING PREEMPT RAMMERS RAPPERS
RAPPORT RATTERS RATTERY RIBBERS RIDDERS RIGGERS RIMMERS RIPPERS ROBBERS ROBBERY
RODDERS ROLLERS ROTTERS RUBBERS RUBBERY RUDDERS RUGGERS RUNNERS RUTTERS SADDEST
SOTTISH SUGGEST SUNNISH SUPPOSE TUFFETS TURRETS WALLOWS WILLOWS WILLOWY WINNOWS

ABCCDBA SETTLES

ABCCDBC BERRIER FERRIER FERRYER MEDDLED MERRIER PEDDLED PERRIER TERRIER

ABCCDBE ALOOFLY BELLIED BELLIES BELLMEN BENNIES BERRIED BERRIES BEZZLED BEZZLES
DEBBIES DISSHIP FALLWAY FERRIED FERRIES FETTLED FETTLES FLEETLY GESSOED HALLWAY
HENNAED HERRIED HERRIES JAZZMAN JEFFREY JELLIED JELLIES JENNIES JERRIES JETTIED
JETTIES KETTLER KETTLES KNEEING LEGGIER MAFFIAS MEDDLER MEDDLES MARRIED MERRIES
MESSIER METTLED METTLES NELLIES NETTIER NETTLED NETTLER NETTLES PASSMAN PASSWAY
PEBBLED PEBBLER PEBBLES PEDDLER PEDDLES PIRRHIC PISSOIR PULLOUT ROLLMOP ROLLTOP
SETTLED SETTLER SLEEKLY SUCCOUR TEDDIES VILLAIN WEBBIER

ABCCDCA GUNNING SLEEVES SNEEZES

ABCCDCB ADEEMED BREEDER CREEKER CREEPER FREEZER GREENER GREETER PENNINE PREENER

ABCCDCC POSSESS

ABCCDCD BLEEDED CHEERER CHEESES CREEDED QUEERER SHEERER SNEERER SPEEDED STEERER
TWEEDED

ABCCDCE BANNING BASSIST BLEEDER BREEZED BREEZES BURRERS CANNING CANNONS CHEEKED
CHEEKER CHEEPED CHEEPER CHEERED CHEESED CHEESER CHEETED CHEETER CONNING CREEKED
CUNNING DENNING DUNNING FANNING FLEECED FLEECER FLEECES FLEETED FLEETER FREEMEN
FREEZES FUNNING GREENED GREETED JOLLILY KLEENEX KNEELED KNEELER LUGGAGE MANNING
MARRERS MIRRORS MIRRORY PANNING PENNANT PENNING PENNONS PREENED PUNNING PURRERS
QUEENED QUEERED RUNNING SHEERED SHEETED SHEETER SKEETED SKEETER SLEEKED SLEEKEN
SLEEKER SLEEPER SLEETED SLEEVED SLEEVER SNEERED SNEEZED SNEEZER SPEEDER STEELED
STEELER STEEPED STEEPEN STEEPER STEERED SUNNING SWEEPED SWEEPER SWEETED SWEETEN
SWEETER TANNING TANNINS TARRERS TERRORS TREEMEN TWEEZED TWEEZER TWEEZES WANNING
WHEELED WHEELER WHEEZED WHEEZER WHEEZES

ABCCDDA SITTEES SUTTEES   **ABCCDDC** LASSOOS

ABCCDDE BALLOON BASSOON BUFFOON CALLEES COFFEES COLLEEN MARROON PUTTEED PUTTEES
RACCOON SUCCEED TOFFEES

ABCCDEA DABBLED DALLIED DAPPLED DAZZLED DITTOED DOLLIED DROOLED DROOPED DULLARD

DUMMIED GABBING GADDING GAFFING GALLING GASSING GELLING GEMMING GETTING GLEEING
GOBBING GULLING GUMMING GUTTING GYPPING HAGGISH HELLISH HENNISH HOGGISH HOTTISH
HUNNISH LOSSFUL MOBBISM RABBLER RAFFLER RAGGIER RALLIER RAMMIER RATTIER RATTLER
RIDDLER RIFFLER RIPPLER RUBBLER RUDDIER RUFFLER RUMMIER RUNNIER RUTTIER SADDENS
SADDLES SAGGERS SALLIES SALLOWS SAPPERS SAPPHOS SAVVEYS SAVVIES SHIITES SIMMERS
SIMMONS SINNERS SIPPERS SITTARS SITTERS SIZZLES SKIIERS SKIINGS SMOOTHS SNOOZES
SOBBERS SOCCERS SODDENS SOFFITS SONNETS SOPPERS SORRELS SORRIES SOTTERS STOOGES
SUCCORS SUDDENS SUFFERS SULLENS SULLIES SUMMERS SUMMITS SUMMONS SUPPERS SUPPLES
SURRAHS SURREYS SUTTLES TALLEST TANNEST TORRENT YELLOWY

ABCCDEB BROODER BROOMER CELLITE CELLOSE CHEETAH CROONER DROOPER FERRATE FERRITE
FERRULE GLEEFUL GROOMER GROOVER LETTUCE MESSAGE PERRINE PROOFER SERRATE SPEEDUP
TERRACE TERRINE TROOPER

ABCCDEC AUSSIES BAGGING BARRIER BASSETS BEGGING BOGGING BOSSERS BOSSIES BUGGING
BURRIER CADDIED CARRIER CODDLED COGGING COSSETS CUDDLED CURRIER CUSSERS DAGGING
FAGGING FATTEST FIDDLED FITTEST FOGGING FOSSILS FUDDLED FURRIER FUSSERS GASSERS
GOSSIPS GUSSETS GUSSIES HARRIER HASSIDS HASSLES HISSERS HOGGING HOTTEST HUDDLED
HUGGING HURRIER HUSSARS HUSSEYS HUSSIES HYSSOPS JAGGING JOGGING JOSSERS JUGGING
KISSERS LAGGING LASSIES LASSOES LEGGING LESSONS LESSORS LISSOMS LOGGING LOSSERS
LUGGING MARRIER MARRYER MIDDLED MISSALS MISSELS MUDDIED MUDDLED MUGGING MUSSELS
PADDLED PASSELS PASSERS PEGGING PIDDLED POSSETS POSSUMS PREEMIE PUDDLED PURRIER
PUSSIES RADDLED RAGGING RIDDLED RUDDIED RUDDLED RUGGING RUSSELS RUSSETS RUSSIAS
RUSSKIS SADDLED SAGGING SOGGING SORRIER STEEPLE SWEETIE TAGGING TARRIER TASSELS
TISSUES TODDLED TOSSERS TOSSUPS TUGGING TUSSAHS TUSSLES TWEENIE WADDIED WADDLED
WAGGING WALLFUL WARRIOR WHEEDLE WILLFUL WORRIER ZAGGING

ABCCDED BLOODED BROODED CHOOSES COLLEGE FLOODED FLOORER PICCOLO SPOORER

ABCCDEE GODDESS OILLESS SHOOTEE WANNESS WHOOPEE

ABCCDEF BADDISH BAFFLED BAFFLER BAFFLES BAGGERS BAGGIER BAGGIES BAGGILY BALLERS
BALLETS BALLING BALLOTS BANNERS BANNOCK BARRELS BARRING BARROWS BATTENS BATTERS
BATTERY BATTIER BATTING BATTISH BATTLED BATTLER BATTLES BEDDING BEGGARS BEGGARY
BELLHOP BELLING BELLMAN BELLOWS BETTORS BIDDERS BIGGERS BIGGEST BILLERS BILLETS
BILLETY BILLOWS BILLOWY BITTERS BLOOMED BLOOMER BLOOPED BLOOPER BODDICE BOFFINS
BOGGIER BOGGISH BOGGLED BOGGLER BOGGLES BOLLING BONNETS BONNIER BONNILY BOPPERS
BOPPING BOSSIER BOSSING BOTTEGA BOTTLED BOTTLER BOTTLES BROOKED BROOMED BUDDAHS
BUDDERS BUDDHAS BUDDIER BUDDIES BUDDING BUFFALO BUFFETS BUFFIER BUFFING BUFFONT
BUGGERY BUGGIER BUGGIES BULLDOG BULLERS BULLETS BULLETY BULLIED BULLIER BULLIES
BULLING BULLION BULLISH BULLOCK BULLPEN BUMMERS BUMMING BUNNIES BURRING BURROWS
BUSSING BUTTERS BUTTERY BUTTING BUTTOCK BUTTONS BUTTONY BUZZARD BUZZERS BUZZIER
BUZZIES BUZZING CABBIES CABBING CADDIES CADDING CADDISH CALLBOY CALLERS CALLING
CALLOUS CANNERS CANNERY CANNIER CANNILY CAPPING CARRIED CARRIES CARRION CARROTS
CARROTY CATTIER CATTILY CATTING CATTISH CELLARS CELLING CELLIST CELLOID CESSANT
CESSPIT CHEERIO CHEERLY CHEETAS CHOOSER CHOOSEY CIRRHUS COBBERS COBBIER COBBING
COBBLED COBBLER COBBLES CODDERS CODDING CODDLER CODDLES COFFERS COFFINS COFFRES
COGGERS COGGERY COGGLED COGGLES COLLARD COLLARS COLLATE COLLERY COLLIDE COLLIED
COLLIER COLLINS COLLUDE COMMAED COMMAES COMMAND COMMEND COMMENT COMMIES COMMITS
COMMUNE COMMUTE CONNATE CONNERS CONNIES CONNIVE COPPERS COPPERY COPPING CORRALS
CORRUPT COTTAGE COTTERS COTTISE CROOKED CROONED CUBBIES CUDDING CUDDLES CUFFING

```
CULLERS CULLIED CULLING CUMMINS CUPPERS CUPPIER CUPPING CURRAGH CURRANT CURRENT
CURRIED CURRIES CURRISH CUSSING CUTTERS CUTTING CUTTLES DABBERS DABBIER DABBING
DABBLER DABBLES DAFFIER DAFFISH DAFFLES DAGGERS DAGGIER DALLIER DALLIES DAMMERS
DAMMING DAMMISH DAPPLES DAZZLER DAZZLES DERRICK DEWWORM DIFFERS DIFFUSE DIGGERS
DIMMERS DIMMEST DINNERS DIPPERS DISSECT DITTOES DIVVERS DOBBERS DOBBIES DOBBING
DOBBINS DOFFING DOGGERS DOGGERY DOGGIER DOGGIES DOGGISH DOLLARS DOLLEYS DOLLIES
DOLLING DOLLISH DOPPLER DOSSIER DOTTERS DOTTIER DOTTILY DOTTING DUBBERS DUBBIER
DUBBING DUBBINS DUFFELS DUFFERS DUFFING DUFFLES DULLERS DULLERY DULLEST DULLIFY
DULLING DULLISH DUMMIES DUNNERS DUNNEST EARRING FADDIER FADDING FADDISH FADDISM
FADDIST FAGGOTS FAGGOTS FALLERS FALLING FALLOUT FALLOWS FANNERS FANNIER FANNIES
FARRING FARROWS FATTENS FATTERS FATTIER FATTIES FATTILY FATTING FATTISH FELLING
FELLOWS FENNISH FERRING FERROUS FIBBERS FIBBERY FIDDLER FIDDLES FIDDLEY FILLERS
FILLETS FINNERS FISSURE FISSURY FITTERS FIZZERS FIZZLED FIZZLES FLEEING FLOODER
FLOORED FLOOSIE FLOOZIE FOBBING FODDERS FOGGERS FOGGIER FOGGILY FOGGISH FOKKERS
FOLLIED FOLLIES FOPPERY FOPPING FOPPISH FOSSICK FREEDOM FREEING FREEISH FREEMAN
FREESIA FREEWAY FUDDLES FULLERS FULLEST FULLISH FUNNELS FUNNIER FUNNIES FUNNILY
FURRILY FURRING FURROWS FURROWY FUSSIER FUSSILY FUSSING FUSSPOT FUZZIER FUZZIES
FUZZILY FUZZING GABBERS GABBIER GABBLED GABBLER GABBLES GADDERS GADDISH GAFFERS
GALLEON GALLERS GALLERY GALLEYS GALLIER GALLISH GALLIUM GALLONS GALLOPS GALLOWS
GARRETS GARROTE GARROTS GASSIER GEMMILY GIBBERS GIBBETS GIBBONS GIBBOSE GIBBOUS
GILLERS GILLNET GINNERS GINNERY GIPPERS GIZZARD GLOOMED GOBBERS GOBBLED GOBBLER
GOBBLES GOLLIES GOSSIPY GREENLY GROOMED GROOVED GROOVES GUFFAWS GULLETS GULLEYS
GULLIED GULLIES GUMMERS GUMMIER GUMMILY GUNNELS GUNNERS GUNNERY GUNNIES GUPPIES
GUTTERS GUTTERY GUTTIER GUZZLED GUZZLER GUZZLES GYPPERS HADDOCK HAGGLED HAGGLER
HAGGLES HALLING HALLOWS HAMMERS HAMMIER HAMMING HAMMOCK HAPPENS HAPPIED HAPPIER
HAPPILY HAPPING HARRIED HARRIES HARROWS HASSLED HASSOCK HATTERS HATTERY HATTING
HELLCAT HELLING HELLION HEMMING HERRING HESSIAN HICCUPS HILLMAN HILLMEN HILLOCK
HILLTOP HITTERS HOBBIED HOBBIES HOBBITS HOBBLED HOBBLER HOBBLES HOGGERS HOGGIES
HOLLAND HOLLERS HOLLIES HOPPERS HOPPIER HOPPING HOPPITY HORRIFY HUBBARD HUBBERS
HUBBIES HUBBING HUDDLER HUDDLES HUFFERS HUFFIER HUFFILY HUFFING HUFFLED HUGGERS
HULLERS HULLING HUMMERS HUMMING HUMMOCK HURRIED HURRIES JABBERS JABBING JAGGERY
JAGGIER JAMMERS JAMMIER JAMMING JARRING JAZZERS JAZZIER JAZZILY JAZZING JAZZIST
JAZZMEN JELLIFY JELLING JETTING JIBBERS JIGGERS JIGGLED JIGGLES JITTERS JOBBERS
JOBBERY JOBBING JOBBISH JOGGERS JOGGLED JOGGLER JOGGLES JOLLIED JOLLIER JOLLIES
JOLLIFY JOSSING JOTTERS JOTTING JUGGERS JUGGLED JUGGLER JUGGLES JUTTIED JUTTIES
JUTTING KADDISH KAFFIRS KIBBLED KIBBLER KIBBLES KIBBUTZ KIDDERS KIDDOES KILLERS
KILLJOY KIPPERS KITTENS KITTERS KNEECAP KNEEPAD KRAALED KUMMELS LADDERS LADDERY
LADDIES LADDISH LAGGERS LAPPERS LAPPING LAPPISH LASSOER LATTENS LATTICE LEGGINS
LEMMING LESSING LETTING LIBBERS LIDDERS LIGGATS LIMMERS LIPPERS LISSOME LITTERS
LITTERY LOBBERS LOBBIED LOBBIES LOBBING LOBBISH LOBBYER LOGGERS LOGGIAS LOGGISH
LOPPERS LOPPING LORRIES LOTTERS LOTTERY LOTTING LUBBERS LUDDISM LUDDITE LUFFERS
LUFFING LUGGERS MADDENS MADDEST MADDING MADDISH MAGGOTS MAGGOTY MALLETS MALLOWS
MANNERS MANNISH MAPPERS MAPPING MAPPIST MARRIED MARRIES MARRING MARROWS MARROWY
MASSEUR MASSIER MASSILY MASSING MASSIVE MATTERS MATTERY MATTING MATTOCK MECCANO
MELLONS MELLOWS MELLOWY MERRILY MESSBOY MESSIAH MESSILY MESSINA MESSING MIDDAYS
MIDDENS MIDDLES MILLERS MILLETS MINNOWS MISSARY MISSEND MISSENT MISSOUT MISSTAY
MISSTEP MITTENS MIZZENS MOBBERS MOBBING MOBBISH MOBBIST MOLLIES MOLLIFY MOLLUSC
MOLLUSK MOPPERS MOPPETS MOPPIER MOPPING MOSSIER MOSSING MOTTLED MOTTLER MOTTLES
MUDDERS MUDDIER MUDDIES MUDDILY MUDDING MUDDISH MUDDLER MUDDLES MUFFETS MUFFING
MUFFINS MUFFISH MUFFLED MUFFLER MUFFLES MUGGERS MUGGIER MUGGILY MUGGISH MULLERS
MULLETS MULLING MULLION MUSSIER MUSSILY MUSSING MUTTERS MUTTONS MUTTONY MUZZIER
```

MUZZILY MUZZLED MUZZLER MUZZLES NABBERS NAGGERS NAGGIER NAGGISH NAPPERS NAPPIER
NAPPIES NARROWS NARROWY NATTERS NATTIER NATTILY NAVVIED NAVVIES NIBBLED NIBBLER
NIBBLES NIGGARD NIGGLED NIGGLER NIGGLES NIPPERS NIPPLED NIPPLES NODDERS NOZZLED
NOZZLER NOZZLES NUBBIER NUBBLES NUGGETS NUGGETY NULLAHS NULLIFY NULLITY NUTTERS
NUTTERY NUTTIER NUTTILY NUTTISH NUZZLED NUZZLES OFTTIME OUTTAKE OWLLIKE PADDERS
PADDIES PADDING PADDLER PADDLES PADDOCK PALLETS PALLIUM PALLORS PALLOUR PANNERS
PANNERY PANNIER PARRIED PARRIES PARROTS PARROTY PASSING PASSION PASSIVE PASSKEY
PASSMEN PASSOUT PATTERN PATTERS PATTIES PATTING PECCARY PESSARY PETTILY PETTING
PETTISH PIDDLER PIDDLES PIGGERY PILLAGE PILLARS PILLARY PILLBOX PILLERS PILLERY
PILLORS PILLORY PILLOWS PILLOWY PINNACE PINNATE PINNERS PITTERS PODDERS PODDIER
PODDING PODDISH POLLAXE POLLENS POLLERS POLLING POLLUTE POMMELS POMMIES POTTAGE
POTTERS POTTERY POTTIES POTTING PREEDIT PROOFED PUDDING PUDDLER PUDDLES PUFFERS
PUFFERY PUFFIER PUFFILY PUFFING PUFFINS PUGGISH PUGGLED PULLENS PULLERS PULLERY
PULLETS PULLEYS PULLING PULLMAN PUMMELO PUMMELS PUMMICE PUNNERS PUNNIER PURRING
PUTTERS PUTTIED PUTTIER PUTTIES PUTTING PUZZLED PUZZLER PUZZLES PYRRHIC QUEENLY
QUEERLY RABBITS RABBITY RAFFISH RAFFLED RAFFLES RAGGEDY RAGGILY RAGGLED RALLIED
RALLIES RAMMING RAPPELS RAPPING RATTING RATTISH RATTLED RATTLES RAZZING RAZZLES
REDDING REDDISH REVVING RHEEBOK RIBBALD RIBBONS RIBBONY RIDDLES RIFFLED RIFFLES
RIPPLED RIPPLES RISSOLE RIZZOMS ROBBING ROBBINS RODDING ROLLICK ROLLING ROLLMAN
ROLLMEN ROLLWAY ROTTENS ROTTING RUBBING RUBBISH RUBBLES RUDDIES RUDDILY RUDDING
RUDDISH RUFFIAN RUFFING RUFFINS RUFFLED RUFFLES RUMMAGE RUMMAGY RUMMIES RUMMILY
RUNNELS RUSSETY RUSSIAN RUSSIFY RUTTING RUTTISH SADDLER SAFFIRE SAFFRON SAGGIER
SALLIED SALLIER SALLOWY SAPPHIC SAPPIER SAPPING SAVVIED SCOONER SCOOPED SCOOPER
SCOOTED SCOOTER SELLING SELLOUT SETTING SHEERLY SHOOFLY SHOOING SHOOTER SIZZLED
SIZZLER SLEEKIT SLOOPED SMOOCHY SMOOTHY SNOOKER SNOOPED SNOOPER SNOOZED SNOOZER
SOBBIER SOBBING SOGGILY SOPPING SORRIED SORRILY SOTTING SPOOFED SPOOFER SPOOKED
SPOOLED SPOOLER SPOONED SPOONER SPOORED STEEPLY STOOGED STOOKED STOOKER STOOLED
STOOLIE STOOPED STOOPER SUBBING SUFFICE SUFFOLK SULLIED SUMMARY SUMMATE SUMMERY
SUMMING SUNNIER SUNNILY SUPPING SUPPLED SUPPLER SUPPORT SWEETLY SWOONED SWOONER
SWOOPED SWOOPER TABBERS TABBIED TABBIES TABBING TAFFIES TAGGERS TALLBOY TALLIED
TALLIER TALLIES TALLISH TALLMEN TALLOWS TALLOWY TALLYHO TANNERS TANNERY TANNIER
TANNISH TANNOID TANNYLS TAPPERS TAPPING TARRIED TARRIES TARRING TARRISH TASSELY
TELLING TENNISY TERRAIN TERRIFY THEEING TIDDLER TIDDLEY TIFFANY TILLAGE TILLERS
TILLMAN TILLMEN TINNERS TINNERY TIPPERS TIPPLED TIPPLER TIPPLES TISSUAL TISSUED
TISSUEY TODDIES TODDLER TODDLES TOFFIES TOGGERY TOGGLED TOGGLER TOGGLES TOLLAGE
TOLLERS TOLLERY TOLLING TOLLMAN TOLLMEN TOLLWAY TOMMIES TONNAGE TOPPERS TOPPING
TOPPLED TOPPLER TOPPLES TOSSING TREEING TREEMAN TROOPED TUBBIER TUBBIES TUBBING
TUBBISH TUGGERS TUMMIES TUNNELS TUSSLED TUSSOCK VACCINE VALLEYS VATTERS VATTING
VELLUMS VELLUMY VETTING VILLAGE VILLAGY VILLANS VOLLEYS VOLLIED VOLLIES WADDERS
WADDIES WADDING WADDLER WADDLES WAFFLED WAFFLES WAGGERS WAGGIER WAGGISH WAGGLED
WAGGLES WAGGONS WALLERS WALLETS WALLING WALLOPS WARRENS WARRING WARRISH WATTLED
WATTLES WEBBING WEDDING WELLING WELLMAN WETTING WETTISH WHOOPED WHOOPER WIGGERS
WIGGERY WIGGLED WIGGLER WIGGLES WIGGLEY WILLERS WINNERS WOBBLED WOBBLER WOBBLES
WOPPERS WOPPING WORRIED WORRIES YAKKERS YAKKING YAPPERS YAPPIER YAPPING YAPPISH
YARROWS YELLING YELLOWS YESSING YUMMIER ZIPPERS

ABCDAAB ENGREEN LABELLA   **ABCDAAC** LOYALLY OUTFOOT OUTROOT

ABCDAAE ENSWEEP ENTREES LEGALLY LOCALLY LOCELLI LOWELLS OAKWOOD OUTBOOK OUTDOOR
OUTFOOL OUTLOOK OUTROOM OUTWOOD OXBLOOD RECARRY REMARRY

ABCDABA DECIDED DECODED DELUDED DEMODED DENUDED DERIDED ENSCENE RETIRER

ABCDABB REAGREE RENTREE RETIREE

ABCDABC BELIBEL DERIDER HOTSHOT INGOING PHOSPHO REDARED   **ABCDABD** ERASERS

ABCDABE AIRMAIL ARTWARE BEROBED BOURBON CHURCHY CORNCOB DECADES DECIDER DECIDES
DECODER DECODES DELUDER DELUDES DENUDER DENUDES DERIDES DRUIDRY EMBLEMS GEORGES
HEATHEN HEATHER IMPRIME INBRING INCHING INCLINE INJOINT INKLING INLYING INSWING
INTWINE INURING INVEINS ITALITE KIDSKIN LEAFLET LIMELIT LINOLIC MAILMAN MALTMAN
MARKMAN MASHMAN MASTMAN MAXIMAL MEATMEN MIASMIC NOMINOR ORATORS ORATORY ORIFORM
OUTPOUR PLUMPLY REBORED REBORES RECURED RECURES REDARES REFIRED REFIRES REHIRED
REHIRES RENFREW RETHREW RETIRED RETIRES REWIRED REWIRES SILESIA TEMPTED TEMPTER
UNBOUND UNCLUNG UNDRUNK UNFOUND UNMOUNT UNROUND UNSLUNG UNSOUND UNSTUNG UNSWUNG
UNWOUND UNWRUNG VETIVER WALKWAY WASHWAY

ABCDACA DREADED ESTHETE   **ABCDACB** DREADER REGORGE REGURGE TREATER

ABCDACC TREATEE   **ABCDACD** COERCER IRANIAN MIASMAS

ABCDACE ABIGAIL ACTUATE AIRWARD ANYWAYS BEANBAG CHANCAS COERCED COERCES DRESDEN
EARNERS EASIEST INKLIKE INTUITS IRAQIAN ITALIAN MIASMAL OILHOLE OUTVOTE PREOPEN
PRIAPIC RETORTS SPONSOR THEATER TREATED UNCOUCH UNTRUTH UPCHUCK

ABCDADC ACETATE   **ABCDADD** LIBELEE

ABCDADE AGITATE ANTIAIR ASONANT CODICIL CURACAO DECADAL DRUIDIC EMINENT IRONING
LABELED LABELER LAPELER LIBELED LIBELER LOCULUS LORELEI MOVEMEN MULEMEN NOVENES
NUMINIA OUTPOPS RIVERED

ABCDAEA EPICENE ETAGERE EXCRETE EXTREME ITALICI MAXIMUM ORINOCO RUMORER SADISTS
SCHISMS SCHISTS SINUSES SPARSES SPOUSES STYPSIS SUFISMS

ABCDAEB ASHPANS ASHRAMS ASTRALS ASTRAYS ATHWART CEVICHE DEBADGE ESCHEWS GRUDGER
IMAGISM PROSPER RECARVE RECURSE RECURVE REFORCE REFORGE REMORSE REPURGE RESURGE
ROSARIO TRACTOR TRAITOR TRUSTER TRYSTER UNCHURN

ABCDAEC ARCHAIC AVERAGE AVOCADO DECADIC DUNEDIN EASTERS ENSUERS ENTREAT HARSHER
HATCHET ICELIKE INSHIPS INSTILS INTWIST ITEMIZE LANOLIN LOYALTY MINTMAN MINTMEN
OUTMOST OUTPORT OUTPOST RESORBS RESORTS SWANSEA THEATRE TRESTLE UNPLUMP UNSHUTS
UNTRUST WIDOWED

ABCDAED ACREAGE AGITANT DISEDGE GRUDGED ICENIAN ICONIAN IMAGING IMPLIAL NOVENAE
OUTROAR SPARSER TRENTON

ABCDAEE BUGABOO EARLESS ELDRESS EMPRESS ENDLESS ENSHELL EXPRESS INSTILL NOMINEE
OUTPOLL OUTROLL TOASTEE TRUSTEE UNGRUFF UNSTUFF UNTRUSS UPTRUSS

ABCDAEF ABEYANT ABREAST ABSTAIN ABUSAGE ACETALS ACTUALS ACTUARY ADORANT ADULATE
AERIALS AFGHANI AFGHANS AFTWARD AIRWAVE AIRWAYS ALEGARS ALREADY AMIDASE AMINASE
ANIMALS ANIMATE ANOMALY ANORAKS ARMBAND ASHCAKE ASPHALT ASPRAWL AVOCATE AVOCATS

```
AVOWALS AVOWANT BANDBOX BELABOR BLURBED BORABLE BOWABLE BRAMBLE BRAMBLY BUSHBOY
BUYABLE CALICOS CHALCID CHANCED CHANCEL CHANCER CHANCES CHANCEY CHANCRE CHOICER
CHOICES CODICAL CODICES COLICKY COMICAL CONICAL COPYCAT COTICES COUNCIL CROTCHY
CRUNCHY CUBICAL CUBICAS CUBICLE CUBICLY CUTICLE CYNICAL DAZEDLY DECIDUA DIHYDRO
DIRNDLS DRYADES DRYADIC DUKEDOM DWINDLE DYNODES EAGLETS EARNEST EASTERN ECHOERS
EDGIEST ELATERS ELOPERS ELUDERS EMBREWS EMOTERS ENAMELS ENCREST ENDSEAL ENVIERS
EPIDEMY ERODENT ESCHEAT ESOTERY ETCHERS EUCHERS EUPHEMY EVADERS EVIDENT EVILEST
EVOKERS EXCRETA EXIGENT EXILERS EXODERM EXOGENS EXOGENY EXONERS FACTFUL FAMEFUL
FATEFUL FEARFUL FIREFLY FISTFUL FOREFIT FORKFUL FRETFUL GEORGIA GEORGIC GLASGOW
GRANGES GRINGAS GRINGOS GRUDGES HARSHLY HATCHED HATCHER HATCHES HAUGHTY HEIGHTS
HIPSHOT HITCHED HITCHER HITCHES HUMPHED HUNCHED HUNCHES HUTCHED HUTCHER HUTCHES
IAMBICS IAMBIST IAMBIZE IBERIAN ICEFISH ICONISM ICOSINE IDOLIFY IDOLISH IDOLISM
IDOLIST IDOLIZE IMAGINE IMAGIST IMBUING IMPAIRS IMPLIED IMPLIES IMPRINT INAGILE
INBUILT INFLICT INLAIDS INQUIET INQUIRE INQUIRY INSPIRE INVEIGH INVEILS INVOICE
IPSWICH IRONIES IRONISH IRONIZE ISCHIAL ISCHIUM ITALICS ITCHIER ITCHILY ITCHING
ITEMING IVORIED IVORIES IVYLIKE KLINKED KLINKER KLUNKED KNACKED KNACKER KNICKED
KNICKER KNOCKED KNOCKER KNUCKLE KNUCKLY LAMPLIT LANGLEY LAZULES LAZULIS LOBULAR
LOBULES LOCALED LOCALES LOCULAR LOCULED LOCULES MAHOMET MAILMEN MALTMEN MARKMEN
MAXIMUS MELAMIN MILKMAN MOLDMAN MOLDMEN MYXEMIA NAMINGS NOMINAL NOVENAS NYLONED
OARHOLE OARLOCK OBVIOUS OCELOID OCELOTS OMINOUS ONEFOLD ONEROUS ONFLOWS ONSHORE
OPALOID OPTIONS OSTEOID OSTEOMA OUTBORE OUTBOWS OUTCOME OUTDOER OUTDOES OUTDONE
OUTFOLD OUTFORM OUTGOER OUTGOES OUTGONE OUTHOLD OUTHOWL OUTMODE OUTROWS OUTWORN
OVALOID OVIFORM OXYTONE PANOPLY PLAYPEN PLUMPED PLUMPEN PLUMPER POLYPED POLYPES
PORKPIE PRIAPES PRIAPUS PRIMPED PROMPTS PUSHPIN RAZORED REBIRTH REBURNS REBURNT
REBURST RECARTS RECORDS RECORKS RECURLS REDARNS REDARTS REFORDS REFORMS REFURLS
REGARDS REHARMS REMARCH REMARKS REMORAS REPORTS RESCRUB RESPRAY RESTRAP RESTRIP
RETARDS RETHROW RETURFS RETURNS REWARDS REWARMS REWARNS REWORDS REWORKS ROSTRUM
RUMORED SAMPSON SATISFY SCHISMA SIMPSON SINUSAL SOAPSUD SPLASHY SPLOSHY SPOUSAL
SPOUSED SQUASHY SQUISHY STEPSON TACITLY TAINTED TAINTER TAUNTED TAUNTER THEATRY
THISTLE THISTLY TIBETAN TIGHTEN TIGHTER TIGHTLY TIMOTHY TINCTED TIPSTER TOASTED
TOASTER TONITES TRACTED TROUTED TRUSTED TRYSTED TWISTED TWISTER UMLAUTS UNACUTE
UNADULT UNCOUTH UNCRUDE UNCRUEL UNEQUAL UNFLUID UNFLUSH UNGLUED UNGLUES UNIQUES
UNMOULD UNPLUGS UNPLUMB UNSTUCK UNTOUCH UNTOUGH UNTRULY UPFLUNG UPSWUNG UPWOUND
URNFULS WIDOWER WINDWAY WIREWAY
```

ABCDBAA LOGROLL SEALESS SEWLESS SEXLESS   **ABCDBAB** NEOCENE NEOGENE

ABCDBAC GASBAGS MISAIMS MUSEUMS RESTERS   **ABCDBAD** TILSITS WARSAWS

ABCDBAE ANGINAL ANGINAS ARBORAL BARNABY DIACIDS DIAMIDE DIAMIDS DIAZIDE DIAZIDS
DIOXIDE DIOXIDS DOGBODY ENGINED ENGINES ENTONED ENTONES ENTUNED ENTUNES ENZONED
ENZONES EVOLVED EVOLVER EVOLVES GARBAGE HALVAHS LABIALS LIMPILY MACRAME NIACINS
NICKING NITRINE NOTIONS NOTIONY PERCEPT READERS REAMERS REAPERS REAVERS REAVERY
RENDERS RENTERS RETIERS RUMOURS RUPTURE SARCASM SEAREST SECRESY SEQUEST SEXIEST
SICKISH SIGNIST SIKHISM SILOIST SURFUSE TIDBITS ZINCIZE

ABCDBBA ANTENNA DECREED DEGREED DOGWOOD RECHEER SEABEES SENDEES

ABCDBBC HOTFOOT JESTEES MONSOON PONTOON REDWEED VESTEES   **ABCDBBD** DECREER

ABCDBBE BETWEEN BOYHOOD DEBTEES DECREES DEGREES FEUDEES FORSOOK FOXWOOD GENTEEL

LENDEES MENDEES POTHOOK REFLEED REFLEES RENTEES RESTEEL RESWEEP SEAWEED UNBONNY
UNCANNY VENDEES WEBFEET

ABCDBCA GINSING SANPANS SERGERS SERVERS   **ABCDBCB** BENZENE SANTANA

ABCDBCC DISMISS

ABCDBCD BINGING DENSENS DINGING HINGING KANSANS NAYSAYS PINGING RINGING SINGING
TINGING UNSENSE VERSERS WINGING ZINGING

ABCDBCE BARNARD BERSERK BIAXIAL BIGWIGS BINDING CARFARE CITYITE CONDONE CUTOUTS
DIARIAL DIARIAN DIAXIAL DINTING EARMARK FATUATE FERNERY FILMILY FINDING FORBORE
FORLORN FORWORE FORWORN GERBERA HARVARD HERDERS HEROERS HEYDEYS HINTING HOBNOBS
INTENTS JERKERS KERNERS KOUDOUS KOWTOWS LENIENT LINKING LINTING LONDONY LOWDOWN
MAYDAYS MERGERS MILKILY MINCING MINDING MINTING MISLIST MUKLUKS NERVERS NITRITE
NITWITS NURTURE OUTCUTS OUTHUTS OUTJUTS OUTPUTS PAYDAYS PENDENT PERVERT PICNICS
PIETIES PINKING PINWING PREDREW RAGBAGS RAGTAGS RECHECK RINDING RINKING RINSING
RISKISH SATIATE SECRECY SERVERY SILKILY SINKING STIPTIC TERMERS TORPORS UNCINCH
UNIONIC VERGERS VERGERY VIEWIER VITRITE WARFARE WAYLAYS WHETHER WINCING WINDING
WINKING WISPISH XYLOYLS YARDARM ZINCING

ABCDBDA SEARERS SEPTETS SEXTETS TENSEST TERSEST   **ABCDBDB** CANTATA ORDERER

ABCDBDC ORDERED SIGNING

ABCDBDE AGREGES APROPOS BEARERS BRIERED CANTATE DENSEST DIONINE FEARERS HEARERS
KILNING LACTATE LIGNINS LIMNING LOBCOCK NOCUOUS PIANINO PIONING PRAIRIE SALTATE
STRATAL TEARERS TOWCOCK WEARERS

ABCDBEA DASTARD DAYWARD DESCEND DINGIED DIRTIED DRAWROD ENHANCE GIFTING GILDING
GIMPING GIRDING PREWRAP RECLEAR RESHEAR RESWEAR RIDGIER RINGIER RISKIER RITZIER
SAMBALS SAMOANS SAMPANS SANDAKS SANDALS SATRAPS SCONCES SEABEDS SEALERS SEAMERS
SEATERS SECRETS SEINERS SEIZERS SENDERS SEQUELS SILKIES SIXTIES STRATUS SUBDUES
SULFURS TEMPEST TOPCOAT TOPMOST TOWBOAT

ABCDBEB ARBORER ARMORER ASEPSIS BAKLAVA BELIEVE BESIEGE CAUSATA DEPLETE FABIANA
GENOESE MANDALA MARSALA MASCARA METHENE RELIEVE REPIECE REPLETE SECRETE

ABCDBEC BADLAND BEDHEAD BESPEWS BIRDIER BOSTONS CASBAHS CONJOIN DIELIKE DIRTIER
DISTILS FESTERS FORGOER JESTERS MISFITS MISHITS MISTICS NESTERS ORDURED OUTHUNT
PESTERS PISTILS PURSUER RASCALS REDHEAD RESKEWS RESPEWS RESTEMS RESTEPS ROSCOES
SIGHING SUNBURN UNTINCT VESPERS VESTERS WESTERS WOESOME

ABCDBED BALSAMS BILGING BIRDIED CAESARS CASEATE CAUSALS CENSERS CONSOLS CONTORT
DEFTEST DIPSIES DIRGING DOBSONS FEATEST FLATLET GEYSERS GIPSIES INCENSE INGENUE
INSENCE INTENSE JERSEYS LACTANT LEASERS LEFTEST NEATEST OUTSUMS PERSEUS PERTEST
PIETIST POISONS PURSUES RIDGING RIOTIST SCARCER SIEGING SOMEONE STARTER SUBDUED
TARSALS TEASELS TEASERS TENSERS TIPSIES TONSORS UNFENCE UNTENSE WEASELS WEASERS

ABCDBEE AIRBILL BEARESS BEDLESS BEDRESS BEPRESS BESHELL BESMELL BESPELL BOYCOTT
CATFALL DAREALL DEANESS DEPRESS DESWELL DEWLESS DISTILL FEWNESS FEYNESS GEMLESS

- 35 -

HEIRESS HERDESS JACKASS JEWLESS KEYLESS MIDRIFF MISBILL MISKILL NEGRESS OUTBUZZ
OUTCULL OUTPULL PEGLESS PEWLESS RANDALL REBLESS REDNESS RESMELL RESPELL RESWELL
WEBLESS WETNESS

ABCDBEF ADJUDGE AIRLIFT AIRLIKE AIRLINE AIRSICK AIRVIEW AISLING ALKYLIC ANOINTS
ANTONYM ARBORED ARMORED ATWITCH BALSAMY BANDAGE BANTAMS BANZAIS BARGAIN BARMAID
BARWAYS BASCART BASTARD BEADERY BEANERY BEAVERS BENDERS BEQUEST BESMEAR BESPEAK
BETHELS BIASING BIFOILS BILKING BIOPICS BIOTICS BIOTINS BIOTIZE BIOXIDE BIPRISM
BIRDIES BIRDING BOGHOLE BORZOIS BOUDOIR BRIARED BUGOUTS BULGURS BULRUSH CADEAUX
CALGARY CALVARY CAMBARS CAPTAIN CARNAGE CARNATE CARPALS CARTAGE CATNAPS CATWALK
CAUSATE CAVEATS CAVIARS CAYMANS CEILERS CENTERS CITRINE CITYISH COLPORT COMFORT
COMPONE COMPORT COMPOSE COMPOST COMPOTE COMPOTS CONDORS CONFORM CONSOLE CONSORT
CONTOUR CONVOKE CONVOYS COPIOUS CORDOBA CORDONS CORDOVA COSMOID COUPONS COWBOYS
COWPOKE CULTURE CUPFULS CURIUMS DEAFENS DEAFEST DEALERS DEAREST DECKERS DECREAM
DEFIERS DEFLEAS DEFLECT DEFLESH DEICERS DELVERS DENIERS DENSELY DENTERS DENVERS
DESCENT DEWIEST DEXTERS DIALING DIALIST DIAMINE DIARIES DIARIST DIARIZE DICKIES
DICTION DIETING DIGNIFY DIGNITY DIMWITS DINGIER DINGILY DINKIER DIRTIES DIRTILY
DISHING DISKING DISLIMB DISLINK DOCTORS DREARLY DUGOUTS EARLAPS EASWARD ENCINAL
ENCINAS ENDINGS ENFANTS ENLINKS ENRANKS ENRINGS ENWINDS FABIANS FACIALS FANTAIL
FANTASM FANTASY FELTERS FENCERS FENDERS FERMENT FERVENT FIBRILS FIBRINE FICOIDS
FICTION FIGLIKE FILMIER FILMING FILMISH FILMIST FINLIKE FIRMING FISHIER FISHILY
FISHING FLAILED FOGHORN FOLDOUT FOLIOED FORBODE FORDOES FORDONE FORGOES FORGONE
FORMOSA FORMOUS FOXHOLE FRIARLY FUNGUSY GALWAYS GARLAND GATEAUX GELDERS GENDERS
GEODESY GIFTIES GIRLIES GIRLISH GIRLISM GONDOLA HALYARD HANGARS HANSARD HATBAND
HAULAGE HAYCART HAYRACK HAYRAKE HAYWARD HEADERS HEALERS HEAPERS HEATERS HEAVENS
HEAVERS HEBREWS HEDGERS HEFTERS HEIFERS HELMETS HELPERS HENPECK HERSELF HESPERA
HICKIES HOEDOWN HOLDOUT HOMEOID HORLOGE HORMONE HOTDOGS HOUNOED HUMBUGS INCANTS
INCENDS INDENTS INFANCY INFANTS INHANCE INJUNCT INLANDS INTONED INTONER INTONES
INUENDO INURNED INVENTS JACKALS JAGUARS JANUARY JAYHAWK JAYWALK JIGLIKE JILTING
JOYSOME JUGFULS JUMBUCK KEDGERS KERNELS KERNELY KILTIES KILTING KUMQUAT LABIATE
LACTARY LACTASE LAMBAST LANYARD LARIATS LARVATE LAYBACK LEADENS LEADERS LEAFERS
LEAFERY LEAKERS LEANERS LEANEST LEAPERS LEAVENS LEAVERS LECHERS LECHERY LECTERN
LEDGERS LENDERS LEWDEST LICKING LIFTING LIGNIFY LIGNITE LIMBIER LIMBING LIMPING
LIMPISH LINKIER LINTIER LIONIZE LIPOIDS LIQUIDS LIQUIDY LIQUIFY LISPING LISTING
LITHIUM LOCKOUT LOGWORK LOTIONS LOWBORN LOWBOYS MADCAPS MAGNATE MAGYARS MAIDANS
MALTASE MANDATE MANIACS MANSARD MANUALS MANWAYS MARGATE MARIANO MARIANS MAYFAIR
MAYHAPS MEANERS MEANEST MEDLEYS MELDERS MELTERS MENDERS MEWLERS MIDLINE MIDRIBS
MIDWIFE MIDWIVE MILDISH MILKIER MILKING MILKISH MINCIER MINKISH MINXISH MISFILE
MISFIRE MISGIVE MISLIKE MISLINE MISTIER MISTIFY MISTILY MISTING MONGOLS MOTIONS
MOUTONS MUGFULS NARWALS NEAREST NECKERS NEGLECT NEPHEWS NEUTERS NICEISH NIFTIER
NIFTIES NITRIDE NITRIFY NOISOME NORFOLK NOXIOUS OAHUANS OAKLAND OATCAKE OILFISH
OILYISH ORATRIX ORDERLY ORDURES OUTGUNS OUTPUSH OUTRUNS OUTRUSH PACKAGE PADRAIC
PADRAIG PADUANS PAGEANT PALMATE PANCAKE PARBAKE PARFAIT PARLAYS PARTAKE PATHANS
PAYBACK PEAHENS PEAKERS PEALERS PEATERY PEAVEYS PECKERS PEDLERS PELFERY PELMETS
PELTERS PERCENT PERFECT PETRELS PEWTERS PEWTERY PIANIST PICKIER PICKING PIDGINS
PIECING PIERING PIETISM PIGMIES PIMLICO PINKIER PINKIES PINKILY PINKISH PIQUING
PISCIAN PISCINE PISCIUM PITHIER PITHILY PITHING PITLIKE PITSIDE PITYING PIXYISH
PLAYLET POGROMS POISONY POTHOLE POTIONS PREARMS PREDRAW PREORAL PRIORAL PRIORLY
PROARMY PROGRAM PURSUAL PURSUED PURSUIT PUSAUNT PUSTULA PUSTULE RADIALE RADIALS
RADIANS RADIANT RADIATE RAGLANS RAMPAGE RAMPANT RANSACK RATBAGS REAGENT REALEST
REAMEND REBLEND RECHEAT RECHEWS RECLEAN REFLECT REFUELS RELIEFS REOPENS REPLEAD

REPLEAT REQUEST RESPEAK RESPECT RESTEAL RESWEAT RESWEPT REVIEWS REWHELP RHYTHMS
RIBLIKE RIFLING RIFTING RIOTING RIPTIDE RISKILY RISKING RITZILY RITZING ROANOKE
ROWBOAT ROWLOCK RUNOUTS SAGUARO SALVAGE SATRAPY SAWBACK SCARCED SCARCEN SCONCER
SCOTCHY SEALERY SECHELT SECRETA SEGMENT SEQUENT SERPENT SIBLING SIEVING SIFTING
SIGNIFY SILKIER SILKING SILOING SILTING SKULKED SKULKER SKUNKED SMARMED STARTED
STARTLE STILTED STILTER STILTON STINTED STINTER STOUTEN STOUTER STOUTLY STRATUM
STRETCH STUNTED STUNTER STYPTIC SUBDUAL SUBDUCT SUBDUER SUBDURE SUBRULE SULFURY
TAILAGE TAIPANS TANKARD TARMACS TARZANS TEAMERS TEMPERA TEMPERS TEMPERY TENDERS
TENSELY TERCELS TERSELY THIGHED TICKIER TICKIES TICKING TIDYING TIERING TIGRISH
TIPSIER TIPSILY TOEHOLD TOMBOYS TOPSOIL TOPWORK TOWROPE TRIARCH TUBFULS TUMOURS
TURNUPS UNAWNED UNBANKS UNBENCH UNBENDS UNBINDS UNBONED UNBONES UNCANED UNFANCY
UNFINED UNHANDS UNHANDY UNHANGS UNHONED UNIONED UNLINED UNLINES UNLINKS UNMANED
UNMANLY UNMINED UNOWNED UNPANEL UNRANKS UNRINDS UNRINGS UNSINEW UNTINED UNTINES
UNTONED UNTONES UNVENOM UNWINDS UNWINDY UNZONED UNZONES VACUATE VAGRANT VALIANT
VALUATE VANDALS VANTAGE VARIANT VARIATE VEILERS VEINERS VENDERS VENGERS VENTERS
VERBENA VERIEST VERMEIL VESPERY VETOERS VICTIMS VIEWING VINDICT VIOLINS VIRGINS
VITRIFY VITRIOL VULTURE WAGTAIL WARPATH WASTAGE WAYBACK WAYFARE WAYLAID WEAKENS
WEAKEST WEANERS WEAVERS WEDGERS WELDERS WELTERS WESTERN WETHERS WHITHER WICHITA
WICKING WICKIUP WIGLIKE WILDISH WILTING WINDIER WINDILY WINGIER WISHING WISPIER
WISPILY WISPING WORKOUT YARDAGE ZACHARY ZINCIFY ZINCITE ZIONISM ZIONIST ZIONITE

ABCDCAB EDIFIED ESTATES REAWARE   **ABCDCAD** OPINION

ABCDCAE ALMSMAN ANTITAX ARIDIAN AURORAE AURORAL AURORAS CLINICS CRITICS DUOPODS
EDIFIER EDIFIES ENGAGED ENGAGER ENGAGES ESTATED GEOLOGY LIEGELY NAILING NOISING
PHILIPS PRECEPT REALARM REAWARD RIEVERS SLIMISH SNIPISH SPITISH SWINISH TENANTS
THERETO TRILITE TRILITS TRINITY

ABCDCBA DEIFIED REPAPER REVIVER ROTATOR   **ABCDCBB** USELESS

ABCDCBE ANILINE ANILINS BACKCAP BEPAPER BREWERS BREWERY CAMPMAN COTUTOR CREWERS
DEIFIER DEIFIES DEITIES DRAWARM GLYCYLS GRANARY HAITIAN KNIFING KNIVING LAMPMAN
MITOTIC NOTATOR OSIRISM PETITES PREFERS PREYERS REPIPED REPIPES REPOPED REPOPES
REVIVED REVIVES SLIMILY SNIPING SYNONYM TENONED TENONER UNEVENS UNICING UNITING
URETERS UTILITY VEINIER

ABCDCCE LIENEES PRESEEN   **ABCDCDA** GAINING   **ABCDCDC** UKELELE

ABCDCDE ALINING AMIDIDE ASININE BRINING CHINING COINING EMANANT JOINING LINENER
OPINING PAINING PHONONS QUININA QUININE QUININS RAINING REINING REMIMIC RUINING
SEINING SHINING SHTETEL TIERERS TWINING UNPAPAL UNVIVID VEINING ZENANAS

ABCDCEA BATHTUB CANONIC DAISIED DISUSED EDIFICE EMANATE ENTITLE EXALATE GAITING
GLIDING GRIDING GRIMING GUIDING GUILING GUISING LIFEFUL RAINIER REVIVOR ROILIER
SCARABS SEABAGS SEAWAYS SHAMANS SHEDERS SHEKELS SIEGERS SIEVERS SKEWERS SONANTS
SPEWERS SPIRITS SPOROUS SPUTUMS STEREOS STEVENS STOLONS TEACART

ABCDCEB BETITLE BRIMIER BRINIER FAUNULA GRIMIER GRIPIER ISOLOGS ISOPODS ISOPORS
LEADAGE LEAFAGE LEAKAGE MYOLOGY MYOTONY PENANCE PHARAOH PRICIER REAWAKE RECYCLE
SEAFARE SEAWARE TEAWARE WHITISH

ABCDCEC DESISTS DISUSES GRANADA GUAYANA MISUSES NIAGARA OKAYAMA PRECEDE RESISTS

ABCDCED ANIMISM BLATANT BONANZA DAISIES DIESELS HAIRIER PRESETS PRETEST PRETEXT
PRONOUN RAISINS THESEUS

ABCDCEE AGELESS AWELESS AWENESS BAILIFF BLOWOFF FOELESS GALILEE HUELESS ICELESS
IRELESS ORELESS PIELESS POETESS PRESELL PRETELL REAMASS ROTATEE SEAWALL TOELESS

ABCDCEF ABIDING ABILITY ACIDIFY ACIDITY ACIDIZE AGILITY AIRCREW AIRDROP ALIBIED
ALIBIES ALMSMEN AMIDINE AMINIZE AMITIES AMOROUS ANILIDE ANILIDS ANIMIST ANIMIZE
APIOIDS APOLOGY ARIDITY ARISING AURORES AVIDITY AWNINGS BAILING BAITING BICYCLE
BIOLOGY BIONOMY BIOTOMY BLOWOUT BOATAGE BOILING BOUQUET BRAVADO BREVETS BRIMING
BRINIES BRINISH BRITISH CAINITE CANINES CANONED CANONRY CEILIDH CEILING CHAPATI
CHARADE CHEWERS CHIDING CHILIES CHIMING CHOROID CLAMANT CLAVATE CLEMENT COADAPT
COEXERT COIFING COILING COUTURE CRAVATS CREWELS CREWETS CUISINE CURARES CURARIN
CYANATE DAILIES DAIRIES DECOCTS DEICING DELILAH DIETERS DIOBOLS DOILIES DRAYAGE
DRIVING DROPOUT DUELERS DUMPMAN DUMPMEN DUOTONE EARDROP EARDRUM ECOLOGY ECONOMY
EDITING EDITION ELICITS ELITISM ELIXIRS EPICISM EPICIST EVILING EXCOCTS EXILING
EXITING EXOPODS FADEDLY FAILING FAIRIES FAIRILY FAIRING FAIRISH FEASANT FINANCE
FLAMANT FOILING FORERUN FRISIAN FUELERS FURORES GEOFORM GRADATE GREYEST GRIMILY
HAILING HAIRIES HAIRING ICEBERG ICELEAF ICHTHUS IDOLOUS ISODONT ISOLOGY ISOTOME
ISOTONE ISOTONY ISOTOPE ISOTOPY JADEDLY JAEGERS JAILING JAILISH JUICIER JUICILY
JUICING LAICISM LAICITY LAICIZE LAIRING LAITIES LAMPMEN LIEFEST LIEGERS LYOPOMA
MAIDING MAIDISH MAILING MISUSED MISUSER MUTATED MUTATES NEOLOGY NEOTOMA NEOZOIC
NOISIER NOISILY NOTATED NOTATES OBEYERS OLIVINE OMAHANS OMELETS ONESELF OPENERS
OPENEST OPTATED OPTATES ORIFICE ORIGINS OSIRIAN OSIRIFY OUTSTAY OUTSTEP OVEREAT
OVICIDE OVIDIAN OXALATE OXIDIZE PAILING PAIRING PEASANT PENANCY PENANGS PHALANX
PHOTOED PHOTONS PIECERS PLACARD PLACATE PLANATE PLATANS PLAYACT PONENTS PORTRAY
PREBEND PRECENT PREDEFY PREDENY PREFECT PREHEAL PREHEAT PREMEDS PRESEAL PRESENT
PRETEND PREVENT PREVETO PREWELT PRICING PRIDING PRIMING PRISING PRIZING PROLOGS
PROLONG PROMOTE PROTONS PROVOKE PROVOST PSIDIUM QUAYAGE RAIDING RAILING RAINILY
RAISING RAISINY RAMPMEN READAPT RECOCKS RECOCTS REICING RETOTAL REVIVAL RIOTOUS
ROEIEST ROILING ROTATED ROTATES SAILING SCAVAGE SCENERY SEAMARK SEAWARD SEIZING
SEMIMAT SHINIER SHINILY SKIMING SLICING SLIDING SLIMIER SLIMING SLIPING SLITING
SMILING SMITING SOILIER SOILING SONANCE SONANCY SPICIER SPICILY SPICING SPIKIER
SPIKILY SPIKING SPINIER SPIRING SPIRITY SPITING STIKINE SUICIDE SUITING SUMPMAN
SUMPMEN SWIPING TAILING TENANCY THEMERS THEREAS THEREBY THEREIN THEREOF THEREON
TIARAED TOILING TONINGS TRAVAIL TRIVIAL TUNINGS TWINIER TWINISM TWOFOLD TWOSOME
UNADAPT UNALARM UNAPART UNAWAKE UNAWARE UNCOCKS UNELECT UNERECT UNIFIED UNIFIER
UNIFIES UNITIES UNITIZE UNPAPER UNPIPED URNINGS UROLOGY UROPODS UTAHANS UTILIZE
VEILING VIEWERS VINTNER VOICING VOIDING WAILING WAITING WAIVING WANINGS WEIRING
WHEREAS WHEREAT WHEREBY WHEREIN WHEREOF WHEREON WHERETO WHINIER WHITING WIENERS
WRITING ZONINGS

ABCDDAE ABUTTAL AVERRAL AXILLAE AXILLAR AXILLAS EMITTED EMITTER EVILLER IDYLLIC
SUFIISM

ABCDDBA REOFFER REUTTER STREETS   **ABCDDBC** UNSEENS

ABCDDBE BEURRES BLUFFLY MEISSEN PAELLAS REANNEX SCREECH TEAMMEN

ABCDDCA DRESSED DUELLED DUETTED DWELLED STEPPES

ABCDDCB CHALLAH DRESSER FRETTER GRAMMAR PRESSER TREKKER

ABCDDCD BLESSES CRESSES DRESSES GUESSES LOESSES PRESSES SHEDDED SKEDDED SLEDDED
TRESSES

ABCDDCE ABERRED ABETTED ABETTER AGREERS APOLLOS AVERRED BLESSED BLESSER BLOSSOM
CAREERS CHIPPIE CRESSED DUELLER FLUMMUX FRETTED FUELLED FUELLER GOANNAS GRIFFIN
GROTTOS GUESSED GUESSER INDEEDY KNELLED PIAZZAS PRESSED QUELLED QUELLER REASSAY
RETOOTH SHABBAT SHEDDER SHELLED SHELLER SLEDDER SMELLED SMELLER SPELLED SPELLER
STEMMED STEMMER STEPPED STEPPER SWELLED SWELLER TEAMMAN TREKKED TRESSED TRESSEL
TROLLOP UNARRAY UNEBBED UNTOOTH WHETTED WHETTEN WHETTER

ABCDDEA CLASSIC DIALLED DRAGGED DRATTED DRILLED DRIPPED DROLLED DROPPED DROSSED
DRUBBED DRUGGED DRUMMED LOESSAL REOCCUR SALOONS SATEENS SCHOOLS SCHOONS SCREENS
SCYLLAS SIENNAS SIERRAS SPLEENS STELLAS STUCCOS TRIVVET

ABCDDEB BAZOOKA BEHOOVE BRAGGER BRASSER BRIMMER CRABBER CRAMMER CRASSER CRIBBER
CRITTER CROPPER CROSSER CRULLER CRUMMER DRABBER DRAGGER DRAMMER DRILLER DRIPPER
DROLLER DROPPER DROSSER DRUGGER DRUMMER FLANNEL FRILLER FRIPPER FRITTER GRABBER
GRASSER GRIDDER GRILLER GRIMMER GRINNER GRIPPER GRITTER GROSSER GRUBBER KRULLER
PRIGGER PRIMMER PRODDER PROFFER PSYLLAS REISSUE SEATTLE SWALLOW TRAMMER TRAPPER
TRIGGER TRILLER TRIMMER TRIPPER TROLLER TRUSSER WRAPPER

ABCDDEC BESOOTS ODYSSEY TRESSLE

ABCDDED ABYSSES AMISSES BIASSES BLISSES BLURRER BRASSES CHARRER CHASSIS CLASSES
CLODDED CROSSES CRUDDED DROSSES FLOSSES GLADDED GLASSES GLISSES GLOSSES GRASSES
GRIDDED GROSSES MOUSSES PLODDED PLUSSES PRODDED QUADDED SCARRER SCUDDED SHIRRER
SKIDDED SPARRER SPUDDED SPURRER SQUEEGE SQUEEZE STARRER STIRRER STUDDED THUDDED
TRUSSES ULYSSES UNADDED

ABCDDEE CHITTEE GRILLEE QUIZZEE SHUTTEE SKIDDOO SNUBBEE THUGGEE

ABCDDEF ABUTTED ABUTTER ABYSSED ALYSSUM ARIPPLE ASIMMER ASUDDEN BIASSED BLADDER
BLIPPED BLOTTED BLOTTER BLUFFED BLUFFER BLURRED BRAGGED BRASSED BRASSEY BRIMMED
BRITTLE BRITTLY CABOOSE CAHOOTS CAISSON CAREENS CHAFFED CHAFFER CHALLIS CHANNEL
CHAPPED CHAPPER CHAPPIE CHARRED CHATTED CHATTEL CHATTER CHEDDAR CHIFFON CHIGGER
CHILLED CHILLER CHINNED CHIPPED CHIPPER CHIRRUP CHITTED CHITTER CHOPPED CHOPPER
CHUBBED CHUDDER CHUFFED CHUGGED CHUGGER CHUKKER CHUMMED CHUMMER CLABBER CLAMMED
CLANNED CLAPPED CLAPPER CLASSED CLASSER CLATTER CLIFFED CLIPPED CLIPPER CLOBBER
CLOGGED CLOGGER CLOPPED CLOTTED CLOTTER CLUBBED CLUBBER CLUTTER COANNEX COIFFED
COIFFES CRABBED CRAGGED CRAMMED CRAPPED CRAPPIE CRASSLY CRIBBED CRIPPLE CROPPED
CROSSED CROSSLY DIALLER DRIBBLE DRIZZLE DRIZZLY DUENNAS DUETTOS ENCOOPS ENROOTS
EXMOORS FAILLES FLACCID FLAGGED FLAGGER FLAPPED FLAPPER FLATTED FLATTEN FLATTER
FLATTOP FLIPPED FLIPPER FLITTED FLITTER FLIVVER FLOGGED FLOGGER FLOPPED FLOPPER
FLOSSED FLOSSER FLUBBED FLUMMOX FLUTTER FRAZZLE FRILLED FRISSON FRIZZED FRIZZES
FROGGED GALOOTS GAZOOKS GHETTOS GLADDEN GLADDER GLASSED GLASSER GLIBBER GLIMMED
GLIMMER GLITTER GLOMMED GLOSSED GLOSSER GLOTTIS GLUMMER GLUTTED GLUTTER GLUTTON
GNOCCHI GRABBED GRANNIE GRAPPLE GRASSED GRASSIE GRIDDLE GRIFFON GRILLED GRILLES

GRINNED GRIPPED GRIPPES GRITTED GRIZZLE GRIZZLY GROMMET GROSSED GROSSLY GRUBBED
GRUFFLY IDYLLER INDOORS INHOOPS INLOOKS INROOMS JOHNNIE KNAPPED KNAPPER KNITTED
KNITTER KNOBBED KNOBBER KNOBBLE KNOBBLY KNOLLED KNOTTED KNOTTER KNUBBED KNUBBLY
LAGOONS LATEENS LOESSIC MAILLOT MAROONS MUEZZIN NAZIISM ODESSAN OMITTED OVALLED
OVERRAN OVERRID OVERRUN PFENNIG PHALLIC PHALLUS PHYLLIN PIERROT PLANNED PLANNER
PLATTED PLATTEN PLATTER PLODDER PLOTTED PLOTTER PLUGGED PLUGGER PLUMMED PLUMMER
PLUMMET PLUSSED POTEENS POUFFED POUFFES PRAMMED PRATTED PRATTLE PRATTLY PRIGGED
PRUSSIC PSYLLIA PSYLLID QUAFFED QUAFFER QUARREL QUIBBLE QUILLED QUILLER QUIPPED
QUIPPER QUITTAL QUITTED QUITTER QUIZZED QUIZZER QUIZZES RACOONS REALLOT REALLOW
REANNOY REAPPLY REBOOKS RECOOKS RECOOLS REDOOMS REFOOLS REHOODS REHOOKS REHOOPS
RELOOKS RETOOLS REWOODS SCABBED SCALLOP SCANNED SCANNER SCARRED SCATTED SCATTER
SCOFFED SCOFFER SCOTTIE SCREENY SCROOGE SCUDDER SCUFFED SCUFFER SCUFFLE SCUFFLY
SCULLED SCULLER SCUMMED SCUMMER SCUPPER SCUTTLE SHAGGED SHALLOT SHALLOW SHAMMED
SHAMMER SHATTER SHELLAC SHILLED SHILLER SHIMMED SHIMMER SHINNED SHINNER SHINNEY
SHIPPED SHIPPER SHIRRED SHODDEN SHOPPED SHOPPER SHOTTER SHUDDER SHUFFLE SHUNNED
SHUNNER SHUTTER SHUTTLE SIERRAN SKIDDER SKIFFED SKILLED SKILLET SKIMMED SKIMMER
SKINNED SKINNER SKIPPED SKIPPER SKITTER SKITTLE SLABBED SLABBER SLAGGED SLAGGER
SLAMMED SLAPPED SLAPPER SLATTED SLATTER SLIMMED SLIMMER SLIPPED SLIPPER SLITTED
SLITTER SLOBBER SLOGGED SLOGGER SLOPPED SLOTTED SLOTTER SLUBBED SLUBBER SLUFFED
SLUGGED SLUGGER SLUMMED SLUMMER SLURRED SMALLED SMALLER SMATTER SMITTEN SMUGGLE
SMUTTED SMUTTER SNAFFLE SNAGGED SNAGGER SNAPPED SNAPPER SNIFFED SNIFFER SNIFFLE
SNIFFLY SNIGGER SNIPPED SNIPPER SNIPPET SNIVVLE SNOBBED SNOBBER SNUBBED SNUBBER
SNUFFED SNUFFER SNUFFLE SNUFFLY SNUGGED SNUGGER SNUGGLE SOUFFLE SPANNED SPANNER
SPARRED SPARROW SPATTED SPATTER SPIFFED SPIGGOT SPILLED SPILLER SPINNER SPINNEY
SPITTED SPITTEN SPITTER SPITTLE SPLEENY SPORRAN SPOTTED SPOTTER SPUDDER SPURRED
SPUTTER SQUEEZY STABBED STABBER STAFFED STAFFER STAGGER STALLED STALLER STAMMER
STARRED STELLAR STIFFED STIFFEN STIFFER STIFFLY STILLED STILLER STIPPLE STIPPLY
STIRRED STIRRUP STOLLEN STOPPED STOPPER STUBBED STUBBER STUBBLE STUBBLY STUDDER
STUFFED STUFFER STUNNED STUNNER SWABBED SWABBER SWABBIE SWADDLE SWAGGED SWAGGER
SWANNED SWAPPED SWAPPER SWATTED SWATTER SWILLED SWILLER SWIMMED SWIMMER SWIPPER
SWIZZLE SWOBBER SWOLLEN SWOTTED SWOTTER TABOOED TAXIING THALLUS THINNED THINNER
THUGGED TRAFFIC TRAMMED TRAMMEL TRAPPED TRELLIS TRILLED TRIMMED TRIPPED TRODDEN
TROLLED TROLLEY TRUFFLE TRUNNEL TRUSSED TUREENS TWADDLE TWADDLY TWIGGED TWIGGER
TWILLED TWINNED TWINNER TYCOONS UNALLOW UNCOOPS UNHEEDS UNHEEDY UNHOODS UNHOOKS
UNHOOPS UNLOOPS UNLOOSE UNMOORS UNPEELS UNREELS UNROOFS UNROOMY UNROOST UNROOTS
UNSOOTY UNWOOED UNWOOLY UPALLEY UPATTIC UPLOOKS UPROOTS VACUUMS VAMOOSE VIALLED
WHAMMED WHIPPED WHIPPER WHIPPET WHIRRED WHIRREY WHIZZED WHIZZER WHIZZES WHOPPER
WRAPPED WRIGGLE WRIGGLY WRITTED WRITTEN YAHOOED

ABCDEAA EMIGREE ESCAPEE EVACUEE EVICTEE EXALTEE EXPIREE LEGPULL LOWBALL SADNESS
SAPLESS SCHLOSS SHYNESS SINLESS SKYLESS SLYNESS SODLESS SONLESS SUMLESS SUNLESS
SURPASS

ABCDEAB ALBINAL ALUMNAL ANGLIAN AREOLAR ASTHMAS CARIOCA DEBRIDE DEGRADE ENDOGEN
ENLIVEN ENRIPEN ENWIDEN ENWOVEN ESCAPES ESCRIES HIBACHI INCHAIN INCHPIN INGRAIN
INSULIN LEGIBLE LENTILE LYINGLY NEGRINE NEPTUNE NEURINE NEURONE REDWARE REQUIRE
RESCORE RESHARE RESPIRE RESTORE RESWORE SEAWISE SECLUSE SHAWISH SHOWISH STALEST
STYLIST SYNOPSY TENUATE TERMITE UNBEGUN

ABCDEAC ACLINAL ANTIFAT AREOLAE AUTOMAT CREVICE DESANDS DISBUDS EARLIER ENDOWED
ENDURED ENROBER ENSURES LINCOLN MOSLEMS MUSLEMS MUSLIMS OUTBLOT OUTPLOT OUTSHOT

OVERTOE PRECIPE RASHERS RASPERS RASTERS REDBIRD RESPARS RESTIRS RHYMERY RISKERS
ROSIERS ROSTERS RUSHERS SETFAST SITFAST

ABCDEAD AMOEBAE CADENCE COGENCE CONTACT ENISLES EPITHET IGNATIA LADYFLY NELSONS
NUDGING RAISERS RESTART RHUBARB RINSERS ROUSERS SALTEST SECTIST SKATIST SOFTEST
TRIESTE UNSTOUT

ABCDEAE ECTASES ELAPSES ENCASES ENCODED ENDURER ENSURER EVULSES EXCIDED EXCISES
EXCUSES EXPIRER EXPOSES MONISMS MUTISMS NIRVANA SIAMESE TANISTS TAOISTS TAPISTS
THEISTS THEMATA THIRSTS THRUSTS TUNISTS TYPISTS ULTIMUM

ABCDEAF ABYSMAL ACROBAT ADMIRAL ADRENAL ADVISAL AFRICAN AGENDAS AIRHEAD ALGEBAR
ALUMNAE AMOEBAN AMOEBAS ANEMIAS ANGORAS ANGULAR ANORMAL ANOXIAS ANTEWAR ANTHRAX
ANTIWAR ARCHWAY AREOLAS ARMLOAD ARNICAS AROUSAL ARSENAL ARTISAN ASEXUAL ASHTRAY
ASOCIAL AUSTRAL AZOREAN AZORIAN AZTECAN AZTECAS AZUREAN CAPLOCK CAPRICE CARSICK
CELTICS CHALICE CHEMICS CLERICS CLIENCY COENACT COGENCY COGNACS COMPACT CONDUCE
CONDUCT CONFECT CONJECT CONVECT CONVICT CORNICE COWLICK CUTBACK DAYBEDS DAYSIDE
DAYTIDE DEMANDS DEVOIDS DISBODY DOTARDS DOTARDY DROMEDS EARLIES EARTHED EARTHEN
EBONIES ECTYPES EDIBLES EGOIZED EGOIZER EGOIZES ELAPSED ELBOWED ELBOWER ELONGED
EMBOLES EMBOWED EMBOWEL EMIGRES EMPALED EMPANEL EMPIRED EMPIRES EMPOWER EMPTIED
EMPTIER EMPTIES ENABLED ENABLER ENABLES ENACTED ENARMED ENARMES ENCAGED ENCAGES
ENCAKED ENCAKES ENCASED ENCAVED ENCAVES ENCODER ENCORED ENCORES ENDIVES ENDOWER
ENDURES ENJOYED ENJOYER ENLACED ENLACES ENLIVED ENLIVES ENRAGED ENRAGES ENROBED
ENROBES ENSURED ENTICED ENTICER ENTICES ENTIRES ENTRIES ENZYMES EPAULET EPOCHES
EQUALED EQUATED EQUINES ERMINED ERMINES ERUPTED ESCAPED ESCAPER ESCRIED EUCHRED
EUCHRES EVACUES EVALUED EVALUES EVANGEL EVICTED EVINCED EVINCES EXACTED EXACTER
EXALTED EXALTER EXCIDES EXCISED EXCITED EXCITER EXCITES EXCUSED EXCUSER EXHALED
EXHALES EXHUMED EXHUMES EXISTED EXISTER EXPIRED EXPIRES EXPOSED EXPOSER EXULTED
FALSIFY FANCIFY FARCIFY FORTIFY GAMINGS GATINGS HAUNCHY HEALTHS HEALTHY HEARTHS
HOWDAHS IMBROIL IMPERIL INERTIA INHABIT INHERIT INTERIM INVALID ISLAMIC ISMATIC
ISOPTIC ISTHMIA ISTHMIC KODIAKS KOPECKS LACTYLS LANCELY LANKILY LAPFULS LARGELY
LAURELS LEGIBLY LENTILS LETHALS LIGHTLY LINTELS LIONELS LITHELY LIVABLE LIVABLY
LOAMILY LOATHLY LOFTILY LOREALS LOSABLE LOUSILY LOVABLE LOVABLY LOVERLY LUCIDLY
LUCKILY LUMPILY LURIDLY LUSTILY MAGNUMS MAYTIME MEDIUMS MEGRIMS MISNAME MYELOMA
NAPKINS NASCENT NATIONS NEARING NEATING NECKING NERVING NESTING NEURONS NEWTONS
NORMAND NORMANS NOTHING NUBIANS NUMBING NURSING OMNIVOR ORATION OUTCROP OUTDROP
OUTFLOW OUTGLOW OUTGROW OUTSHOW OVATION OVERBOW OVERGOD OVERJOY OVERPOT OVERTOP
PERHAPS PLATYPI PREAMPS PRECOPY PROTYPE RACKERS RAFTERS RAGWORT RAIDERS RAILERS
RAINERS RAMPERS RANCORS RANGERS RANKERS RANTERS RAPIERS RAPTERS RAPTORS RAPTURE
RATHERS READORN REBOARD RECHURN RECTORS RECTORY REGUARD REHAIRS REPAIRS REPOURS
REQUIRY RESWARM RESWORN RETOURS REWHIRL RHYMERS RIBWORK RICHARD RIDGERS RIFLERS
RIFLERY RIFTERS RIGOURS RINGERS RINKERS RIOTERS RIVALRY ROAMERS ROCKERS ROCKERY
ROGUERY ROMPERS ROUTERS ROXBURY RUINERS SAGIEST SAIDEST SALTISH SANDISH SAWDUST
SAWFISH SCABISH SCENIST SCOTISH SECTISM SELFISH SERVIST SICKEST SLATISH SLAVISH
SLAVISM SLAVIST SLOWEST SLOWISH SMOKISH SNAKISH SNIDEST SNOBISM SNOWISH SOFTISH
SOPHISM SOPHIST SOULISH SOUREST SOURISH SPANISH SPAREST SPORTSY SPRIEST SPRYEST
STEWISH STYLISH STYLISM SUAVEST SUBCASE SUBCAST SUCROSE SUNFISH SUNRISE SUNROSE
SURMISE SWEDISH SYNAPSE TABLETS TALENTS TARGETS TARPOTS TEAPOTS TENSITY THIRSTY
THREATS THRIFTS THRIFTY THROATS THROATY THRUSTY THWARTS TICKETS TOILETS TOMCATS
TOWPATH TRIACTS TRIBUTE TRICOTS TRIVETS TRUANTS TRYOUTS TURBOTS TWELFTH TYRANTS
UMBROUS UNAWFUL UNCLOUD UNPIOUS UNPROUD UNVALUE URANIUM URANOUS URGEFUL URINOUS
WINDOWS WINDOWY

ABCDEBA CARDIAC DEAIRED DEASHED DEBASED DEBATED DEBITED DEBONED DEBUSED DEBUTED
DECAYED DECISED DECKLED DECOKED DECORED DECOYED DECRIED DEFACED DEFAMED DEFILED
DEFINED DEFUSED DEIGNED DELAYED DELIMED DELINED DELUGED DEMOTED DENOTED DEPOSED
DEPOTED DEPUTED DERATED DERIVED DESIRED DESIZED DETAXED DETUNED DEVILED DEVISED
DEVOTED DEVOWED DEWAXED DIPLOID DIPNOID EMPLUME ENPLANE ENTWINE ERASURE ESPOUSE
EVASIVE FANLEAF FIXATIF GAMEBAG GNAWING LACTEAL LATERAL LATRIAL LUNGFUL LUSTFUL
NETSMEN NEWSMEN NICOTIN RADULAR RAILCAR REACHER READIER REALTER REBATER REBUKER
RECITER RECOVER REDUCER REFINER REFUSER REFUTER REGALER REIGNER REINFER REINTER
RELATER RELAXER RELAYER RELINER RELIVER RELOWER REMAKER REMOTER REMOVER RENTIER
REPINER REPLIER REPOSER RESAWER RESCUER RESIDER RESINER RESIZER RESTIER RESUMER
RETAKER REVILER REVISER REVIZER REVOKER REWAGER REWATER SALINAS SALIVAS SALMIAS
SALVIAS SANDRAS SCENICS SEANCES SECURES SEDATES SEDUCES SEMBLES SEMITES SENATES
SERAPES SEWAGES SHEATHS SHEIKHS SOLANOS STARETS STILETS STRAITS STUARTS STYLETS
SURPLUS SWATOWS TEARLET TEMPLET THOUGHT TOPKNOT TRIPART TURNOUT

ABCDEBB ASHLESS DEVISEE DEVOTEE FLYBALL LEGATEE PERIGEE REFUGEE REVISEE SEDUCEE

ABCDEBC ABSORBS ANEMONE ANGLING BANDMAN BANKMAN BEDAZED BERTHER BESIDES BESPIES
BRAVURA CEDARED DERATER DERIVER DERNIER DESIRES DESIZES DESUMES ENSIGNS ENTRANT
FLEXILE GERMIER HANGMAN HANUMAN HERBIER HUMDRUM INSPANS ITERATE JERKIER KANTIAN
KINGPIN LANDMAN LENSMEN LOWBROW MEDALED MERITER MILFOIL NERVIER NESTLES NICOTIC
PEDALED PERCHER PERKIER PERUSER PESTLES PINGUIN PLANULA POTSHOT PRECURE PRETIRE
PREWIRE REDATED REDIVED REDUCED RELABEL RESALES RESCUES RESHOES RESIDES RESITES
RESIZES RESOLES RESPUES RESUMES SALIVAL SANDMAN SEDATED SEDUCED SERVIER TANKMAN
UNSKINS UNSPANS UNSPINS UNTAINT UPSKIPS UPSLIPS

ABCDEBD BARNMAN BEARDER COPYBOY DECRIER DOGTROT FOXTROT FRASERS HANGTAG INSTANT
INTERNE JOHNSON LEARNER LEASHES MEASLES NAUSEAS PEARLER PERSUES PROSARS PROSERS
PUNTOUT READIED SALTFAT SCIENCE TARSIAS TEARIER TEASLES UNAGING UNISONS VERSTES
VESTLET WEARIER WEIRDER WELSHES YEARNER

ABCDEBE ATHLETE BEARDED BEMUSES CENTRER CERISES COJUROR DEBASES DECISES DEFUSES
DEMISES DEMURER DEPOSES DESIRER DEVISES DIOPSIS FETUSES GRUYERE HABITAT KETOSES
KINESIS LEWISES LIMOSIS LIPOSIS MEIOSES MELOSES MITOSIS NEXUSES PERUSES REBASES
REBUSES RECASES RECODED REFUSES RELADED RELOSES REMISES REPOSES RESIDED REVISES
REWADED SECURER STOMATA UTMOSTS VENUSES WEIRDED

ABCDEBF AIRFOIL AIRSHIP ALERTLY ALONELY ALPHYLS ANCIENT ANDRONS ANELING ANEMONY
ANODYNE APOTYPE ARBITRE ARBITRY ARCHERS ARCHERY ARDOURS ARGUERS ARMOIRE ARMOURS
ARMOURY ASHIEST AUTOBUS BACKSAW BACKWAY BAKEPAN BALUGAS BANDEAU BASEMAN BASILAR
BASINAL BASURAL BATHMAN BATSMAN BEACHED BEACHES BEADIER BEADLET BEAGLED BEAGLER
BEAKIER BEAMIER BEAMLET BEANIER BECOMED BECOMES BECRIED BECRIES BEDGOER BEDIZEN
BEFAMED BEFAMES BEHAVED BEHOVED BELATED BELAYED BELCHED BELCHER BELCHES BELOVED
BELTMEN BEMUSED BEMUTED BENCHED BENCHER BENCHES BERATED BERATES BERIDES BERIMED
BERTHED BERTHES BESOMER BESPIED BETIDES BEWARED BEWARES BIFOLIA BIGAMIC BILOXIS
BIONTIC BISCUIT BLACKLY BLANDLY BLANKLY BLEAKLY BLINDLY BLOWFLY BLUNTLY BOERDOM
BOLEROS BOREDOM BOWKNOT BOWSHOT BRACERS BRAKERS BRAVERS BRAVERY BRAYERS BRAZERS
BRINERS BROKERS BROKERY BUILDUP BULIMUS BUREAUS BUREAUX BURNOUS BURNOUT BUSHFUL
BYPLAYS CADMEAN CADMIAN CAGEMAN CALDEAN CAMBIAL CAMERAS CANULAR CAPITAL CARDIAE
CARDIAL CARLOAD CAROLAN CARTMAN CARTWAY CAVEMAN CAYUGAN CAYUGAS CENTRED CENTRES
CERATED CERATES CERITES CERULES CLAVELS CLEANLY CLEARLY CLERKLY CLOSELY CONFLOW

```
CONTROL COPILOT CORAZON COREBOX CRANERS CRATERS CRAVERS CRAYERS CURIOUS CURVOUS
DAHLIAS DAKOTAS DARESAY DARTMAN DATCHAS DATIVAL DATURAS DAYSMAN DEARIES DEBASER
DEBATER DEBATES DEBONES DEBOWEL DEBRIEF DECAYER DECIBEL DECILES DECIMES DECISER
DECKIES DECKLES DECKMEN DECOKES DECORES DECRIES DEFACER DEFACES DEFAMER DEFAMES
DEFIBER DEFILER DEFILES DEFINER DEFINES DEFIXES DELATES DELAYER DELIMES DELINES
DELUGES DEMOTES DENOTES DEPOSER DEPUTES DERIVES DESKMEN DETAXES DETUNES DEVICES
DEVILER DEVISER DEVIZES DEVOTER DEVOTES DEWATER DEWAXES DIACTIN DIAMBIC DIAZOIC
DIGOXIN DIPLOIC DISHEIR DISJOIN DISPAIR DISTAIN DOMINOS DONATOR DOVECOT DRAPERS
DRAPERY DRAWERS DRIVERS DRONERS DROVERS DUBIOUS DUTIFUL ECSTACY EMBALMS ENCHANT
ENGLAND ENJOINS ENLIMNS ENODING ENRUINS ENSUANT ENSUING ENURING ENVYING ENWOUND
EPITAPH FACEMAN FACTUAL FACULAR FAIRWAY FARCIAL FAREWAY FARINAS FASCIAE FASCIAL
FATHEAD FEATHER FEIGNED FEIGNER FEINTED FEINTER FELINES FELTIER FEMALES FERULED
FERULES FETCHED FETCHER FETCHES FIBROID FIBROIN FIDUCIA FIRELIT FLAKILY FLASHLY
FLESHLY FLORALS FLUIDLY FLUKILY FLYABLE FLYBELT FOREBOW FORETOP FRAMERS FRAZERS
FULCRUM FUNGOUS FURIOUS GAINSAY GASTRAL GATEMAN GATEWAY GEARMEN GEARSET GENOMES
GENTLED GENTLER GENTLES GHURKHA GLAZILY GLOBULE GLYCOLS GONAPOD GRACERS GRADERS
GRATERS GRAVERS GRAVURE GRAZERS GRIPERS GROCERS GROCERY GROPERS GROWERS GUSTFUL
HACKMAN HACKSAW HAIRCAP HALFWAY HALIFAX HANDBAG HANDCAR HANDJAR HANDSAW HARDPAN
HARDWAY HAVERAL HEADIER HEADMEN HEADSET HEARKEN HEARSED HEARTED HEARTEN HEAVIED
HEAVIER HEAVIES HECKLED HECKLER HECKLES HEDGIER HEFTIER HEISTED HEISTER HELIXES
HERBMEN HERDMEN HEXADES HEXANES HEXINES HEXITES HEXODES HEXONES HISTRIO HORIZON
HUMERUS HURTFUL IMBALMS IMPALMS INBOUND INBURNT INCHANT INFERNO INTERNS INTURNS
INWOUND IRONERS JACKDAW JACKMAN JACKSAW JERKIES JEWRIES KELPIES KELTIES KESTREL
KETCHED KETCHES KETONES KEWPIES KINESIC KINETIC KINSHIP KNAVING KNOWING LACEMAN
LACTEAN LAIRMAN LAMBDAS LAMINAE LAMINAR LAMINAS LANDWAY LANEWAY LAOTIAN LATVIAN
LAUDEAN LAUDIAN LEACHED LEACHER LEACHES LEADIER LEADMEN LEAFIER LEAGUED LEAGUER
LEAGUES LEAKIER LEARNED LEASHED LEATHER LEAVIER LEDGIER LEFTIES LEGATED LEGATES
LEGUMEN LEGUMES LEISTER LEMONED LEMURES LEVITES LIBERIA LITCHIS LITHOID LOCATOR
LOCKBOX LOCUTOR LONGBOW LUTEOUS MACERAL MAGICAL MAHICAN MAILBAG MANILAS MANTEAU
MANTRAP MANTRAS MANTUAS MAORIAN MARINAS MARITAL MARSHAL MARTIAL MARTIAN MARXIAN
MAYORAL MEAGRED MEALIER MEALIES MEANDER MEANIES MEASLED MEATIER MENACED MENACER
MENACES MENAGES MERCIED MERCIES MERITED MESHIER MESTIER METALED METALER MIDSHIP
MIDVEIN MISCOIN MISEDIT MISJOIN MISLAID MISPAID MONGHOL MONITOR MOUFLON MUGSFUL
MUSEFUL MUTINUS NARWHAL NATURAL NEBULES NECKLET NEGATED NEGATER NEGATES NEGROES
NEIGHED NEIGHER NEITHER NEPOTES NESTLED NESTLER NEWFIES NEWSIER NICOSIA NIGERIA
NIGHTIE NUCLEUS OAKLEAF OARSMAN OATMEAL OEUVRES OILSKIN OMNIUMS ONSTAND ORALERS
ORCHARD ORGANRY OUTFLUE OUTFLUX OUTHAUL OUTSPUE OUTSWUM PACKMAN PACKWAX PACKWAY
PAGINAE PAGINAL PAGODAS PAKEHAS PALEMAN PARKWAY PARTIAL PARTWAY PATHWAY PATINAS
PATRIAL PAYLOAD PAYOLAS PEACHED PEACHEN PEACHER PEACHES PEAKIER PEARLED PEATIER
PEATMEN PECKIER PEDALER PENILES PEONIES PERCHED PERCHES PERUSED PESTLED PETALED
PEYOTES PIGSKIN PIGTAIL PILGRIM PINRAIL PINTAIL PIRAMID PIRATIC PLAINLY PLIABLE
PLIABLY PLUMBLY PLURALS PLUSHLY POETDOM POLIGON POLYCOT POLYGON POLYZOA POMELOS
POMEROY PONCHOS PORTHOS PORTION POSITON POSITOR POSTBOX POSTBOY PRATERS PRAYERS
PREBORN PREBURN PREDARK PREFORM PRETORY PREWARN PRICERS PRIMARS PRIMARY PRIMERS
PRIZERS PRIZERY PROBERS PROCURE PROFERS PROFERT PROVERB PROVERS PROWERS PRUDERY
PRUNERS QUANTUM QUAYFUL QUIPFUL RACEWAY RACKWAY RADICAL RADULAE RAFTMAN RAILFAN
RAILMAN RAILWAY RAMHEAD REABLED REABLES REACHED REACHES REACTED READIES REASKED
REBAKED REBAKES REBALED REBALES REBASED REBATED REBATES REBITES REBOXED REBOXES
REBUKED REBUKES REBUSED REBUTES RECAGED RECAGES RECASED RECIPED RECIPES RECITED
RECITES RECODES RECOKED RECOKES REDATES REDIVES REDUCES REFACED REFACES REFILED
REFILES REFINED REFINES REFIXED REFIXES REFLIES REFUGED REFUGES REFUSED REFUTED
```

```
REFUTES  REGALED  REGALES  REGIMEN  REGIMES  REGIVES  REGLUED  REGLUES  REHALED  REHALES
REHIDES  REIGNED  REIMPEL  REINKED  RELADEN  RELADES  RELATED  RELATES  RELAXED  RELAXES
RELAYED  RELIMED  RELIMES  RELINED  RELINES  RELIVED  RELIVES  RELOVED  RELOVES  REMAKES
REMATES  REMISED  REMIXED  REMIXES  REMODEL  REMOTES  REMOVED  REMOVES  RENAMED  RENAMES
REOILED  REOWNED  REPACED  REPACES  REPAGED  REPAGES  REPANEL  REPAVED  REPAVES  REPAYED
REPILED  REPILES  REPLIED  REPLIES  REPOSED  REPUTED  REPUTES  REQUIEM  RESAWED  RESCUED
RESINED  RESIZED  RESOLED  RESOWED  RESPUED  RESUMED  RETAKEN  RETAKES  RETAMED  RETAMES
RETAPED  RETAPES  RETAXED  RETAXES  RETCHED  RETCHES  RETILED  RETILES  RETIMED  RETIMES
RETUBED  RETUBES  RETUNED  RETUNES  RETYPED  RETYPES  REVILED  REVILES  REVISED  REVOKED
REVOKES  REVOTED  REVOTES  REWADES  REWAKED  REWAKEN  REWAKES  REWAVED  REWAVES  REWAXED
REWAXES  REWIDEN  REWOKEN  REWOVEN  REYOKED  REZONED  REZONES  ROADEOS  ROMANOS  RUINOUS
RUSTFUL  SALTMAN  SALTPAN  SAMOVAR  SAMURAI  SANDBAG  SANDBAR  SCIENCY  SCRATCH  SCRUNCH
SEAGOER  SEAMIER  SEAMLET  SECURED  SEDATER  SEDGIER  SEDUCER  SELTZER  SEMBLED  SEMINED
SEPALED  SERVIET  SETOVER  SEWAGED  SHEATHY  SIBERIA  SILURIC  SINAPIC  SINOVIA  SIPHOID
SIRENIC  SIRLOIN  SKYLIKE  SLACKLY  SLANTLY  SLICKLY  SLOPELY  SNAKING  SNARING  SNORING
SNOWING  SOAPBOX  SOMEHOW  SOUPCON  STEALTH  STOMATE  STRIATE  STYLATE  STYLITE  SUPLHUR
TABLEAU  TABULAE  TABULAR  TACOMAN  TAPEMAN  TAPSMAN  TAUREAN  TAURIAN  TAXICAB  TAXIMAN
TAXIWAY  TEACHER  TEACHES  TEASIER  TEMPLED  TEMPLES  TENDREL  TENURES  THRUSHY  TINFOIL
TIVOLIS  TOLEDOS  TOREDOS  TORSION  TOYSHOP  TRACERS  TRACERY  TRADERS  TREMORS  TRICORN
TRIFORM  TRIMERS  TUBEFUL  TUNEFUL  UNALONE  UNAMEND  UNBEING  UNBLIND  UNBORNE  UNBRAND
UNCLANG  UNCLING  UNCOINS  UNDAMNS  UNDOING  UNDOWNY  UNDYING  UNEYING  UNFAINT  UNFIEND
UNFLANK  UNFRANK  UNGOWNS  UNGRAND  UNHORNY  UNJOINS  UNJOINT  UNLYING  UNMEANT  UNOPENS
UNPAINT  UNPAWNS  UNPLANK  UNPLANS  UNPLANT  UNPRINT  UNRAINY  UNREINS  UNSAINT  UNSCENT
UNSLING  UNSPENT  UNSTING  UNSTONE  UNSTONY  UNSWING  UNTHANK  UNTHINK  UNTOWNS  UNTREND
UNTWINE  UNTYING  UNWARNS  UPLEAPS  UPSLOPE  UPSWEPT  URETHRA  URINARY  VAGINAE  VAGINAL
VARICAL  VATICAL  VATICAN  VEIGLED  VENICES  VENOMED  VENOMER  VERITES  VINYLIC  VISCOID
VITALIC  VITAMIN  WARDIAN  WARDMAN  WAREMAN  WARHEAD  WASHDAY  WASHMAN  WASHRAG  WEARIED
WEARIES  WEATHER  WEBSTER  WEDGIER  WEDGIES  WEIGHED  WEIGHER  WELCHED  WELCHER  WELCHES
WELSHED  WELSHER  WEMBLEY  WENCHED  WENCHER  WENCHES  WIGTAIL  WOLFDOM  WORKBOX  WRITERS
YAKIMAS  YARDMAN  YEARNED  YEASTED  ZINCOID
```

```
ABCDECA  DREAMED  ENGORGE  ESTUATE  GINSENG  MOSAISM  NAILBIN  SAGINGS  SCABIAS  SETOUTS
SHEAVES  SHELVES  SKYWAYS  SLEAVES  SLEDGES  SORCERS  SORTERS  SPECIES  SPENCES  SPURIUS
STADIAS  STANZAS  SUNTANS  SURFERS  SWERVES  TANGENT  TENDANT
```

```
ABCDECB  ADIPOID  ASTINTS  BEDSIDE  BELADLE  BENZINE  BREAKER  CANTINA  CLAUSAL  CLAVIAL
CREAKER  CREAMER  CREASER  DEGORGE  DELIBLE  DESPISE  DESPOSE  DEVOLVE  DRAWBAR  DREAMER
FRESHER  GENUINE  GLACIAL  GLYOXYL  GREASER  GREATER  GRENIER  HENBANE  PENTANE  PERDURE
PERJURE  PLASMAL  PREMIER  PROCTOR  REGAUGE  RETASTE  REVOLVE  SCIATIC  STEMLET  STICKIT
TRAMCAR  TREADER  UNAVIAN  UNEATEN  VERDURE  WEIRDIE  WREAKER  WRECKER  WRESTER
```

```
ABCDECC  ABSCESS  CHEATEE  DISCUSS  GASLESS  HOLDALL  HOSTESS  OVERSEE  PLEDGEE
```

```
ABCDECD  ALUMIUM  AVERTER  BANGING  BUNGING  BURSARS  CONTENT  CORSERS  CURSERS  CURSORS
DISEASE  FASTEST  FIERCER  FLEDGED  FLESHES  FRESHES  HANGING  HORSERS  INEDGED  JUSTEST
LICENCE  LONGING  LUNGING  MISEASE  NURSERS  ORESTES  OUTSETS  OUTSITS  OVENMEN  PARSERS
PIERCER  PLASMAS  PLEDGED  POESIES  PURSERS  RANGING  SHUTOUT  SLEDGED  SOULFUL  STERNER
SWERVER  TENSONS  UGANDAN  UNEDGED  URANIAN  VASTEST  VENGING  VERSORS  WORSERS
```

```
ABCDECE  AMENDED  ARTISTS  AUTISTS  AVERSES  BLEARER  BLENDED  BREADED  CLEARER  CONVENE
CRAWDAD  CREASES  CURIARA  CYTOSTS  FIELDED  FUEHRER  GRANDAD  GREASES  KNEADED  LATESTS
```

LUTISTS MEIOSIS MONTANA MUTISTS NOMISMS NOTISTS PLEADED PLEASES SHEARER SMEARER
SPEARER SPENDED STEADED SWEARER TREADED TRENDED UNEASES UPENDED VOTISTS WIELDED
YIELDED

ABCDECF ABIOTIC AIRPORT ALERTED ALUMNUS AMENDER AMINOID AMNIONS ARCTICS AREOLES
ARTISTE ATELIER AVENGED AVENGER AVENGES AVENUED AVERSED AVERTED AVIONIC AZUROUS
BALKILY BALMILY BANDING BANKING BANTING BARKERS BARONRY BARTERS BARTERY BATISTE
BENDING BIAURAL BIOPHOR BIRDERS BIVALVE BLEAKED BLEARED BLEATED BLEATER BLENDER
BLETHER BOATMAN BONDING BORDERS BRAHMAN BRAHMAS BRITAIN BROCHOS BRONCOS BRUSQUE
BULGILY BULKILY BUNIONS BUNKING BUNTING BURGERS BURIERS BURNERS BURSARY BUSIEST
BUSYISH CANTING CANTINO CANYONS CARBURE CARPORT CATGUTS CHAPEAU CHAPMAN CHATEAU
CHEAPED CHEAPEN CHEAPER CHEATED CHEATER CHELSEA CHEQUER CHEQUES CHEQUEY CHESTED
CHESTER CHEVRES CHEWIER CHINOIS CHITLIN CHORION CIERGES CINZANO CITRATE CLAYMAN
CLAYPAN CLEANED CLEANER CLEARED CLEATED CLEATER CLEAVED CLEAVER CLEAVES CLEFTED
CLERKED COALBAG COASTAL COAXIAL COBWEBS CONFINE CONKING CONSENT CONTEND CONVENT
CORDERS CORKERS CORNERS COSIEST CRABMAN CRANIAL CRAWDAB CREAKED CREAMED CREASED
CREATED CREATES CREOLES CRESTED CREWMEN CROFTON CROUTON CROYDON CURBERS CURLERS
CURSORY CURVERS CUTLETS CZARIAN DANCING DARNERS DARTERS DEISTIC DENTING DENYING
DIAGRAM DIESTER DIETHER DISBASE DISEASY DISGUST DISMASK DISMAST DISNEST DISPOST
DISREST DOGLEGS DORMERS DOTANTS DOYLEYS DRACMAS DRAPEAU DRAWMAN DRAYMAN DUNCING
DUNKING DURBARS DUSKISH ECSTASY EDGINGS ELUVIUM EMOTION EQUINUS EROSION EXTORTS
FAERIES FALSELY FARCERS FARMERS FARMERY FASCISM FASCIST FASTISH FATUITY FELONLY
FENCING FENDING FENIANS FERVORS FIELDER FINLAND FIREARM FITOUTS FLAGMAN FLATCAR
FLATMAN FLATWAY FLAXMAN FLECKED FLECKEN FLECKER FLENSED FLENSER FLESHED FLESHEN
FLESHER FLEXIER FLOTSON FLYBOYS FONDANT FONTINA FONTING FORBARE FORCERS FOREARM
FORGERS FORGERY FORKERS FORMERS FORWARD FORWARN FREAKED FRESHED FRESHEN FRESHET
FUNDING FUNKING FURLERS GARNERS GARNERY GARTERS GEARMAN GELIDLY GIRDERS GLEAMED
GLEANED GLEANER GLUTEUS GRADUAL GREASED GREATED GREATEN GREAVED GREAVES GUESTED
GUILDIC GUNHAND HAIRPIN HANDING HARBORS HARBORY HARMERS HARPERS HAUTEUR HEADCAP
HEADMAN HEADSAW HEADWAY HEARSAY HECTICS HENCING HENDING HERBARY HERONRY HEYDAYS
HONKING HORNERS HUNTING HURLERS HURTERS HUTLETS HYAENAS HYDRIDE HYDRIDS IDAHOAN
INEDGES INGORGE INTEXTS INTORTS INTRATE INVOLVE ISOTRON JENKINS JUNKING KANTING
KENTING KEYWAYS KITCATS KNEADER LANCING LANDING LARDERS LARKERS LATENTS LEADMAN
LEADWAY LEAKMAN LEIPZIG LENDING LENSING LINDENS LINGENS LUCENCY LURKERS LUSHEST
LYNCINE MALTOLS MANHUNT MANKIND MARKERS MARKERY MARTYRS MENDING MINOANS MINYANS
MISCAST MITRATE MORTARS MORTARY MOSAIST MUNDANE MUNIONS MUNTING MURDERS MUSCOSE
MUSKISH MUTANTS NITRATE NORWARD NOSIEST NURSERY NUTLETS OAKLIKE OBEISED OCEANED
OCTANTS OPIATIC OPTANTS OSTIATE OUTACTS OUTDATE OUTEATS OUTFITS OUTGATE OUTHITS
OUTJETS OUTLETS OUTPATH OUTPITY OUTWITH OUTWITS OVARIAL OVARIAN OVERFED OVERJET
OVERNET OVERSEA OVERSET OVERSEW OVERWEB OVERWET OVISTIC PAGINGS PANTING PARKERS
PARLORS PARTERS PATENTS PEACOAT PEATMAN PENDANT PENDING PERFORM PERJURY PERTURB
PHARIAN PHASEAL PIERCED PIERCES PINKENS PINYONS PIRATRY PLANTAR PLATEAU PLAYMAN
PLEADER PLEASED PLEASER PLEATED PLEATER PLEDGER PLEDGES PLOWBOY PLUMOUS POESIED
POLARLY PONDING PONTINE PONTINS PONYING PORKERS PORKERY PORTERS POTENTS POUTFUL
PREDIET PREIDEA PREKNEW PREMIES PRETZEL PREVIEW PREVUES PUDENDA PUNGENT PUNTING
PURGERS PURGERY PURLERS QUADRAL QUADRAN QUANTAL QUATRAL QUAYMAN QUEASED QUERIED
QUERIES QUESTED QUESTER QUICKIE RANKING RANTING RASHEST RASPISH RATBITE RAUCOUS
RECATCH RECHUCK RECOACH REDBUDS REKICKS RENDING RENOWNS RENTING REPUMPS RESLASH
RHEUMED RHIZOID RHOMBOS ROADMAN ROADWAY ROSIEST ROTGUTS ROUNDUP RUANDAS RULABLE
RULABLY SALTILY SANDING SATIETY SCANDAL SCENTED SCENTER SCEPTER SENDING SERIARY
SHEAFED SHEARED SHEAVED SHELFED SHELTER SHELVED SHELVER SHERBET SHINDIG SHOPBOY

SHOWDOM SITUATE SKEINED SKEINER SKELTER SLABMAN SLAGMAN SLEAVED SLEDGER SLENDER
SMEARED SMELTED SMELTER SMIDGIN SNAPBAG SNEAKED SNEAKER SOLIDLY SOLUBLE SOLUBLY
SORCERY SPACIAL SPARTAN SPATIAL SPEAKER SPEARED SPECKED SPECKER SPECTER SPENCER
SPENDER SPEWIER STADIAL STEAKED STEALER STEAMED STEAMER SULKILY SURGERY SVELTER
SWAGMAN SWEATED SWEATER SWELTER SWERVED SYNCING TAILPIN TANKING TENDING TENDONS
TENPINS TENSING THEOREM THERMEL THIAMID THIAMIN THIAZIN THIOLIC THOMSON TIERCED
TIERCEL TOLABLE TOLUYLS TONSING TOPCAPS TRAMWAY TRAUMAS TREBLED TREBLES TRIACID
TRIAMID TRIAMIN TRIFOIL TRISAIL TRIZOIC TURNERS TUSKISH TWEAKED TWEAKER TWELVER
TWELVES TWIFOIL UNBARBS UNCHECK UNCLICK UNCOACH UNEAGER UNEARED UNEASED UNEDGES
UNGORGE UNISOIL UNLAWLY UNLOWLY UNPROPS UNTASTE UNTASTY UNTILTS UNTRITE UNTROTH
UPREARS UPROARS UPTILTS VALIDLY VARIERS VENDING VENTING VINCENT VISCOSE VOLABLE
VOLABLY VOLUBLE VOLUBLY WAMPUMS WANDING WANTING WANTONS WARBURG WARDERS WARLORD
WARMERS WARNERS WARPERS WASPISH WEIGHIN WENDING WHEALED WHEATEN WHELMED WHELPED
WHELVED WHENCES WIELDER WORDERS WORKERS WORMERS WREAKED WREAKEN WRECHED WRECKED
WRESTED WYNDING YAHWEHS YANKING YARDERS YARNERS YIELDER YORKERS

ABCDEDA ALPINIA ANCILIA DOWELED DOWERED DOZENED ENSTATE GARNING GOWNING NEVADAN
NOTEMEN RAVELER RAVENER RECOLOR REHONOR RIPENER RIVETER SCHEMES SCORERS SHARERS
SHORERS SINUOUS SIRENES SLIPUPS SNARERS SNORERS SOARERS SONATAS SOURERS SPARERS
SPHERES STARERS STORERS TYPESET

ABCDEDB ACLINIC ACRIDIC ADHERED ALCOHOL BRIEFER CANDIDA CRUELER DENTATE EMBOSOM
FAMILIA FRIEZER GESTATE GRIEVER GRUELER LEONINE NAPHTHA PARTITA PECTATE RESTATE
SEPTATE UNPAGAN

ABCDEDC ADENINE CRYBABY FLYAWAY FOREVER INDEXED KITAMAT LADENED LINEMEN MODELED
PACIFIC PHENINE PREGAGE SCREWER STREWER TINEMEN TIREDER UNCIVIC UNDEWED UNLEVEL
UNSEXES VINEMEN WIDENED YODELED

ABCDEDD ATHENEE FORESEE JUDICII

ABCDEDE ADHERER ALTERER ARGININ AUGERER CATERER COHERER COVERER HOVERER HYPERER
IMPEDED INCEDED LOWERER MITERER RAMESES SOBERER TAPERER UKALELE UNCEDED UNDERER
USHERER WAFERER WAGERER WATERER WAVERER

ABCDEDF ADHERES ADORERS ADULTLY AEROSOL AGILELY ALBINIC ALIENED ALIENER ALTERED
AMBERED AMPERES ANGELED ANGERED APIECES ARBUTUS ARDUOUS ASPIRIN ATONING AUGERED
BACULUS BAGPIPE BASEMEN BASILIC BEANING BICOLOR BIGEYES BILCOCK BISEXED BISTATE
BOGEYED BOLIVIA BOWELED BOWERED BRIEFED BUGEYES BULIMIA BULIMIC BURLILY BURNING
CAGEMEN CAMELED CAPELET CAPERED CATERED CATEYES CAVEMEN CEDUOUS CHILDLY CHROMOS
CHRONOS CINEREA CLOSEST CLOSISH COGENER COHERED COHERES COHIBIT COKEMEN COLITIS
CONSIST COPEMEN CORNING COSTATE COVERED COVETED COVETER COVEYED COWERED COZENED
COZENER CRANING CREOSOL CUBELET CUPOLOS CURETES CURLILY CUTAWAY CYANINE DARNING
DAWNING DECOLOR DEFICIT DELIMIT DICTATE DISGAGE DOMICIL DOMINIE DOVEKEY DOVELET
DOWELER DOWNING DOZENER DRONING EARBOBS EARLILY EARNING EIGHTHS EMPIRIC ETHYNYL
EXHIBIT FACEMEN FACETED FAIRERS FALSEST FATUOUS FAWNING FELICIA FIBERED FIREMEN
FIRESET FLARERS FLEABAG FLUEMEN FLUIDIC FORELEG FOREMEN FORESET FRIEZED FRIEZES
GAMETES GASPIPE GATEMEN GAVELED GAVELER GETAWAY GLUEMEN GONIDIC GRIEVED GRIEVES
GRUELED GUANINE HASIDIC HASIDIM HAYCOCK HAZELED HELIOID HELIXIN HEMOPOD HEMOZOA
HEXANAL HOMINID HONEYED HORNING HOSEMEN HOVELED HOVELER HOVERED HOWEVER HUMIFIC
HYMNING HYPERED IDLEMEN IDLESET IGUANAS IMHETEP IMPALAS IMPEDER IMPEDES INCEDES

INCUBUS INDEXER INDEXES INSTATE INTEGER IPECACS ISLEMEN ISLETED ITHACAN JICAMAS
JOINANT JUDAEAN JUDICIO KERNING KIMONOS LACEMEN LADEMEN LAGERED LAPCOCK LATEXED
LATEXES LATINIC LAYERED LEANING LEVITIC LIBRARY LIFEMEN LIGNONE LIKENED LIQUEUR
LIVENED LIVERED LOANING LOVERED LOWERED LUCAYAN MEALILY MEANING MITERED MITRERS
MOANING MODELER MODULUS MONACAL MONEYED MONEYER MONILIA MORNING MOSEYED MOTIFIC
MOTIVIC MUNIFIC NAVELED NODULUS NOSEYED NOVELET NOWADAY OCHERED OCTAVAL OCTENES
OLEANAS OMENING OPENING OUTPIPE OVENING OVERARM OVERDRY PABULUM PACIFID PAIRERS
PANELED PANELER PARTITE PAWNING PEACOCK PERIWIG PERSIST PHENINS PHIALAE PHLEMES
PHOEBES PHONING PHRASAL PICENES PIGNONS PIRANAS PIRENES PLANING POKERED POLEMEN
POLITIC POURERS POWERED PRONING PROSISH PROSIST PRUNING PUGNANT PYJAMAS PYRENES
PYRITIC QUIETED QUIETEN QUIETER QUINONE RABITIC RAVELED REGULUS RELIGIO RELIMIT
REMNANT RESILIA RESINIC REVISIT RIPENED RIVETED ROPEMEN RUNAWAY SABERED SAFENED
SAFENER SALICIN SALOMON SATIRIC SCENING SCHEMED SCHEMER SCREWED SEMIFIT SEMITIC
SHOEMEN SHREWED SIDEMEN SINEWED SIRENED SOBERED SOLICIT SPHERED SPIEGEL SPIELED
SPIELER STALELY STONING STREWED SURLILY SURVIVE TAMILIC TAPEMEN TAPERED TENUOUS
THIEVED THIEVER THIEVES TIGERED TIREMEN TOKENED TOURERS TOWELED TOWERED TRIAXAL
TUNISIA TURNING ULCERED UMBILIC UNBESET UNCIVIL UNHEWED UNHEXED UNIAXAL UNJEWEL
UNKEYED UNMETED UNMEWED UNREBEL UNRIGID UNSEWED UNSEXED UNSTATE UNVEXED UPCANAL
UPSTATE URINANT USHERED VACUOUS VALETED VISEMEN VISERED VOWELED WAFERED WAGERED
WAKENED WAKENER WAPITIS WARNING WATERED WAVERED WEANING WHELPLY WHOEVER WHOLELY
WHORERS WHYEVER WIDENER WIREMEN WISEMEN WISENED WIZENED WORLDLY YARNING YAWNING
YODELER YUCATAN

ABCDEEA ANCILLA ANDORRA DISPEED DISWOOD MISDEEM OTHELLO REFLOOR SARCEES SCROLLS
SCRUFFS SETOFFS SHAVEES SHRILLS SIGNEES SKIDOOS SOIREES SQUALLS STROLLS TAPROOT

ABCDEEB CAMILLA GYRALLY LORETTO MADONNA MANILLA MAXILLA PELISSE RAVENNA SEVILLE
SKYHOOK SKYLOOK TOBACCO TYRANNY UNGREEN UPCREEP UPSWEEP VANESSA VANILLA

ABCDEEC CANTEEN DASHEES DUSTEES LISTEES MISADDS MUDWEED RANGOON REDWOOD ROYALLY
RUSHEES UNSELLS

ABCDEED AMUSEES BACILLI CAYENNE CURETTE DINETTE DOYENNE DURESSE FINESSE GAZELLE
GAZETTE HOSANNA LAYETTE MISDEED MOSELLE OUTPEEP OUTSEES PALETTE PARSEES RISOTTO
ROSELLE ROSETTE SIROCCO

ABCDEEF ANGELLY ANISEED APOGEES ARGONNE ARGYLLS AVOWEES AWFULLY BAILEES BARKEEP
BEDROOM BEGORRA BIGOTTY BINGEES BIZARRE BRAILLE BUNGEES BURGEES CARTOON CHEROOT
CHINOOK COATEES CONGEED CONGEES CORINNA CORINNE COULEES CRUELLY CULOTTE CUTOFFS
DAYROOM DEBLOOM DEBURRS DEHULLS DILEMMA DISALLY DISROOF DISROOT DRAGEES DRAGOON
DUCALLY EMBASSY ENROLLS EQUALLY EXTOLLS FELUCCA FESTOON FINALLY FOCALLY FRAILLY
FUSILLY GAROTTE GIRAFFE GLACEED GOATEED GOATEES GORILLA GRUELLY HAPENNY HARPOON
HAYSEED HAZELLY HOAXEES IDEALLY IMPASSE INBREED INFALLS INROLLS IVYWEED IVYWOOD
JAYCEES JAYVEES JILTEES KILDEER LAMPOON LAYOFFS LEGROOM LETOFFS LICHEES LOANEES
LYCHEES MANHOOD MARKEES MEDULLA MELISSA MIDWEEK MISALLY MISCOOK MISKEEP MISTOOK
MODALLY MOIREED MOLASSY MORALLY MORASSY MULATTO MURALLY NOVELLA NOVELLY NUTSEED
OATSEED OILSEED OUTHEEL PADFOOT PARCOOK PARTOOK PAWNEES PAYBOOK PAYOFFS PENALLY
PICKEES PIGWEED PINHOOK PIONEER PLATOON PLYWOOD PONGEES PREALLY PRECOOK PRECOOL
PREDOOM PREFOOL PROCEED PUNTEES PURGEES QUOTEES RAGWEED RAVELLY REBILLS REBLOOM
REBUFFS RECALLS REFALLS REFILLS REFLOOD REGALLY REKILLS REMILLS REPOLLS REPUFFS
RESHOOK RESHOOT RETILLS REWALLS RICOTTA ROSELLA ROSETTA ROSETTY RUBELLA RUNOFFS

```
SAUTEED SCRAGGY SCRAPPY SCROLLY SCRUBBY SCRUFFY SEAFOOD SHREDDY SHRILLY SHRUBBY
SIXTEEN SONALLY SPRIGGY SQUALLY SUBROOT SUBTEEN SUNROOM TARIFFS TEAROOM THRILLS
THRILLY TIDALLY TONALLY TOUPEED TOUPEES TYPHOON UMPTEEN UNBELLS UNBLOOM UNBOGGY
UNFILLS UNFLOOR UNFOGGY UNFREED UNFREES UNHAPPY UNJOLLY UNMERRY UNROLLS UNSHEET
UNSHOOK UNSLEEK UNSOGGY UNSTEEP UNSWEET UNTREED UNWALLS UNWITTY UPCREEK UPROLLS
UPWELLS VENALLY VITALLY VOCALLY VOIDEES VOWELLY WEBFOOT WRITEES YANKEES ZONALLY
```

```
ABCDEFA ADENOMA ADERMIA AEROBIA ALBERTA ALEGBRA ALUMINA AMERICA AMNESIA AMNIOTA
AMORPHA AMPHORA ANGIOMA ANTHEMA APHORIA ARIZONA ATRESIA ATROPIA AURELIA AUREOLA
AUSTRIA CALORIC CAMBRIC CATONIC CAUSTIC CENTRIC CERAMIC CHAOTIC CHASMIC CHLORIC
CHOLEIC CHROMIC CHRONIC CLASTIC CRYPTIC CYSTEIC CYTASIC DANGLED DARTOID DAUNTED
DAVITED DEFRAUD DELTOID DEMIGOD DERMOID DESPOND DIAMOND DICHORD DIEHARD DILATED
DILUTED DIMPLED DISCARD DISCORD DISTEND DITCHED DOGHEAD DOGSLED DONATED DOUBLED
DOUBTED DOUCHED DOUGHED DOWRIED DRAFTED DRAINED DRAWLED DRIFTED DROWNED DROWSED
DRYLAND DUMPLED DUNKARD DUTCHED DWARFED EARHOLE EARLIKE EARLOBE EBONITE EBONIZE
ECLIPSE ECOTYPE EDUCATE EDUCIVE EGALITE ELATIVE ELOCUTE ELUSIVE EMBLAZE EMBRACE
EMBURSE EMIRATE EMOTIVE EMPLANE EMULATE ENCLAVE ENCLOSE ENDABLE ENDORSE ENDWISE
ENFLAME ENFORCE ENGRAVE ENLARGE ENLODGE ENQUIRE ENSLAVE ENTHUSE EPICURE EPIDOTE
EPILATE EPISODE EPISTLE EPITOME EPOXIDE EQUABLE ERATIVE EROSIVE EROTIZE ERUDITE
ESCRIBE ESQUIRE ETHNIZE EVOCATE EVOLUTE EXAMINE EXAMPLE EXCLUDE EXPANSE EXPARTE
EXPIATE EXPLODE EXPLORE EXPULSE EXPUNGE EXPURGE EXTRUDE EXUDATE GARBING GASHING
GASPING GAUZING GAWKING GEARING GELDING GERMING GLARING GLAZING GLOBING GLOVING
GLOWING GLUEING GOADING GOALING GOLDBUG GOSLING GRACING GRADING GRATING GRAVING
GRAYING GRAZING GREYING GROPING GROWING GULFING GULPING GUSHING HAWKISH HENFISH
HOARISH HOGWASH INTARSI ISRAELI KEYLOCK KINFOLK LEXICAL LIBERAL LINGUAL LITERAL
LOBTAIL LOCHIAL LOGICAL LUGSAIL LYRICAL MARXISM MIDTERM MISFORM MISTERM MODICUM
MUDWORM MYOGRAM MYTHISM NEBULON NEPHRON NETSMAN NEUTRON NEWBORN NEWSMAN NOCTURN
NOTEMAN ONTARIO OREGANO ORVIETO PIESHOP PINESAP PRESHIP PREWHIP RAMBLER RANCHER
RANCOUR RANGIER RANGLER RAPIDER RAPINER RASPIER REACTOR REALTOR REGULAR REINCUR
RELATOR REVIGOR REVISOR RIGHTER ROASTER ROCKIER ROISTER ROUGHER ROUNDER ROUSTER
ROUTIER ROWDIER RUMBLER RUMPIER RUNOVER RUNTIER RUSHIER RUSTIER RUSTLER SABINES
SACHEMS SACHETS SACKERS SAILERS SAILORS SALINES SALMONS SALTERS SALUTES SALVERS
SALVOES SAMPLES SANCTUS SANDERS SAPIENS SARONGS SATIRES SATORIS SATURNS SAUCERS
SAVINGS SAVIORS SAVOURS SAWINGS SAWYERS SAYINGS SCABIES SCALERS SCAPELS SCARVES
SCATHES SCAULDS SCHEIKS SCHIZOS SCHOLAS SCLERAS SCOTIAS SCRAPES SCRAWLS SCREAMS
SCRIBES SCRIMPS SCRIPTS SCULPTS SCYTHES SEADOGS SEBAITS SECANTS SECONDS SECTORS
SEIZORS SENIORS SENORAS SEPTICS SEPTUMS SEQUINS SERAPHS SERIALS SERIOUS SERMONS
SEWINGS SEXPOTS SEXTANS SEXTONS SHADERS SHADOWS SHAKERS SHALOMS SHAPERS SHAVERS
SHERPAS SHIELDS SHINERS SHINTOS SHOGUNS SHOVELS SHOVERS SHOWERS SHRIEKS SHRIMPS
SHRINES SHRINKS SHROUDS SHROVES SHYINGS SICKENS SICKERS SICKLES SIDLERS SIFTERS
SIGHERS SIGNALS SIGNERS SIGNETS SILENTS SILKENS SILKERS SILVERS SIMPERS SIMPLES
SINGERS SINGLES SINKERS SIPHONS SKAGITS SKATERS SKYCAPS SLAKENS SLAKERS SLATERS
SLAVERS SLAVICS SLAYERS SLEIGHS SLEUTHS SLICERS SLIDERS SLIGHTS SLIMERS SLIVERS
SLOGANS SLOPERS SLOUGHS SLOVACS SLOVAKS SLOVENS SLUDGES SLUICES SMIDGES SMILERS
SMITERS SMOKERS SMUDGES SMYRNAS SNAKERS SNIPERS SNIVELS SNOWIES SOAKERS SOAPERS
SOCIALS SOCKERS SOCKETS SODIUMS SOFTENS SOFTIES SOLACES SOLDERS SOLEMNS SOLIDUS
SOLVERS SOMBERS SOPHIAS SOPHIES SORBETS SORTIES SOULERS SOUPERS SOURCES SOVIETS
SOWINGS SPACERS SPADERS SPAULDS SPICERS SPIDERS SPIGOTS SPIKERS SPINALS SPINETS
SPINOUS SPIRALS SPLICES SPLINTS SPONGES SPRAINS SPRAWLS SPREADS SPRINGS SPRINTS
SPRITES SPROUTS SPRUCES SQUARES SQUAWKS SQUEAKS SQUEALS SQUEAMS SQUINTS SQUIRES
SQUIRLS SQUIRMS SQUIRTS STABLES STAGERS STAKERS STAMENS STAMINS STANCES STAPLES
```

```
STARVES STAVERS STAYERS STIFLES STIGMAS STINGES STOGIES STOKERS STONERS STOREYS
STORIES STOWERS STRAFES STRAINS STRANDS STREAKS STREAMS STRIDES STRIKES STRINGS
STRIPES STRIVES STROBES STROKES STRONGS STRUCKS STUDIES STUDIOS STUPIDS STUPORS
STYLERS STYMIES SUBACTS SUBGODS SUBLETS SUBLOTS SUBMITS SUBORNS SUBWAYS SUCKERS
SUCKLES SUDANIS SUITERS SUITORS SULKERS SULKIES SULTANS SULTIES SUNDAES SUNDAYS
SUNDOGS SUNRAYS SUPINES SURVEYS SWARTHS SWATHES SWAYERS SWIPERS SWIVELS SYLVANS
SYLVIAS SYLVIDS SYMBOLS SYRIACS SYRIANS THICKET TONIEST TONIGHT TOPMAST TORMENT
TOURIST TRAJECT TRANSIT TRAVEST TRIDENT TRINKET TRIOLET TRIPLET TRISECT TRUMPET
TUGBOAT TWIGLET TZARIST WHIPSAW WINDROW


ABCDEFB ACERBIC ACHOLIC ACRYLIC ACYSTIC ADENOID ADJURED ADMIRED ADMIXED ADOPTED
ADORNED ADVISED ALMSFUL ANDIRON ANGEVIN ANTIGEN ANTISUN ARBITER AROUSER ASCENDS
ASCENTS ASHPITS ASPECTS ASPIRES ASYLUMS ATHEIST ATOMIST BANKSIA BEASTIE BECAUSE
BEDMATE BEDRAPE BEDSITE BEDSORE BEDTIME BEGRIME BEGUILE BEGUINE BERHYME BESPOKE
BEZIQUE BRAIDER BRAILER BRAINER BRAKIER BRANDER BRASHER BRAWLER BRAWNER BRAZIER
BRIDGER BRIDLER BRINGER BRISKER BROADER BROGUER BROILER BRONZER BROTHER BROWNER
BROWSER BRUISER BRUSHER CADENZA CAESURA CALDERA CAMBRIA CAPSULA CARBONA CENSURE
CENTIME CHERISH COLUMBO CRADLER CRAFTER CRAMPER CRANKER CRASHER CRAWLER CRAZIER
CREATOR CRIMPER CRINGER CRIPSER CRISPER CROAKER CROFTER CROUPER CROWBAR CROWDER
CROWNER CRUISER CRUMBER CRUSHER CRUSTER DEBACLE DEBURSE DECIMAE DECLARE DECLINE
DEFLATE DEGLAZE DELOUSE DENSATE DENTURE DEPHASE DEPLANE DEPLORE DEPLUME DEPRAVE
DEPRIVE DEPULSE DEPURGE DEPURSE DERANGE DESCALE DESLIME DESPITE DESPUME DETINUE
DEVALUE DEVIATE DEVOICE DEWLIKE DRAFTER DRAINER DRAWLER DRIFTER DRINKER DRONIER
DROWNER DRUNKER DYARCHY DYINGLY DYNASTY ECTOPIC ELUVIAL ENCHAIN ENCROWN ENGRAIN
ENTRAIN ENVIRON ESCARPS ESCORTS ESCROWS ESKIMOS ESPRITS ESTROUS FEATURE FEBRILE
FENAGLE FENSIVE FERTILE FESTIVE FLOREAL FLUIDAL FLUVIAL FLYTAIL FRAILER FRANKER
FRAUDER FRINGER FRISKER FRONTER FROTHER FROWNER FRUITER GEMLIKE GENTILE GEORDIE
GERMANE GESTURE GETABLE GLUTEAL GRAFTER GRAILER GRAINER GRANDER GRANTER GRANTOR
GRASPER GRAZIER GRINDER GROANER GROUPER GROUSER GROUTER GROVIER GROWLER GRUNTER
HECTARE HELMAGE HEMLINE HENLIKE HEPTANE HEPTOSE HERBAGE HEROINE HEROIZE HEWABLE
HORATIO HYDROXY HYMNARY HYMNODY INBLOWN INDOGEN INDRAWN INGROWN INHUMAN INKHORN
INWOVEN ISABELS ISLANDS ISOBARS ISOGAMS ISOGENS ISOMERS ISONYMS ISRAELS ISTHMUS
ITERANT JACOBEA JEWLIKE JUNGFRU KACHINA KEYHOLE KEYNOTE KNOXIAN LECTURE LEISURE
LOCARNO MADEIRA MADRONA MAGENTA MATILDA MAZURKA MEASURE MEDIATE MELANGE MERCATE
METHANE MYSTERY MYSTIFY MYTHIFY NEBULAE NECKTIE NEOCYTE NEOTYPE NETLIKE NEURITE
NEWCOME NEWGATE OCEANIC OCTADIC OCTAVIC OMENTUM ORACLER ORBITER ORGANER OSPREYS
OSTENDS OSTLERS OYSTERY PALMIRA PALMYRA PANDORA PEALIKE PECTASE PECTIZE PECTOSE
PEDICLE PEGLIKE PENDICE PENDULE PENLIKE PENLITE PENSILE PENSIVE PEONAGE PEONIZE
PERBOLE PERCALE PERFIDE PERFUME PERFUSE PERLITE PERMUTE PEROGUE PERVADE PEWMATE
PIGNOLI PLAYFUL PLIMSOL PLUVIAL PORTICO PRAETOR PRAISER PRANCER PRANKER PRATLER
PRAWNER PRICKER PRINTER PRONGER PROUDER PROWLER PSEUDOS PSYCHES PSYCHOS PURLIEU
REABUSE REALINE REALISE REALIVE REALIZE REAMUSE REAWOKE REBATHE REBLADE REBLAME
RECABLE RECHASE RECHOSE RECLINE RECLUSE REDLINE REDPOLE REFLAME REFLATE REGLAZE
REGLOVE REGUIDE REHINGE REHOUSE REIMAGE REJOICE REJUDGE RELAPSE RELODGE RENOBLE
REPASTE REPHASE REPLACE REPLANE REPLATE REPLUME REPTILE REPULSE REQUITE REQUOTE
RESCALE RESHAKE RESHAPE RESHAVE RESHINE RESHONE RESIDUE RESLATE RESLIDE RESMILE
RESOLVE RESPACE RESPADE RESPITE RESPOKE RESTAGE RESTAKE RESTIVE RESTYLE RETABLE
RETICLE RETINUE RETWINE REUNITE REVALUE REVOICE REVULSE ROTUNDO SAMBUCA SARCOMA
SCEPTIC SEALIKE SECLUDE SEIZURE SELVAGE SEPTANE SEPTILE SEPTIME SERIATE SERINGE
SERVAGE SERVICE SERVILE SETLINE SEWABLE SEXLIKE SEXTILE SKYLARK SLEDFUL SNOWMAN
SNOWMEN SOPRANO STARLET STARLIT STEWART STEWPOT STUDENT SYNERGY SYNOECY TAPIOCA
```

```
TENABLE TENACLE TENSILE TENSIVE TENSURE THROUGH TIMPANI TORNADO TORPEDO TRACKER
TRAILER TRAINER TRAMPER TRAWLER TRICKER TRIFLER TRIPLER TROUPER TROUSER TRUCKER
TRUDGER TRUMPER UGLYING UNADORN UNBLOWN UNBROWN UNCHAIN UNCLEAN UNCROWN UNCTION
UNDRAWN UNFLOWN UNGIVEN UNGRAIN UNGROWN UNICORN UNLADEN UNLEARN UNLIKEN UNPLAIN
UNRISEN UNSHORN UNSHOWN UNSLAIN UNSTAIN UNSTERN UNSWORN UNTAKEN UNTHORN UNTRAIN
UNWOVEN USAGERS USANCES UTOPIST UTRECHT VALERIA VASCULA VECTURE VEHICLE VENDAGE
VENTAGE VENTURE VERBATE VERBOSE VERMINE VERSATE VESICLE VESTIGE VESTURE VOLCANO
VYINGLY WEBLIKE WELCOME WELFARE WETABLE WRACKER WRINGER WRISTER WRONGER ZEOLITE
```

```
ABCDEFC ABSENTS ACETIZE ACETONE ACRIDER ADENOSE AFTMOST ALTOIST AMENUSE ANDROID
ANSWERS ANYBODY APELIKE ARGUING ARTIEST ASCETIC AUDITED AUTOIST AWESOME BALEFUL
BANKMEN BARKIER BARNIER BASHERS BASKERS BASKETS BASQUES BASTERS BEDWARD BENISON
BENZOIN BESOILS BESTIRS BESTOWS BETWIXT BEWIDOW BISECTS BISHOPS BISQUES BISTROS
BODICED BOGUING BONDMAN BONDMEN BREATHE BREWAGE BRONCHO BUCOLIC BUGLING BURGHER
BURGLAR BURLIER BURNIER BURSTER BUSHELS BUSHERS BUSHIES BUSKERS BUSTERS BUSWAYS
BUTMENT CALOMEL CAMBIUM CAROLER CARTIER CASEINS CASULES CESIUMS CHEAPIE CHELATE
CHEMISE CHENILE CHIANTI CHLORAL CHLORYL CHORISO CHORIZO CLEANSE COAGULA COENURE
CONDEMN CONDIGN CONSIGN CONTAIN CORDIER CORKIER CORNIER CORSAIR COSEATS COSINES
COSTALS COSTARS COSTERS CREMATE CREMONE CRENATE CURATOR CURBIER CURDIER CURDLER
CURLIER CURVIER CUSPIDS CUSTOMS CYSTOUS CZARINA DASHERS DESALTS DESCUMS DESIGNS
DESILTS DESOILS DESPOTS DETRACT DEWCLAW DISARMS DISBARS DISHERS DISKERS DISMALS
DISMAYS DISOWNS DISPELS DOLEFUL DOSAGES DOTIEST DRACHMA DRACULA DUNGEON DUSTERS
DYEABLE EASINGS EJACULA ENTRUST ENTWIST EXTINCT EXTRACT FARTHER FASCETS FASTENS
FASTERS FERVOUR FISCALS FISHERS FISTERS FLEXIVE FLEXURE FOELIKE FORAGER FORAYER
FORBEAR FORKIER FOSTERS FRECKLE FULCRAL FURTHER FURZIER FUSIONS GARBLER GASEOUS
GASKETS GASPERS GENTIAN GIRDLER GODHEAD GODSEND GODSPED GODWARD GORSIER GOSPELS
GRANDMA GRANDPA GRANULA GRENADE GUNSMAN GUNSMEN GUSHERS GUSTOES HANDGUN HANGMEN
HARBOUR HARDIER HARPIER HASTENS HELICAL HELPFUL HERITOR HORNIER HORSIER HOSIERS
HOSTELS HOSTERS HURDLER HUSKIES HUSTLES HYDROID ICEBONE IDLEFUL INDUCED INDURED
INSEAMS INSECTS INSERTS INSHOES INSOLES INSTALS INSTEPS INSULTS INSURES INTREAT
INTREST INTRUST JACOBIC JASMINS JASPERS JEHOVAH JESUITS JOSEPHS JOSHERS JOSTLES
JUNGIAN JUNKMAN JUNKMEN KINSMAN KINSMEN KISMETS KOSHERS LACONIC LANDMEN LANTERN
LARDIER LARKIER LASHERS LASTERS LATCHET LENSMAN LESIONS LINEMAN LINKMAN LINKMEN
LISPERS LISTENS LISTERS LOSINGS LOTMENT LURCHER LUSHERS LUSTERS LUSTRES LYSINES
MANDRIN MANSION MARBLER MARCHER MARINER MASCOTS MASHERS MASKERS MASTERS MASTICS
MENTION MIDLAND MIDWARD MISCUES MISGOES MISHAPS MISLAYS MISPAYS MISPELS MISPUTS
MISRUNS MISTERS MISTLES MODULED MORALER MOSAICS MOSQUES MURKIER MUSCATS MUSCLES
MUSHERS MUSINGS MUSKATS MUSKEGS MUSKETS MUSLINS MUSTERS MYCOLIC MYCOTIC MYELINE
MYSTICS NAIROBI NODATED NODULED NORTHER NOUVEAU NUCLEIC NUTMEAT OBDURED OBELIZE
OBSIGNS OESTRUS OLEFINE ONETIME ONYMITY OPERATE ORIGAMI OUSTERS OUTBENT OUTCANT
OUTCAST OUTLAST OUTSENT OUTSERT OUTSIFT OUTSPIT OUTWAIT OVERAGE OVERATE OVERAWE
OVERDUE OVERDYE OVERLIE OVERUSE OYSTERS PALMFUL PARCHER PARDNER PARLOUR PARTNER
PASTELS PASTIES PASTILS PASTORS PATIENT PATRIOT PENGUIN PENSION PHAEDRA PHRASER
PHYLOGY PIANOLA PIERAGE PISTLES PISTOLS PISTONS PLANERA PLATINA PLEIDAE PONDMAN
PONDMEN PORKIER POSEURS POSINGS POSTALS POSTERS POSTIES PREBAKE PRECISE PREDATE
PREDINE PREFACE PREFINE PREGAME PRELATE PRELIFE PRELUDE PREMAKE PREMATE PREMISE
PREMOVE PRENAME PRENOTE PRESAGE PRESIDE PRESUME PREVOTE PREZONE PROVISO PUERILE
PUNTMAN PUNTMEN PURSIER PUSHERS RADIOED RATCHET RESACKS RESAILS RESALTS RESCANS
RESHIPS RESHOWS RESHUNS RESHUTS RESIFTS RESIGNS RESINGS RESINKS RESKINS RESLAYS
RESLOTS RESNAPS RESNUBS RESOAKS RESOAPS RESOILS RESPANS RESPINS RESPOTS RESTOWS
RESUCKS RESUITS RESULTS RESWIMS RETAUNT RETOAST RINGMAN RINGMEN RINKMAN RINKMEN
```

ROELIKE ROGUING RUNDOWN RUSTICS RUSTIES RUSTLES SALICYL SANDMEN SANGUIN SATIENT
SCANDIA SCAPULA SCENITE SCEPTRE SCLERAL SCORPIO SCRAPER SCRIBER SEGUING SHELTIE
SHRINER SHRIVER SHROVER SIRUPER SONGMAN SONGMEN SPATULA SPECKLE SPECTRE SPRAYER
SPRUCER STAMINA STERILE STIMULI STRAWER STRAYER STRIDER STRIKER STRIPER STRIVER
STROKER SUEABLE SUNDOWN SURFIER SURGIER SURLIER SYMPTOM SYRUPER TANKMEN TARDIER
TASKERS TECHNIC TENDRON TENSION THRIVER THROWER TINEMAN TINHORN TISANES TOELIKE
TORCHER TRACHEA TREACLE TREADLE TREMBLE TRIPOLI TSARINA TURFIER TUSCANS TUSKERS
TZARINA ULSTERS UNCOMIC UNDARED UNDATED UNDAZED UNDIKED UNDOMED UNDOPED UNDOSED
UNDRIED UNHARSH UNHITCH UNLEGAL UNLOCAL UNLOYAL UNSACKS UNSEALS UNSEAMS UNSEATS
UNSELFS UNSHIPS UNSHOES UNSHOPS UNSHOTS UNSLIPS UNSLOTS UNSOILS UNSOLES UNSORTS
UNSPARS UNSPITS UNSPOTS UNSTARS UNSTEPS UNSTOPS UNSTOWS UNTIGHT UNTWIST UPGOING
UPRISER UPRIVER UPSHOTS UPSIDES URATOMA USEABLE UTERINE VENISON VESTALS VETOIST
VINEMAN VISAGES VISCOUS VISUALS VOCALIC VOGUING WARBLER WARTIER WASHERS WASHUPS
WASTERS WESKITS WILEFUL WINGMAN WINGMEN WIREBAR WISDOMS WISHERS WISKERS WITHOUT
WORDIER WORMIER WREATHE WRESTLE XANTHIN XYLENOL XYLITOL

ABCDEFD ABSENCE ABUSERS ADORNER ADVERSE AMUSERS ANGRIER ATHEIZE ATOMISM AUBERGE
AUREOLE BADGING BANDIED BAPTIST BARGING BEKNOWN BLUSHES BOARDER BORSHTS BOWLFUL
BOWSERS BRANDON BRASHES BRASILS BRIDGED BRIDLED BRONZEN BRUSHES BUDGING BULGING
BUNDLED CADGING CADMUIM CANDIED CANDLED CATSUPS CAUSERS CELSIUS CELTIST CENSORS
CHANSON CHARGER CHARMER CHARTER CHASERS CHASTES CHIRPER CHISELS CHURNER CHUTIST
CLASHES CLINTON CLOSERS CLOSETS COARSER CODEINE CONSULS CONTEST CONTEXT CORNBIN
CORSETS COTERIE COURIER COURSER COURTER COUSINS CRADGED CRADLED CRUSHES CRUSOES
CULTIST CUNEATE CURDLED CURTEST DAMSELS DAMSONS DENTIST DISPULP DISTANT DISTORT
DIVERGE DIVERSE DORSALS DORSETS DOUSERS DOWSERS DRUNKEN DUNKIRK DWARFER EGOTIST
ETONIAN FAIENCE FALSENS FALSERS FALSETS FALSIES FATSOES FIASCOS FIESTAS FLASHES
FLIRTER FLOTANT FLUENCE FLUSHES FLUTIST FONDLED FOREUSE FORGING FORTUIT FRESCOS
FRESNOS FRIDGED FRISCOS FRISONS FROGLEG FUDGING GAUDIED GEISHAS GELATIA GESTALT
GESTANT GIBSONS GIRDLED GLARIER GNASHES GOTHISH GRUNION GUARDER GUISERS GYPSIES
GYPSUMS HANDLED HANGDOG HANSOMS HAWSERS HEDGING HOARDER HOARIER HOARSER HOLYDAY
HOUSERS HOWDIED HUNDRED HURDLED INVERSE INWEAVE IRONMAN IRONMEN JADEITE JETSOMS
JIGSAWS JUDAICA JUDGING KAISERS KATSUPS KEDGING KILNMAN KILNMEN KINDLED KINDRED
KNISHES LAPSERS LATENCE LAWYERY LEDGING LEFTIST LICENSE LINEAGE LINEATE LODGING
LOZENGE LUCERNE MAFIOSI MARSHES MAUSERS MEGALIA MENISCI MERGING METAZOA MILEAGE
MODERNE MORSELS MOURNER MOUSERS MOUSEYS NUCLEAL OBSERVE OBVERSE ORGANZA OUTEDGE
OUTGANG OUTKICK OUVERTE OUVRIER OVENMAN OVISACS PAILFUL PALSIES PANSIES PARSONS
PATSIES PAUSERS PELAGRA PERSONS PHASERS PHYSICS PLAYBOY PLUSHES POLEAXE PORGING
PORTENT POTENCE PRACTIC PREMIUM PRISONS PROTECT PROTEST PROTEXT PSYCHIC PULSERS
PUNTIST PURGING QUARTER QUASHES QUIESCE RANDIED RANSOMS RAVIOLI REASONS REGALIA
REKNOWN RESTANT REUNION RIKSHAS RIPSAWS ROADBED ROMANIA ROSEATE ROUGING ROWDIED
RUMANIA SCALPEL SCARIER SCORNER SEDGING SELKIRK SERGING SEXTANT SHARKER SHARPER
SHIPLAP SHIRKER SHORTER SIGNMAN SIGNMEN SILENCE SINDBAD SKILFUL SKIRTER SLUDGED
SMARTER SMIRKER SMUDGED SNARLER SNORTER SOMALIA SPARKER SPORTER SPURNER SPURTER
STAGING STARKER STARVER STOPGAP STORIER STORMER STUDIED SUBTEXT SUMATRA SURGING
SWARMER SWIRLER SYDNEAN TANSEYS TANSIES TARDIED TENSORS TINSELS TOADIED TONSILS
TOUSLES TOWNMAN TOWNMEN TRASHES TRISHAS TRUDGED TWIRLER UNHEDGE UNMERGE UNORDER
UNSEIZE UNWEAVE UNWEDGE UPHEAVE UPSTART URGENCE VALENCE VERANDA VERGING VERSALS
VIALFUL WAILFUL WEDGING WHATNOT WHATSIT WHIRLER WHITEST WORSENS

ABCDEFE ABILENE ABJURER ACHIEVE ADJURER ADJUROR ADJUSTS ADMIRER ADVISES AGNOSIS
ARGUSES AROUSES ASPHYXY ASPIRER AUSTERE AUTISMS AVOIDED BANGKOK BIRDEYE BLINDED

```
BLOUSES BOARDED BOGUSES BOKHARA BONUSES BOUNDED BOURSES BRAIDED BRAISES BRANDED
BREASTS BRINDED BROWSES BRUISES BURMESE CAIRENE CATYDID CAYUSES CHAIRER CHAISES
CHINESE CHORDED CHRISTS CIENAGA CITRENE CLAUSES CLOUDED CLOVENE CODISTS COMPERE
COMPETE CORPSES CORTEGE COTISES COURSES CROESUS CROWDED CRUISES CUBISMS CUBISTS
CURIOSO CYNISMS CYRUSES DECASTS DEHUSKS DELISTS DEMAGOG DEMASTS DIBASES DICASTS
DIGESTS DIOCESE DIORAMA DIVESTS DOGMATA DROWSES DYNASTS EGOISMS EGOISTS ENCYSTS
ENHUSKS ENIMAGA ENLISTS ENMASKS ENMISTS EPHRATA EUONYMY FAVORER FIGURER FIORDED
FISHEYE FOCUSES FORESTS FOUNDED FRAUDED FRONDED GHANESE GOANESE GOLDEYE GOURDED
GRINDED GROUSES GUARDED GUILDED HAWKEYE HOARDED HONESTS HUMISTS HYGIENE IGNORER
IMPOSES INCASES INCASKS INCASTS INCESTS INFESTS INFUSES INGESTS INJURER INMASKS
INSURER INVADED INVESTS JURISTS KETOSIS KUWAITI LABORER LEBANON LEGISTS LIPASES
LIPOSES LOCUSTS LOTUSES LYRISTS MACHETE MAFIOSO MALTESE MARTINI MATURER MELANIN
MINUSES MIOCENE MOLESTS MOULDED MOUNDED MUCOSAS MUTASES MYCOSES MYCOSIS NAIVETE
NAZISMS NOWHERE NUDISMS NUDISTS OBSCENE OBTUSES OPTIMUM OVIPARA PANIOLO PEDAGOG
PEGASUS PHONEME PHRASES PINKEYE PLAUDED PLAUSES POMADED POUNDED PRAISES PRIESTS
PROBATA PROTEGE PURISTS QUARTET QUINTET RACISMS RAPISTS RECASTS RELASTS RELISTS
REMASKS REMASTS REOSTAT REPASTS REPOSTS RIPOSTS ROUNDED SAPONIN SAVORER SCALDED
SCOLDED SCOURER SHARDED SINCERE SOCIETE SOCKEYE SOLEDAD SOUNDED SPRAYEY SQUARER
STYRENE SUGARER SULTANA SUPREME SWAHILI SYNAGOG TAOISMS THEISMS TIRADED TOLUENE
TRAPEZE TREMOLO TRIANON TRUISMS UMPIRER UNAIDED UNCASES UNCASKS UNCASTS UNCODED
UNCOSTS UNFADED UNHASPS UNHOSES UNJADED UNLADED UNLISTS UNMASKS UNMASTS UNOBESE
UNPIECE UNRESTS UNSHYLY UNSIDED UNSIEGE UNVESTS UNWADED UPCASTS UPRISES VALIDED
VALISES VAPORER VIRUSES WOUNDED
```

```
ABCDEFF ACTLESS ACTRESS ADOPTEE ADVISEE ADVOWEE AIDLESS AIMLESS AIRLESS AMPUTEE
ANTHILL APTNESS ARMLESS ARTLESS ASPIREE AWNLESS BADNESS BANSHEE BEDROLL BIGNESS
BIOMASS BITLESS BOWLESS BUDLESS BURGESS CAPLESS CARDIFF CARLESS CHARGEE CHORDEE
CLASHEE COBLESS COMPASS CONFESS COYNESS CREVASS CUIRASS CUPLESS CUTLASS CYPRESS
DAYLESS DECLASS DESKILL DEWFALL DIGRESS DILUTEE DIMNESS DISTAFF DOGLESS DONATEE
DOTLESS DRAFTEE DRAWOFF DRYNESS DUCHESS DULNESS EARMUFF ENGROSS ENSTALL ESCROLL
FARNESS FATLESS FATNESS FIANCEE FIGLESS FINLESS FITNESS FOGLESS FULNESS GANTREE
GAYNESS GODLESS GRANDEE GRANTEE GUARDEE GUMLESS GUNLESS GUTLESS HAPLESS HARNESS
HATLESS HIPLESS HITLESS HOTNESS ICEFALL IMPRESS INDWELL INGRESS INKLESS INKWELL
INSHELL INSTALL INSWELL JAGLESS JARLESS JAWLESS JOBLESS JOYLESS JUBILEE LARGESS
LAXNESS LEADOFF LIONESS LOWNESS MADNESS MANLESS MARQUEE MASTIFF MATINEE MATLESS
MAXWELL MIDLESS MISCALL MISFALL MISFELL MISPELL MONKESS MOUNTEE MUDLESS MUNCHEE
NAPLESS NARCISS NETBALL NUTFALL OARLESS OBLIGEE OFTNESS OLDNESS ORBLESS ORDINEE
OUTFALL OUTSELL OUTWALL OUTWELL OVERALL PAROLEE PAYROLL PILOTEE PINBALL PINFALL
PINLESS PITFALL PITLESS PONTIFF PREBILL PRELOSS PREMISS PRITHEE PROCESS PROFESS
PROWESS PUNLESS RAWNESS RAYLESS REBLUFF RECLASS REDBILL REGLOSS RESTAFF RESTIFF
RESTUFF RESWILL RIBLESS RIMLESS RODLESS RUMLESS RUMNESS RUNLESS SAWBILL SAWMILL
SCHLEPP SCHNELL SHAMPOO SHAWNEE SHERIFF SHUTOFF SKYFULL SOIGNEE STAMPEE STANDEE
SUBCELL SUBHALL SUBTILL SUNFALL TAKEOFF TAXLESS THANKEE TIGRESS TIPLESS TOPFULL
TOPLESS TOURNEE TOYLESS TRAINEE TRUCKEE TUGLESS TURNOFF UNBLESS UNCROSS UNDRESS
UNFRILL UNGLOSS UNICELL UNSHELL UNSKILL UNSPELL UNSTILL UNSWELL UPDRESS UPSWELL
VOTRESS VOUCHEE VOWLESS WARLESS WASHOFF WAXBILL WAYBILL WIGLESS WITLESS WITNESS
WRYNESS
```

EIGHT-LETTER PATTERN WORDS

AABACDEF OOGONIAL OOGONIUM OOLOGIST   **AABCADEB** OOSPORES

AABCDABE AARDVARK   **AABCDAEE** EERINESS   **AABCDEFB** OOCYSTIC OOSPERMS

AABCDEFC EELSKINS   **AABCDEFF** EELGRASS OOZINESS

AABCDEFG EELWORMS OOPHYTES OOPHYTIC   **ABAABCAD** SISSIEST

ABAABCBC PEPPERER   **ABAABCBD** PEPPERED

ABAABCDE COCCOIDS LILLIPUT LOLLOPED NONNOBLE PIPPIEST   **ABAACBAD** SISSYISH

ABAACBDA GIGGLING

ABAACBDE DIDDLING GIGGLIER GIGGLISH NINNYISH NINNYISM PEPPIEST

ABAACCDE LILLOOET PAPPOOSE TATTOOED TATTOOER

ABAACDAE DODDARDS SASSIEST   **ABAACDBD** LALLYGAG LOLLIPOP LOLLYPOP

ABAACDBE MAMMULAR   **ABAACDCA** DODDERED SUSSEXES

ABAACDCD DODDERER TATTERER TITTERER TOTTERER

ABAACDCE MAMMITIS NONNASAL NONNAVAL TATTERED TITTERED TOTTERED

ABAACDEA GAGGLING GOGGLING SESSIONS

ABAACDEF BABBLING BABBLISH BOBBINER BOBBINET BOBBLING BUBBLERS BUBBLIER BUBBLIES
BUBBLING BUBBLISH DIDDLERS GAGGLERS GIGGLERS GOGGLERS LOLLARDS MAMMOTHS MUMMINGS
MUMMYING POPPABLE POPPINGS POPPLING PUPPETLY PUPPETRY PUPPYDOM PUPPYING PUPPYISH
PUPPYISM TATTERLY TATTINGS TATTLERS TATTLERY TATTLING TITTLERS TOTTINGS TOTTLING
TOTTLISH

ABABBCBD REREELED REREEVED REREEVES   **ABABBCDE** COCOONED

ABABCADE ACACIANS NONOWNER   **ABABCBAD** REREFERS   **ABABCBDA** MIMICISM

ABABCBDE REREBELS REREJECT REREPEAT REREPENT RERESENT REREVEAL VIVIDITY VIVIFIED
VIVIFIER VIVIFIES

ABABCCBA SUSURRUS   **ABABCCDE** SUSURRED   **ABABCDAB** RERETIRE

ABABCDAE RERECORD REREFORM REREPORT RERETURN REREWARD TITIVATE

ABABCDBA REREADER RERENDER   **ABABCDBE** RERELIED RERELIES RERENTED TITIANIC

ABABCDEA REREPAIR SYSYGIES

ABABCDEB RERECITE REREDUCE REREFINE REREFUSE RERELATE REREMOVE RERESCUE RERESIDE
REREVISE

ABABCDED DADAISMS DADAISTS

ABABCDEF BOBOLINK COCOANUT COCOMATS COCONUTS CUCUMBER MEMENTOS MIMICKED MIMICKER
MIMINGLY PAPACIES PAPALISM PAPALIST PAPALITY PAPALIZE PEPERINO PEPERONI PIPINGLY
POPOVERS RERECKON REREIGNS RERELISH REREMAIN REREMIND REREMITS RERENTAL RERESIGN
TATARIZE ULULATED ULULATES UNUNITED VAVASOUR VIVIDEST VIVIPARY VIVISECT

ABACAACD EYETEETH   **ABACABDE** LILYLIKE   **ABACACDE** NONENEMY

ABACADAD EXEGESES   **ABACADAE** EBENEZER ELEVENER EYELETED EYELETER

ABACADBA NONUNION   **ABACADBC** INITIANT   **ABACADBE** COCKCROW INITIONS

ABACADCE INITIATE   **ABACADDE** EVERETTS   **ABACADEC** IRIDIZED

ABACADED ANABASES EXEGESIS IRICISMS

ABACADEF ADAMANCY ADAMANTS AMARANTH ANABATIC ANAPAEST ARAPAHOE AWAKABLE AWAKABLY
ELEMENTS ELEVENTH EYEWEARS INIMICAL INITIALS INITIARY IRICIZED IRICIZES IRIDIATE
IRIDICAL IRIDIOUS IRIDITES IRIDIUMS IRIDIZES NONENTRY

ABACBACD NONIONIC   **ABACBADE** AWAYWARD NONZONAL   **ABACBBDE** NONWOODY

ABACBDAD TITLISTS TITOISTS   **ABACBDAE** NONDOING NONROUND

ABACBDBE MEMBERED TETHERED UNURNING   **ABACBDCE** FIFTIETH

ABACBDEA NONWOVEN SISTINES SYSTYLES   **ABACBDEC** BIBLICAL NONLOCAL

ABACBDED BIBLISTS TITOISMS

ABACBDEF NONBOARD NONFOCAL NONLOSER NONLOVER NONMODAL NONMOLAR NONMORAL NONPOETS
NONPOLAR NONPOWER NONROYAL NONSOLAR NONSOLID NONTOXIC NONVOCAL NONVOTER POPCORNS
POPHOLES POPJOYED SASHAYED TITHINGS TITLINGS

ABACCADD EVENNESS   **ABACCDBE** REROOFED REROOTED

ABACCDEC AMASSERS OPOSSUMS   **ABACCDED** PAPOOSES

ABACCDEF ABATTOIR AMASSING TATOOERS TATOOING   **ABACDAAE** ELECTEES

ABACDABA AMALGAMA   **ABACDABE** AMALGAMS ERECTERS   **ABACDACB** CYCLICLY

ABACDACD NONSENSE   **ABACDACE** IRISHISM   **ABACDADE** ADAPTATE

ABACDAEA EYEPIECE   **ABACDAEB** ODONTOID

ABACDAEC ALASKANS CYCLICAL NONSYNCS   **ABACDAED** NONDENSE

ABACDAEE EYEDNESS

ABACDAEF ACADIANS ANAGRAMS ANAGRAPH ANAPHASE ARABIANS CYCLECAR EMENDERS EMERGENT IDIOCIES IDIOTING IDIOTISH IDIOTISM IDIOTIZE ILIADIST ILIADIZE INIQUITY IRISHIZE IRISLIKE NANKINGS NONGENIC NONPENAL NONTUNED OTOSCOPE OTOSCOPY TETRITOL TITRATED TITRATES

ABACDBAC POPSHOPS   **ABACDBAE** NINEPINS TITANITE   **ABACDBBE** POPEHOOD

ABACDBCD TITANIAN   **ABACDBCE** NINETIES PIPERIES POPULOUS TITANIAS

ABACDBDE ATAXITIC CICADIDS   **ABACDBEA** ANACONDA

ABACDBEC NONSTOPS PIPELIKE PIPELINE

ABACDBEF ATAXITES COCTIONS DIDUCING LILYFIED LILYFIES NONCLOSE NONQUOTA NONSTOCK OTOPATHY OZONIZED OZONIZER OZONIZES PAPULATE PIPEFISH PIPERINS POPEDOMS RERIVETS TITANISM TITANIUM TITULING VIVACITY VIVARIES VIVARIUM

ABACDCCA NINETEEN   **ABACDCDE** NONPAPAL PAPERERS UKULELES

ABACDCEE IMITATEE PIPELESS POPELESS RARENESS

ABACDCEF ARAISING AVAILING AWAITING CECILIAN EVENINGS IDIOZOME IMITATED IMITATES IMITATOR NINEPEGS NONELECT NONRURAL PAPILIOS POPEHEAD POPELERS POPIFIED POPIFIES PUPILIZE RARIFIED RARIFIES RARITIES RERISING SYSTATIC TETRARCH

ABACDDBA REROLLER

ABACDDBE MAMILLAE PAPILLAE PAPILLAR RERIGGED REROBBED REROLLED RERUBBED

ABACDDCD POPESSES   **ABACDDCE** EYETOOTH PIPETTED PIPETTES SUSANNAH

ABACDDEF CUCKOOED FIFTEENS NONAPPLY NUNHOODS PAPILLON PUPILLAR PUPILLED TOTALLED

ABACDEAA SASHLESS   **ABACDEAB** ACARDIAC EDENIZED NONAMINO USURIOUS

ABACDEAC ANALOGAL EYESORES ODORATOR TOTEMITE   **ABACDEAD** SUSPENSE

ABACDEAF ACANTHAS ALAMEDAS ANALGIAS ANARCHAL ANASTRAL ARABICAL ARAMIDAE EDENITES EDENIZES ELECTRES ELEGIZED ELEGIZES ELEUTHER ELEVATED ELEVATES EMERITED EMERIZED EMERIZES ENERGIES EPERGNES EVETIDES EXECUTED EXECUTER EXECUTES EXEMPTED IRIDEMIA NONAGENT NONBEING NONPLANE NONSPINY NONUSING OZONATOR TETRACTS TITRANTS TOTALITY UNUSEFUL

ABACDEBA DEDUCTED EVERSIVE RERACKER RERAILER   **ABACDEBB** COCKATOO

ABACDEBC IRISHERS PEPSINES   **ABACDEBD** DIDACTIC UNURGING

ABACDEBE ANALGENE ATAVISTS JUJITSUS NONJUROR RERAISES

ABACDEBF ACAPULCO ALATEDLY BEBRINED BEBRINES ENEMYING ENERVING ERECTORS ETERNITY
GIGANTIC MEMORIED MEMORIES MOMENTOS NANOGRAM NONHEROS PAPRIKAS PAPYREAN PAPYRIAN
PEPLUMED PEPTIDES PEPTIZED PEPTIZER PEPTIZES PEPTONES RERACKED RERAILED RERAISED
RERANKED REROUTED REROUTES TETCHIER TETRANES TETRODES TETROLES UNURBANE UNURGENT
USUALISM

ABACDECA EVERMORE RAREFIER   **ABACDECB** USURPERS USURPORS

ABACDECF ABANDING ABANDONS AMANDINE AWARDERS BIBULOUS CYCADEAN EMENDING EVENHAND
EVENSONG EVENTING EVERTORS GIGANTAL IMITANTS NONTRUTH PAPISTIC PAPULOUS PIPEAGES
PIPESTEM POPERIES PUPARIAL RAREFIED RAREFIES

ABACDEDA CYCLITIC NONPAGAN SASHIMIS   **ABACDEDB** ANALOGON OROMETER

ABACDEDC NONLEVEL

ABACDEDF ACADEMES AWAKENED AWAKENER CACHETED COCKERED COCKEREL COCKEYED COCKEYES
CYCLENES CYCLITIS EREMITIC INIQUOUS NONFATAL NONHUMUS NONREBEL NONRIGID ODOMETER
ODORIFIC SISTERED SYSTEMED TETRINIC TETRODON TUTORERS

ABACDEEA NONGREEN   **ABACDEED** CACHETTE

ABACDEEF AMARILLO AWARDEES BABYHOOD EYEBALLS LILYWOOD NONFATTY NONGASSY PIPEWOOD

ABACDEFA ACADEMIA ACAMPSIA ACANTHIA ANALOGIA ANAPHORA ANATHEMA CYCLADIC CYCLONIC
CYCLOPIC EGESTIVE EJECTIVE ELECTIVE ELEGANCE ELEGANTE EMERAUDE ENERGISE ENERGIZE
ENERVATE ERECTILE ERECTIVE EREWHILE ETERNIZE EVENTIDE EVERTILE EVERYONE EXECRATE
EXERCISE EXERCITE EXERTIVE EYESHADE MOMENTUM NONGRAIN NONHUMAN NONURBAN SASHINGS
SISYPHUS SUSCEPTS SUSPECTS SUSPENDS SUSPIRES SUSTAINS SYSTOLES TOTEMIST

ABACDEFB ACADEMIC ADAUNTED ANABOLIN ANATOXIN BABUSHKA DEDICATE DEDUCIVE EGESTING
ELECTRAL MEMBRANE MEMORATE MEMORIZE MEMPHITE ODORIZED USUARIES

ABACDEFC ABASINGS ACANTHIN ANAEROBE BABELIKE BOBSLEDS BOBSTAYS CICERONE CYCLITOL
CYCLONAL ELECTRIC EVENDOWN EVESONGS EVESTARS EXEMPLUM EYESHOTS EYESPOTS GAGELIKE
GAGSTERS NONLEGAL NONSALES NONSKEDS NONSKIDS NONSUITS PIPERATE POPELIKE POPELINE
TUTELAGE UNUSAGES

ABACDEFD ALARMISM ANARCHIC COCKERIE COCREATE ELECTANT EMERGING EVERYDAY IRIDESCE
NONGYPSY NONTRIER NONUSERS ODONTIST PAPISHES TOTEMISM

ABACDEFE ABACISTS ABACUSES AGAMISTS AMANISTS ANALYSES ANALYSIS ANALYSTS ANAPESTS
ANATHEME ARABISMS ARABISTS ATAVISMS CACTUSES COCAUSES COCHLEAE COCKADED CYCLISMS
CYCLISTS ELEGISTS NONPASTS OBOEISTS OLOGISTS POPEISMS

ABACDEFF BABYNESS EVENFALL EYEGLASS NONGRASS NONPRESS NONSPILL ODORLESS TITANESS
TUTORESS

ABACDEFG ABALONES ABASEDLY ABASHING ABATURES ACANTHUS ADACTYLE ADAMITES ADAPTERS
ADAPTING ADAPTION ADAPTIVE AGASTRIC AGATIZED AGATIZES ALACRIFY ALACRITY ALARMING
ALARMIST ALASKITE AMADINES AMATEURS AMATRICE AMAZEDLY AMAZEFUL ANABOLIC ANAGLYPH

ANALGIZE ANALOGIC ANALOGUE ANALYSED ANALYSER ANALYTIC ANALYZED ANALYZER ANALYZES
ANATOLIC ANATOMIC APARTING APATHISM ARABIZED ARABIZES ARACEOUS ARACHIDE ARACHNES
ARACHNID ARANEOUS AVARICES AVAUNTED AVAUNTER AWAITERS AWARDING BABELISH BABYFIED
BABYLIKE BIBELOTS BIBENZYL BOBFLIES BOBTAILS BOBWHITE CACHEPOT CACKLERS CACKLING
COCAINES COCHLEAR COCHLEAS COCKADES COCKBIRD COCKIEST COCKINGS COCKLERS COCKLETS
COCKNEYS COCKPITS COCKSPUR COCKSURE COCKTAIL CUCKHOLD CUCKOLDS CUCKOLDY CYCLADES
CYCLAMEN CYCLAMIN CYCLEDOM CYCLIDES CYCLINGS CYCLIZED CYCLIZES CYCLOIDS CYCLONED
CYCLONES CYCLOPIA DEDICANT DEDUCING DEDUCTIO DIDACTYL DIDUCTOR DODECANT DODGEFUL
DODGIEST DUDGEONS EGESTION EJECTING EJECTION EJECTORS ELECTING ELECTION ELECTORS
ELECTRON ELECTROS ELECTRUM ELEGANCY ELEGANTS ELEGIACS ELEGIAST ELEGIOUS ELEPHANT
ELEVATOR EMERALDS EMERITUS EMERSING EMERSION EMETICAL ENERGISM ENERGIST ERECTING
ERECTION ETERNALS ETERNIFY ETERNISH EVENGLOW EVENTFUL EVENTUAL EVERSING EVERSION
EVERTING EVERYMAN EXECUTOR EXEMPLAR EXERTING EXERTION EYEBROWS EYEDROPS EYESIGHT
IDIOTYPE IMITABLE IMITABLY IRIDATES IRIDEOUS IRISHMAN IRISHMEN MAMBOING MEMORAND
MEMORIAL MEMORIAS MEMORIST MEMSAHIB MIMOTYPE MOMENTAL MOMENTLY MUMBLERS MUMBLING
NINEFOLD NONACUTE NONADULT NONBASIC NONBLACK NONCASTE NONCLAIM NONDEIST NONEQUAL
NONESUCH NONETHYL NONFALSE NONFLAKY NONFLUID NONGLARE NONGUARD NONHARDY NONIDEAL
NONLICET NONLIVES NONMETAL NONPARTY NONPAUSE NONPLATE NONRATED NONRAYED NONRIVAL
NONSERIF NONSHAFT NONSUGAR NONTAXES NONTERMS NONTIDAL NONTRADE NONTRIAL NONTRUMP
NONUSAGE NONUTILE NONVALUE NONVITAL NONWHITE NUNBIRDS NUNCIATE OBOLIZED ODORABLE
ODORABLY ODORANTS ODORIZES OROGENIC OROPHYTE OTOGENIC OVOCYTES OVOLYTIC OZONATED
OZONATES OZONIDES OZOTYPES PAPERFUL PAPERING PEPTALKS PEPTICAL PEPTONIC PEPYSIAN
PIPEFULS PIPEWORK POPINJAY POPISHLY POPLARED POPULACE POPULACY POPULARS POPULATE
POPULISM POPULIST PUPATING PUPATION PUPIFORM PUPILAGE PUPILARY PUPILATE PUPILDOM
RAREBITS RERAKING RERATING RERIVALS REROBING REROPING REROWING RURALISM RURALIST
RURALITE RURALIZE SISTERLY SYSTALIC SYSTEMIC SYSTOLIC TETANOID TETCHILY TETRACID
TETRADIC TETRAGON TETRAMIN TETRAPOD TETRAZIN TETRAZYL TETRICAL TETRIFOL TITANOUS
TITANYLS TITHABLE TITHABLY TITLARKS TITMOUSE TITRABLE TITRABLY TITULARS TITULARY
TOTALING TOTALISM TOTALIZE TUTORAGE TUTORIAL TUTORING TUTORISM TUTORIZE UNUSABLE
UNUSABLY USURPANT USURPATE USURPING

ABBABACD DEEDEDLY   **ABBABBCD** ASSASSIN   **ABBABCBC** TEETERER

ABBABCBD TEETERED   **ABBABCDE** REERECTS

ABBACADE APPARATE ARRAYALS EFFERENT EFFETELY IMMIXING IRRIDING IRRIDIUM NOONINGS
TEETOTAL

ABBACBDD DEEDLESS   **ABBACBDE** DEEDIEST PEEPIEST TEETHERS

ABBACCDE APPALLED   **ABBACDAB** ESSENCES

ABBACDAE EFFECTED EFFECTER EGGEATER ENNERVED ENNERVES ESSENCED ILLINOIS ILLIQUID

ABBACDBD ASSAMESE

ABBACDBE ANNALINE ARRAYERS ATTAINTS ENNEWING SEESAWED TEETHIER

ABBACDCE IMMINENT IRRITATE OPPONENT   **ABBACDEA** ESSENIZE

ABBACDEB ARRANGER ASSAULTS ASSAYERS PEEPHOLE

ABBACDEC IRRITANT OPPOSALS OPPOSERS TOOTSIES   **ABBACDED** ANNAMESE APPAIRER

ABBACDEF ALLAYERS ALLAYING ANNALISM ANNALIST ANNALIZE APPAIRED APPARELS APPARENT APPAYING ARRAIGNS ARRANGED ARRANGES ARRANTLY ARRAYING ASSAILED ASSAILER ASSAYING ATTACHED ATTACHER ATTACHES ATTACKED ATTACKER ATTAINED ATTAINER ATTASKED DOODLERS DOODLING EFFECTOR EFFENDIS ESSENTIA IMMINGLE IRRIGANT IRRIGATE NOONDAYS NOONTIDE NOONTIME OPPOSING OPPOSITE OPPOSURE OTTOMANS TEETHFUL TEETHILY TEETHING TOOTEDLY TOOTHCUP TOOTHERS TOOTHFUL TOOTHIER TOOTHILY TOOTHING TOOTINGS TOOTLERS TOOTLING TOOTLISH UNNUMBED

ABBCABBC POOHPOOH   **ABBCABDE** BOOTBOYS FOOTFOLK WOODWORK WOODWORM WOOLWORK

ABBCADBE ATTRACTS REEARNED SEEDSMEN   **ABBCADCD** APPEARER APPEASES

ABBCADCE ANNEALED ANNEALER APPEALED APPEALER APPEARED APPEASED APPEASER OPPROBRY

ABBCADDE ANNUALLY EGGBERRY   **ABBCADEB** ASSUAGES

ABBCADEC AFFRAYER OFFGOING WOODWARD WOODWIND   **ABBCADED** AGGRADED

ABBCADEE FOOTFALL REENROLL WOODWALL

ABBCADEF ACCLAIMS AFFIANCE AFFIANTS AFFLATED AFFLATES AFFRAYED AGGRADES AGGRATED AGGRATES ALLIANCE APPLAUDS APPLAUSE APPRAISE ASSUAGED ASSUAGER EGGHEADS LOOPLETS LOOPLIKE OFFCOMES SEEDSMAN WOODWISE WOOLWICH

ABBCBADB REEMERGE   **ABBCBADE** REEXERTS   **ABBCBBCB** ASSESSES

ABBCBBCC ASSESSEE   **ABBCBBCD** ASSESSED   **ABBCBBDC** HOODOOED VOODOOED

ABBCBBDE ASSESSOR BOOHOOED   **ABBCBCDE** HEEDEDLY SEEDEDLY WEEDEDLY

ABBCBDBA DEEPENED   **ABBCBDBE** DEEPENER KEEPERED MEEKENED

ABBCBDEA ALLELUIA ALLELUJA

ABBCBDEF ASSISTED ASSISTER ASSISZED ASSISZER ASSISZOR ATTITUDE BEEPEDLY COOKOUTS ERRORFUL FOOYOUNG LOOKOUTS PEEVEDLY REEJECTS REELECTS REEXEMPT WEEKENDS ZOOGONIC ZOOLOGER ZOOLOGIC ZOOMORPH ZOONOMIA ZOONOMIC ZOONOTIC ZOOTOMIC ZOOTOXIN

ABBCCBDD KEELLESS KEENNESS   **ABBCCDCB** ADDEEMED   **ABBCCDCD** UNNEEDED

ABBCCDEC AFFEEBLE REESSAYS   **ABBCCDEE** TOOLLESS

ABBCCDEF COOEEING FOOLLIKE ROOMMATE UNNOOKED UNNOOSED WOOLLENS WOOLLIER WOOLLIES WOOLLIKE WOOLLISH

ABBCDAAE LEEFULLY OFFSHOOT   **ABBCDABE** ACCROACH ACCURACY HOOKSHOP

ABBCDACE ILLUVIUM   **ABBCDADE** ANNOTATE ASSONANT IMMUNING OFFERORS

ABBCDAEB ASSEGAIS ESSAYERS ILLUVIAL   **ABBCDAEC** ALLEGATE ALLEVATE

ABBCDAED ACCUSALS   **ABBCDAEE** EGGSHELL

ABBCDAEF ACCOLADE ACCRUALS ACCURATE ACCUSANT AFFIDAVY ALLIGATE ALLOCATE AMMONATE
ANNULATE APPLIANT APPROACH ARRIVALS ARROGANT ARROGATE ASSURANT ASSURATE BOOKABLE
BOOMABLE DOOMEDLY DOOMSDAY EFFACERS EFFLUENT ILLOGICS ILLUDING ILLUMINE ILLUMING
ILLURING ILLUSION ILLUSIVE IMMAZING IMMERITS IMMOBILE IMMUNITY IMMUNIZE IMMURING
IMMUTING MOORSMAN MOORSMEN NEEDINGS NOOKINGS OFFSHORE OSSIFORM SOOTHSAY UNNATURE
UPPLOUGH

ABBCDBAA SEEDLESS SEEDNESS   **ABBCDBAC** REESTERS

ABBCDBAE ATTRITAL LOOPHOLE REENTERS ROOTWORM SEEDIEST SEEPIEST

ABBCDBBC COOKBOOK

ABBCDBBE BOOKROOM COOKROOM DOOMBOOK FOOTROOM LEECHEES POOLROOM REESTEEM TOOLROOM

ABBCDBCA DEERHERD SEEDBEDS   **ABBCDBCE** ATTESTED ATTESTER FOOTNOTE REEDBEDS

ABBCDBDE AGGREGED AGGREGES WOODCOCK

ABBCDBEA REENDEAR SEEDLETS SEETHERS TEENIEST

ABBCDBEC BEETIEST BOOKWORK FOOTPOST HOOSGOWS KEESTERS   **ABBCDBED** REEXTENT

ABBCDBEE BEEFLESS DEEPNESS FEETLESS HEEDLESS HEEDNESS MEEKNESS NEEDLESS PEERLESS
REEDLESS WEEDLESS

ABBCDBEF ADDENDUM ANNOUNCE ATTESTOR ATTRITED ATTRITUS BEEFIEST BEERIEST BOOKLORE
BOOKWORM BOOMTOWN BOONDOCK BOOTHOSE DEERMEAT DOORBOYS DOORPOST EGGINGLY FEEBLEST
FOOTHOLD FOOTLOCK FOOTLOGS FOOTROPE FOOTSORE FOOTWORK FOOTWORN GOODSOME HOOKNOSE
HOOKWORM INNUENDO LEECHERS LEECHERY LEERIEST LOOKDOWN MOORFOWL NEEDIEST NEEDLERS
PEERIEST REEDIEST REEFIEST REEKIEST REEMBEDS REEXCELS REEXPECT REEXPELS REEXTEND
ROOFTOPS ROOTHOLD WEEDIEST WEEPIEST WOODLOTS WOOLROCK ZOOPHORE ZOOSCOPY ZOOSPORE

ABBCDCAE EFFIGIED EFFIGIES   **ABBCDCCE** OFFEREES

ABBCDCDE AFFINING OFFERERS OTTERERS UPPERERS UTTERERS

ABBCDCEB ASSEVERS OSSIFIES

ABBCDCEF ACCEDERS ACCITING ACCOMODE ADDITION ADDITIVE AFFINITE AFFINITY AFFIXING
ALLEGERS AMMETERS AMMINIDE AMMONOID ANNEXERS ARRIDING ARRIVING ARRIVISM ASSIMILE
ATTICIZE ATTIRING DOOMSMAN DOOMSMEN EFFIGIAL FOOTSTEP HOODEDLY IMMUTUAL KEENINGS
MOONINGS OCCIPITA ODDITIES OFFICIAL OFFICING OSSIFIED OSSIFIER OTTAWANS UPPEREST
WOODEDLY

ABBCDDCC APPELLEE   **ABBCDDCD** ABBESSES ACCESSES

ABBCDDCE INNETTED UNNETTED   **ABBCDDEE** ACCOLLEE ALLOTTEE

ABBCDDEF ALLOTTED ALLOTTER ANNULLED ANNULLER OCCURRED UNNABBED UNNAGGED UNNAPPED
UNNARROW UNNIBBED UNNIPPED

ABBCDEAA SOOTLESS

ABBCDEAB ALLODIAL ALLUVIAL IRREPAIR KEELRAKE KEEPSAKE LEEANGLE SEEDCASE

ABBCDEAC ACCLINAL ROOSTERS SOOTHEST SOOTIEST   **ABBCDEAD** ALLEYWAY AMMONIAN

ABBCDEAE APPESTAT EFFUNDED ELLIPSES MOORISMS

ABBCDEAF ACCRETAL ALLUVIAN AMMONIAC AMMONIAL AMMONIAS APPRISAL APPRIZAL APPROVAL
ASSIDUAL ASSIGNAT ASSYRIAN EDDYITES EFFLATED EFFLATES EFFLOWER EFFLUVES EFFLUXED
EFFLUXES EFFORCED EFFORCES EFFORMED EFFULGED EFFULGES EMMANUEL ENNICHED ENNICHES
ENNOBLED ENNOBLER ENNOBLES GOODINGS KEEPSAKY LOOPEDLY LOOPFULS LOOSEDLY LOOTABLE
LOOTABLY LOOTEDLY NEEDLING OCCASION OCCLUSOR REEDWORK REEMBARK REEXPORT ROOFWARD
ROOMWARD ROOTWARD UDDERFUL UPPERCUT

ABBCDEBA SEEDAGES SEEPAGES   **ABBCDEBC** REEDITED

ABBCDEBE ATTRISTS REEVADED

ABBCDEBF ANNEXING ANNOYING ARRIVERS ATTEMPTS BEECHIER BOOKSHOP COOKSHOP COOPTION
DOORKNOB DOORSTOP ERRANTRY ESSAYISH ESSAYISM FEEDSMEN FEETAGES HOOSEGOW INNOCENT
INNOVANT MOONGLOW PEERAGES REECHOED REECHOES REENAMEL REETCHED REETCHES REEVADES
REEVOKED REEVOKES SEEMLIER TEENAGES UNNAMING UNNOSING UNNOTING WEEKLIES WEEVILED
WOODSHOP

ABBCDECA DOORWARD SEEDPODS

ABBCDECB ARRESTER FEELABLE PEELABLE REELABLE REENGINE

ABBCDECC ARRESTEE ATTENDEE KEELBILL WOOLBALL

ABBCDECD AMMONION ASSERTER IMMESHES

ABBCDECE ACCENDED APPENDED ATTENDED ELLIPSIS IMMENSES IMMERSES OFFENDED OFFENSES

ABBCDECF ACCENTED ACCEPTED ACCEPTER ACCRUERS AFFECTED AFFECTER AGGESTED ALLERGEN
ALLUVIUM AMMINOID ARRECTED ARRENTED ARRESTED ARROSION ASSENTED ASSENTER ASSERTED
ATTEMPER ATTENDER BOOKLIKE DEERHORN ELLIPTIC FOOTBATH FOOTPATH GOOSIEST HOOKLIKE
IMMERGED IMMERGES IMMERSED IMMESHED INNERVED INNERVES INNESTED MOONVINE MOORBIRD
NOOKLIKE OFFENCES OFFENDER ROOKLIKE UNNEALED UNNEAPED UNNEARED UNNERVED UNNERVES
UNNESTED UNNEWSED WOODSIDE

ABBCDEDB ASSURERS REENGAGE REESTATE   **ABBCDEDC** APPETITE WOODENED

ABBCDEDE COOPERER

ABBCDEDF ACCRETED ACCRETES ALLURERS ATTIRERS ATTUNING COOPERED EFFICACY FOOTERED
HOOKUPUS IMMANENT LAAGERED LOOSENED LOOSENER MOONEYES OCCULTLY ZOOLITIC ZOOMETER

ABBCDEEC BEETROOT   **ABBCDEED** ROOMETTE

ABBCDEEF ALLOTEES ODDBALLS POONGEES WEEVILLY

ABBCDEFA ALLERGIA ANNELIDA DOORMAID EFFUSIVE EGGCRATE EMMANTLE EMMARBLE KEELBACK
MOONBEAM PEERSHIP REENAMOR SEEKINGS SEEMINGS SEEPINGS SOOTHERS

ABBCDEFB ADDICTED ADDORSED ADDUCTED ADDULCED AMMONIUM ARRESTOR ASSUMERS ASSURGES
BEEFCAKE BEEHOUSE FEEDABLE JEEPABLE KEEPABLE MEETABLE NEEDSOME REEDLIKE REEFABLE
REENABLE REENTICE REESCAPE REEXCITE REEXHALE REEXPOSE SEEDCAKE SEEDLIKE SEEDTIME
SEERLIKE UNNATION VEERABLE WEEDABLE WEEDLIKE WEEPABLE

ABBCDEFC ACCESIVE AMMELINE ANNEXIVE APPETIZE APPRIZER APPROVER ASSEMBLE BOOKMARK
BOOKRACK BOOSTERS COONSKIN COOTIEST DEERHAIR FOOTBEAT FOOTREST HOOSIERS KEELHAUL
LOOSINGS OCCLUSAL OFFSIDES OFFSPINS REENJOIN ROOTFAST ROOTIEST UNNESTLE WOODBIND
WOODLAND WOODMAID WOODSHED WOODYARD

ABBCDEFD ACCORDER ACCUSERS AFFIRMER ALLEGING APPOSERS ASSERTOR ASSORTER FOOTSIES
ILLUSORS MOONSETS WOOLSEYS

ABBCDEFE ACCORDED ACCURSES AFFORDED AGGRIEVE ALLOGENE APPRISES APPULSES BOOKISMS
EDDYISMS ILLAPSES IMMOLDED LOOPISTS OCCLUDED OCCURSES OFFCASTS REEXISTS ZOOCYSTS

ABBCDEFF ABBOTESS ASSIGNEE BEERPULL BOOKFULL BOOMLESS BOONLESS BOOTLESS COOKLESS
COOLNESS DEERKILL DOORBELL DOORLESS DOORSILL FOODLESS FOOTBALL FOOTHILL FOOTLESS
FOOTWELL GOODLESS GOODNESS GOODWILL GOOFBALL HOODLESS HOOFLESS HOOKLESS HOOPLESS
MOONBILL MOONFALL MOONLESS MOOTNESS PEEKABOO POORNESS POORWILL ROOFLESS ROOMLESS
ROOTLESS SEEDBALL SEEDFALL SOOTFALL WOODFALL WOODLESS WOODNESS WOODRUFF

ABBCDEFG ACCEDING ACCENSOR ACCENTOR ACCEPTOR ACCESION ACCIDENT ACCINGED ACCINGES
ACCLOYED ACCLOYER ACCOILED ACCOILER ACCOSTED ACCOUNTS ACCCUPLE ACCREDIT ACCRUING
ACCUMBER ACCURSED ACCUSING ACCUSIVE ACCUSTOM ADDICTER ADDITORY ADDUCENT ADDUCERS
ADDUCING ADDUCTOR AFFINELY AFFIRMED AFFIXERS AFFLICTS AFFLUENT AFFLUING AFFLUXES
AFFORCED AFFORCES AFFRIGHT AFFRONTS AFFRONTY ALLEGORY ALLEGROS ALLERGIC ALLERGIN
ALLNIGHT ALLODIUM ALLONYMS ALLOTYPE ALLOVERS ALLOWING ALLOYING ALLSPICE ALLTHING
ALLUDING ALLUMINE ALLURING ALLUSION ALLUSIVE ALLUSORY ALLUVION AMMONIDE AMMONIFY
AMMONITE AMMONITY ANNELIDS ANNELISM ANNELOID ANNOYERS ANNOYFUL ANNULISM ANNULOID
APPENDIX APPERILS APPLENUT APPLIERS APPLIQUE APPLYING APPOINTS APPORTED APPOSING
APPOSITE APPRISED APPRIZED APPRIZES APPROVED APPROVES ARRODING ARROSIVE ARROWING
ARROWLET ASSEMBLY ASSENTOR ASSIGNED ASSIGNER ASSIGNOR ASSOILED ASSOILER ASSORTED
ASSUMING ASSURING ATTORNEY BEECHNUT BEETLING BOOKCASE BOOKENDS BOOKFAIR BOOKIEST
BOOKINGS BOOKLAND BOOKLETS BOOKLING BOOKMATE BOOKREST BOOKWARD BOOKWAYS BOOKWISE
BOOMIEST BOOMINGS BOOMLETS BOOSTING BOOTINGS BOOTLACE BOOTLEGS BOOTLICK BOOZIEST
COOINGLY COOKABLE COOKINGS COOKMAID COOLANTS COOLIDGE COONIEST COONTAIL COOPTIVE
DEEPINGS DEERSKIN DOOMLIKE DOOMSTER DOORCASE DOORJAMB DOORLIKE DOORMATS DOORNAIL
DOORSMAN DOORSMEN DOORSTEP DOORWAYS DOORWISE EFFACING EFFLUVIA EFFRONTS EFFUDING
EFFUMING EFFUSING EFFUSION EGGFRUIT EGGPLANT ERRANTLY ERRATICS ERRATISM ERRINGLY
ESSAYING FEEBLING FEEBLISH FEEDBACK FEEDBINS FEEDINGS FEEDLOTS FEEDSMAN FEEDWAYS

FEELINGS FOOLHEAD FOOLINGS FOOLSCAP FOOLSHIP FOOTAGES FOOTBACK FOOTBAND FOOTGEAR
FOOTGRIP FOOTINGS FOOTLIKE FOOTLING FOOTMARK FOOTPACE FOOTPADS FOOTPICK FOOTRACE
FOOTRAIL FOOTWALK FOOTWAYS FOOTWEAR FOOYUNGS GOODHAPS GOODLIER GOODLIKE GOODWIFE
GOODYEAR GOODYISH GOOFIEST HEELBAND HEELCAPS HEELGRIP HEELINGS HEELPOST HEELTAPS
HOODCAPS HOODFULS HOODINGS HOODLIKE HOODLUMS HOODWINK HOODWISE HOOFBEAT HOOFLIKE
HOOFMARK HOOKIEST HOOKLAND HOOKLETS HOOKTIPS HOOKWISE HOOLIGAN HOOPINGS HOOPLIKE
HOOPSTER ILLFARED ILLFARES ILLUDERS ILLUMERS ILLUSORY ILLUSTRE IMMANTLE IMMARBLE
IMMASKED IMMATURE IMMERSAL IMMODEST IMMOLATE IMMORALS IMMORTAL INNATELY INNOVATE
INNYARDS IRRUPTED ISSUABLE ISSUABLY ISSUANCE KEELBOAT KEEPINGS KEESHOND KEEWATIN
KOOTENAY LEEBOARD LEECHING LEECHMAN LEEWARDS LOOKINGS LOOMINGS LOONIEST LOOPIEST
LOOTSMAN MEETINGS MOOCHERS MOOCHING MOODIEST MOONCALF MOONDIAL MOONFACE MOONFISH
MOONIEST MOONLIKE MOONRISE MOONTIDE MOONWARD MOORAGES MOORBAND MOORHENS MOORIEST
MOORINGS MOORLAND MOORSHIP MOOTABLE MOOTABLY MOOTINGS NEEDFULS NEEDHAMS NOOKIEST
NOOKLETS NOOTSACK OCCIDENT OCCIPUTS OCCLUDES OCCULTED OCCULTER OCCUPANT OCCUPATE
OCCUPIED OCCUPIER OCCUPIES ODDMENTS OFFBEATS OFFBREAK OFFERING OFFGRADE OFFICERS
OFFISHLY OFFPRINT OFFSCAPE OFFSIDER OFFSTAGE OFFTAKES OFFTYPES OFFWARDS OSSICULE
OTTERING OTTINGER PEELINGS PEERDOMS POODLERS POODLING POOLIEST POOLINGS POOLSIDE
REEDINGS REEDLING REEFINGS REEMBODY REEMPLOY REENACTS REENDOWS REENJOYS REENLIST
REENTOIL REENTOMB REEQUIPS REEXALTS REEXPAND ROOFAGES ROOFINGS ROOFLETS ROOFLIKE
ROOFWISE ROOKIEST ROOKLETS ROOMAGES ROOMFULS ROOMIEST ROOMLETS ROOSTING ROOTAGES
ROOTCAPS ROOTEDLY ROOTLIKE ROOTLING ROOTWISE SEEDLING SEEINGLY SEEMABLY SEETHING
SOOTHFUL SOOTHING SOOTLIKE SOOTYING TOOLHEAD TOOLINGS TOOLMARK TOOLSHED UNNAILED
UNNATIVE UNNEATLY UNNICELY UNNICHED UNNICKED UNNIMBLE UNNIMBLY UNNOBLED UNNOBLES
UNNOISED UNNORMAL UNNOTIFY UPPERDOG UPPISHLY UTTERING VEERINGS WEEDLING WEEKDAYS
WOODBARK WOODBINE WOODBINS WOODBUSH WOODCUTS WOODENLY WOODGATE WOODGRUB WOODIEST
WOODINGS WOODLIKE WOODPECK WOODPILE WOODRACK WOODRICK WOODSIER WOODSMAN WOODSMEN
WOOINGLY WOOLHEAD WOOLIEST WOOLPACK WOOLSACK WOOLSHED WOOLSKIN ZOOGENIC ZOOLITES
ZOOSPERM ZOOTYPES ZOOTYPIC

ABCAABDE REARREST   **ABCAACDE** REARRAYS TWITTIER TWITTING

ABCAADAD EXCEEDED   **ABCAADAE** ESTEEMED ESTEEMER EXCEEDER

ABCAADBE FLUFFILY GROGGERY PROPPERS TROTTERS

ABCAADEA ENFEEBLE GROGGING SCISSORS   **ABCAADEB** GROGGIER REARRIVE

ABCAADEF BLABBERS BLABBING BLOBBIER BLUBBERS BLUBBERY BLUBBING CHICCORY EMCEEING
FLUFFERS FLUFFIER FLUFFING GROGGILY HIGHHOLE ONLOOKER PLOPPING PREPPING PROPPING
TROTTING TWITTERS TWITTERY TWITTLED TWITTLES

ABCABAAD LOBLOLLY   **ABCABADE** CONCOCTS ETCETERA INFINITE INFINITY

ABCABBDB REFREEZE   **ABCABBDE** REBREEDS REGREENS REGREETS UNSUNNED

ABCABCAD ALFALFAS ENTENTES   **ABCABCBD** ONIONING

ABCABCCD BERBERRY BONBONNE   **ABCABCDB** REDREDGE   **ABCABCDC** MURMURER

ABCABCDE BARBARIC BULBULES MIAMIANS MURMURED SHOSHONE SHOSHONI TARTARIC TARTARIN
TARTARLY TARTARUS TINTINGS WARWARDS

ABCABDAD TINTISTS   **ABCABDAE** ALCALZAR ENCENTER ENGENDER ENTENDER

ABCABDBA DEADENED REPREFER   **ABCABDBD** REGREDED TENTERER

ABCABDBE CONCOLOR DEADENER DEADEYES REBREWED RECREWED TENTERED UNTUNING VELVETED

ABCABDCE INTINCTS PALPABLE PALPABLY RETREATS   **ABCABDDE** CATCALLS PRYPROOF

ABCABDEA ENDENIZE SAPSAGOS SAUSAGES SHUSHERS SUBSULTS SUBSUMES SUNSUITS

ABCABDEB ECLECTIC RECREASE RECREATE UNSUNKEN

ABCABDEC CASCADES INSINEWS PREPRICE PREPROVE UNDUNGED

ABCABDED CAPCASES CASCADED UNFUNDED   **ABCABDEE** INKINESS

ABCABDEF ALKALIED ALKALIES ALKALIFY ALKALINE ALKALIZE ALKALOID ARTARINE BARBADOS
BOXBOARD CHECHAKO CIRCINAL CONCORDS CONCOURS COXCOMBS COXCOMBY DAEDALIC DAEDALUS
ENLENGTH ENVENOMS FANFARED FANFARES GEOGENIC GINGIVAE GINGIVAL HOTHOUSE INKINDLE
INKINGLY INRINGED INVINATE KICKIEST KINKIEST MATMAKER MESMERIC OSMOSING PALPATED
PALPATES PORPOISE PREPRINT RECREANT RECREDIT REDREAMS REDREAMT REFRENZY REFRESCO
REPREACH RETREADS RETRENCH SENSEFUL SHASHLIK SHUSHING SUBSUMED TACTABLE TAGTAILS
TANTALUS TARTANES TASTABLE TASTABLY TENTEDLY TESTEDLY THITHERS TILTINGS TORTOISE
TOYTOWNS UNBUNDLE UNBUNGED UNHUNTED

ABCACADE IMBIBING   **ABCACBAD** TARTRATE   **ABCACBDE** PROPORTS TILTLIKE

ABCACCDE UPBUBBLE   **ABCACDAE** AGRARIAN TARTRITE   **ABCACDCE** THATAWAY

ABCACDEB ASTATICS PROPONER PROPOSER   **ABCACDEC** PREPENSE

ABCACDED CAUCUSES PROPOSES   **ABCACDEE** BULBLESS PALPLESS PULPLESS

ABCACDEF ARMAMENT BULBLETS BULBLIKE CAUCUSED EUPEPTIC IMBIBERS INSISTED INSISTER
INTITLED INTITLES MAIMINGS PROPONED PROPONES PROPOSAL PROPOSED PROPOUND PULPLIKE
TRITIDES TUITIONS

ABCADABC INGIVING TESTATES

ABCADABE INCIDING INCISING INCITING INDITING INTICING INVITING TESTATED

ABCADACB IGNITING   **ABCADACC** EASELESS   **ABCADACE** INTIMITY IONIZING

ABCADADE ENTERERS   **ABCADAEA** SENSISTS SUBSISTS

ABCADAEB INCISION INSITION   **ABCADAEC** IGNITION INSIPIDS INTIMIST PREPUPAE

ABCADAEE EDGELESS EMPERESS

ABCADAEF ALCAZARS ALMANACS ALTARAGE AREAWAYS BRIBABLE BRIBABLY EAGEREST EASEMENT
ENJEWELS EPHEMERA ETHEREAL ETHEREAN IGNIFIED IGNITIVE INCISIVE INCITIVE INCIVISM

INDICIAL INDICIAS INDICIUM INDIVISM INHIBITS INVIRILE IODIZING IONICISM IONICIZE
IOTIZING OCTOPODA OCTOPODS OENOLOGY OPTOLOGY OSMOLOGY PANPIPES PREPUPAL TACTITES
TESTATOR TESTATUM UNMUTUAL

ABCADBAE EMBEAMED ENKERNEL INSIGNIA KIRKLIKE REDRIERS REORDERS TEXTLETS

ABCADBBD INDIENNE   **ABCADBCA** DEADHEAD TESTIEST   **ABCADBCB** PREPARER

ABCADBCE CINCHING DEADBEAT GANGLAND ONGOINGS PINPOINT PREPARED PREPARES RUNROUND

ABCADBDB INDIANAN PROPERER   **ABCADBDE** INDIANAS KICKPIPE PROPERED TORTUOUS

ABCADBEA ENCEINTE SEWSTERS   **ABCADBEB** REPRIEVE RETRIEVE

ABCADBEC ALTARLET DISDAINS   **ABCADBEE** CATCHALL DEADNESS SEASHELL TENTLESS

ABCADBEF ATLANTIC ATLANTIS CIRCLING CIRCUING CIRCUITS CIRCUITY COACTORS GANGWAYS
GORGEOUS HIGHLINE HIGHTIDE INDIGNES INDIGNLY INSIGNED KOLKHOZY MNEMONIC PEOPLERS
PERPLEXT PIMPLIER PIMPLING PINPRICK PREPARTS PROPERLY PROPERTY REORIENT THATCHED
THATCHER THATCHES TORTIONS TORTIOUS TORTUOSE TRITORAL TRITURAL TRITURES UNBURNED
UNGUENTS UNRUINED UNTURNED

ABCADCAE GANGINGS NOINTING REARWARD

ABCADCBE ASIANISM DREDGERS GEWGAWED REBRIBED REBRIBES TACTICAL VALVULAE VALVULAR

ABCADCCE BARBERRY BURBERRY FULFILLS PULPALLY ZIGZAGGY

ABCADCDE BARBERED CALCULUS VOLVULUS   **ABCADCEA** EMPEOPLE SENSINGS

ABCADCEB ASIATICS SEASCAPE   **ABCADCEC** TORTURER

ABCADCED EUTECTIC UNFULFIL   **ABCADCEE** DEADFALL

ABCADCEF APIARIES APIARIST AQUALUNG AVIARIES AVIARIST AXIALITY AXIATION CHECKERS
CHICKIES CHICKING CLICKING CONCENTS CRICKING DEADPANS FORFARED FORFARES INCIRCLE
INDIADEM PUMPSMAN PUMPSMEN PURPARTS PURPARTY PURPORTS SWISHIER SWISHING TONTINES
TORTURED TORTURES UNHUSHED UNPULPED UNPUMPED UNTUFTED VALVULES

ABCADDAA EXPELLEE   **ABCADDAD** EGRESSES EMBEDDED EXCESSES

ABCADDAE EGRESSED ENCELLED ENFETTER ENGEMMED EXCELLED EXCESSED EXPELLED EXPELLER

ABCADDBE UNQUEENS   **ABCADDEA** EMBEZZLE   **ABCADDEB** UNBUTTON UNSULLEN

ABCADDEC EGRESSOR INRIGGER UNDUBBED UNDULLED

ABCADDED ALKANNIN UNBUDDED UNMUDDED

ABCADDEF ACHATTER AXHAMMER EMBEGGAR IMBITTER INFILLED INFITTED INFITTER INRIGGED
RECROONS REDROOTS REPROOFS UNBUFFED UNBURROW UNCUBBED UNCUFFED UNCULLED UNCUPPED

```
UNFULLED   UNFURRED   UNFURROW   UNFUSSED   UNGUMMED   UNGUTTED   UNHUDDLE   UNHUGGED   UNHULLED
UNLUGGED   UNMUDDLE   UNMUFFLE   UNMULLED   UNMUSSED   UNMUZZLE   UNPUFFED   UNPULLED   UNPUZZLE
UNRUBBED   UNRUFFED   UNRUGGED   UNSUMMED   UNSUPPLE   UNTUBBED   UNTUGGED   UNTUPPED
```

ABCADEAB TENTMATE TERTIATE   **ABCADEAC** ENDEARED ENDEBTED

ABCADEAD ALBANIAN APHASIAS APLASIAS ARKANSAN ENHEDGED ENMESHES SUBSENSE

ABCADEAE ARKANSAS EXPENDED EXPENSES

```
ABCADEAF   ACRANIAL   ALSATIAN   AQUARIAL   AQUARIAN   ARBACIAS   ARCADIAN   ARCADIAS   ARMAGNAC
EATERIES   EDGERMEN   ELDERMEN   ELSEWHEN   ENFESTED   ENFESTER   ENHEDGES   ENHELMED   ENLEAFED
ENMESHED   ENSEALED   ENSEAMED   ENSEARED   ENSEATED   ENVEILED   ENWEAVED   ENWEAVES   EXCEPTED
EXCEPTER   EXCERPED   EXPECTED   EXPECTER   EXPENDER   EXPENSED   EXPERTED   EXSECTED   EXSERTED
EXTENDER   INVISCID   NUANCING   PITPROPS   SUDSIEST   TARTLETS   TUFTLETS   UNDULOUS   UNRUEFUL
```

ABCADEBA ETHERATE RECRATER REDRAWER REGRATER REPRIMER REPROVER REWRITER SEASIDES
SENSATES SENSIZES SPYSHIPS

ABCADEBC CZECHIZE GANGSMAN REDRAPED SUBSHRUB TESTONES TESTULES TOSTADOS

ABCADEBD GANGLIAL INCITANT INVITANT

ABCADEBE INDIGENE REGRADED REPRISES RETRADED

```
ABCADEBF   ARMATURE   BARBICAN   CATCHMAN   COACTION   CRACKERS   CROCKERY   DAYDREAM   DEADLIER
DRUDGERS   DRUDGERY   DUODENUM   ENDERONS   ENTERING   GANGLIAC   GANGLIAR   INCIDENT   INDICANS
INDICANT   INDIGENA   INDIGENS   INDIGENT   INVIRONS   NEONATES   ONCOMING   POMPANOS   REARGUED
REARGUES   REARISEN   REARVIEW   REBRACED   REBRACES   RECRATED   RECRATES   REDRAPES   REDRIVEN
REDRIVES   REFRAMED   REFRAMES   REGRADES   REGRATED   REGRATES   REGRAVEL   REPRAYED   REPRICED
REPRICES   REPRIMED   REPRIMES   REPRISED   REPROVED   REPROVES   REPRUNED   REPRUNES   RETRACED
RETRACES   RETRADES   RETRAVEL   RETRAYED   REWRITES   SEASIDER   SEASONED   SEASONER   SENSATED
SENSIZED   SETSCREW   SLOSHILY   SLUSHILY   TEATIMES   TEXTILES   TEXTURED   TEXTURES   UNBUYING
UNDUKING   UNDULANT   UNHUMANS   UNLUCENT   UNLUTING   VALVEMAN   ZANZIBAR
```

ABCADECA GANGLING KICKBACK TASTIEST   **ABCADECD** ABRASERS

ABCADECE GANGRENE PORPHYRY PREPOSES RETRUSTS

```
ABCADECF   ABRADERS   AERATORS   AQUARIUM   AQUARIUS   AVIATRIX   AWEARIED   AWEATHER   BARBWIRE
CHECKIER   CHECKMEN   CINCHONA   CIRCLERS   COACHMAN   COACHWAY   CONCERNS   CONCHING   CRACKJAW
DANDLING   DANDYING   DENDRONS   DREDGIES   GARGLERS   GROGSHOP   HASHIEST   HITHERTO   IDLINGLY
INTIMATE   KIRKWARD   KIRKYARD   NURNBERG   OBLONGLY   PORPHYRA   PREPAVED   PREPAVES   PREPOSED
PREPUBES   PREPUCES   PROPANOL   PROPYLON   RETRACTS   RETRAITS   SEASONAL   SUNSHINE   SUNSHINY
TERTIARY   TILTABLE   TILTEDLY   TRUTHFUL   TURTLERS   UNLUCKLY
```

ABCADEDA CALCIFIC CALCITIC DANDERED DIADEMED SENSUOUS   **ABCADEDB** INDIAMAN

ABCADEDC GADGETED TOSTADAS   **ABCADEDE** CONCEDED PAMPERER

ABCADEDF CANCELED CANCELER CANCERED CIRCAEAN CIRCULUS CONCEDER CONCEDES CONCILIA

CRUCIFIX EMPERORS GINGERED HIGHERED HYPHENED NEONATAL PAMPERED PAUPERED POMPEYED
POMPILIA PROPANAL PROPENES PULPITIC PULPITIS PURPLELY RUBRIFIC SENSIFIC SUBSEWER
TARTENED TASTENED TAUTENED TILTERED UNFUELED UNRULILY VALVEMEN

ABCADEEA DEADWOOD SUBSILLS   **ABCADEEB** CALCUTTA   **ABCADEEC** BAYBERRY

ABCADEED BARBETTE

ABCADEEF BANBERRY BILBERRY BOWBELLS BOXBERRY BULBERRY COACHEES COACTEES CONCETTI
COUCHEES CRUCILLY DANDILLY FITFULLY INVITEES KICKOFFS KILKENNY MISMARRY PINPROOF
PULPWOOD RAMRODDY REDRILLS RETRALLY SUNSETTY TEXTBOOK TORTILLA

ABCADEFA AGNATHIA ALHAMBRA DENDROID EDGEBONE EDGEWISE ENLEAGUE ENSEMBLE ENTEMPLE
ENVEIGLE ENVELOPE ESTERIZE ETHERIZE EXPEDITE EXTERNAE GARGLING GURGLING HIGHBUSH
LADLEFUL SHUSWAPS SHYSTERS SKYSAILS SLASHERS SLOSHERS SLUSHERS SLUSHIES SMASHERS
SMASHUPS SPASMOUS SPASTICS SUASIONS SUASIVES SUBSALTS SUBSECTS SUBSIDES SUBSIGNS
SUBSOILS SUNSPOTS SWASHERS SWISHERS TEXTUIST TUFTIEST

ABCADEFB ADVANCED ASHANTIS ASKANCES CONCERTO CRACKIER CROCKIER CRUCIFER DEADLINE
DENDRITE HENHOUSE INDIAMEN OENOCYTE REAROUSE REBRIDGE REBRONZE REFRINGE RETRIBUE
SEASHORE SENSABLE SENSIBLE TEATLIKE TENTABLE TENTACLE TENTICLE TENTLIKE TENTWISE
TESTABLE TESTICLE UNBURDEN ZARZUELA

ABCADEFC AGNATION ALTARIST BEDBOARD BURBLIER CHECKAGE CIRCULAR EAGERING EDGELING
EDGELONG ELSEWAYS EXTERNAT GANGLION GANGSMEN HUSHINGS HUSHIONS IGNITRON INDICTED
INSIDERS INSIGHTS MISMAKES MISMATES MISMEANS MISMOVES PREPLACE PURPOSER RETROACT
RETROFIT SWASTIKA TASTINGS TECTONIC TESTINGS UNDULOID UNDUMPED UNDUSTED UNRULIER
UPSURGES

ABCADEFD ABRASHES BARBECUE CONCEIVE CZECHISH DREDGING DRUDGING EXTERIOR INCISORS
KICKSEYS MALMSEYS PROPENSE REURGING SUBSERVE SUBSTANT SUBSTRAT UNBUDGED UNBUSHES
UNBUSIES UNJUDGED UPRUSHES

ABCADEFE BOMBASTS CIRCUSES CONCISES CONCRETE CROCUSES FUNFESTS GANGISMS HYPHAENE
OBSOLETE OCTOPEDE ONLOADED PADPIECE POMPISTS PREPOSTS PURPOSES REGRASPS SUBSIDED
TACTISMS TERTIANA UNCURDED UNCURSES UNGUIDED UNPURSES

ABCADEFF BARBLESS CHECKOFF CHICADEE DANDRUFF HIGHBALL HIGHNESS ICKINESS INDICTEE
KICKBALL KICKLESS NOUNLESS POMPLESS PROPHYLL PROPLESS PUMPLESS TACTLESS TARTNESS
TAUTNESS TINTLESS

ABCADEFG ABLATING ABLATION ABLATIVE ABLATORS ABRADING ABRASING ABRASION ABRASIVE
ACRAZING ACUATING ACUATION ADJACENT ADRAWING ADVANCER ADVANCES AERATING AERATION
AFEARING AIDANCES ALBACORE ALBATROS ALKAMINE AMIABLER ANTACIDS AQUATICS AQUATILE
AQUATING AQUATION AQUATONE ARCADING ARCANELY ARCANIST AREADING AREALITY ARYANISM
ARYANIST ARYANIZE ASLAKING ASPARKLE AUDACITY AUTARCHY AVIATORS AVIATORY BARBIZON
BAUBLERY BAUBLING BIOBLAST BOMBACES BOMBARDS BOMBLINE BOWBACKS BUGBEARS BUGBITES
BULBIEST BUMBLERS BUMBLING CALCEDON CALCINED CALCINER CALCINES CANCROID CARCINUS
CATCHERS CATCHFLY CATCHIER CATCHING CATCHMEN CATCHUPS CHACKERS CHACKING CHACKLED
CHACKLER CHACKLES CHECKING CHECKMAN CHECKROW CHECKUPS CHICAGOS CHICANED CHICANER
CHICANES CHICKENS CHICKERS CHICKERY CHICKORY CHOCKERS CHOCKING CHOCKLER CHOCKMAN

```
CHOCKMEN CHOCTAWS CHUCKERS CHUCKIES CHUCKING CHUCKLED CHUCKLER CHUCKLES CINCHERS
CINCTURE CIRCLETS CIRCULED CIRCULES CIRCUSED CLACKERS CLACKETY CLACKING CLICKERS
CLICKETS CLOCKERS CLOCKING CLUCKING COACHERS COACHFUL COACHIES COACHING COACHMEN
COACTING COACTIVE COLCINES CONCAUSE CONCAVED CONCAVER CONCAVES CONCEALS CONCEITS
CONCEITY CONCEPTS CONCERTI CONCERTS CONCHERS CONCHIES CONCILED CONCILES CONCISED
CONCISER CONCLAVE CONCLUDE CONCRETA CONCREWS COUCHANT COUCHERS COUCHIER COUCHING
CRACKING CRACKLED CRACKLES CRACKNEL CRACKPOT CRICKETS CRICKETY CRICKLED CRICKLES
CROCKETS CROCKING CROCUSED CRUCIANS CRUCIATE CRUCIBLE CUPCAKES DANDIEST DANDLERS
DANDYISH DANDYISM DANDYIZE DAWDLERS DAWDLING DEADBORN DEADLOCK DENDRIUM DEWDROPS
DIADERMS DOLDRUMS DOWDIEST DOWDYISH DOWDYISM DRUDGISM DUODENAL EAVEDROP ECHELONS
EDGERMAN EDGEWAYS ELBERTAS ELDERMAN EMPEARLS ENDEAVOR ENDEMIAL ENDEMICS ENDERMIC
ENHEARTS ENTERICS ENTEROID ENVELOPS EPHEDRIN ESPECIAL ESTERIFY ETHENOLS ETHENYLS
ETHERIAL ETHERIFY ETHERISM ETHEROUS EUGENIAS EUGENICS EUGENISM EUGENIST EXCEPTOR
EXCERPTA EXCERPTS EXPEDING EXPERTLY EXTENDLY EXTENSOR EXTERNAL EXTERNAS EXTERNLY
EXTERNUM FANFOLDS FARFETCH FIEFDOMS FORFEITS FORFENDS GADGETRY GANGLIER GANGSTER
GARGOYLE GINGERLY GINGHAMS GORGEDLY GUDGEONS HIGHBORN HIGHBOYS HIGHBRED HIGHBROW
HIGHLAND HIGHLOWS HIGHMOST HIGHROAD HIGHTOBY HIGHWAYS HOGHEADS HOGHERDS HOPHEADS
HOTHEADS HUSHABLE HUSHABLY HUSHEDLY IGNIFORM IGNITERS IGNITORS IMPINGED IMPINGER
IMPINGES IMPISHLY INBIRTHS INCISELY INCISORY INCISURE INCITERS INCITORY INDICATE
INDICTER INDICTOR INDIGEST INDIGOES INDIRECT INDITERS INFIDELS INFIEDLS INFILTER
INFIRMED INFIRMLY INGIRDLE INGIVERS INLISTED INTIMACY INTIMADO INTIMOUS INTIRELY
INVIABLE INVIABLY INVICTED INVIGORS INVIGOUR INVITERS INVITORS KICKABLE KICKOUTS
KINKABLE KIRKTOWN KWAKIUTL LAPLINGS LEYLANDS LOWLANDS LOWLIEST LOWLIFES LOWLIVES
LOWLYING MAIMEDLY MARMELOS MARMITES MARMOSET MERMAIDS MIDMONTH MIDMORNS MISMATCH
MISMATED MISMOVED MURMANSK NOINTERS NOUNIZED NOUNIZES OBROGATE OCTOBERS OCTOGAMY
ODIOUSLY OLEOSITY ONCOMERS ORDOVIAN OUTOVENS PAMPHLET PEOPLING PEOPLISH PIEPLANT
PIMPLOUS PINPATCH POMPEIAN POMPIERS PORPHINE PORPHINS PREPACKS PREPANIC PREPLANS
PREPLANT PREPLOTS PREPUBIC PREPUBIS PROPAGED PROPAGES PROPALED PROPALES PROPANES
PROPENYL PROPHECY PROPHESY PROPHETS PROPJETS PROPLASM PROPULSE PROPYLIC PULPIEST
PULPITED PULPITER PUMPABLE PUMPABLY PUMPINGS PUMPKINS PUMPLIKE PURPLEST PURPLING
PURPLISH PURPOINT PURPOSED REARINGS REARLING REARMING REARMOST REBRAIDS REBRANCH
REBRANDS REBRICKS REBRINGS REBROACH REBROWNS RECRAMPS RECRANKS RECROWDS RECROWNS
RECRUITS RECRUITY REDRAFTS REDRYING REFRACTS REFRAINS REFROIDS REFRONTS REGRAFTS
REGRANTS REGRINDS REGROUND REGROUPS REGROWTH REORDAIN REPRINTS REPRISAL REPROACH
REPROVAL REPRYING RETRACKS RETRAINS RETRAMPS RETRANCH RETRIALS RETRUING RETRYING
RIBROAST RIMROCKS ROARINGS RUBRICAL RUBRICAS RUBRICED SANSCRIT SANSERIF SANSKRIT
SEASCOUT SENSIBLY SENSICAL SKYSCAPE SKYSHINE SLASHING SLOSHIER SLOSHING SLUSHIER
SLUSHING SLUSHPIT SMASHING SOLSTICE SOLSTICY STASHIED STASHING SUASIBLE SUBSCALE
SUBSHAFT SUBSHIRE SUBSHOCK SUBSIDER SUBSOLAR SUBSOLID SUBSONIC SUBSPACE SUBSTAGE
SUBSTILE SUBSTOCK SUBSTORY SUBSTYLE SUBSYNOD SUNSHADE SWASHIER SWASHING TACTILES
TANTRUMS TASTEFUL TENTFULS TENTWORK TERTIALS TERTIANS TEUTONIC TEXTUALS TEXTUARY
TEXTURAL TILTYARD TINTYPER TINTYPES TOLTECAN TORTUGAS TRITAPHS TRITONAL TRITONES
TROTHFUL TROTHING TROTLINE TRUTHING TUFTINGS TURTLING TWITCHED TWITCHER TWITCHES
TWITLARK UNBUCKLE UNBUILDS UNBUMPED UNBUOYED UNBURIAL UNBURIED UNBURIES UNBUSHED
UNBUSIED UNBUSILY UNBUSKED UNCULTED UNCUMBER UNCURBED UNCURLED UNCURSED UNCUSPED
UNDULATE UNDUTIES UNFURLED UNFUTILE UNGUARDS UNGUILED UNGUILTY UNGULATE UNGULPED
UNHUMBLE UNHUMBLY UNHURLED UNHURTED UNHUSKED UNJUDGES UNJUICED UNJUSTLY UNLUMPED
UNMULISH UNMUSKED UNMUSTED UNPUBLIC UNPUCKER UNPURELY UNPURGED UNPURLED UNPURSED
UNPUSHED UNPUTRID UNQUAYED UNQUIETS UNQUOTED UNQUOTES UNRUMPLE UNRUSHED UNRUSTED
UNRUSTIC UNSUBTLE UNSUBTLY UNSUCKED UNSUGARY UNSUITED UNSULTRY UNSURETY UNTUCKED
UNTURBID UNTURFED UNTURGID UNTUSKED UNVULGAR UPBUILDS UPCURLED UPCURVED UPCURVES
```

UPFURLED UPRUSHED UPSURGED UPTURNED URSULINE VALVIFER VALVINGS WARWICKS WAXWINGS
WAXWORKS WEBWORMS

ABCBAABA REFERRER SECESSES   **ABCBAABD** LEVELLED LEVELLER REFERRED

ABCBAADE REFERRAL   **ABCBABAD** REVERERS

ABCBABBD REFEREED REFEREES REVEREES   **ABCBABCB** BARABARA LAVALAVA TIKITIKI

ABCBABDA MINIMISM

ABCBABDE CIVICISM CIVICIZE DECEDENT DIVIDING FINIFIED FINIFIES LEVELERS MINIMITE
MINIMIZE REFERENT REVEREND REVERENT

ABCBADAE MINIMUMS   **ABCBADBA** RESERVER REVERSER REVERTER SENESCES

ABCBADBB RESERVEE   **ABCBADBC** BEDEBTED RESERVES   **ABCBADBD** REVERSES

ABCBADBE LEVELMEN RADARMAN REJERKED REMERGED REMERGES RENERVED RENERVES RESERVED
REVERBED REVERIES REVERSED REVERTED SEMESTER SENESCED

ABCBADCE TOPOTYPE   **ABCBADEA** DIVIDEND GARAGING RESERVOR STETSONS

ABCBADEB REDERIVE REPERUSE RESERATE TELETAPE TELETYPE

ABCBADEF ARMRACKS CAPACITY CATACOMB DECEDING DIVIDANT DIVIDENT DIVIDERS DIVIDUAL
KAYAKERS KAYAKING LAVALIER LAVALIKE LEVELING LEVELISH LEVELISM LEVELMAN LOYOLISM
LOYOLIST MADAMING MALAMUTE MONOMERS MONOMIAL PARAPETS PARAPHED REPERMIT REVERIFY
REVERING REVERIST REVERSAL REVERTAL SINISTER SINISTRA TAXATION TAXATIVE TAXATORS
TELETHON TERETIAL UNINURED WEREWOLF

ABCBBABA DESEEDED   **ABCBBCBC** REDEEDED   **ABCBBDBA** REDEEMER

ABCBBDBC REDEEMED   **ABCBBDBD** RESEEDED VENEERER

ABCBBDBE REHEELED VENEERED   **ABCBBDEA** STUTTERS

ABCBBDEF BESEEING BESEEMLY LEVEEING RESEEING SALAAMED   **ABCBCDAD** MONONYMY

ABCBCDAE MONONYMS   **ABCBCDBA** REMEMBER   **ABCBCDCB** PREREFER

ABCBCDEE ROTOTILL TININESS

ABCBCDEF CATATONY DININGLY LOGOGRAM PREREADY PREREGAL PREREMIT PRERENAL PRERENTS
PROROGUE PROROYAL QUEUEING REDEDUCT SORORITY SORORIZE STATABLE

ABCBDABA DEFENDED DELEADED DEPENDED STATISTS

ABCBDABE DEFENDER DEGENDER DEPENDER MAHATMAS METERMEN REGEARED

ABCBDACE PRERIPEN   **ABCBDADE** RIVIERES

ABCBDAEA SOLOISTS STATISMS STATUSES   **ABCBDAEB** REHEARSE

ABCBDAEF GIBINGLY GIVINGLY METERMAN MONOAMID MOTORMAN MOTORMEN RELEARNS RESEARCH
RIVIERAS TUMULTED TUMULTER UPSPRUNG

ABCBDBAA SERENESS   **ABCBDBAC** CATARACT RESEVERS

ABCBDBAE CARAPACE MACADAMS MONOSOME RECEDERS REDEFERS RENEGERS RENEWERS REVELERS
SERENEST SEVEREST TIMIDITY

ABCBDBBA REVENEER   **ABCBDBBE** KEGEREES   **ABCBDBCA** TENEMENT

ABCBDBCE DIVISIVE FINIKING FINITING HOMONOMY LAYAWAYS MONOGONY MONOTONE MONOTONY
PANAMANS RELEVELS

ABCBDBDA SEVERERS

ABCBDBDE DEFERERS DIVINING HAVANANS LEVERERS METERERS VENERERS

ABCBDBEA SECEDERS SEVENERS SINIFIES SOLOMONS SONOROUS SOPOROUS STATUTES

ABCBDBEB CARAGANA DOLOROSO GENEVESE MAHARAJA MAHARANA

ABCBDBEC MONOZOAN REDEPEND VENEREAN VIGILING

ABCBDBED FINITIST REBESETS REDETECT   **ABCBDBEE** FETELESS HERENESS

ABCBDBEF AIRIFIED BEVELERS CALABASH CALAMARY CARAVANS CATALANS CEMETERY CITIFIED
CIVILIAN CIVILISE CIVILIST CIVILITE CIVILITY CIVILIZE COLOTOMY DEFERENT DEGENERS
DELETERY DIGITIZE DIMINISH DIMITIES DIVINIFY DIVINITY DIVINIZE DIVISION DOXOLOGY
FARADAYS FARAWAYS FILIPINO FINICISM FINITIES FINITISM FINITIVE FIXIDITY FIXITIES
GALAHADS GALAVANT HOMOLOGS HOMOLOGY HONOROUS HOROLOGE HOROLOGY JEWELERS JEZEBELS
LIAISING LIMITIES LIMITING LIMITIVE LIVIDITY LOBOTOMY LOCOMOTE MALAGASY MALAYANS
MILITIAS MONOLOGS MONOPODE MONOPOLE MONOPOLY MONOSOPE MONOZOIC NAGASAKI NIHILIFY
NIHILISM NIHILIST NIHILITY PAJAMAED PIXIEISH RAMADANS REBEGETS REBEHELD RECEDENT
REDEFEAT RESELECT RIGIDIFY RIGIDIST RIGIDITY SERENELY SEVERELY SICILIAN SILICIDE
SILICIFY SILICIUM SILICIZE SIMILING SIMILITY SIMILIZE STATUTED TAMARACK TOPOLOGY
TOPONOMY TOXOLOGY TUBULURE VEHEMENT VENEREAL VICINITY VIGILIES VILIFIED VILIFIER
VILIFIES VIRILITY VISITING YAMANAIS

ABCBDCBA DETECTED DETESTED RESEISER

ABCBDCBE DETECTER DETENTES DETESTER PARAGRAM RETESTED

ABCBDCCE FILIALLY   **ABCBDCEA** PARADROP RETENTOR

ABCBDCEB DEAERATE DEPEOPLE REPEOPLE

ABCBDCEF CEREBRAL CEREBRIN CEREBRUM DETECTOR HEREFROM ISOSCOPE ISOSPORE MINIONLY
MUTUATED MUTUATES PEREGRIN PINIONED STATUARY SUBURBAN SUBURBED SUBURBIA TELEPLAY
UNINVITE VACANCES VITIATED VITIATES VITIATOR

ABCBDDBA DEBELLED DEFERRED DETERRED HADASSAH REBELLER RECESSER RELETTER REPELLER RESELLER RESETTER REVELLER SAVANNAS

ABCBDDBD BEWEDDED COLOSSOS DEFERRER JEWESSES REBEDDED RECESSES REWEDDED

ABCBDDBE BEFETTER BEFEZZED BEGEMMED BEGETTER BELETTER BEPENNED BESETTER BEVELLED BEVELLER BEWETTED BEZELLED HAWAIIAN JEWELLED JEWELLER MALACCAS MOROCCOS REBEGGED REBELLED RECESSED REFELLED REPEGGED REPELLED REPENNED REVELLED REVETTED REWETTED SAVANNAH TOMORROW

ABCBDDEA COLOSSIC DIMISSED REBEGGAR RECESSOR RELESSOR   **ABCBDDEB** RESETTLE

ABCBDDEC COLOSSAL HARASSER   **ABCBDDED** COLOSSUS HARASSES PARALLEL

ABCBDDEF AUBUSSON CABALLED CABALLER CANALLED CANALLER CATARRHS COROLLAS DECESSOR DEFERRAL GOMORRAH GOMORRHA HARASSED JAPANNED JAPANNER LIPIZZAN MOROCCAN PARAFFIN TOBOGGAN TOBOGGIN

ABCBDEAA SAVAGESS SIZINESS

ABCBDEAB LEVEABLE PENELOPE REBEMIRE RECENTRE REDESIRE VEGETIVE

ABCBDEAC ENSNARES SATANIST   **ABCBDEAE** ENSNARER NAZARENE

ABCBDEAF ANONYMAL AUGURIAL AUGUSTAL AUGUSTAN AUTUMNAL EARACHES EATABLES ENDNOTES ENSNARED ENSNOWED EUNUCHED LIKINGLY LIVINGLY MINICAMS MONOGAMY NOMOGENY PARATYPE POROTYPE RAVAGERS REVESTRY SATANISM SAVAGEST SAVAGISM SEVERISH SODOMIST SOLONIST TABARETS TELEPATH TEMERITY TUBULATE TUBULETS UPSPROUT

ABCBDEBA DECEASED DECEIVED DEFEATED DEFECTED DEFENCED DEFENSED DEGERMED DEJECTED DEMEANED DEMENTED DEMERGED DEMERSED DEPERMED DESEAMED DESERTED DESERVED DETERMED DEVESTED MOTORDOM NATALIAN NAZAREAN REBEAMER RECEIVER RECENTER REGENDER REGESTER REHEATER REJECTER RELEASER REPEALER REPEATER REPENTER RESEIZER RESENTER RETEMPER RETENDER REVEALER REVENDER REVENGER REVENUER REVESTER SEDENTES SEVERIES SEWERIES

ABCBDEBB REJECTEE RELEASEE SELECTEE

ABCBDEBC BEDECKED BEREAVER CANADIAN DESERVES GALAXIAL MALARIAL PALATIAL PANACEAN REDECKED REDEFIED REDENIED RESEIZES

ABCBDEBD AUGUSTUS BEHEDGED CANASTAS CELESTES DEMESNES DESERTER DESERVER REHEDGED REMEDIED UNINTENT

ABCBDEBE BEHEADED DECEASES DEFENSES LEGENDED REBENDED RECENSES REHEADED RELEASES REMEADED REMENDED REPEASES REWELDED REWENDED

ABCBDEBF AUGUROUS BAHAMIAN BAVARIAN BEFERNED BEHEDGES BEMEANED BEREAVED BEREAVEN BESEAMED BEVEILED CEMENTED CEMENTER CUMULOUS DECEIVER DECEIVES DECEMBER DECENTER DEFEATER DEFENCES DEFENSER DEMERGES DETENUES DETERGES FENESTER FILICOID GALACTAN GALATEAS GALAXIAN INUNDANT JAMAICAN JAMAICAS LEVERMEN MALARIAN MALARIAS MARATHAS PANACEAS PARAGUAY PARAXIAL PARAZOAN PETERMEN REBEATEN REBELIEF RECEIVED RECEIVES

RECENSED RECEPTED REDEFIES REDENIES REFECTED REFENCED REFENCES REGENTED REGESTED
REHEALED REHEAPED REHEATED REHEDGES REHELMED REJECTED RELEAPED RELEASED RELENTED
RELEVIED RELEVIES REMEDIES REMELTED RENESTED REPEALED REPEASED REPEATED REPENTED
RESEALED RESEAMED RESEATED RESECTED RESEIZED RESENTED RETENUES REVEALED REVEILED
REVENGED REVENGES REVENTED REVENUED REVENUES REVESHED REVESTED REWEAKEN REWEAVED
REWEAVES SELECTED SEWERMEN TELEVIEW TUBULOUS TUMULOUS UNENDING UNINSANE UNKNOWNS
VAGARIAN VENERIES VISIONIC VISITRIX

ABCBDECA SONORANS   **ABCBDECB** HEREFORE REDECIDE

ABCBDECD MANAGING MONOTINT RENEGING

ABCBDECF COLONELS CORONARY CORONERS FATALITY FUTURITY HEREFORD HEREWARD HOMOGAMY
HOMONYMS HONORING KITIMATS LINIMENT LITIGATE MITIGATE MONOGENA MONOGENY NATALITY
OILINGLY OLDLANDS PARADERS PARAFORM RENEWING RETEMPTS SELECTLY SONORANT STATEWAY
STATICAL TELEFILM UNENVIED UNINLAID UPSPLASH VENERANT VENERING

ABCBDEDB VEGETATE   **ABCBDEDC** DETENANT RETENANT

ABCBDEDE DEMERARA HONOLULU

ABCBDEDF COLORERS DIGITATE HONORARY HONORERS LIMITATE MILITATE PAEANING PROREBEL
PRURITIC REVENANT SERENING SEVENING TRIREMES UNANELED VIRILELY VISITATE

ABCBDEEB REVEILLE   **ABCBDEEC** VISITEES

ABCBDEEF CARAGEEN HONOREES LOCOWEED MACAROON MUTUALLY PARAKEET SPYPROOF UNKNOTTY

ABCBDEFA CELERIAC CEREALIC DAMASKED DIMINUED HEREWITH MONOGRAM MORONISM MOTORISM
MOTORIUM NOVOCAIN RECENSOR RECEPTOR REJECTOR RELEASOR SABAYONS SALARIES SARACENS
SEVENTHS SEVERALS SILICONS SIMILARS SIMITARS SODOMIES SOJOURNS STATICES STATIONS
STATIVES STATIZES STATURES STITCHES SUBUNITS TELECAST TELEPORT TELEPOST TIMIDEST

ABCBDEFB BENEFICE BEVERAGE CASANOVA CAVATINA COLORADO CORONADO DECENTRE DEFECATE
DELEGATE DELETIVE DENEGATE DEVELOPE FEDERATE GALACTIA GENERALE GENERATE HEGELIZE
HETERIZE ISOSTERS LEGENDRE LEVERAGE METERAGE PARABOLA PARANOIA PARASITA PASADENA
PRORATER REBECAME REBECOME REBETAKE REDEBATE REDEFINE REDEMISE REDEVISE REDEVOTE
REGELATE RELEGATE RELEVATE REMENACE RENEGADE RENEGATE RESEMBLE SARATOGA SELENIDE
SELENITE SERENADE SERENIZE SEVERANE SEVERATE SEVERIZE SEWERAGE TELEVISE VENERATE
YEMENITE

ABCBDEFC AUGURING BOSOMERS CASAQUES CATALYST CATAPULT COLONIAL COLORFUL ENSNARLS
FATALIST FUTURIST INSNARES INSNARLS JOYOUSLY LITIGANT MARAUDER MITIGANT MOTORIST
PAEANIZE PARAMOUR PREROUTE REDEMAND TAGALONG UNENTIRE UNSNARES UNSNARLS UPSPEARS
VENERIAN VENETIAN VISIBLES VISITERS VISITORS

ABCBDEFD DAMAGING DAMASCUS DIVISORS FINISHES GALACTIC GAMASHES HAZARDER HIBISCUS
LIAISONS MALAPROP MILITANT MONOSKIS MOTORCAR PARASOLS RAVAGING SAVAGING SOLONIAN
TABASCOS VEGETANT VISITANT

ABCBDEFE ARMRESTS CANARDED COLOURER CORONATA FUGUISTS FUTURAMA HAVANESE HAZARDED

HOMOGENE HOMOTYPY HONOURER HUMULENE INSNARER ISOSCELE JAPANESE JAVANESE MALAISES
MARAUDED MATABELE NAVALESE POLOISTS POLONESE RECENSUS TABARDED TOGOLESE YOKOHAMA

ABCBDEFF AIRINESS DIVINESS EPIPHYLL FILIGREE HONORESS OILINESS PITILESS TIDINESS
WILINESS WIRINESS

ABCBDEFG ANONYMES APOPLEXY ASHSTONE ASYSTOLE AUGURIES AUGURISM AUGURIST AUGURIZE
AUGUSTLY AUTUMNER BALANCED BALANCER BALANCES BANALITY BASALTIC BENEDICT BENEFACT
BENEFITS BEVELING BEZELING BILIATED BILIATES BILINEAR BITINGLY BIWINTER BOLOGNAS
BOLONEYS BOROUGHS BOSOMING CABALISM CABALIST CABALIZE CABARETS CADAVERS CALADIUM
CALAMINE CALAMITE CALAMITY CALANDER CANALIZE CANARIES CANARIUM CANASTER CARABINE
CARABOID CARAVELS CATALOGS CATALYZE CAVALIER CELERITY CEMENTAL CEREMONY CILIATED
CILIATES CILIFORM CITIZENS COJOINED COLOGNES COLOMBIN COLONATE COLONIES COLONIST
COLONIZE COLORANT COLORATE COLORIES COLORING COLORISM COLORIST COLORIZE COLORMAN
COLORMEN COLOURED CONOIDAL CORONALS CORONATE CORONELS CORONETS CORONIUM COYOTING
CUMULANT CUMULATE CUMULOSE CUPULATE DAMAGERS DAMASKIN DECENARY DECENTLY DEFECANT
DEFECTOR DEFENSOR DEJECTLY DELEGACY DELEGANT DELETING DELETION DELETORY DEMEANOR
DEMENTIA DEMENTIS DEMERITS DERELICT DESERTIC DESEXING DEVELOPS DIGITALS DILIGENT
DIMINUTE DIRIGENT DISINTER DISINURE DIVINELY DIVINERS DIVINEST DIVINYLS DIVISORY
DOLOMITE DOLOMIZE EPIPHANY EPIPLASM EUNUCHAL EUNUCHRY FACADING FANATICS FANATISM
FATALISM FATALIZE FEDERACY FEDERALS FEVERING FEVERISH FEVEROUS FILIATED FILIATES
FINIALED FINICKED FINISHED FINISHER FINITARY FINITELY FINITORS FINITUDE FUTURELY
FUTURING FUTURISM FUTURIZE GADABOUT GALATINE GALAXIES GARAMOND GENERALS GENERICS
GENEROUS GENETICS GONOTYPE GURUSHIP HARANGUE HEGELIAN HEGEMONS HEGEMONY HEREDITY
HEREINTO HERETICS HEREUNTO HEREUPON HETERISM HOLOTYPE HOMOGENS HOMOGENY HOMOTAXY
HOMOTYPE HONORIAL HONOURED HUGUENOT ICECRAFT INUNDATE JALAPENO JAPANERS JAPANESY
JAPANISM JAPANIZE JEREMIAH JEWELING JOCOSELY JOCOSITY JUGULARS JUGULARY JUGULATE
KIBITZED KIBITZER KIBITZES KITISHLY LAMASERY LAVATORY LAXATING LAXATION LAXATIVE
LAZARIST LEGENDIC LEGENDRY LEPERDOM LEPEROUS LEVERING LEVERMAN LIMITARY LIMITEDS
LIMITERS LOGOTYPE LUXURIES LUXURIST LUXURITY MACARONI MACARONS MAGAZINE MAGAZINY
MALADIES MALARKEY MANACLED MANACLES MANAGERS MANAGERY MARABOUS MARANTIC MARATHON
MATADORE MATADORS METEORIC METERING MIDIRONS MILITARY MINICARS MINISTER MINISTRY
MINIVERS MISINFER MISINTER MOLOKANI MONOACID MONOBASE MONOCLED MONOCLES MONOCRAT
MONOCULE MONOCYTE MONODISC MONODISK MONODIZE MONOFILS MONOFUEL MONOLITH MONOPACK
MONOPTIC MONORAIL MONOTYPE MONOXIDE MORONITY MOROSELY MOROSITY MOTOCARS MOTORBUS
MOTORCAB MOTORIAL MOTORING MOTORIZE MOTORWAY NAPALMED NASALITY NASALIZE NAVAHOES
NAVAJOES NAVALISM NAVALIST NOBODIES NUCULIDS NUCULOID PACATELY PACATING PACATION
PACATIVE PAEANISM PAGANDOM PAGANISH PAGANISM PAGANIST PAGANITY PAGANIZE PALACING
PALADINE PALADINS PALAMINO PALATINE PALATIVE PALATIZE PALAVERS PANACHED PANACHES
PARABLED PARABLES PARADIGM PARADING PARADISE PARADOXY PARAGONS PARALOGY PARALYSE
PARALYZE PARANOIC PARANOID PARASITE PATAGONS PEDERAST PEDESTAL PELERINS PETERING
PETERMAN PICIFORM PILIFERS PILIFORM PIMIENTO PITIABLE PITIABLY PITIEDLY POLONIUM
POLONIUS POLONIZE POROSITY POROUSLY PRERADIO PREROYAL PRORATED PRORATES PRURIENT
RAPACITY REBEGINS REBEHOLD REBELDOM REBELONG REBESTOW REBEWAIL RECEDING RECEIPTS
RECEIVAL RECENTLY REDEBITS REDELAYS REDEPLOY REDESIGN REFEIGNS RELEVANT REMEDIAL
REMEDING REMETALS REMEWING REPEWING RESEWING RESEXING REVELANT REVELING REVELOUS
REVETING REWEIGHS REWEIGHT RIDICULE ROBOTIAN ROBOTISM ROBOTIZE ROTONDAS SAGAMORE
SALACITY SALADING SALAMING SALARIED SANATORY SARAJEVO SATANIZE SAVAGELY SAVAGERY
SAVAGIZE SECEDING SELECTOR SELENIUM SERENDIP SERENIFY SERENITY SEVERING SEVERITY
SEWERING SEWERMAN SIBILANT SIBILATE SILICATE SILICEAN SILICONE SIMILARY SIMILATE
SODOMITE SODOMIZE SOJOURED SONORITY SONORIZE STATELDY STATEFUL STATIZED STATUING

STATURED STITCHED STITCHER SUTURING TAMARIND TAMARINS TAMARISK TAXABLES TELEGRAM
TELEMARK TIMIDOUS TIRINGLY TOBOGANS TUBULARY TUBULOSE UNANCHOR UNGNAWED UNINODAL
UNKNAVES UNKNIGHT UNKNOWER UNSNARED UNSNATCH UNSNOWED UPSPREAD VACANTED VACANTER
VACANTLY VACANTRY VACATING VACATION VAGABOND VAGARIED VAGARIES VAGARISH VAGARIST
VAGARITY VALANCED VALANCES VANADIUM VEGETALS VEGETISM VENERIAL VENEROUS VENETICS
VETERANS VIGILANT VIGILATE VINIFERA VIRIDANS VIRIDATE VISIGOTH VISIONAL VISIONED
VISIONER WEBERIAN YOHOURTS

ABCCABCC CHOOCHOO WELLWELL **ABCCABDE** LITTLING LITTLISH RATTRAPS

ABCCACDE TWEETERS **ABCCADCB** HELLHOLE TELLTALE

ABCCADCC LOSSLESS RIFFRAFF **ABCCADCE** TWEETLED TWEETLES

ABCCADEA SWOOSHES **ABCCADEB** MESSMATE **ABCCADEC** LITTLEST

ABCCADEF BELLBIRD FULLFACE MISSMARK OUTTOWER PASSPORT SETTSMAN SLOOSHED SWOOSHED
TREETOPS TWEETING WALLWISE WALLWORK

ABCCBADA SUFFUSES **ABCCBADD** RAPPAREE

ABCCBADE BARRABLE BATTABLE BATTABLY NIPPINGS SUFFUSED TANNATES TINNITUS

ABCCBBDE LOWWOODS **ABCCBCAD** GINNINGS **ABCCBCDA** SINNINGS

ABCCBCDE BAGGAGER BAGGAGES HITTITES MINNINGS PINNINGS POWWOWED POWWOWER TINNINGS
WEDDEDLY WINNINGS

ABCCBDAD MILLIEME **ABCCBDAE** LEGGEDLY MILLIAMP SILLIEST

ABCCBDBA HAGGADAH SUCCUBUS **ABCCBDBC** FERRETER REDDENED

ABCCBDBD FETTERER LETTERER

ABCCBDBE BACCARAT BILLIKIN CARRAWAY FALLAWAY FERRETED FETTERED HELLENES KENNELED
LESSENED LESSENER LETTERED PELLETED PELLETER VESSELED

ABCCBDCE BARRATRY BIGGINGS CALLABLE DIGGINGS FALLABLE FALLABLY FIGGINGS HOLLOWLY
PIGGINGS RIGGINGS WIGGINGS

ABCCBDDE KENNELLY

ABCCBDEA DOGGONED DOLLOPED SABBATHS SIPPINGS SITTINGS SKOOKUMS SUCCUMBS TINNIEST
TIPPIEST

ABCCBDEB BARRANCA BATTALIA

ABCCBDEC BORROWER CORROBER CORRODER DESSERTS FISSIONS HISSINGS MASSAGES MISSILES
MISSIONS MISSIVES NARRATER NARRATOR NITTIEST PASSAGES PASSANTS SORROWER WASSAILS
WITTIEST

ABCCBDED BALLADED BALLASTS CORRODED HARRASES   ABCCBDEE MACCABEE

ABCCBDEF BALLADER BALLADIC BALLADRY BARRACKS BARRAGED BARRAGES BIDDINGS BILLIARD
BILLINGS BILLIONS BITTINGS BORROWED BOTTOMED BOTTOMER CABBAGED CABBAGER CABBAGES
CANNABIS CATTAILS COLLOIDS COLLOQUY COMMODES COMMONED COMMONER COMMONLY CONNOTED
CONNOTES CORRODES COTTONED COTTONER DILLINGS DIPPIEST DIPPINGS DIZZIEST FATTABLE
FERREOUS FIGGIEST FILLINGS FINNICKY FINNIEST FITTINGS FIZZIEST FOLLOWED FOLLOWER
GALLANTS GIDDIEST GIMMICKS GIMMICKY GINNIEST GUTTURAL HAGGARDS HELLENIC HILLIEST
HIPPIEST HOLLOWED HOLLOWER JIBBINGS JILLIONS KILLINGS LAGGARDS LIPPIZAN MALLARDS
MAPPABLE MASSACRE MASSAGED MASSAGER MILLIBAR MILLIERS MILLINER MILLINGS MILLIONS
MILLIPED MISSIBLE MISSIBLY NARRATED NARRATES NETTEDLY NIPPIEST OUTTURNS PASSABLE
PASSABLY PASSAGED PASSAGER PATTABLE PETTEDLY PIGGIEST PILLIONS PITTINGS RATTAILS
RATTANED RIBBIEST RIBBINGS RIDDINGS RIPPINGS SABBATIC SARRAZIN SORROWED SUCCUBAE
TANNABLE TAPPABLE TARRAGON TILLICUM TIPPINGS VALLANCE VALLANCY VASSALED VASSALIC
VASSALRY VETTEDLY WAGGABLE WAGGABLY WARRANTS WARRANTY WATTAGES WETTEDLY WIGGIEST
WILLIAMS WILLINGS WINNIPEG WITTINGS ZEPPELIN ZILLIONS ZIPPIEST ZIPPINGS

ABCCCDEE WALLLESS   ABCCDABE MERRYMEN TAFFETAS

ABCCDACE BILLABLE BILLABLY NAGGINGS NOGGINGS OUTTROTS

ABCCDACE COSSACKS PITTYPAT   ABCCDADA ROLLERER RUBBERER

ABCCDADC RUDDERED   ABCCDADE ROLLERED RUBBERED SUBBASAL TURRETED WELLAWAY

ABCCDAEA SUBBASES SUGGESTS SUMMISTS SUPPOSES   ABCCDAEB BEGGABLE FLEETFUL

ABCCDAED BILLYBOY BULLYBOY

ABCCDAEF BIDDABLE BIDDABLY BUFFABLE BUFFABLY COLLECTS CONNECTS COPPICED COPPICES
CORRECTS COTTICES DAFFODIL DOGGEDLY HURRAHED HUZZAHED MERRIMAC MERRYMAN NAPPINGS
NETTINGS NODDINGS NULLINGS NUTTINGS PREEMPTS RAPPORTS SUPPOSED SUPPOSER WALLOWED
WHEELWAY WILLOWED WILLOWER WINNOWED WINNOWER

ABCCDBAC NIGGLING TOSSPOTS   ABCCDBAE NIBBLING NIPPLING SILLYISH

ABCCDBBE BELLWEED TOLLBOOK   ABCCDBCB DERRIERE

ABCCDBCC LESSNESS PELLMELL

ABCCDBCE FERRIERS MESSIEST MISSYISH PERRIERS TERRIERS   ABCCDBDE BULLPUPS

ABCCDBEA GIDDYING SETTLERS SUCCOURS

ABCCDBEC BOSSDOMS DISSHIPS DISSUITS JIGGLING NETTIEST PASSWAYS PETTIEST WIGGLING

ABCCDBED DISSEIZE MALLEATE WHOOSHES   ABCCDBEE CARRYALL WELLNESS

ABCCDBEF BACCHANT BILLFISH BOLLWORM BULLDUST BULLNUTS BULLRUSH BURROUGH CARRIAGE
DILLYING DITTOING DITTYING DIVVYING DIZZYING FALLBACK FALLWAYS FIDDLING FIZZLING
GAFFSAIL GEMMIEST GIDDYISH HALLIARD HALLMARK HALLWAYS HILLBIRD HILLSIDE JIGGLIER

JIMMYING KETTLERS KIDDYING LEGGIEST MARRIAGE MEDDLERS MERRIEST MESSDECK MIDDLING
MILLSITE MISSFIRE NETTLERS OUTTRUMP PALLIATE PASSBACK PASSBAND PASSWALK PEBBLERS
PEDDLERS PEDDLERY PIDDLING PIFFLING PULLOUTS RIBBLING RIDDLING RIFFLING RILLWISE
RIPPLING ROLLMOPS SILLYING SIZZLING SURROUND TIDDLING TIPPLIER TIPPLING TISSUING
VILLAINS VILLAINY WEBBIEST WELLHEAD WELLNEAR WHOOSHED WILLYING

ABCCDCAB STEEPEST   **ABCCDCAD** SWEETEST

ABCCDCAE GUNNINGS SHEEREST SLEEKEST TREELETS

ABCCDCBE BREEDERS CREEKERS CREELERS CREEPERS FREEZERS GREEKERY GREENERS GREENERY
GREETERS PENNINES PENNONED PREENERS TERRORED

ABCCDCDA SNEERERS STEERERS   **ABCCDCDE** CHEERERS FLEERERS QUEERERS

ABCCDCEA SHEETERS SKEETERS SLEEKENS SLEEKERS SLEEPERS SLEEVERS SNEEZERS SPEEDERS
STEELERS STEEPENS STEEPERS SWEEPERS SWEETENS

ABCCDCEB CELLULAE   **ABCCDCEC** BASSISTS MISSUSES

ABCCDCED CHEESERS FLEETEST TERRARIA   **ABCCDCEE** FREENESS GREEKESS TREELESS

ABCCDCEF BLEEDERS BUDDEDLY BUNNINGS CANNINGS CANNONED CANNONRY CELLULAR CHEEKERS
CHEEPERS CHEESERY CHEETERS CONNINGS CUNNINGS FANNINGS FLEECERS FLEETERS GREENEST
KENNINGS KNEELERS LUGGAGES MANNINGS MIRRORED PANNINGS PENNANTS PENNINGS PILLULAR
PREELECT QUEEREST RUNNINGS TANNINED TANNINGS TUBBABLE TWEEZERS WHEELERS WHEELERY
WHEEZERS

ABCCDDAC MISSEEMS   **ABCCDDCE** SHEEPPEN   **ABCCDDEA** SUCCEEDS

ABCCDDEC BASSOONS

ABCCDDEF BALLOONS COLLEENS COWWEEDS HALLOOED LASSOOED MARROONS PROOFFUL RACCOONS

ABCCDEAA SUPPRESS   **ABCCDEAB** LETTABLE SHEEPISH

ABCCDEAC GASSINGS GREENAGE NAGGLING

ABCCDEAD COMMENCE COMMERCE SHOOTIST SUCCEASE

ABCCDEAF CURRENCY DISSUADE DULLARDS GALLINGS GETTINGS GOBBINGS GUBBINGS GUMMINGS
LATTERLY LOGGEDLY NAVVYING NETTLING NOBBLING NOZZLING NUZZLING OUTTHROB OUTTHROW
RABBITRY RABBLERS RAFFLERS RALLIERS RATTLERS RIBBONRY RIDDLERS RIFFLERS RIPPLERS
RUBBLERS RUFFLERS SAGGIEST SAPPHISM SAPPHIST SAPPIEST SLEEPISH SOBBIEST SODDIEST
SOGGIEST SOPPIEST SORRIEST SORRYISH SPOOFISH SPOOKISH SPOOKISM SPOOKIST SPOONISM
STEEPISH SUNNIEST SUPPLEST SUPPRISE SWEETISH TOLLGATE TORRENTS

ABCCDEBA GOLLIWOG SERRATES SPEEDUPS TOMMYROT

ABCCDEBC CORRIDOR LESSIVES MESSAGES MILLTAIL TERRACER

ABCCDEBE BEGGARER CELLARER CELLOSES TENNISES

ABCCDEBF BEGGARED BELLOWED BELLOWER BELLYMEN BLOODILY BROODERS BROOMERS CANNIBAL
CANNULAE CANNULAR CELLARED CELLATED CELLITES CHEETAHS COLLATOR CROOKERY CROONERS
DALLYMAN DROOPERS FARRUCAS FELLOWED FELLSMEN FERRATED FERRATES FERRITES FERRULED
FERRULES FERRYMEN FLEECILY FREEBORN FREEWARD GAFFSMAN GALLOWAY GLOOMILY GROOMERS
GROOVERS HARRIDAN KNEELING KNEEPANS LESSONED LETTICES LETTUCES MELLOWED MELLOWER
MESSAGED NETTLIER PEBBLIER PIZZERIA POLLIWOG POLLYWOG POMMELOS PREENTRY PROOFERS
SERRATED SLEEPILY SNEERING SNEEZING SNOOPING SNOOTING SNOOZING SUCCINUM TALLYMAN
TALLYWAG TENNISED TERRACED TERRACES TERRINES TREEWARD TROOPERS VACCINAL VACCINAS
YELLOWED YELLOWER

ABCCDECA SAGGINGS SPEECHES STEELIES STEEPLES SWEEPIES SWEETIES YELLOWLY

ABCCDECB BREEDIER BREEZIER CREEPIER FELLABLE FREEZIER GREEDIER GREENIER PELLICLE
PREENTER SELLABLE TELLABLE WELLHOLE

ABCCDECC BASSNESS BELLPULL MASSLESS MOSSLESS PASSLESS TOLLHALL

ABCCDECD CHEERIER KNEESIES MASSEUSE SHEETLET SNEERIER TWEEDLED WHEEDLED

ABCCDECF BAGGINGS BARRIERS BILLFOLD BOSSIEST BREECHED BREECHES CHEEKIER CHEEPIER
CHEESIER CHEETIES COGGINGS CREEPIES CURRIERS CURRIERY DAGGINGS DOSSIEST FALLIBLE
FALLIBLY FARRIERS FARRIERY FELLOWLY FILLABLE FILLABLY FLEECIER FOLLICLE FREEDMEN
FURRIERS FURRIERY FUSSIEST GASSIEST GREENIES GULLABLE GULLABLY GULLIBLE GULLIBLY
HARRIERS HENNAING HOGGINGS HURRIERS JOGGINGS KILLABLE KILLABLY LAGGINGS LEGGINGS
LOGGINGS MARRIERS MARRYERS MASSIEST MELLOWLY MILLABLE MILLFULS MOSSIEST MUGGINGS
MUSSIEST NULLABLE PALLIDLY PARRIERS PARROTRY PEGGINGS POLLABLE PREEXCEL PULLABLE
PULLABLY PUSSIEST RAGGINGS ROLLABLE ROLLABLY RUGGINGS SELLABLY SHEENIER SHEEPIER
SHEEPMEN SHEETIER SLEEKIER SLEEPIER SLEETIER SLEEZIER SNEEZIER SPEECHED SPEECHER
SPEEDIER STEELIER STEELMEN STEEPLED STEERMEN SUCCINCT SULLENLY SWEEPIER SYLLABLE
TARRIERS TERROURS TILLABLE TILLABLY TOLLABLE TOLLABLY TUGGINGS TWEEDIER TWEEDLES
TWEENIES WAGGINGS WALLFULS WARRIORS WHEEDLER WHEEDLES WHEELMEN WHEEZIER WHEEZLED
WHEEZLES WILLABLE WILLABLY WILLFULS WORRIERS

ABCCDEDA DAGGERED DIFFERED DOTTERED GREENING RAGGEDER ROTTENER SPOORERS SWEEPUPS
TASSELET

ABCCDEDB CESSPIPE VACCINIA

ABCCDEDC BARRELER BARRENER FODDERED LADDERED MADDENED MANNIKIN PANNIKIN SADDENED
SODDENED SUCCINIC TODDERED WARRENER

ABCCDEDE BANNERER BUTTERER COBBERER COFFERER COPPERER DAPPERER FODDERER GUTTERER
HAMMERER JABBERER JIGGERER KIPPERER LITTERER MUTTERER PATTERER POTTERER PUTTERER
SUFFERER SUMMERER TAPPERER

ABCCDEDF BANNERED BARRELED BARRELET BATTENED BATTENER BATTERED BILLETED BILLETER
BITTERED BONNETED BONNETER BUFFETED BUFFETER BULLETED BUTTERED CINNABAR COFFERED
COLLEGED COLLEGER COLLEGES CONNEXED CONNEXES COPPERED COSSETED COTTERED COTTEREL
CROONING DISSEVER DOGGEREL FATTENED FATTENER FIGGERED FILLETED FILLETER FITTENED

FITTERED FLOORERS FULLERED FUNNELED GARRETED GARRULUS GIBBERED GIBBETED GULLETED
GUSSETED GUTTERED HAPPENED HASSIDIC HATTERED HOLLERED HORRIFIC HOTTENED HUMMELED
HUMMELER JABBERED JELLABAS JIBBERED JIGGERED JITTERED KIPPERED KITTENED LAGGERED
LIPPERED LITTERED LOBBERED LOPPERED MALLETED MANNERED MATTERED MISSTATE MITTENED
MUSSELED MUSSELER MUTTERED NATTERED NIGGERED NIPPERED PARRELED PASSENED PATTENED
PATTENER PATTERED PERRIWIG PICCOLOS PITTERED POLLENED POMMELED POMMELER POSSEMEN
POSSETED POTTERED PREENING PULLAWAY PUMMELED PUTTERED QUEENING RABBETED RABBINIC
RATTENED ROLLAWAY ROTTENED SAGGERED SCOONING SIMMERED SINNERED SONNETED SONNETER
SPOONING SUFFERED SULLENED SULLENER SUMMERED SUPPERED SUPPLELY SWOONING TASSELED
TASSELER TERRIFIC TILLERED TUNNELED TUNNELER TUNNERED VALLEYED VOLLEYED VOLLEYER
WALLEYED WALLEYES YABBERED YAMMERED YATTERED ZIPPERED

ABCCDEEA DILLSEED DILLWEED MESSROOM SHOOTEES   **ABCCDEEC** MILLPOOL PASSELLS

ABCCDEED BARRETTE BILLETTE PALLETTE

ABCCDEEF BALLROOM BASSWOOD BELLWOOD BILLHOOK CESSPOOL FREEBOOT KILLDEER MESSCOOK
MILLFEED MISSPEED OUTTELLS PASSBOOK POMMELLY SUBBREED TASSELLY TERRAZZO TIPPROOF
TUNNELLY TUPPENNY WHOOPEES

ABCCDEFA COMMATIC DIFFAMED DIFFUSED DISSAVED DULLHEAD DUNNAGED GABBLING GESSOING
GLOOMING GOBBLING GREEDING GREENBUG GREETING GROOMING GROOVING GULLYING GUZZLING
HARRUMPH HICCOUGH LITTORAL MANNHEIM PREEQUIP RABBITER RIBBONER RUMMAGER SADDLERS
SAFFLORS SAFFLOWS SAFFRONS SAPPHICS SAPPINGS SAWWORTS SCOONERS SCOOPERS SCOOTERS
SELLINGS SELLOUTS SETTINGS SHOOTERS SIZZLERS SMOOCHES SNOOKERS SNOOPERS SNOOZERS
SODDINGS SOFFITES SPOOFERS SPOOKIES SPOOLERS SPOONERS SPOONEYS SPOONIES STOOKERS
STOOLIES STOOPERS SUBBANDS SUBBANKS SUBBINGS SUFFICES SUFFIXES SUFFOLKS SUMMATES
SUPPAGES SUPPINGS SUPPLIES SUPPORTS SURREPTS SWOONERS SWOOPERS SYLLABES SYLLABUS
SYLLOGES TARRIEST TUBBIEST

ABCCDEFB BELLVINE BELLWARE BELLWINE BROODIER BROOKIER BROOMIER CATTLEYA CHEEKISH
COMMANDO DROOLIER DROOPIER GALLERIA GETTABLE GLOOMFUL GROOVIER MISSOURI NETTABLE
PECCABLE PETTABLE PROOFIER SETTABLE SHEELAGH SLEEPFUL SORRENTO SYMMETRY TERRIBLE
WELLSIDE WELLSITE WETTABLE

ABCCDEFC BASSINGS BATTIEST BELLICAL BELLTAIL BELLYFUL BOGGLING BOSSINGS BURROWER
BUSSOCKS CADDISED CARROTER CATTIEST CESSPITS CINNAMON COGGLING COTTIEST DISSEATS
DISSECTS DISSENTS DISSERTS DOSSIERS DOTTIEST FATTIEST FISSURES FOSSICKS FUNNYMAN
FUNNYMEN FURROWER FUSSPOTS GARROTER GREEKIZE GUTTIEST HAGGLING HARROWER HASSOCKS
HESSIANS HUGGLING JOGGLING JUGGLING KNEEHOLE LASSOERS MASSEURS MASSINGS MASSIVES
MESSBOYS MESSIAHS MESSINGS MESSTINS MISSENDS MISSORTS MISSTAYS MISSTEPS NARROWER
NATTIEST NUTTIEST PARROTER PASSINGS PASSIONS PASSIVES PASSKEYS PASSOUTS PEGGLING
PISSANTS POLLICAL PREEXILE RAGGLING RATTIEST RISSOLES RUGGLING RUSSIANS RUSSKIES
RUTTIEST STEERAGE SWEEPAGE TAGGLING TOGGLING TORRIDER TOSSINGS TREELIKE TUSSOCKS
WAGGLING WHEELAGE

ABCCDEFD BLOODIED BLOODRED CAFFEINE CHOOSERS COMMERGE DISSERVE DOLLYWAY FLOOSIES
FREESIAS MAFFIOSI MISSERVE OUTTEASE PELLAGRA QUEENPIN SPOOLFUL STOOGING SUPPLIAL
TUPPENCE

ABCCDEFE BALLISTS CALLUSES CELLISTS COLLIDED COLLUDED COMMISES COTTISES CULLISES

- 77 -

DIFFUSES FADDISMS FADDISTS HOBBISTS JAZZISTS LUDDISMS MAFFIOSO MAPPISTS MOBBISTS
MOLLUSKS MORRISES NULLISMS OUTTASKS SILLABUB SUCCORER SUPPREME SYLLABUB TOPPIECE
TYRRHENE ZUCCHINI

ABCCDEFF BALLYHOO BROOKESS BUTTRESS COLLATEE DULLNESS FREEWILL FULLNESS FUZZBALL
MATTRESS MISSPELL PUFFBALL TALLNESS VACCINEE WILLNESS

ABCCDEFG ADEEMING BACCHIUS BAFFLERS BAFFLING BAGGIEST BALLINGS BALLOTED BALLOTER
BALLYING BARRENLY BASSINET BATTINGS BATTLERS BATTLING BEDDINGS BEGGARLY BELLHOPS
BELLINGS BELLSMAN BELLWIND BELLYING BELLYMAN BERRYING BETTINGS BIDDANCE BILLOWED
BITTERLY BLEEDING BLOODIER BLOODIES BLOODING BLOOMAGE BLOOMERS BLOOMERY BLOOMIER
BLOOMING BLOOPERS BLOOPING BOGGIEST BOGGLERS BOGGLISH BONNIEST BONNYISH BOTTLERS
BOTTLING BREEDING BREEZILY BREEZING BROOCHED BROOCHES BROODING BROOKING BROOKLET
BROOKLYN BROOMING BUCCANED BUDDHISM BUDDHIST BUDDIEST BUDDYING BUFFALOS BUFFCOAT
BUFFIANS BUFFIERS BUFFIEST BUFFINGS BUFFLERS BUFFWARE BUGGIEST BUGGYMAN BUGGYMEN
BULLCART BULLDOGS BULLDOZE BULLETIN BULLFROG BULLHEAD BULLHIDE BULLHORN BULLIEST
BULLINGS BULLIONS BULLNECK BULLOCKS BULLOCKY BULLPENS BULLRING BULLSKIN BULLTOAD
BULLWHIP BULLWORK BULLYDOM BULLYING BULLYISM BUMMLERS BURRIEST BURRINGS BURRLIKE
BURROWED BUTTINGS BUTTLING BUTTOCKS BUTTONED BUTTONER BUTTYMAN BUTTYMEN BUZZARDS
BUZZIEST BUZZINGS CABBLERS CABBLING CADDYING CALLBOYS CALLINGS CALLIOPE CALLIPER
CALLOWER CALLUSED CANNIEST CAPPIEST CARROTED CARRYING CATTYMEN CELLOIST CHEEKILY
CHEEKING CHEEPING CHEERILY CHEERING CHEERIOS CHEESILY CHEESING CHOOSING CIRRHOUS
COBBIEST COBBINGS COBBLERS COBBLERY COBBLING CODDLERS CODDLING COLLAGEN COLLAGES
COLLAPSE COLLARDS COLLARED COLLATED COLLATES COLLEGIA COLLIDES COLLIERS COLLIERY
COLLIEST COLLINES COLLINGS COLLUDER COLLUDES COLLUVIA COMMAING COMMANDS COMMEDIA
COMMENDA COMMENDS COMMENTS COMMISED COMMIXED COMMIXES COMMUALS COMMUNAE COMMUNAL
COMMUNED COMMUNER COMMUNES COMMUTED COMMUTER COMMUTES CONNIVED CONNIVER CONNIVES
COPPINGS CORRUPTS COTTAGED COTTAGER COTTAGES COTTAGEY CREEPILY CREEPING CROOKING
CUDDLIER CUDDLING CUFFLING CUFFYISM CULLINGS CULLYING CUPPIEST CUPPINGS CURRANTS
CURRENTS CURRYING CUSSEDLY CUTTABLE CUTTAGES CUTTAILS CUTTINGS CUTTLERS CUTTLING
DABBIEST DABBLERS DABBLING DAFFIEST DAFFINGS DALLIERS DALLYING DAPPERLY DAPPLING
DAZZLERS DAZZLING DERRICKS DIBBLERS DIFFLATE DIFFRACT DIFFUSER DIFFUSOR DIGGABLE
DISSOLVE DOGGIEST DOGGRELS DOLLFACE DOLLIERS DOLLSHIP DOLLYING DOLLYMAN DOLLYMEN
DROOLING DROOPING DUBBIEST DUBBINGS DULLSOME DUMMYING EARRINGS FADDIEST FAGGOTED
FALLOUTS FALLOWED FARROWED FELLAHIN FELLATIO FELLINGS FERRYING FERRYMAN FIDDLERS
FIDDLERY FISSURAL FISSURED FITTABLE FITTAGES FLEECING FLEETING FLOODAGE FLOODERS
FLOODING FLOODWAY FLOORAGE FLOORING FLOORMAN FLOORMEN FLOORWAY FLOOZIES FOGGIEST
FOLLYING FOSSILED FREEDMAN FREEDOMS FREEHAND FREEHOLD FREELOAD FREEWAYS FREEZING
FULLBACK FULLDONE FULLINGS FUNNIEST FURRIEST FURRINGS FURROWED FUZZIEST FUZZLING
FUZZTAIL GABBIEST GABBLERS GAFFSMEN GALLEONS GALLIPOT GALLIUMS GALLOMEN GALLONER
GALLOPED GALLOPER GAMMONED GAMMONER GARRISON GARROTED GILLMORE GILLNETS GIZZARDS
GLOOMIER GOBBLERS GOSSAMER GOSSIPED GOSSIPER GREEDILY GREEKISH GREENISH GROOMISH
GUFFAWED GULLIVER GUMMIEST GUTTABLE GUZZLERS HADDOCKS HAGGIEST HAGGLERS HALLBOYS
HALLINGS HALLOWED HALLOWER HAMMIEST HAMMOCKS HANNOVER HAPPIEST HAPPINGS HAPPYING
HARROWED HARRYING HASSLING HASSOCKY HATTINGS HATTIZED HATTIZES HATTOCKS HELLCATS
HELLIONS HELLWARD HEMMINGS HERRINGS HICCUPED HIDDENLY HILLOCKS HILLOCKY HILLSMAN
HILLSMEN HILLTOPS HILLWARD HOBBLERS HOBBLING HOBBYING HOBBYISM HOBBYIST HOLLANDS
HOPPIEST HORRIBLE HORRIBLY HORRIDLY HUBBARDS HUDDLERS HUDDLING HUFFIEST HUFFLERS
HUFFLING HUMMABLE HUMMINGS HUMMOCKS HUMMOCKY HURRYING HUZZARDS JAGGEDLY JAGGIEST
JAMMIEST JARRINGS JAZZIEST JELLOIDS JELLYING JETTISON JETTYING JOLLIERS JOLLIEST
JOLLITRY JOLLYING JOTTINGS JUGGLERS JUGGLERY JUTTINGS JUTTYING KELLYING KILLJOYS

KISSABLE KISSABLY KNEECAPS KNEEPADS KRAALING KREELING LAPPINGS LASSOING LATTICED
LATTICES LEMMINGS LETTINGS LOBBYERS LOBBYING LOBBYISM LOBBYIST LOBBYMAN LOBBYMEN
LOPPINGS LORRAINE LORRYING LUDDITES LUGGARDS MAGGOTRY MANNERLY MARRIEDS MARROWED
MARRYING MASSLIKE MATTEDLY MATTINGS MATTOCKS MEDDLING MERRYING MIDDLERS MILLPOND
MILLPOST MILLRACE MILLWARD MILLWORK MISSABLE MISSAYER MISSHAPE MISSPEAK MISSPELT
MISSPEND MISSPENT MISSPOKE MISSUADE MISSWORD MOCCASIN MONNIKER MOPPIEST MOPPINGS
MORRISED MOSSBACK MOSSHEAD MOSSLIKE MOTTLERS MOTTLING MUDDLERS MUDDLING MUDDYING
MUFFLERS MUFFLING MUGGIEST MULLIGAN MULLIONS MUSSABLE MUSSABLY MUZZIEST MUZZLERS
MUZZLING NAGGIEST NAPPIEST NARROWED NARROWLY NIBBLERS NIGGARDS NIGGARDY NIGGLERS
NOBBIEST NOBBLERS NOBBLIER NOLLEITY NOZZLERS NUBBIEST OFTTIMES OUTTAKEN OUTTAKER
OUTTAKES OUTTALKS OUTTHINK OUTTIRED OUTTIRES OUTTRADE OUTTRAIL OUTTRICK OUTTWINE
OWLLIGHT PADDIEST PADDINGS PADDLERS PADDLING PADDOCKS PADDYISM PALLINGS PALLIUMS
PARROTED PARRYING PASSERBY PASSIBLE PASSOVER PASSWORD PATTERNS PATTERNY PEBBLING
PEDDLING PEMMICAN PETTIFOG PETTINGS PIDDLERS PIFFLERS PILLAGED PILLAGER PILLAGES
PILLARED PILLOWED PINNACES PINNACLE PITTANCE POLLAXED POLLAXES POLLINGS POLLSTER
POLLUTED POLLUTER POLLUTES PORRIDGE POSSABLE POSSIBLE POSSIBLY POSSUMED POTTAGES
POTTANCE POTTINGS PREEDITS PREENACT PREENJOY PREEXIST PROOFING PUDDINGS PUDDINGY
PUDDLERS PUDDLIER PUDDLING PUFFIEST PUFFINGS PULLBACK PULLDOWN PULLMANS PULLOVER
PUMMICES PUNNIEST PURRIEST PURRINGS PUSSLIKE PUSSYCAT PUTTINGS PUTTYERS PUTTYING
PUZZLERS PUZZLING PYRRHICS PYRRHITE PYRRHOUS PYRROLES PYRROLIC PYRROLIN QUEERING
QUEERISH QUEERITY RABBITED RABBLING RAFFLING RAGGEDLY RAGGIEST RALLYING RAMMIEST
RAPPINGS RATTLING REDDINGS RETTINGS RIBBANDS RIBBONED RIDDANCE RIPPABLE RIZZOMED
ROBBINGS RODDINGS ROLLBACK ROLLICKS ROLLICKY ROLLINGS ROLLSMAN ROLLSMEN ROLLWAYS
ROTTENLY ROTTINGS ROTTLING RUBBINGS RUBBISHY RUDDIEST RUDDYING RUDDYISH RUFFABLE
RUFFIANS RUFFLIKE RUFFLING RUGGEDLY RUMMAGED RUMMAGES RUMMIEST RUNNABLE RUNNIEST
RUTTLING SADDLERY SADDLING SAFFRONY SALLOWED SALLOWER SALLYING SALLYMEN SAPPHIRE
SARROWED SATTLING SAVVYING SCOOPFUL SCOOPING SCOOTING SETTLING SHEENFUL SHEEPING
SHEEPMAN SHEERING SHEERMAN SHEETFUL SHEETING SHOOTING SHOOTMAN SHOOTMEN SINNABLE
SITTABLE SKEETING SLEEPIFY SLEEPING SLEETING SLEEVING SLOOPING SLOOPMAN SLOOPMEN
SMOOCHED SMOODGER SMOOTHED SMOOTHER SMOOTHIE SMOOTHLY SNEERFUL SNOOPERY SNOOPIER
SNOOTFUL SNOOTIER SNOOTILY SNOOZIER SODDENLY SORRYING SPEEDFUL SPEEDILY SPEEDING
SPEEDWAY SPOOFERY SPOOFING SPOOKERY SPOOKIER SPOOKILY SPOOKING SPOOLING SPOONFUL
SPOONIER SPOONILY SPOORING STEELING STEELMAN STEEPING STEERING STEERMAN SUCCORED
SUDDENLY SUFFICED SUFFICER SUFFIXAL SUFFIXED SUFFOKED SUFFRAGE SULLYING SUMMABLE
SUMMATED SUMMATOR SUMMERLY SUMMITAL SUMMITRY SUMMONED SUMMONER SUPPABLE SUPPLANT
SUPPLICE SUPPLIED SUPPLIER SUPPLING SWEEPING SWEETFUL SWEETING SWOOPING SYLLABIC
TABBYING TALLBOYS TALLOWED TALLYHOS TALLYING TALLYMEN TANNIERS TANNOIDS TAPPINGS
TARRYING TELLINGS TERRAINS TERRIBLY TILLAGES TIPPABLE TIPPLERS TODDLERS TODDLING
TODDYING TODDYMAN TODDYMEN TOFFYMAN TOFFYMEN TOGGLERS TOLLAGES TOLLINGS TOLLWAYS
TONNAGED TOPPINGS TOPPLERS TOPPLING TORRIDLY TREEFULS TROOPING TUBBINGS TUMMOCKS
TUNNAGES TUPPINGS TUSSLING TUSSOCKY TWEEZING VACCINES VILLAGED VILLAGER VILLAGES
VILLAGEY WADDINGS WADDLERS WADDLING WAFFLIER WAFFLING WAGGIEST WAGGONED WAGGONER
WAGGONRY WALLINGS WALLOPED WALLOPER WALLYING WATTLING WEBBINGS WEDDINGS WELLBORN
WELLINGS WELLMOST WELLYARD WETTINGS WHEELBOX WHEELING WHEELMAN WHEEZILY WHEEZING
WHOOFING WHOOPERS WHOOPING WIGGLERS WOBBLERS WOBBLIER WOBBLIES WOBBLING WORRYING
YAPPIEST YUMMIEST ZIGGURAT

ABCDAABA RECURRER   **ABCDAABE** ENGREENS LAMELLAR REBARRED RECURRED

ABCDAACE OUTFOOTS OUTROOTS   **ABCDAADA** SAGESSES SIRESSES STRESSES

ABCDAADC STRESSER   **ABCDAADD** LIBELLEE

ABCDAADE LABELLED LABELLER LAPELLED LIBELLED LIBELLER REBORROW STRESSED TILETTES
TONETTES

ABCDAAEA ENFREEZE REMIRROR SCHUSSES SUMASSES   **ABCDAAEB** BEDABBLE

ABCDAAEC ENSWEEPS

ABCDAAEF ENWHEELS LABELLUM LOCALLED LOCELLUS OAKWOODS OUTDOORS OUTFOOLS OUTLOOKS
OUTROOMS OXBLOODS REHARROW THROTTLE

ABCDABAC ENSCENES

ABCDABAE EMBLEMED ENSCENED IMPRIMIS INOSINIC LIVELILY RETIRERS

ABCDABBE ESPRESSO FOREFOOT REAGREED REAGREES RENTREES RESCREEN RETIREES ROSEROOT
ROTPROOF WORMWOOD

ABCDABCD BERIBERI CHOWCHOW COUSCOUS HOTSHOTS MAHIMAHI SINGSING

ABCDABCE BELIBELS DERIDERS HINCHING INGOINGS LINOLINS PHOSPHOR SHOESHOP TINCTING

ABCDABDB ADREADED   **ABCDABDC** BILABIAL   **ABCDABDD** LENSLESS

ABCDABDE CETACEAN CONICOID INVEINED LANDLADY LIKELIER LIVELIER LOBULOUS LOCULOUS
RIPARIAL RIPARIAN

ABCDABEA ORATORIO SILESIAS SOURSOPS   **ABCDABEB** OSTEOSIS

ABCDABEC CYTOCYST INSWINGS OUTCOURT SINESIAN TIGHTING TINCTION VETIVERT WASHWAYS

ABCDABED CHITCHAT FLIMFLAM INSTINCT KIDSKINS LIFELIKE LIFELINE LIMELIKE RETHRESH
RIVERINE TIGHTISH WILDWIND

ABCDABEE BASEBALL LEADLESS LEAFLESS LEAKLESS NEARNESS NEATNESS NEXTNESS RECTRESS

ABCDABEF ABIDABLE ABIDABLY ABUSABLE ABUSABLY AIRMAILS ARTWARES ATOMATIC BACKBAND
BAREBACK BOURBONS CARDCASE CHANCHES CHINCHAS CHURCHED CHURCHES CHURCHLY CORNCOBS
CUBICULE CUTICULA DECADENT DECIDENT DECIDERS DECODERS DELUDERS DENUDERS DIPODIES
DISEDIFY DISODIUM ENFRENZY ENTRENCH EPILEPSY EPILEPTS FOURFOLD HARDHACK HEATHENS
HEATHERS HEATHERY HITCHIER HITCHILY HITCHING ICONICAL IMPRIMED IMPRIMES INBEINGS
INBRINGS INCLINED INCLINER INCLINES INFRINGE INGUINAL INJOINTS INKLINGS INLYINGS
INPAINTS INTWINED INTWINES KAMIKAZE LAKELAND LEAFLETS LIBELIST LIONLIKE LOCULOSE
LOVELOCK LOVELORN MAINMAST MAXIMATE NOMINORS ORATORIC OUTBOUND OUTHOUSE OUTPOURS
OUTSOUND PHOSPHID PHOSPHYL POSTPONE REDIRECT REFOREST RESPREAD RESTREAM RETHREAD
RIGORISM RIGORIST RIVERING RIVERISH SEMISERF SILESIAN TEMPTERS TINCTILE TOMATOES
TRACTRIX UNBOUNDS UNFOUNDS UNHAUNTS UNJAUNTY UNMOUNTS UNPLUNGE UNPRUNED WALKWAYS
WARDWALK WAVEWARD WIDOWING WIDOWISH

ABCDACAE TRACTATE   **ABCDACBA** RETORTER

ABCDACBE DREADERS KNICKING PROSPORT REGORGED REGORGES REGURGED REGURGES RETORTED
TREATERS

ABCDACCE TREATEES   **ABCDACDA** REMURMUR

ABCDACDE ANTEATER COERCERS IRANIANS KLINKING PUERPERA PUERPERY TAINTING

ABCDACEA SPONSORS   **ABCDACEB** RECIRCLE REPURPLE   **ABCDACED** TWISTIES

ABCDACEE KNOCKOFF

ABCDACEF ABIGAILS ACTUATED ACTUATES ACTUATOR AIRMARKS AIRWARDS BEANBAGS COINCIDE
CORNCRIB CRESCENT ESTHETIC INTUITED ITALIANS KNOCKOUT OILHOLES ORTHOTIC OUTVOTED
OUTVOTER OUTVOTES PREOPENS PRIAPISM PRIAPIUM PRIMPING SHIPSIDE STAYSAIL THEATERS
THIRTIES TWISTIER TWISTILY TWISTING UBIQUITY UNGAUGED UNGOUGED UNIQUITY UNSOUSED
UNTRUTHS UPCHUCKS WHIPWISE

ABCDADBB BLUEBELL   **ABCDADBE** ELUDEDLY LACELEAF RUMOROUS TAHITIAN

ABCDADCE ACETATED   **ABCDADDE** FOREFEET HEROHOOD LIBELEES WIREWEED

ABCDADEA EMINENCE   **ABCDADEB** REPARATE

ABCDADEE LACELESS LAKELESS LIFELESS LIMELESS LINELESS LOBELESS LORELESS LOVELESS
NICENESS NUDENESS RIDERESS

ABCDADEF AGITATED AGITATES AGITATOR CHOICIER CODICILS COLICINE CUBICITY CYNICISM
DECADARY DECIDING DERIDING DRUIDISM EMINENCY EVADEDLY EXUDEDLY FOREFELT FOREFEND
IRONINGS LABELERS LABILITY LABILIZE LAPELERS LIBELERS LIFELETS LINELETS LORELEIS
MAXIMIST MAXIMITE MOVEMENT NOMINIES OARCOCKS OUTDODGE REFIRING REHIRING RETIRING
REWIRING RIGOROUS RIVERETS TOXITIES

ABCDAEAB ASHRAMAS   **ABCDAEAD** EXCRETER EXTREMER

ABCDAEAF ARCHAEAN EASTERED ECUMENES EMBREWED ENAMELED ENAMELER EPICENES ESCHEWED
ESCHEWER ETAGERES EUCHERED EXCRETED EXCRETES EXTREMES HEIGHTHS IMPLICIT INSPIRIT
MAXIMUMS ORTHODOX PLAYPIPE RUMORERS SENUSISM SPARSEST TRACTITE TRISTATE UNCTUOUS

ABCDAEBA DEBADGED RECORDER REFORGER REFORMER REGARDER REMARKER REPORTER RESORTER
RETARDER RETURFER RETURNER REWARDER REWARPER

ABCDAEBB BLOWBALL BLUEBILL REPARTEE RETURNEE

ABCDAEBC ADELAIDE HENCHMEN REDARNED REDARTED RESURGES ROSARIOS UNEQUINE UNGLUING
UNTRUANT

ABCDAEBD HARDHEAD PRESPURS PROSPERS TIENTSIN TRUSTERS TRUSTORS TRYSTERS

ABCDAEBE IMAGISMS ITACISTS REBURSES RECORDED RECURSES REFORDED REGARDED REMORSES
RETARDED REWARDED REWORDED

ABCDAEBF BRADBURY CEVICHES COERCION COFACTOR DEBADGES DIHYDRIC ELATEDLY ELOPEDLY
GRANGERS GRUDGERS GRUDGERY HATCHMAN HATCHWAY HEATHIER HEIGHTEN IAMBICAL IATRICAL
KNACKING KNOCKING LINOLEIC MILKMAID PNOMPENH RAZORMAN REBURDEN REBURIED REBURIES
REBURNED REBURSED RECARPET RECARTED RECARVED RECARVES RECORKED RECURLED RECURSED
RECURVED RECURVES REDARKEN REFORCED REFORCES REFORGED REFORGES REFORGET REFORMED
REFURLED REHARDEN REHARMED REMARKED REMARKET REMORSED REPARKED REPARTED REPORTED
REPURGED REPURGES RESORBED RESORTED RESURGED RESURVEY RETURFED RETURNED REVARIED
REVARIES REWARMED REWARNED REWORKED SAILSMAN SALESIAN SALESMAN SALISHAN SEAMSTER
SEATSMEN SIDESLIP SIDESPIN SINUSOID TRACTORS TRACTORY TRAITORS TRAITORY TROUTERS
UNCHURNS UNFLUENT

ABCDAECA EXCRESCE   **ABCDAECB** DEMIDOME PERSPIRE

ABCDAECC LASHLESS LISTLESS LUSTLESS NOSINESS

ABCDAECD AVERAGER DINGDONG INEDITED ITALICAL LAKELIKE MISHMASH NICKNACK RICKRACK
SINGSONG TICKTACK TICKTOCK TRESTLES UNCHURCH UNEDUCED

ABCDAECE INTWISTS OUTPOSTS UNELUDED UNEXUDED UNTRUSTS

ABCDAECF ACERATES AVERAGED AVERAGES AVOCADOS CHARCOAL CLENCHED CLENCHER CLENCHES
DENUDANT DENUDING ENTREATS ENTREATY EPIDEMIC EXTREATS HATCHETS HATCHETY HUNCHING
HUTCHETS IMAGINAL ITALICAN ITEMIZED ITEMIZER ITEMIZES LANDLINE LANOLINE LANOLINS
LONGLINE MONAMINE MONUMENT OUTCOATS OUTFORTH OUTFORTS OUTPORTS OUTWORTH PERSPIRY
SAILSHIP SEATSMAN SLIPSKIN SNOWSHOE SWAGSMAN SWIMSUIT THEATRES TREATIED TREATIES
TRESTLED TRUSTFUL TWENTIES UNCLUTCH UNPLUMPS UNTRUSTY WIREWORK

ABCDAEDA DISEDGED HARSHISH SCORSERS

ABCDAEDB REPURSUE SCHISMIC SCHISTIC TERMTIME

ABCDAEDC DISEDGES ROSERIES TRENTINE VESUVIUS   **ABCDAEDD** CODECREE

ABCDAEDF ACREAGES ADRIATIC AGITANTS ANTIACID AUREATED AUREATES CABOCHON CHANCING
CHINCONA DRAWDOWN EXILEDLY HARSHEST HATCHECK IMPLIALS IMPOISON INVEILED KLUNKING
LARKLIKE LONELIER LONGLEGS LOVELIER LOVELIES MOLDMADE OUTPOMPS OUTROARS REFORGOT
RIVERBED RIVERLET RIVERMEN ROSARIAN ROSTRATE ROTARIAN SADISTIC SALESMEN SIDESMEN
SIDESTEP SPONSING TAUNTING THEATRAL TOGETHER TRENTONS TROUTFUL

ABCDAEEB ASHFALLS   **ABCDAEEC** ENSHELLS INSTILLS UNSTUFFS WEDGWOOD

ABCDAEED BANKBOOK FLATFEET FLATFOOT TOASTEES TRUSTEES WILDWOOD WORKWEEK

ABCDAEEF ABORALLY ACTUALLY AERIALLY AMORALLY ANIMALLY ASTRALLY BLUEBOOK BUGABOOS
NOMINEES OUTPOLLS OUTROLLS RATPROOF RUNPROOF THIRTEEN TRUSTEED UNCLUBBY UNSMUTTY
USEFULLY

ABCDAEFA APHRASIA DWINDLED EMPIERCE EVANESCE EVIDENCE EXIGENCE EXUDENCE GRUDGING
NERONIAN SIMPSONS SIWASHES SOAPSUDS SPLASHES SPOUSALS SQUASHES SQUISHES STEPSONS
TIGHTEST TRACTLET TROUTLET

ABCDAEFB ADULATED ASHCAKES ASPHALTS ASTRAINS CROUCHER CRUNCHER CRUTCHER DECIDUAE
DENUDATE ECUMENIC ESCHEATS IDOLIZED IDYLIZED IRONIZER ISOLINES ITCHIEST LEADLINE
LEAFLIKE LEGALIZE LENSLIKE LEVULOSE MELAMINE OSTEOIDS OSTEOMAS PROMPTER REMARQUE
RENGRADE REPHRASE RESCRIBE RESHRINE RESTRIKE RESTRIVE RESTROKE RESTROVE RETHRIVE
RETHRONE RETIRADE SELFSAME SYNASTRY TEINTURE TROUTIER TRUSTIER WEFTWISE

ABCDAEFC ABEYANCE ABSTAINS ACETABLE AMENABLE ARCHAEIC BUSHBOYS COERCIVE CORACLER
EASTERNS ENTREPOT FISTFULS HENCHMAN INEDIBLE INSPIRES LORDLIER OUTPOINT PUSHPINS
RESCRUBS RESPRAYS RESTRAPS RESTRIPS RETHRUST RETIRANT ROSARIES ROSTRUMS TREATISE
UNDAUBED UNTAUGHT

ABCDAEFD ABEYANCY ABUSAGES ACREABLE BAREBONE BUSYBODY CROTCHET ENDSEALS EXSHEATH
FOREFACE GLASGOWS HANDHOLD HARSHENS HINDHEAD HOGSHIPS HOUGHING ICOSINES INOSITES
INVEIGLE LACELIKE LANDLORD MALEMUTE MIASMOUS OUTGOING OUTROPER OUTSOARS OUTSOLES
PINSPOTS PRAEPUCE RESTRICT RETHRASH SCANSION TAPSTERS THISTLES TIPSTERS TOASTERS
TRUSTIES TWISTERS TWISTLES WAVEWISE WINDWARD

ABCDAEFE AMIDASES AMINASES EARNESTS ENCHESTS ENQUESTS ENURESIS IAMBISTS IBERISMS
ICONISMS IDOLISMS IDOLISTS IMAGISTS IMPAIRER INEXISTS INQUIRER INSPIRER IRANISTS
IRONISTS ITACISMS IVORISTS NOMINATA OUTMODED REBURSTS UNHOUSES UNLAUDED

ABCDAEFF DRUIDESS FIREFALL LADYLESS LAIRLESS LAMPLESS LANDLESS LIFTLESS LIMBLESS
LINTLESS LOADLESS LOAMLESS LOCKLESS LOFTLESS LORDLESS LUCKLESS LUNGLESS NUMBNESS
OPTIONEE RETARIFF RETHRILL RYEGRASS

ABCDAEFG ABIDANCE ACQUAINT ADORABLE ADORABLY ADORANTS ADULATES ADULATOR AFGHANIS
AFTWARDS AGITABLE AIRWAVES ALICANTE ALPHABET AMBIANCE AMENABLY AMICABLE AMICABLY
AMINATED AMINATES AMOVABLE AMUSABLE AMYLATES ANIMABLE ANIMATED ANIMATER ANIMATES
ANIMATOR ANTIARCH APHRASIC ARCHAISM ARCHAIST ARCHAIZE ARGUABLE ARGUABLY ARMBANDS
AROMATIC ASTRAYED ATONABLE AVIGATOR AVOWABLE AVOWABLY AVOWANCE AVOWANTS BACKBEND
BACKBITE BACKBLOW BACKBONE BANDBOXY BASEBORN BELABOUR BIRDBATH BLOWBACK BLUEBACK
BLUEBIRD BLURBING BLURBIST BRAMBLED BRAMBLES BRISBANE BROWBEAT BRUMBIES BUSHBEAT
CABOCHED CADUCITY CALICOED CALICOES CALYCINE CALYCOID CANICULE CAPUCHIN CAPUCINE
CARICOUS CHALCIDS CHALCONE CHANCELS CHANCERS CHANCERY CHANCIER CHANCILY CHANCRES
CHOICELY CHOICEST CLATCHES CLINCHED CLINCHER CLINCHES CLUTCHED CLUTCHES COARCTED
COASCEND COLICKER CONICLES COPYCATS CORACITE CORACLES CORNCAKE COSECANT COUNCILS
COWICHAN CROTCHED CROTCHES CROUCHED CROUCHES CRUNCHED CRUNCHES CRUNCHLY CRUTCHED
CRUTCHES CUBICLES CUBICONE CURACIES CUTICLES CYTOCIDE DARNDEST DECADIST DECIDUAL
DECODING DEFADING DELUDING DIHEDRAL DIHEDRON DISADORN DISADVER DOWNDALE DREADFUL
DREADING DUKEDOMS DUPEDOMS DWINDLES EASTERLY ENFIELDS ENURETIC EPIGEOUS EROGENIC
EROTEMAS ESCHEWAL ESOTERIC EUCLEIDS EVIDENCY EVIDENTS EXCRETAL EXFLECTS EXIGEANT
EXIGENCY EXIGENTS EXILEDOM EXODERMS EXOGENIC EXOTERIC FIVEFOLD FLAGFISH FLATFISH
FOREFLAP FORKFULS FROGFISH FUSIFORM GEORGIAN GEORGINA HAIPHONG HANDHOLE HATCHERS
HATCHERY HATCHING HATCHMEN HAWTHORN HEADHUNT HENCHBOY HITCHERS HOGSHEAD HUMPHING
HUTCHING IAMBIZED IAMBIZES IBERIANS ICHNITES IDOLIZER IDOLIZES IDYLIZES IMAGINED
IMAGINER IMAGINES IMPAIRED IMPRINTS IMPRISON INFLICTS INQUIETS INQUIRED INQUIRES
INRAILED INSPIRED INTRIGUE INVEIGHS INVOICED INVOICES INWEIGHT IRANIZED IRANIZES
IRONICAL IRONIZED IRONIZES ISORITHM ISOTIMAL ITCHINGS ITEMINGS IVORINES KLINKERS
KLUCKERS KNACKERS KNACKERY KNACKIER KNICKERS KNOCKERS KNOCKUPS KNUCKLED KNUCKLER
KNUCKLES KODAKERS KODAKING KODAKIST LABELING LADYLIKE LADYLOVE LAMBLIKE LANDLERS
LANDLIKE LANDLOCK LANGLEYS LANOLIZE LASHLITE LAWNLIKE LAZULINE LAZULITE LEGALISM

```
LEGALIST LEGALITY LIBELANT LIBELOUS LIFELONG LIGULATE LINOLATE LINOLEUM LIVELONG
LOBELIAS LOBELINS LOBULATE LOCALING LOCALISM LOCALIST LOCALITE LOCALITY LOCALIZE
LOCKLETS LOCULATE LONGLEAF LORDLIKE LORDLING LOYALISM LOYALIST LOYALIZE LUNGLIKE
LYNXLIKE MAHOMETS MANUMISE MANUMITS MONAMIDE NASONITE NICKNAME NOCENTLY NOMINALS
NOMINATE NOVENARY OARHOLES OARLOCKS OILCOATS OPTIONAL OPTIONED OUTBOARD OUTBORNE
OUTBORNS OUTBOWED OUTBOWLS OUTBOXED OUTBOXES OUTCOMER OUTCOMES OUTDOING OUTFOLDS
OUTFORMS OUTFOXED OUTFOXES OUTGOERS OUTHORNS OUTHOWLS OUTLOPER OUTLOPES OUTLOVED
OUTLOVES OUTMODES OUTMOVED OUTMOVES OUTNOISE OUTPOISE OUTPORCH OUTPOWER OUTROADS
OUTROWED OUTROYAL OUTSOLER OUTVOICE OUTWORKS OUTWORLD OXYGONAL OXYTOCIA OXYTOCIN
OXYTONED OXYTONES OXYTONIC PANOPTIC PERIPLUS PLAYPENS PLUMPERS PLUMPEST PLUMPIER
PLUMPING PLUMPISH POLYPEDS POLYPIAN POLYPIDE POLYPITE PORKPIES POSTPAID PREOPTIC
PRESPOIL PROMPTED PROMPTLY PROSPECT PROSPICE RACKRENT RAZORING REBIRTHS REBORING
REBURIAL RECARBON RECURING REDARING REDBRUSH REFORBAD REFORBID REMARGIN REPURIFY
REPURING RESCRIPT RESPRING RESPROUT RESPRUNG RESTRAIN RESTRING RESTRUCK RESTRUNG
RETARING RETHROWN RETHROWS RETIRALS RETURBAN RIVERMAN RIVERWAY ROSARIUM ROSTRULA
ROTARIES RUMORING SACKSFUL SAILSMEN SANDSHOE SANDSPIT SANDSPUR SCHISMED SCORSING
SCOTSMAN SCOTSMEN SEALSKIN SELFSAID SEMISOFT SEMISPAN SERFSHIP SHOTSMAN SHOTSMEN
SIDESHOW SIDESMAN SIDESWAY SILKSMAN SILKSMEN SIWASHED SLIPSHOD SLIPSHOE SNAPSHOT
SNOWSHED SNOWSUIT SONGSTER SPARSELY SPARSING SPARSITY SPINSTER SPINSTRY SPLASHED
SPLASHER SPLOSHED SPOTSMAN SPOTSMEN SPOUSING SQUASHED SQUISHED STAGSKIN STARSHIP
STAYSHIP STUNSAIL SWAGSMEN SYNUSIAL TACITURN TAINTURE TAUNTERS TEMPTING TERATOID
THEATRIC THISTLED TIBETANS TIGHTEND TIGHTENS TIGHTERS TIGHTNER TIGHTWAD TINCTURE
TIPSTOCK TOASTIER TOASTING TOMATINE TONETICS TRACTILE TRACTING TRACTION TRACTIVE
TREATING TRIETHYL TRIPTONS TRIPTYCH TROUTING TRUSTILY TRUSTING TRUSTMAN TRUSTMEN
TRYPTASE TRYPTONE TRYSTING TURNTAIL UMLAUTED UNABUSED UNADULTS UNBOUGHT UNBRUTED
UNBRUTES UNCAUGHT UNCAUSED UNCOUPLE UNCOUTHS UNCTUOSE UNDOUBLE UNEQUALS UNEQUITY
UNFAULTY UNFEUDAL UNFLUKED UNFLUTED UNFOUGHT UNFOULED UNFRUGAL UNFRUITY UNHAULED
UNHOUSED UNIPULSE UNIQUELY UNITUDES UNLAUGHS UNMAULED UNMOULDS UNMOULDY UNOCULAR
UNPLUMBS UNPLUMED UNPOURED UNROUGED UNROUSED UNROUTED UNSAUCED UNSLUICE UNSOUGHT
UNSOULED UNSOURED UNSQUARE UNSQUIRE UNSTUPID UNTOURED UNTRUCED UNTRUCKS UNTRUISM
UPCAUGHT UPCOURSE UPROUSED UPROUTED UPROUTES UPSOUGHT UPTRUNKS VESUVIAN VOTIVELY
WAGEWORK WARPWISE WASHWORK WESTWARD WIDEWORK WIDOWERS WIDOWERY WIDOWMAN WIDOWMEN
WINDWAYS WIREWAYS WITHWARD WORKWAYS WORKWISE
```

ABCDBAAE ENGINEER LABIALLY LAICALLY LOGROLLS REDBERRY SARGASSO

ABCDBABA REAMERER RENDERER   **ABCDBABD** DIACIDIC RENDERED

ABCDBABE ARBORARY INTONING INURNING NEATENED NEOCENES REAMERED REITERED RENTERED
WALKAWAY WASHAWAY

ABCDBACB RESPERSE   **ABCDBACE** DELVEDLY OUTQUOTE

ABCDBADE BAILABLE BAILABLY ORDUROUS UNVENUED

ABCDBAEA BELZEBUB RUMOURER SARCASMS SARCASTS SEQUESTS SIGNISTS SIKHISMS SILOISTS
SURFUSES

ABCDBAEC ARTCRAFT MISTIMES OVERVOTE UNBENUMB   **ABCDBAED** ANTENAVE HEDGEHOG

ABCDBAEF ALKYLATE BANKABLE BANKABLY CATFACED CATFACES CONFOCAL DEBTEDLY DENTEDLY

DEUCEDLY DIAMIDES DIAZIDES DIOXIDES EVOLVERS FENCEFUL GARBAGED GARBAGES INSANITY
MACRAMES MISAIMED MISTIMED NICKINGS NOTIONAL NOTIONED OMNIMODE PERCEPTS RAMPARTS
RUMOURED RUPTURED RUPTURES SURFUSED TOPNOTCH WHICHWAY ZINCIZED ZINCIZES

ABCDBBAD ANTENNAE   **ABCDBBAE** ANTENNAL ANTENNAS DOGWOODS RECHEERS

ABCDBBCD MONSOONS   **ABCDBBCE** GODHOODS HOTFOOTS PONTOONS REDWEEDS

ABCDBBDC UNDENNED   **ABCDBBDE** DECREERS DOGTOOTH UNKENNED UNKENNEL UNPENNED

ABCDBBEA SEAWEEDS   **ABCDBBEB** DEFREEZE

ABCDBBEC RESTEELS RESTEEPS RESWEEPS STRUTTER UNDONNED

ABCDBBEF ATWITTER BEGREENS BETWEENS BOXROOMS BOXWOODS BOYHOODS DEGREENS DEQUEENS
DOGFOOTS FORSOOTH INCONNUS LOGBOOKS MONGOOSE POTHOOKS REQUEENS SEAWEEDY STRUTTED
TOMFOOLS UNBONNET UNCANNED UNCONNED UNFANNED UNGINNED UNMANNED UNMANNER UNPANNEL
UNPINNED UNSINNED UNTANNED UNTINNED

ABCDBCAE STILTISH   **ABCDBCBA** DENSENED SANTANAS

ABCDBCBE LANTANAS PENTENES   **ABCDBCCB** BANDANNA VALHALLA

ABCDBCCE PRECREED PREGREET TENPENNY   **ABCDBCDA** SINGINGS

ABCDBCDC INSENSES UNSENSES

ABCDBCDE INSENSED INTENTED PINGINGS RINGINGS STINTING UNSENSED UNTENTED

ABCDBCEA SATIATES SINKINGS

ABCDBCEB LARVARIA LENIENCE PENDENTE PERVERSE SENTENCE TENDENCE TENPENCE

ABCDBCEC COSMOSES MISLISTS NURTURER WARFARER

ABCDBCED CONDONED PREDREAD PRETREAT RINSINGS THIGHING

ABCDBCEF BACKACHE BACKACHY BIAXIATE BINDINGS CONDONER CONDONES CORPORAL DISVISOR
EARMARKS FANDANGO FIERIEST FINDINGS FLATLAND FRAGRANT FRIARING GERBERAS HEDGEDLY
INTENTLY KOWTOWED LENIENCY LENIENTS LINKINGS LONDONER LOWDOWNS MINCINGS MINDINGS
MINTINGS NAYSAYED NAYSAYER NITRITES NURTURAL NURTURED NURTURES OVERVEIL PENDENTS
PERVERTS PICNICKY PINKINGS PINWINGS PLAYLAND PREBREAK PRIORIES PRIORITE PRIORITY
RECHECKS SATIATED SEABEACH SHEPHERD SHIPHIRE SHOEHORN SLIMLINE SLITLIKE STILTIER
STILTIFY STILTING SUBPUBIC TARYARDS TENDENCY TOULOUSE UNCANCEL UNGANGED UNIONISM
UNIONIST UNIONIZE UNKINKED UNTINTED VIEWIEST VITRITES WARFARED WARFARES WARFARIN
WAYLAYER WHETHERS WINCINGS WINDINGS WINKINGS YARDARMS

ABCDBDAE LEADEDLY   **ABCDBDBC** ENGINING

ABCDBDBE CANTATAS ORDERERS UNLINING UNTINING

ABCDBDCE MELDEDLY UNIONOID WELDEDLY   **ABCDBDDB** SEPTETTE SEXTETTE

ABCDBDEB UNPINION   **ABCDBDEE** FLUELESS

ABCDBDEF ARBOROUS BEADEDLY BLUELEGS CANTATES DISTITLE FEUDEDLY FLAILING FOLIOING
HERDEDLY LACTATED LACTATES LOBCOCKS MENDEDLY MISTITLE OUTPUPIL PRAIRIED PRAIRIES
RENDEDLY RETIEING SUBTUTOR TOWCOCKS UNFINISH UNFINITE VENDEDLY

ABCDBEAA SLAGLESS SLIPLESS SLITLESS SNUGNESS   **ABCDBEAB** STOUTEST STUNTIST

ABCDBEAC DASTARDS DESCENDS RESHEARS RESWEARS   **ABCDBEAD** SILTIEST

ABCDBEAE ENSANDED TEMPESTS

ABCDBEAF ARBOREAL ARBOREAN ARBORWAY ARTERIAC ARTERIAL DASTARDY ENDANGER ENHANCED
ENHANCER ENLINKED ENRANKED ENRINGED GILDINGS GIRDINGS INCENDIA LAUDABLE LAUDABLY
LEADENLY LIMPIDLY LIQUIDLY PREWRAPS RASCALRY RECLEARS RUPTUARY SCARCEST SILKIEST
SKUNKISH STARTISH STOUTISH SUNBURST TEMPESTY TOPCOATS UNGENIUS UNMANFUL UNSINFUL
UNTONGUE

ABCDBEBA DEAFENED DECKERED DECREWED DEFLEXED DEPLETED RELIEVER REOMETER REOPENER
REVIEWER SECRETES SINUITIS

ABCDBEBB KEDGEREE TENDEREE

ABCDBEBC LEDGERED MASCARAS MEDLEYED MUSCULUS RAZMATAZ UNTENANT VERTEBER

ABCDBEBD FENDERED GENDERED LEADENED MARSALAS SECRETER TENDERED

ABCDBEBE BESTERER CENTERER CITRININ GENDERER LECHERER PELTERER PESTERER PEWTERER
TEMPERER TENDERER

ABCDBEBF ARBORERS ARMORERS BEAVERED BELIEVED BELIEVER BEPIECED BEPIECES BESIEGED
BESIEGER BESPEWED BESTERED BICLINIA CADMAEAN CATHAYAN CENTERED DECRETES DEFLEXES
DEPLETES DIAPIRIC DISPIRIT ENTONING ENTUNING ENZONING FADEAWAY FELTERED FENCELET
FESTERED FUNDULUS GEODETES GEOMETER GESTENED GEYSERED HAULAWAY HEAVENED HELMETED
JERSEYED KELTERED KERNELED LACKADAY LEAVENED LECHERED LEDGEMEN LIGNITIC LIPOIDIC
MANDALAS MANDALAY MANIACAL METHENES NEUTERED NIGRITIC PALMATAE PEACEMEN PELTERED
PESTERED RECHEWED REFLEXED REFLEXES REFUELED RELIEVED RELIEVES REOPENED REPIECED
REPIECES REPLETED REPLETES RESPEWED REVIEWED SECRETED SIGNIFIC SIGNIFIE TEASELED
TEASELER TEMPERED UNBONING UNOWNING UNSONANT UNTONING UNWANING UNZONING VERSEMEN
VERTEXES VIRGINIA WEAKENED WEAKENER WEASELED WEAZENED WELTERED WESTERED

ABCDBECA SIGHINGS SUNBURNS   **ABCDBECB** DESCENSE DREARIER PREORDER VERTEBRE

ABCDBECD MISTIEST PREDRIED PURSUERS SALEABLE

ABCDBECF BADLANDS BELTEDLY CONFOUND CONJOINS CONJOINT FISHIEST FORGOERS INSANEST
INTONATE LAUDANUM LEASEMAN LITHIATE MALTABLE MELTEDLY OUTHUNTS OVERVIEW PEACEMAN
PREARMED PREDRIES PRETRIED PRETRIES REDHEADS RISKIEST SALTABLE SALVABLE SALVABLY
SUNBURNT TALKABLE TRAMROAD UNLONELY VALUABLE VALUABLY VENGEANT VERTEBRA WALKABLE

WALKABLY WISPIEST

ABCDBEDA STARTERS STARTORS TIPSIEST   **ABCDBEDB** ORNERIER

ABCDBEDC INDENTED MOREOVER UNDENIED   **ABCDBEDD** CAVEATEE INDENTEE

ABCDBEDE DIETISTS INCENDED INCENSES INTENDED PIETISTS RIOTISTS UNBENDED UNMENDED
UNTENDED UNVENDED

ABCDBEDF ARDUROUS ARTERIED ARTERIES ASEISMIC CASEATED CAVEATED CONTORTS CONVOLVE
DRYERMEN FAILABLE FAILABLY FLATLETS GYPSYISH GYPSYISM HEALEDLY HETAERAS INCENSED
INCENSER INCENTER INDENTER INGENDER INGENUES INTENDER INTENSER INVENTED INVENTER
ISLESMEN LIQUIDUS MAILABLE MAILABLY MALEATES PEALEDLY REFLEXLY SAILABLE SCONCING
SIXTIETH SKUNKING STUNTING SUBAURAL UNBENDER UNCENTER UNFENCED UNFENCES UNLENSED
UNMANIAC UNRENTED UNTENDER UNVENGED UNVENTED VAILABLE VEILEDLY WAYGANGS

ABCDBEEA YEWBERRY

ABCDBEEB ANTENOON DENTELLE MARIANNA SERGETTE SERVETTE VERSETTE

ABCDBEEC DESWELLS DISTILLS MISBILLS MISKILLS RESMELLS RESPELLS RESWELLS

ABCDBEEF BEDWELLS BEPRETTY CANVASSY CARNALLY CATFALLS CAUSALLY CONSOMME DEWBERRY
FACIALLY FAUNALLY FENBERRY FIBRILLA GRUBROOT KERNELLY LAUSANNE MADGASSY MADRASSI
MANUALLY MARIANNE MIDRIFFS OUTBULLY OUTCULLS OUTPULLS PEABERRY RACIALLY RADIALLY
RANDALLS RASCALLY REDBELLY RUEFULLY SEABERRY SORBONNE SPALPEEN TARNALLY TEABERRY
UNIONEER VENDETTA WEASELLY

ABCDBEFA ARBORETA DECREPID DIARIZED DISLIKED DISLIVED DOCTORED ENKINDLE ENTANGLE
GYPSYING LIPOIDAL RADIATOR RAMPAGER SACKAGES SAGUAROS SAILAGES SALIANTS SALVAGES
SAWBACKS SCARCENS SCONCERS SCORCHES SCOTCHES SEGMENTS SEQUENTS SERPENTS SETHEADS
SEXTERNS SIBLINGS SIDLINGS SIEVINGS SIFTINGS SILTINGS SKULKERS SODWORKS STARTLES
STILTERS STILTONS STINTERS STOATERS STOUTERS STRATOUS STUNTERS STYPTICS SUBCUTIS
SUBDUALS SUBDUCES SUBDUCTS SUBDUERS SUBRULES TICKIEST

ABCDBEFB ADJUDGED ASBESTOS CAMPAGNA DECREASE DEGREASE FANTASIA FANTASMA FERVENCE
MERGENCE PERCEIVE PERMEATE REFLEDGE REPLEDGE RESHELVE SECRETAE SELVEDGE SEQUENCE
TASMANIA UNBENIGN UNWANTON VENDEUSE VERGENCE

ABCDBEFC AIRLINER AISLINGS ATESTINE BESMEARS BESPEAKS BESPENDS BESTEALS BOSPORUS
CHESHIRE CULTURAL DESCENTS DISLIKES DISLIMBS DISLIMNS DISLIVES ECTOCYST FISHINGS
FISTINGS FURCULAR LISPINGS LISTINGS LITHIEST MANDARIN MASTAGES MIDFIELD MIDWIFED
MIDWIVED MISBINDS MISCITES MISFILES MISFIRES MISGIVES MISLIKES MISLINES MISPICKS
MISTIDES MUDGUARD MUSCULES OUTBUILT OUTBURNT OUTBURST PANTALON PARTAKER PITHIEST
PREBROKE PREDRIVE PREDROVE PREGRADE PRETRACE PUSTULES RADIATED RESPEAKS RESPECTS
RESTEALS RESWEATS RITZIEST SLEDLIKE TASKAGES UNDINTED UNLINEAL UNSINEWS VARIATOR
WARMAKER WESTERNS WISHINGS WISTINGS

ABCDBEFD AIRTIGHT ALOELIKE ARTERIZE ATHETIZE BANDAGED CASTANET CAUDATED CAUSATES
COADORED CONDOLED CONSOLES CONSORTS CORDONED DATEABLE DIRTIEST DISTINCT FACEABLE
FORGOING HANSARDS HATEABLE HAVEABLE HETAERIA INCENTRE KEYSEATS LABRADOR LINTIEST

MANDATED MANSARDS MARIACHI MATSAILS MILTIEST MINTIEST NAMEABLE NIFTIEST OILTIGHT
OUTSUCKS OUTSULKS PAISANOS PAREABLE PERSEIDS PROTRACT PURSUALS PURSUITS PYGMYDOM
PYGMYISM RANSACKS RATEABLE SANDALED SATRAPER SAVEABLE SCORCHER SECRETOR SHEDHAND
SMARMIER STARTLER SUBDUCED SUBRULER TAKEABLE TAMEABLE TOPSOILS UNCENTRE UNGENTLE
WADEABLE WAGEABLE WAVEABLE

ABCDBEFE ALKYLENE ANTONYMY BEQUESTS BIPRISMS BRAIRDED CENTESIS COMPOSES COMPOSTS
DIALISTS DIARISTS FANTASMS FILMISTS FORMOSAS FUNGUSES HOMEOSIS INFUNDED LACTASES
LAMBASTS LIONISMS MALTASES MISTIDED PIANISMS PIANISTS PIETISMS REQUESTS RUCKUSES
RUMPUSES UNBANDED UNBONDED UNCANDID UNHANDED UNLANDED UNMINDED UNRINDED UNSANDED
UNWINDED VIOLISTS WAYFARER ZIONISMS ZIONISTS

ABCDBEFF BLOTLESS CLANLESS CLAWLESS CLOYLESS FLAGLESS FLAWLESS GLADLESS JACKAROO
KANGAROO MANDATEE ONLINESS ORATRESS OUTGUESS OUTQUAFF PLANLESS PLAYLESS PLOTLESS
PLOWLESS PLUGLESS PLUMLESS PREDRILL PRIORESS PROGRESS SALVAGEE

ABCDBEFG ADJUDGER ADJUDGES AETHERIC AETHERIN AIRFIELD AIRLIFTS AIRLINES AIRVIEWS
ALDOLIZE ALKYLIZE ANOINTED ANOINTER ANTINODE ANTINOMY ANTONYMS APORPHIN ARBORIES
ARBORISE ARBORIST ARBORIZE ARMORIED ARMORIES ARMORING ARMORIST ASBESTIC ASPISHLY
BAGMAKER BALKANIC BALSAMER BALSAMIC BANDAGER BANDAGES BARGAINS BARMAIDS BARNACLE
BASTARDY BEFLECKS BEPREACH BEQUEATH BETREADS BEWREAKS BEWREATH BEWRECKS BILKINGS
BIOCIDES BIOLITES BIOLITHS BIOTICAL BIOTIZED BIOTIZES BIOXIDES BIRDIEST BIRDINGS
BLOWLAMP BLOWLINE BOGHOLES BOILOVER BONHOMIE BOSPORAN BOUDOIRS BOXWORKS BULRUSHY
BURGUNDY CAFTANED CALKAGES CALVADOS CAMPAIGN CANMAKER CAPMAKER CAPTAINS CARNAGED
CARTABLE CARVAGES CASTABLE CATWALKS CAUSABLE CAUSATED CAVEATOR CERVELAT CIRTINES
CLAYLIKE CLODLETS CLOGLIKE CLUBLAND COADORES COBWORKS CODWORMS COENOBIA COLPORTS
COMFORTS COMPOLES COMPONED COMPONES COMPORTS COMPOSED COMPOSER COMPOTED COMPOTES
COMPOUND CONDOLER CONDOLES CONFORMS CONSOLED CONSOLER CONVOKED CONVOKER CONVOKES
CONVOYED CORDOBAN CORDOBAS CORDOVAN COUPONED COWBOYED COWHOUSE COWPOKES CULTURED
CULTURES DAMNABLE DAMNABLY DECREPIT DEFLECTS DETRENCH DEUTERIC DEUTERON DIALINGS
DIAMINES DIARIZES DINGIEST DINKIEST DISCIPLE DISLIKEN DISLIKER DOCTORAL DOCTORLY
DOGBOLTS DOGHOLES DOGHOUSE DOGMOUTH DORMOUSE DRAGROPE DRAWROPE DREARILY DREARING
DRIERMAN DRYBRUSH DRYERMAN ENCINALS ENGINOUS EUPHUISM EUPHUIST EVOLVING FACTABLE
FANBACKS FANMAKER FANTAILS FANTASIE FARMABLE FEAREDLY FENCEROW FERMENTS FERVENCY
FICOIDAL FICOIDES FICTIONS FICTIOUS FILMIEST FILMIZED FILMIZES FLAGLETS FLAGLIKE
FLATLING FLATLOCK FLAXLIKE FLYBLOWN FLYBLOWS FOGBOUND FOGHORNS FOLDOUTS FORBODES
FORMOSAN FORWOUND FOXHOLES FOXHOUND FUMOUSLY FUNGUSED GAINABLE GALVANIC GARBANZO
GARLANDS GASMAKER GAZPACHO GEODESIA GEODESIC GEODETIC GEOMETRY GEYSERAL GEYSERIC
GLADLIER GONDOLAS GONDOLET GYPSYDOM HALYARDS HANDARMS HANGABLE HANGARED HATBANDS
HATRAILS HAULAGES HAYBANDS HAYMAKER HAYRACKS HAYWARDS HEATEDLY HEAVENLY HEDGEROW
HELVETIA HELVETIC HENPECKS HERMETIC HERPETIC HESPERIA HESPERIC HESPERID HETAERIC
HETAERIO HEURETIC HIPLINES HOEDOWNS HOGBOATS HOLDOUTS HOLDOVER HOMEOIDS HOMEOTIC
HORMONAL HORMONES HORMONIC HOTBOXES HUMOURAL HUMOURED INCANTED INCENSOR INCENTOR
INDANGER INDENTOR INFANTED INFANTLY INFANTRY INHONEST INJUNCTS INLANDER INORNATE
INSANELY INTANGLE INTONERS INUENDOS INVENTAR INVENTOR ISLESMAN JANUARYS JAYHAWKS
JAYWALKS JERSEYAN JETBEADS JILTINGS JOYHOUSE JUMBUCKS KATMANDU KILTINGS KUMQUATS
LABIATED LABIATES LAMBASTE LANDAGES LANYARDS LARIATED LARVATED LAUDATOR LAURATES
LAWMAKER LAYBACKS LECTERNS LEDGEMAN LEUKEMIA LEUKEMIC LICKINGS LIFTINGS LIGNITES
LIMBIEST LIMNIADS LIMNITES LIMPINGS LINGIEST LINKIEST LIONIZED LIONIZER LIONIZES
LIRKINGS LITHIUMS LOCKOUTS LOGWORKS MACKAREL MAENALUS MAGDALEN MAGNATES MANDATES
MANDATOR MANIABLE MANJACKS MANWARDS MARKABLE MEAGERLY MEDIEVAL METHENYL MICHIGAN

```
MIDLINES MIDNIGHT MIDWIVES MILKIEST MILKINGS MINCIEST MISBIRTH MISCIBLE MISCITED
MISFIELD MISFILED MISFIRED MISGIVEN MISLIGHT MISLIKED MISLIKEN MISLIKER MISLINED
MONGOLIA MONGOLIC MONROVIA MOTIONAL MOTIONED MOTIONER MUSCULAR MYOCYTES NAYWARDS
NEGLECTS NEOFETAL NEOFETUS NEOTERIC NEUTERLY NIGRITES NIOBITES NIOBIUMS NITRIDES
NORFOLKS OATCAKES OATHABLE OCRACIES ONHANGER ORATRICE ORDERING OUTBUILD OUTBULGE
OUTBULKS OUTBURNS OUTCURED OUTCURES OUTCURSE OUTCURVE OUTGUARD OUTHURLS OUTJUMPS
OUTPURSE OUTSURGE PACKABLE PACKAGED PACKAGER PACKAGES PAGEANTS PANCAKED PANCAKES
PARBAKED PARBAKES PARFAITS PARLANCE PARSABLE PARTAGES PARTAKEN PARTAKES PAUSABLY
PAWNABLE PAWNAGES PAYBACKS PEACEFUL PEAKEDLY PENHEADS PENTELIC PERCEITS PERCENTS
PERFECTS PICKIEST PICKINGS PIECINGS PIMLICOS PINKIEST PISCINAE PISCINAL PLAYLETS
PLAYLIKE PLOWLAND PLOWLINE PLUGLIKE PLUMLIKE POGROMED POISONED POISONER POISONLY
POTBOILS POTHOLER POTHOLES POTHOUSE POTIONED POTIONER POTWORKS PREDRAFT PREDRAWN
PREDRAWS PREFRACT PREFRAUD PRETRAIN PRETRIAL PRIMROSE PRIMROSY PRIORACY PRIORATE
PROCRIES PROGRADE PROGRAMS PROTRADE PROTRUDE PURSUANT PURSUING PUSTULAR PUSTULED
PYGMYISH RADIABLE RADIANCE RADIANCY RADIANTS RADIATES RAFTAGES RAILAGES RAISABLE
RAMPAGED RAMPAGES RAMPANCY RATEABLY READEPTS REAGENCY REAGENTS REAMENDS REBLEACH
REBLENDS RECHEATS RECLEANS REFLECTS REHOEING REPLEADS REPLEATS REQUENCH RESKETCH
REVIEWAL REWHELPS REYIELDS RHYTHMAL RHYTHMED RHYTHMIC RIDGIEST RIFLINGS RINGIEST
RINSIBLE RIPTIDES ROANOKES ROWBOATS ROWLOCKS RUMPUSED SACKAGED SALVADOR SALVAGED
SALVAGER SATIABLE SATIABLY SATRAPIC SAWMAKER SCARCELY SCARCING SCARCITY SCORCHED
SCOTCHED SCOTCHER SECRETIN SECRETLY SECRETUM SEGUENDO SEPTEMIA SEQUENCY SERGEANT
SIGNIFER SIGNIORY SIGNITOR SINOIDAL SKULKING SKUNKDOM SKUNKERY SKUNKLET SLUGLIKE
SLUGLINE SLUMLAND SMARMING STARTFUL STARTING STARTLED STOUTING STRATEGY STRATIFY
STRETCHY STULTIFY STUNTIER SUBDUING SUBDURAL SUBHUMAN SUBHUMID SUBJUDGE SUBJUGAL
SUBJUGED SUBJUNCT SUBLUNAR SUBPUNCH SUBTUNIC SULFURAN SULFURIC SYNTYPIC TAMEABLY
TANBARKS TANKAGES TANKARDS TANYARDS TAXIABLE TAXIARCH TAXPAYER TEMPERAS TENDERLY
TICKINGS TOEBOARD TOEHOLDS TOPWORKS TOWROPES TOYHOUSE TOYWOMAN TOYWOMEN TRAPROCK
TRIARCHY TRIGRAMS TRIGRAPH TUMOURED UNBANKED UNCANDOR UNDONKEY UNFANGED UNGENIAL
UNGENTLY UNHANGED UNHINTED UNHONEST UNHONIED UNKINDLY UNKINGED UNKINGER UNLANCED
UNLENGTH UNLINKED UNMANTEL UNMENIAL UNMENTAL UNMINCED UNMINGLE UNMINTED UNMONIED
UNMONKLY UNORNATE UNPANELS UNPANGED UNPINKED UNRANCID UNRANDOM UNRANKED UNRINGED
UNRINSED UNSANITY UNSINEWY UNSINGED UNSINGLE UNTANGLE UNTINGED UNVENIAL UNVENOMS
UNWANTED UNWINDER UNWINGED UNWINKED UNWINTER UNWINTRY UNWONDER UNWONTED VACUATED
VACUATES VAGRANCE VAGRANCY VAGRANTS VAGRATED VAGRATES VALIANCE VALIANCY VALIANTS
VALUATED VALUATES VALUATOR VANDALIC VANTAGED VANTAGES VANWARDS VARIABLE VARIABLY
VARIANCE VARIANCY VARIANTS VARIATED VARIATES VARIATUS VATMAKER VENGEFUL VERBENAS
VERMEILS VERSEMAN VESPERAL VICTIMED VIEWINGS VINCIBLE VINCIBLY VINDICES VINDICTA
VINDICTS VIOLINED VIOLINES VIRGINAL VIRGINED VIRGINLY VISCIDLY VITRINES VITRIOLS
VITRIOUS VULTURED VULTURES WAFTAGES WAGTAILS WARDABLE WARDAGES WARMABLE WARPABLE
WARPAGES WARPATHS WASHABLE WASTABLE WAVEABLY WAXMAKER WAYBACKS WAYFARED WAYFARES
WAYMAKER WAYMARKS WESLEYAN WESTERLY WHITHERS WICHITAS WICKINGS WICKIUPS WILDINGS
WILTINGS WINDIEST WINDIGOS WINGIEST WITLINGS WORKOUTS YARDAGES YOGHOURT ZINCIDES
ZINCITES ZIONITES
```

ABCDCAAE FLOWOFFS OUTSTOOD PHILIPPA

ABCDCABE ANTITANK BLAMABLE BLAMABLY TENANTED TENANTER

ABCDCACE PROTOPOD   **ABCDCADE** OPINIONS

ABCDCAEB BEARABLE BEATABLE CLINICAL

ABCDCAEF AIRCRAFT AIRFRAME AIRGRAPH BEARABLY BOATABLE CRITICAL DIETEDLY EDIFIERS
EMPAPERS ENDODERM ENGAGERS ESTATELY GEOLOGIC MYOTOMIC OILCLOTH PHOTOPIC PRECEPTS
REALARMS REAWARDS SPOROSAC TENANTRY

ABCDCBAA SELFLESS   **ABCDCBAE** REPAPERS REVIVERS ROTATORS ROTATORY

ABCDCBBE CORNROOT FOREROOM WORKROOM WORMROOT   **ABCDCBCC** PREFEREE

ABCDCBCE UNEVENED   **ABCDCBDE** MILKLIKE SILKLIKE

ABCDCBEA DAWNWARD SNIPINGS SYNONYMS   **ABCDCBEB** SYNONYMY

ABCDCBEC OUTSTUNT PRESERVE   **ABCDCBED** FILELIKE LINENIZE TILELIKE

ABCDCBEE HELMLESS HELPLESS PELTLESS WELDLESS

ABCDCBEF BACKCAST BAILIAGE BEPAPERS CITATION COITIONS COTUTORS DEIFIERS DISUSING
DRAWARMS FALKLAND FILMLIKE FOLKLORE FORGROWN FORGROWS GRIDIRON GUARAUNO HAITIANS
HANGNAIL HATSTAND LONGNOSE MICACITE MICACIZE MILTLIKE MISUSING MOTATORY MYCOCYTE
NOTATORS OUTSTUDY POTATOED POTATOES POTATORS POTATORY POTSTONE PREMERIT PREVERBS
PROMORAL SILTLIKE SYNONYME TENONERS TIARAING UNEVENLY UNITINGS URETERAL URETERIC
VEINIEST WARCRAFT WILDLIFE WILDLIKE WILDLING

ABCDCCAE OBSESSOR   **ABCDCCBE** BELULLED REBOBBED   **ABCDCCDC** OBSESSES

ABCDCCDE MISASSAY OBSESSED OCTETTES   **ABCDCCEA** EMBUBBLE

ABCDCCEB BOCACCIO REBUBBLE RETATTLE   **ABCDCCEF** ALIBIING UNGAGGED

ABCDCDAA SANENESS SOLELESS   **ABCDCDAB** MESOSOME

ABCDCDAE ENTITIES GAININGS   **ABCDCDBB** ISLELESS   **ABCDCDBE** DIETETIC

ABCDCDCE PHENENES QUININIC UKELELES VENINING   **ABCDCDEB** LENINITE

ABCDCDED CRISISES

ABCDCDEE BALELESS FINENESS GONENESS HOLELESS LONENESS PILELESS POLELESS RULELESS
WILELESS

ABCDCDEF COININGS EMANANTS FOREREAD JOININGS LENINISM LENINIST LINENERS NOTITIAE
PETITION QUININES REMIMICS REPIPING REVIVIFY REVIVING SEMIMILD VEININGS WASHSHED

ABCDCEAA SALTLESS SURPRESS   **ABCDCEAB** EDIFICED HEADACHE LEAPABLE LEASABLE

ABCDCEAC CREDENCE HIAWATHA   **ABCDCEAD** PRETEMPT

ABCDCEAF APICILAR APIOIDAL AUROREAN AURORIAN BATHTUBS CANONICS CLEMENCY CORNRICK
EDIFICES ELICITED EMANATED EMANATES ENTITLED ENTITLES EXCOCTED HEADACHY HUARACHE
LIFEFULS LOANABLE LOANABLY NOTATING NUTATING OPTATION REVIVORS SHINIEST SLIMIEST
SOILIEST SPICIEST SPIKIEST SPINIEST SURPRISE

ABCDCEBA DECOCTED DESISTED DIPEPTID ELIGIBLE NOTATION RESISTER SEAFARES SEAWARES

ABCDCEBC BICYCLIC ENGAGING OUTSTRUT   **ABCDCEBD** FLEYEDLY

ABCDCEBE SEAFARER

ABCDCEBF BETITLED BETITLES BIOLOGIC BIONOMIC CANONIAL CLEVERLY DIABASIC DIABATIC
DIERETIC DUOLOGUE ELIGIBLY FISHSKIN LEADAGES LEAFAGES LEAKAGES PENANCED PENANCER
PENANCES PHARAOHS PLACABLE PLACABLY PLANABLE PLAYABLE REAWAKEN REAWAKES RECOCKED
RECOCTED RECYCLED RECYCLES RESISTED ROTATION SEAWATER SLAKABLE SLAYABLE TEAMAKER
TEAWARES UNPOPING

ABCDCECA ESTATUTE NIAGARAN   **ABCDCECB** ACIDIFIC CREWELER PRECEDER PROMOTOR

ABCDCECD SCENEMEN WHEREVER   **ABCDCECE** CLEVERER PRECEDED SKEWERER

ABCDCECF ANILIDIC BAEDEKER BREVETED CANONING CRENELED CRENELET LIEGEMEN NIAGARAS
OUTSTATE PIECENED PLANAEAS PRECEDES PRETEXED PRETEXES PREVENED PREVENES PROTOCOL
PROTOLOG PROTOZOA QUEBECER RHAMADAN SCALAWAG SKEWERED SOAKAWAY SPOROZOA STEREOED
STEVENED TEARAWAY TENONING WHENEVER

ABCDCEDA DOWNWIND   **ABCDCEDB** DEALABLE HEALABLE MEALABLE SEALABLE

ABCDCEDC LINENMEN   **ABCDCEDE** ANIMISMS ELITISTS PRETESTS

ABCDCEDF BONANZAS DIALABLE FOLKLIKE NOISIEST PRETENTS PRETEXTS PRONOUNS SCALABLE
SCALABLY SEACATCH UNMEMBER UNTETHER

ABCDCEEA SEAWALLS

ABCDCEEC CHEYENNE CRENELLE CREVETTE OMELETTE OPERETTE PIECETTE QUENELLE

ABCDCEED PRESELLS

ABCDCEEF AIRPROOF BAILIFFS BLOWOFFS CARDROOM CHAPATTI CHAPATTY DARKROOM FIREROOM
GALILEES OPERETTA OVEREGGS PRETELLS ROTATEES SPIRILLA TIREROOM WARDROOM WAREROOM
WARPROOF WITHTOOK

ABCDCEFA APOLOGIA DOWNWARD DUOTONED EASTSIDE ERASABLE EVADABLE EXIGIBLE LIEGEFUL
NUTATION PHOTOMAP POSTSHIP RESISTOR SAILINGS SCAVAGES SEALANTS SEAWARDS SEIZINGS
SLICINGS SLIDINGS SOAKAGES SOILINGS SONANCES SPICINGS SPIKINGS SPIRITUS STAKAGES
STIKINES SUICIDES SUITINGS TWILIGHT TWINIEST

ABCDCEFB BEARANCE BELTLINE CRINIGER ECOLOGIC ECONOMIC ECOTOPIC FEARABLE FEASANCE
FELTLIKE GERTRUDE HEARABLE HEATABLE ISOTOPES LEAKANCE NEARABLE PENKNIFE PERORATE
PROMOTER PROVOKER READABLE REAPABLE SELFLIKE TEARABLE TEASABLE THOROUGH TRIFILAR
WEANABLE WEARABLE WEAVABLE

ABCDCEFC ANTITHET DJAKARTA ENCYCLIC EUCYCLIC LINENMAN MISUSERS OUTSTART OUTSTEPT
OVEREDGE PLANARIA PRELEASE PRESENCE PRETENCE PRETENSE STALAGMA TENONIAN UNDODGED
UNSASHES

ABCDCEFD ACIDIZED ANTETYPE ARISINGS BIOSOMES CATSTEPS CUISINES GRADATED HOMEMADE
MOLELIKE OUTSTAYS OUTSTEPS OXIDIZED PEASANTS PHOTOIST PHOTOSET PORTRAIT PRELEGAL
PRESEALS PRESENTS RAISINGS SCENEMAN SKELETAL SPIRITER THEREFOR TWOSOMES WHEREFOR

ABCDCEFE ANIMISTS ANTITYPY APODOSES APODOSIS AUTOTYPY DIABASES DIAPASES ELITISMS
EPICISMS EPICISTS FRACASES HUNANESE MYOCOELE PROVOSTS SUICIDED TAURUSES TRINIDAD
TWINISMS UNICISMS UNICISTS UNITISMS WHIGISMS

ABCDCEFF BOLTLESS CALFLESS CANONESS DANKNESS FOLDLESS FONDNESS FORTRESS GOLDLESS
HARPRESS JOLTLESS KINDNESS LANKNESS LONGNESS MANYNESS MILKLESS MORTRESS MURDRESS
NABOBESS PORTRESS PROMOTEE PROVOKEE PUNINESS RANKNESS SHAWANEE WARDRESS WOLFLESS
YOLKLESS ZANINESS

ABCDCEFG ACIDITES ACIDIZER ADITIONS AIRBRUSH AIRCREWS AIRDROME AIRDROPS ALTITUDE
AMINIZED AMINIZES ANIMIZED ANIMIZER ANIMIZES ANTITYPE APOLOGER APOLOGUE APTITUDE
ARCHCITY ASTUTELY AWNINGED BALDLING BETUTORS BICYCLED BICYCLER BICYCLES BIOTOPES
BIOZONES BITSTONE BLATANCY BLOWOUTS BOATAGES BOILINGS BOLTLIKE BOUQUETS BRAVADOS
BREVETCY BRIMIEST BRIMINGS BRINIEST CAINITES CALFLIKE CALFLING CAMOMILE CANONIST
CANONIZE CEILINGS CHARADES CHASABLE CHEVERIL CHIDINGS CITATORS CITATORY CLAVATED
CLINIQUE COADAPTS COEXERTS COILINGS COUTURES CREDENZA CRIMINAL CRITIQUE CRITIZED
CRITIZES CURARINE CURARINS CURARIZE CYANAMID CYANATES DECOCTUM DEIFICAL DELILAHS
DENUNCIA DICYCLES DISASTER DISUSAGE DOWNWASH DOWNWITH DRAMATIC DRAPABLE DRAWABLE
DRAYAGES DRIVINGS DROPOUTS DUOTONES EARDROPS EARDRUMS EDITIONS ELICITOR EMANATOR
ESTATING FAILINGS FAIRINGS FEASAUNT FILMLAND FINANCED FINANCER FINANCES FLAKAGES
FLITINGS FLOPOVER FLUXURES FOILINGS FOLKLAND FORDRIES FORERANK FORERIBS FORERUNS
FORPRISE FORTREAD FORWRAPS FRAMABLE FRENETIC FRIGIDLY GEOPOLAR GLOBOIDS GNAWABLE
GOLDLIKE GRADABLE GRADATES GRAZABLE GRIMIEST GRIPIEST GUARANTY GULFLIKE HAIRIEST
HALFLING HALOLIKE HANGNEST HAWKWISE HINDNECK HORARIES ICEBERGS INAPATHY INARABLE
ISOGONAL ISOLOGUE ISOMORPH ISOPODAN JUICIEST LAICIZED LAICIZER LAICIZES LATITUDE
LIEGEDOM LIEGEMAN LONGNECK MAILINGS MARKRIES MESOSAUR MISUSAGE MUTATING MUTATION
MUTATIVE MUTATORY MYOLOGIC NABOBISH NABOBISM NEOLOGIC NEOMODAL NEOMORPH NEOZOICS
NOTATIVE OLIVINES OPACATED OPACATES OPIFICES OPINIATE OPTATING OPTATIVE ORIFICES
ORIGINAL ORIGINED ORIGINES OUTSTAID OUTSTAND OUTSTARE OUTSTEAL OUTSTEAM OUTSTING
OUTSTINK OUTSTRIP OVEREASY OVEREDIT OVICIDAL OVICIDES OXALATES OXIDIZER PAIRINGS
PALMLIKE PARERGIC PEASANTY PETITORS PETITORY PHALANGE PHALANGY PHOTOGEN PHOTOING
PHOTONIC PLACARDS PLACATED PLACATER PLACATES PLANATED PLATANES PLAYACTS PLEBEIAN
PLEBEITY POLYLITH PORTRAYS POSTSIGN POTATIVE PRAYABLE PREBENDS PRECENTS PREDEATH
PREDEBIT PREDECAY PREDELAY PREFEAST PREFECTS PREHEALS PREHEATS PREHENDS PRELECTS
PREMEDIA PREMEDIC PRETEACH PRETENDS PREVENTS PREWEIGH PRICIEST PRIDINGS PRIMINGS
PRIVIEST PROFOUND PROLOGUE PROLONGS PROMOTED PROMOTES PROMOVAL PROMOVED PROMOVES
PROTOGEN PROTONES PROTONIC PROTOXID PROVOKED PROVOKES PROVOSTY PROZONES PUTATIVE
QUAYAGES QUINIZED QUINIZES RAILINGS RAINIEST RAISINED READABLY READAPTS REPOPING
RESISTAL RETOTALS REVIVALS RICOCHET RINGNECK ROADABLE ROILIEST ROTATING ROTATIVE
SALTLIKE SCAVAGER SCELETON SCENEFUL SCIMITAR SEAMANLY SETATION SHAKABLE SHAKABLY
SHAMABLE SHAMABLY SHAMANIC SHAPABLE SHARABLE SHARABLY SHAVABLE SIEVEFUL SKELETON
SOARABLE SOARABLY SPADABLE SPADAITE SPARABLE SPINIFEX SPIRITAL SPIRITED STAVABLE
STAYABLE STOPOVER SUICIDAL SURPRIZE SWAYABLE TAILINGS TALCLIKE TARBRUSH TEARABLY
TEASABLY TOWNWARD TOWNWEAR TRADABLE TRAVAILS TRIVIALS TWOFOLDS UNABASED UNABATED
UNADAPTS UNALARMS UNAMAZED UNAWAKED UNAWARED UNAWARES UNCOCKED UNCOCTED UNEXEMPT
UNIFIERS UNIFILAR UNITIZED UNITIZER UNITIZES UNPAPERS UNSASHED UNSISTER UNTITHED
UNTITLED UROLOGIC UROPODAL UROTOXIA UROTOXIC UROTOXIN UTILIZED UTILIZER UTILIZES

VEILINGS VINTNERS VINTNERY VOICINGS VOIDINGS VOILIERS WAITINGS WARDROBE WEIRINGS
WHINIEST WHITINGS WITHTURN WOLFLIKE WRITINGS

ABCDDAAE OVERROOF   **ABCDDAEB** REACCRUE   **ABCDDAEC** ABERRATE OVERRODE

ABCDDAED EMITTENT   **ABCDDAEE** OVERROLL

ABCDDAEF ABERRANT ABUTTALS AXILLARS AXILLARY CROSSCUT EMITTERS EVILLEST EXAGGERS
IDYLLIAN IDYLLISM IDYLLIST IDYLLIZE UNACCUSE

ABCDDBAE REASSERT REOFFERS REUTTERS   **ABCDDBCA** REAPPEAR

ABCDDBCE CROSSROW PIAZZIAN REANNEAL REAPPEAL   **ABCDDBDD** REASSESS

ABCDDBEB REALLEGE   **ABCDDBEC** CIOPPINO   **ABCDDBED** REATTEST

ABCDDBEE LEANNESS MEALLESS MEANNESS REACCESS VEILLESS ZEALLESS

ABCDDBEF BIASSING BIENNIAL BIENNIUM DIALLING GAILLARD GIRLLIKE LOESSOID PRESSRUN
REACCEND REACCEPT REAFFECT REASSENT REATTEND REOFFEND SCREECHY TAILLAGE VIALLING
WASHHAND WITHHIED WITHHIES

ABCDDCAB TEAMMATE   **ABCDDCAC** SIENNESE

ABCDDCAE COEFFECT OMISSION SKITTISH SLIMMISH SNIFFISH SNIPPISH STIFFISH STILLISH
SWELLEST SWIMMIST

ABCDDCBD DRESSERS PRESSERS

ABCDDCBE BRAGGART CHALLAHS FRETTERS GRAMMARS KNITTING SNIFFING SNIPPING STACCATO
TREKKERS

ABCDDCDA GRINNING   **ABCDDCDC** UNDEEDED

ABCDDCDE CAREERED CHILLILY CHINNING FRILLILY SHINNING SKINNING SPINNING THINNING
TWINNING

ABCDDCEA EMISSIVE GLIBBING GRIDDING GRILLING GRIMMING GRIPPING GRITTING RAILLIER
SHEDDERS SHELLERS SHIMMIES SKIVVIES SLEDDERS SMELLERS SPELLERS SPINNIES STEMMERS
STEPPERS SWELLERS TRIPPIST

ABCDDCEB CHILLISH DRIPPIER FLATTAIL FRILLIER FRIZZIER GRINNIER GRIPPIER GRITTIER
REOPPOSE SHABBATH THINNISH VEILLIKE WHIGGISH

ABCDDCEC UNEFFETE VIENNESE

ABCDDCED BLESSERS BLOSSOMS FRIGGING GUESSERS PRIGGING REASSAYS SWIGGING TWIGGING
WHIGGING WRIGGING

ABCDDCEE OPENNESS

ABCDDCEF ABETTERS BLESSETH BLIPPING BLISSING BLOSSOMY BOATTAIL BRIMMING CHILLIER
CHILLING CHIPPIER CHIPPIES CHIPPING CHITTING CLIFFIER CLIFFING CLIPPIES COATTAIL
COIFFING CRIBBING DIALLAGE DRILLING DRIPPING DUELLERS DWELLERS EMISSION EMITTING
FLAMMANT FLIPPING FLITTING FRILLIES FRILLING FRITTING FRIZZILY FRIZZING FUELLERS
GLOWWORM GRIFFINS GRITTILY GROTTOED GROTTOES JAILLIKE NAILLIKE OMISSIVE OMITTING
OVERREAD OVERREDS OVERRENT PIAZZAED PLACCATE PRIGGISH PRISSILY PRISSING QUELLERS
QUILLING QUIPPING QUIPPISH QUITTING QUIZZING QUIZZISH RAILLIED RAILLIES RAILLIKE
REASSAIL REATTACH REATTACK REATTAIN RETOOTHS SCABBARD SHILLING SHIMMIED SHIMMING
SHINNIED SHIPPING SHIRRING SKIDDING SKIFFING SKILLING SKIMMING SKINNIER SKIPPING
SKITTING SLIMMING SLIPPIER SLIPPING SLITTING SMITTING SNIFFILY SNIPPIER SPIFFIER
SPIFFILY SPIFFING SPILLIER SPILLING SPITTING STAFFAGE STALLAGE STIFFING STILLIER
STILLING STIRRING SWILLING SWIMMIER SWIMMILY SWIMMING TAILLIKE TRILLING TRILLION
TRILLIUM TRIMMING TRIPPING TROLLOPE TROLLOPS TWIGGIER TWILLING UNARRAYS UNATTACH
UNTOOTHS WHIMMIER WHIMMING WHINNIED WHINNIES WHIPPIER WHIPPING WHIRRING WHIZZING
WRAPPAGE WRITTING

ABCDDEAA SAILLESS SKILLESS SNOBBESS SOILLESS SOULLESS

ABCDDEAB REASSURE REATTIRE SHOPPISH STIFFEST STILLEST

ABCDDEAC SKEWWISE UNLEEFUL   ABCDDEAD CLASSICS   ABCDDEAE ENWOODED

ABCDDEAF CRANNOCK ENCOOPED ENROOTED GRILLAGE RAILLERY REACCORD REAFFIRM REAFFORD
REAPPORT REASSORT REOCCURS SCOTTISH SLIMMEST SLUGGISH SLUTTISH SMALLEST SMALLISH
SMUGGEST SMUGGISH SNAPPISH SNOBBISH SNOBBISM SNUBBISH SNUFFISH SNUGGEST SNUGGISH
STAFFISH SWANNISH SWELLISH TRIVVETS

ABCDDEBA DEWOOLED LAGOONAL RECOOPER REISSUER SWALLOWS

ABCDDEBC PRESSURE REDOOMED STELLATE STELLITE

ABCDDEBD BRASSERS CROSSERS DROSSERS GRASSERS GROSSERS REISSUES SNAGGING SNUGGING
TRUSSERS

ABCDDEBE REHOODED REWOODED STECCATA STEMMATA

ABCDDEBF BAZOOKAS BEFOOLED BEHOOPED BEHOOVED BEHOOVES BELOOKED BEMOONED BESOOTED
BRAGGERS BRAGGERY BRANNERS BRIMMERS CLAMMILY CLODDILY CLOGGILY CLUBBILY CRABBERS
CRABBERY CRIBBERS CRITTERS CROPPERS CROSSARM CRULLERS DRAGGERS DRAMMERS DRILLERS
DRIPPERS DROLLERS DROLLERY DROPPERS DRUGGERY DRUMMERS FLABBILY FLAGGILY FLANNELS
FLOCCULI FLOPPILY FRILLERS FRILLERY FRIPPERS FRIPPERY FRITTERS FRIZZERS FROGGERS
FROGGERY GLASSILY GLOSSILY GRABBERS GRAPPERS GRIDDERS GRILLERS GRINNERS GRIPPERS
GRITTERS GRUBBERS GRUBBERY INERRANT KNELLING KNOBBING KNOLLING KNOTTING KRULLERS
MOUFFLON PLUMMILY PRIGGERS PRIGGERY PRODDERS PROFFERS REBOOKED RECOOKED RECOOLED
REFOOLED REFOOTED REHOOKED REHOOPED REISSUED RELOOKED REOFFSET RETOOLED SCOTTICE
SLABBILY SLOPPILY SNAPPING SNELLING SNOBBING SNUBBING SNUFFING TRAMMERS TRAPPERS
TRIGGERS TRILLERS TRIMMERS TRIPPERS TRIPPERY TROFFERS TROLLERS UNACCENT UNADDING
UNEBBING UNERRANT UNERRING UNFEEING UNSEEING WITHHEIR WRAPPERS WRITTERS

ABCDDECA SHERRIES SMELLIES SPETTLES

ABCDDECB CRESSIER DREGGIER DRESSIER FRETTIER PRETTIER TRESSIER

ABCDDECD BACKKICK ODYSSEYS SCULLFUL SKULLFUL

ABCDDECF BIANNUAL CHERRIED CHERRIES CHESSMEN CLASSMAN COAPPEAR CROSSBOW CROSSFOW
GHETTOED GHETTOES GLASSMAN GRASSMAN PRESSMEN PRETTIED PRETTIES SHELLIER SHELLMEN
SHERRIED SMELLIER SPELLMEN STAFFMAN STALLMAN STEMMIER UMTEENTH

ABCDDEDA GRUNNING SCARRERS SHIRRERS SPARRERS SPURRERS SQUEEGES SQUEEZES STARRERS
STIRRERS

ABCDDEDC APENNINE CAREENER SCREENER UNDEEMED UNREELER   **ABCDDEDD** SQUEEGEE

ABCDDEDE FRITTATA UNHEEDED UNSEEDED UNWEEDED

ABCDDEDF BLURRERS BRASSISH CAREENED CHARRERS CLANNING CLOGGAGE COASSIST CRASSEST
CROSSEST FLANNING GLOSSIST GROSSEST PLANNING REASSIST SCANNING SCREENED SHUNNING
SPANNING SPLEENED SQUEEGED SQUEEZED SQUEEZER STUNNING SWANNING UNHEELED UNKEELED
UNPEELED UNPEERED UNREEFED UNREELED UNREEVED UNREEVES UNSEELED UNTEEMED

ABCDDEEA SKIDDOOS SNUBBEES   **ABCDDEEF** FISHHOOK LINSSEED SPITTOON THUGGEES

ABCDDEFA DRIBBLED DRIPPLED DRIZZLED GLADDING GLASSING GLOSSING GLUTTING GRABBING
GRASSING GROSSING GRUBBING GRUFFING GUESSING LOESSIAL RAILLEUR SCALLOPS SCANNERS
SCARROWS SCATTERS SCOFFERS SCOTTIES SCROOGES SCUDDERS SCUDDIES SCUDDLES SCUFFERS
SCUFFLES SCULLERS SCUMMERS SCUNNERS SCUPPERS SCUPPETS SCUTTLES SHALLOTS SHALLOWS
SHAMMERS SHATTERS SHELLACS SHIMMERS SHINNERS SHINNEYS SHIPPERS SHOPPERS SHOTTERS
SHUDDERS SHUFFLES SHUNNERS SHUTTERS SHUTTLES SIERRANS SKIDDERS SKILLETS SKIMMERS
SKINNERS SKIPPERS SKITTERS SKITTLES SLABBERS SLAGGERS SLAPPERS SLATTERS SLIPPERS
SLITTERS SLIVVERS SLOBBERS SLOGGERS SLOTTERS SLUBBERS SLUGGERS SLUMMERS SLURRIES
SLUTTERS SMATTERS SMUGGLES SMUTTERS SNAGGERS SNAGGLES SNAPPERS SNIFFERS SNIGGERS
SNIGGLES SNIPPERS SNIPPETS SNOBBERS SNOTTERS SNOTTIES SNUBBERS SNUFFERS SNUFFLES
SNUGGERS SNUGGIES SNUGGLES SOUFFLES SPANNERS SPARROWS SPATTERS SPIGGOTS SPILLERS
SPINNERS SPINNEYS SPITTERS SPITTLES SPORRANS SPOTTERS SPUDDERS SPUTTERS STABBERS
STAFFERS STAGGERS STALLERS STAMMERS STANNOUS STIFFENS STILLERS STIPPENS STIPPLES
STIRRUPS STOLLENS STOPPERS STOPPLES STUBBERS STUBBLES STUCCOES STUFFERS STUNNERS
SWABBERS SWABBIES SWABBLES SWAGGERS SWAGGIES SWANNERS SWAPPERS SWATTERS SWILLERS
SWIMMERS SWIPPERS SWIZZLES SWOBBERS SWOTTERS THINNEST TRAPPIST TRIMMEST TRIPPANT

ABCDDEFB AGREEING BESOOTHE BLISSFUL BRAGGIER BRANNIER BRASSIER BRATTIER CRABBIER
CRAGGIER CRAPPIER CRASSIER CRIPPLER CROSSBAR CRUMMIER DRABBIER DRAGGIER DRIBBLER
DROSSIER DRUGGIER FRIZZLER FROGGIER GLASSFUL GRABBIER GRABBLER GRAPPLER GRASSIER
GRIZZLER GRUBBIER PRATTLER PSYLLIDS REACCUSE REALLUDE REAPPOSE REASSUME REILLUME
RESOOTHE SEALLIKE SNUFFMAN SNUFFMEN THUGGISH TRAPPIER TRUFFLER UNLOOSEN VEALLIKE
WRIGGLER

ABCDDEFC DIARRHEA DRESSAGE DUELLIZE GLESSITE MAROONER OCELLATE OVERRACE OVERRAKE
OVERRATE OVERRIDE OVERRIFE OVERRIPE OVERRISE OVERRUDE OVERRULE PRESSIVE SWELLAGE
UNDOOMED UPROOTER YAHOOISH

ABCDDEFD ALYSSUMS BRAGGING BRASSEYS BRASSIES BRUSSELS CAISSONS CHARRIER CHUGGING

CLASSERS CLOGGING COATTEST DRAGGING DRUGGING DUETTIST FLAGGING FLATTEST FLOGGING
FLOSSERS FROGGING GLASSERS GLOSSERS GRASSIES GRIDDLED INFEEBLE ODESSANS ODYSSEUS
PLUGGING QUARRIER SCURRIER SHAGGING SHELLFUL SHODDIED SKILLFUL SLAGGING SLOGGING
SLUGGING SMELLFUL SMUGGING SPELLFUL SPURRIER STAGGING STARRIER SWADDLED SWAGGING
THUGGING TWADDLED TWIDDLED UNFEEBLE

ABCDDEFE CABOOSES GLASSEYE GRAFFITI NAZIISMS UNHOODED UNLOOSES UNROOSTS UNWOODED
VAMOOSES

ABCDDEFF COALLESS DOWNNESS DUMBBELL GOALLESS IRONNESS MAILLESS NAILLESS OVERRUFF
RAILLESS TAILLESS THINNESS TOILLESS TWINNESS VAINNESS WORNNESS

ABCDDEFG ABERRING ABETTING ABETTORS ABUTTERS ABUTTING ABYSSING ARCHHOST ASWOONED
AVERRING BIRDDOMS BIWEEKLY BLADDERS BLADDERY BLESSING BLIZZARD BLOTTERS BLOTTIER
BLOTTING BLUFFERS BLUFFEST BLUFFIER BLUFFING BLURRING BOUFFANT BOWLLIKE BRAGGISH
BRASSILY BRASSING BRATTISH BRILLANT BRITTANY BRITTLED BRITTLES BROLLIES CABOODLE
CABOOSED CHAFFIER CHAFFING CHAFFMEN CHANNELS CHAPPERS CHAPPIER CHAPPIES CHAPPING
CHAPPIST CHARRING CHATTELS CHATTERS CHATTERY CHATTIER CHATTILY CHATTING CHEDDARS
CHESSDOM CHESSMAN CHIFFONS CHIFFONY CHILLERS CHILLEST CHIPPERS CHIPPEWA CHIRRUPS
CHIRRUPY CHITTERS CHOPPERS CHOPPIER CHOPPING CHUBBIER CHUBBILY CHUFFIER CHUFFILY
CHUFFING CHUGGERS CHUKKERS CHUMMERS CHUMMERY CHUMMIER CHUMMIES CHUMMILY CHUMMING
CLABBERS CLABBERY CLADDING CLAMMIER CLAMMING CLAMMISH CLAPPERS CLAPPING CLASSIER
CLASSIFY CLASSING CLASSMEN CLATTERS CLATTERY CLATTING CLIPPERS CLOBBERS CLODDERS
CLODDIER CLODDING CLODDISH CLOGGERS CLOGGIER CLOPPING CLOTTERS CLOTTING CLUBBERS
CLUBBIER CLUBBING CLUBBISH CLUBBISM CLUBBIST CLUTTERS CLUTTERY COASSERT COASSUME
COATTEND COIFFEUR COIFFURE CRABBING CRABBISH CRAGGILY CRAMMING CRANNIED CRANNIES
CRAPPING CRESSIDA CRIBBAGE CRIPPLED CRIPPLES CROPPING CROSSBIT CROSSING CROSSLET
CROSSTIE CROSSWAY CROSSWEB CRUDDING CRUMMING DEOSSIFY DHURRIES DIALLERS DRABBEST
DRABBING DRABBISH DRABBLES DRAGGILY DRAGGLES DRATTING DREGGILY DREGGISH DRESSILY
DRESSING DRIBBLES DRILLMAN DRILLMEN DRIPPAGE DRIZZLES DROLLEST DROLLING DROLLISH
DROLLIST DROPPAGE DROPPING DROSSING DRUBBING DRUGGIST DRUMMING DUELLING DUELLIST
DUETTING DUETTINO DWELLING EMISSARY FISHHOLD FLABBIER FLAGGERS FLAGGERY FLAGGIER
FLAGGISH FLAPPERS FLAPPIER FLAPPING FLATTENS FLATTERS FLATTERY FLATTIES FLATTING
FLATTISH FLATTOPS FLIPPANT FLIPPERS FLIPPERY FLIPPEST FLITTERS FLIVVERS FLOGGERS
FLOPPERS FLOPPETY FLOPPIER FLOPPING FLOSSIER FLOSSING FLUBBING FLUMMERY FLURRIED
FLURRIES FLURRING FLUTTERS FLUTTERY FRAZZLED FRAZZLES FRETTING FRIZZLED FRIZZLES
FROGGIES FROGGISH GHAFFIRS GLADDENS GLADDERS GLADDEST GLADDONS GLASSIER GLASSINE
GLASSITE GLASSMEN GLIBBEST GLIMMERS GLIMMERY GLISSADE GLITTERS GLITTERY GLOBBIER
GLOSSARY GLOSSATE GLOSSIER GLOTTICS GLOTTIDS GLUMMEST GLUTTERS GLUTTERY GLUTTONS
GNATTERS GNATTIER GRANNIES GRAPPLED GRAPPLES GRASSCUT GRASSHOP GRASSMEN GRASSNUT
GRIDDLES GRIFFONS GRIMMEST GRIZZLED GRIZZLES GROMMETS GROPPLED GROPPLES GROSSIFY
GRUBBIES GRUBBILY GRUFFILY GRUFFISH GRUMMETS HINDDECK IDYLLERS INHOOPED INLOOKED
INLOOKER INROOTED JOHNNIES KABOODLE KNITTERS KNOBBERS KNOBBIER KNOBBILY KNOBBISH
KNOBBLED KNOBBLER KNOBBLES KNOLLERS KNOTTERS KNOTTIER KNOTTILY LAGOONED LAMPPOST
LYONNAIS MAILLOTS MAROONED MUEZZINS ODYSSEAN OVALLING OVERRACK OVERRANK OVERRASH
OVERRICH OVERRUNS OVERRUSH OVERRUST PFENNIGS PHALLISM PHALLIST PHALLOID PHYLLADE
PHYLLARE PHYLLINE PHYLLINS PHYLLITE PHYLLIUM PHYLLODE PHYLLOID PHYLLOME PHYLLOUS
PIERROTS PLANNERS PLATTENS PLATTERS PLATTING PLODDERS PLODDING PLOTTAGE PLOTTERS
PLOTTERY PLOTTIES PLOTTING PLOWWISE PLUGGERS PLUMMERS PLUMMETS PLUMMIER PLUMMING
PLUSSING PRAMMING PRATTING PRATTLED PRATTLES PRESSFUL PRESSING PRESSMAN PRETTIFY
PRETTILY PRIMMEST PRODDING PRUSSIAN PRUSSIFY PSYLLIUM PUISSANT PUREEING PYORRHEA

```
QUADDING QUAFFERS QUAFFING QUARRELS QUARRIED QUARRIES QUARRING QUELLING QUIBBLED
QUIBBLER QUIBBLES QUILLERS QUIPPERS QUITTALS QUITTERS QUITTORS QUIZZERS QUIZZERY
REACCOST READDING REALLOTS REALLOWS REANNOYS REASSIGN REOCCUPY SCABBERY SCABBIER
SCABBILY SCABBING SCABBLED SCABBLER SCAFFOLD SCALLION SCARRING SCATTIER SCATTING
SCHOOLED SCHOOLER SCHOONED SCHOONER SCOFFING SCOFFLAW SCROODGE SCUDDIER SCUDDING
SCUFFIER SCUFFING SCUFFLED SCUFFLER SCULLERY SCULLING SCULLION SCUMMIER SCUMMING
SCURRIED SCUTTLED SCUTTLER SHABBIER SHABBIFY SHABBILY SHADDOCK SHAGGIER SHAGGILY
SHALLOWY SHAMMING SHATTERY SHEDDING SHELLACK SHELLING SHELLMAN SHELLPAD SHELLPOT
SHIMMERY SHIPPAGE SHODDIER SHODDILY SHOPPIER SHOPPING SHOTTIER SHOTTING SHUDDERY
SHUFFLED SHUFFLER SHUTTING SHUTTLED SHUTTLER SKEDDING SKINNERY SKIPPERY SKITTERY
SKITTLED SKITTLER SKULLCAP SKULLERY SLABBIER SLABBING SLAMMING SLAPPIER SLAPPING
SLATTERN SLATTERY SLATTING SLEDDING SLIPPAGE SLIPPERY SLOBBERY SLOBBIER SLOPPAGE
SLOPPERY SLOPPIER SLOPPING SLOTTERY SLOTTING SLUBBERY SLUBBIER SLUBBING SLUFFING
SLUGGARD SLUMMIER SLUMMING SLURRIED SLURRING SLUTTERY SLUTTIER SLUTTING SMALLING
SMALLPOX SMELLING SMOGGIER SMUGGERY SMUGGLED SMUGGLER SMUTTIER SMUTTILY SMUTTING
SNAFFLED SNAGGIER SNAGGLED SNAPPIER SNAPPILY SNAZZIER SNIFFLED SNIFFLER SNIGGLED
SNIGGLER SNIPPETY SNOBBERY SNOTTERY SNOTTIER SNOTTILY SNOZZLED SNUBBIER SNUFFBOX
SNUFFIER SNUFFLED SNUFFLER SNUGGERY SNUGGLED SNUZZLED SOFTTACK SOULLIKE SPARRING
SPARROWY SPELLING SPELLMAN SPIGGOTY SPILLAGE SPILLWAY SPINNERY SPITTLED SPLEENIC
SPOTTAIL SPOTTIER SPOTTILY SPOTTING SPOTTLED SPREEING SPUDDIER SPUDDING SPURRING
SPUTTERY STABBING STAFFIER STAFFING STAFFMEN STAFFORD STAGGIER STALLING STALLION
STALLMEN STARRILY STARRING STEMMING STEPPING STILLAGE STILLERY STILLMAN STILLMEN
STIPPLED STIPPLER STOPPAGE STOPPING STOPPLED STUBBIER STUBBING STUBBLED STUBBORN
STUCCOED STUCCOER STUDDING STUFFIER STUFFILY STUFFING SWABBING SWABBLED SWADDLER
SWANNECK SWANNERY SWAPPING SWATTING SWELLING SWIZZLED SWIZZLER SWOTTING TABOOING
TABOOISM THALLIUM THINNERS THUDDING THUGGERY THUGGISM TRAFFICS TRALLOPS TRAMMELS
TRAMMING TRAPPING TRAPPOID TRAPPOUS TREKKING TRESSFUL TRESSING TRODDING TROLLEYS
TROLLIED TROLLIES TROLLING TROLLMAN TROLLMEN TROMMELS TRUFFLED TRUFFLES TRUMMELS
TRUNNELS TRUSSING TWADDLER TWADDLES TWIGGERS TWIGGERY TWILLERS TWINNERS TWIZZLED
TWIZZLES ULYSSEAN UNACCEPT UNACCORD UNALLIED UNALLOWS UNATTIRE UNBOOKED UNBOOTED
UNCOOKED UNCOOLED UNCOOPED UNFOOLED UNFOOTED UNGOODLY UNHOOFED UNHOOKED UNHOOPED
UNHOOPER UNHOOTED UNLOOKED UNLOOPED UNLOOSED UNLOOTED UNMEEKLY UNMOORED UNMOOTED
UNOFFSET UNPOOLED UNROOFED UNROOTED UNSEEMLY UNWOOFED UPLOOKED UPLOOKER UPROOTAL
UPROOTED VACUUMED VAMOOSED WHAMMING WHAPPING WHETTING WHIGGERY WHINNOCK WHIPPERS
WHIPPETS WHIPPOST WHITTERS WHITTLED WHITTLER WHITTLES WHIZZERS WHIZZLED WHIZZLES
WHOPPERS WHOPPING WINDDOGS WITHHELD WITHHOLD WOLFFIAN WOLFFISH WRAPPING WRIGGLED
WRIGGLES WRITTENS WRIZZLED YAHOOING YAHOOISM
```

ABCDEAAB ESCAPEES LENTILLE   **ABCDEAAC** OUTSHOOT   **ABCDEAAD** OVERDOOR

ABCDEAAE TABLETTE TANKETTE TOILETTE

ABCDEAAF ADVOCAAT EIGHTEEN EMIGREES ENDSHEET ERMINEES EVACUEES EVICTEES EXPIREES
LAWFULLY LEGPULLS LETHALLY LINEALLY LOWBALLS LOWBELLS OILPROOF OUTBLOOM OVERBOOK
OVERBOOT OVERCOOK OVERCOOL OVERFOOT OVERHOOK OVERLOOK OVERTOOK

ABCDEABA ANDRIANA DEBRIDED DECARDED DEGRADED DEMANDED DESANDED DEVOIDED REPAIRER
REQUIRER RESTORER SINOPSIS STOLISTS STYLISTS

ABCDEABC BELIABEL EINSTEIN INGOTING INSULINS MESDAMES OKEYDOKE OUTSCOUT OUTSHOUT
OUTSPOUT RESCORES RESHARES RESPIRES RESTORES ZEROIZER

ABCDEABD DEGRADER   **ABCDEABE** CURLECUE INEDGING ISLAMISM

ABCDEABF ACROBACY ANTIBANK ARMGUARD BENUMBED BETIMBER CARIOCAS CERVICES CLAVICLE
CURLICUE CURLYCUE DEBRIDES DEGRADES DEMANDER DIPLODIA ENASCENT ENDOGENS ENDOGENY
ENLIVENS ENRIPENS ENWIDENS GESTOGEN HIBACHIS INACTING INARMING INBOWING INCASING
INCAVING INCEDING INCHPINS INCOMING INCUBING INCUSING INCUTING INDEXING INDUCING
INDURING INECHING INFACING INFAMING INFUSING INGRAINS INHALING INJURING INLAYING
INMOVING INSHRINE INSURING INTAKING INTUBING INVADING INVOKING INYOKING ISLAMIST
LENTILES MADWOMAN MARCHMAN MARKSMAN MARSHMAN NATIONAL NEPTUNES REHAIRED REPAIRED
REPOURED REQUIRED REQUIRES RESCORED RESHARED RESPIRED RESTORED RETOURED TEAMSTER
TENUATED TENUATES TERMITES TRUANTRY UNFECUND UNGROUND UNJOCUND UNROTUND UNSHRUNK
UNSPRUNG UNSTRUNG WAGONWAY WATERWAY

ABCDEACA AUTOMATA SITFASTS   **ABCDEACB** IGNORING

ABCDEACC EASINESS EASTNESS

ABCDEACD ALTERATE ANTEDATE FAULTFUL OUTSHOTS OVERDOER UNDELUDE

ABCDEACF ACTIVATE AUTOMATE AUTOMATS CREVICED CREVICES EARTHERN ENROBERS ENTIRETY
FRUITFUL IBSENISH IBSENISM IGNOMINY INTRAITS INVASIVE LINCOLNS OUTBLOTS OUTFROTH
OVERDOES OVERGOES PRECIPES REASTRAY REDBIRDS UNACTUAL

ABCDEADA SECTISTS SKATISTS

ABCDEADC CADENCED MONEYMEN OVERBORE OVERMORE OVERWORE RESTARTS

ABCDEADE NASCENCE

ABCDEADF ABUNDANT APOSTASY CADENCES COGENCES CONTACTS CONTECTS DISELDER EPITHETS
FRAUDFUL IGNATIAS INCARIAL ISMALIAN NASCENCY OVERLORD OVERWORD OVERWORK OVERWORN
RHUBARBS RHUBARBY SOMERSET STREUSEL TALENTED TALENTER TAOISTIC TAPESTER THEISTIC
THREATED THREATEN TRUISTIC UNCASUAL UNLIQUID

ABCDEAEB TRIMETER TRIMOTOR   **ABCDEAEC** ASEPTATE ENSURERS

ABCDEAEF ADVOCACY AMPUTATE APOSTATE ENDURERS EXPIRERS EXPONENT IDENTITY LANCELET
LAURELED LINTELED MAYHEMED NIRVANAS PHYSOPOD PRECIPIT RAFTERED RANTERED RAPIERED
RESPIRIT ROCKERED ROSTERED ROUTERED SIAMESED SUBNASAL TABLETED TARGETED TERMITIC
THROATAL TICKETED TICKETER TOILETED WESTAWAY WORKAWAY

ABCDEAFA ASPIRATA AXIOMATA CRETACIC DISMODED EARPIECE ENDOMERE ENDPIECE ENSPHERE
ENTOCELE EPICOELE ETHYLENE SACRISTS SARCOSIS SAWDUSTS SCENISTS SECTISMS SELFISTS
SERVISTS SLAVISMS SLAVISTS SNOBISMS SOPHISMS SOPHISTS STREPSIS STYLISMS STYLUSES
SUBCASES SUBCASTS SUCRASES SUCROSES SUNRISES SURMISES SYNAPSES SYNAPSIS SYNOPSES
SYNOPSIS

ABCDEAFB ARMCHAIR ASHTRAYS BENDABLE CLERICAL ESCAPERS FLESHFUL INACTION INERTION
INFUSION INVASION ISLAMICS OMNIFORM RECHARGE RECOURSE RENFORCE RESOURCE TRIASTER
TRIBUTER TRIBUTOR

ABCDEAFC	ACERBATE	ACERVATE	ADEQUATE	AFTERACT	ALTERANT	ANTEFACT	ANTEPAST	ANTIPART
	AREOLATE	ARSENALS	ARTEFACT	ARTIFACT	IDEALIZE	IDEATIVE	MASTOMYS	MISNAMES	MONEYMAN
	OESTROUS	OUTFLOAT	OUTFRONT	OUTSPORT	OVERCOME	OVERDOME	OVERDONE	OVERDOSE	OVERGONE
	OVERHOPE	OVERPOLE	OVERTONE	RESPORTS	RESWARDS	RESWARMS	SURMISER	THRUSTER	TUNGSTEN
	UNSHOUTS	UNTHRUST	UPTHRUST						

ABCDEAFD	ABNEGATE	ABSTRACT	AIREDALE	ALIENAGE	ALIENATE	AMPERAGE	ANGELATE	ASPERATE
	BITEABLE	BOREABLE	CONDUCED	EMPTIEST	EXISTERS	GASTIGHT	IBSENITE	IMBECILE	IMPEDITE
	IMPERITE	INDERITE	NURSINGS	OKLAHOMA	OVERPOUR	OVERSOAR	OVERSOUR	PASTEPOT	THIRSTER
	UNDEMURE	UNSECURE	UNSEDUCE	WINDOWED					

| ABCDEAFE | ADJUTANT | ADOPTANT | ADVISALS | AROUSALS | ARTISANS | DISORDER | EXACTEST | EXCUSERS |
| | EXISTENT | EXPOSERS | IBSENIAN | INFERIOR | INTERIOR | NOWHENCE | PAINTPOT | THWARTER | |

| ABCDEAFF | ECHOLESS | EDGINESS | EDITRESS | EVILNESS | OUTCROSS | OUTGROSS | OVERMOSS | |

ABCDEAFG	ABDICANT	ABDICATE	ABJUGATE	ABLIGATE	ABROGATE	ACROBATS	ACRYLATE	ADEQUACY
	ADJUTAGE	ADMIRALS	ADRENALS	ADVOCATE	AERONATS	AERONAUT	AESTUARY	AFRICANS	AIRBOATS
	AIRHEADS	AIRPLANE	AIRSCAPE	AIRSPACE	ALGINATE	AMBULANT	AMBULATE	AMPERAND	AMPLIATE
	ANGULARS	ANGULATE	ANTEMASK	ANTIBALM	ANTIFACE	ANTIFAME	ANTIHALO	ANTIMARK	ANTIMASK
	ANYPLACE	APOSTACY	ARCHBAND	ARCHWAYS	ARCTIANS	ARGONAUT	ARIOLATE	ARMLOADS	ARMPLATE
	ASHPLANT	ASPIDATE	ASPIRANT	ASPIRATE	AUCKLAND	AUTOBAHN	AUTOCABS	AUTOCADE	AUTOCAMP
	AUTOCARS	AUTOHARP	AUTOMACY	AUTORAIL	AVERSANT	BEACHBOY	BIRTHBED	BIVERBAL	BLACKBOY
	BONDABLE	BREADBOX	BRICKBAT	BURNABLE	CANTICLE	CAPERCUT	CAPLOCKS	CAPSICUM	CERVICAL
	CHALICED	CHALICES	CHEMICAL	CLAVICOR	COENACTS	COMANCHE	COMPACTS	CONDUCER	CONDUCES
	CONDUCTS	CONFACTS	CONFECTS	CONJECTS	CONVECTS	CONVICTS	CORNICED	CORNICES	CORNICHE
	CORSICAN	CORTICAL	CORTICES	COSMICAL	COWLICKS	CUTBACKS	DASHEDLY	DAYTIDES	DEVILDOM
	DISENDOW	DISLODGE	DOMESDAY	DOTARDLY	EARLIEST	ECTODERM	EGOIZERS	ELBOWERS	ELOQUENT
	EMBOWELS	EMBOWERS	EMPANELS	EMPIREAN	EMPOWERS	EMPTIERS	EMPYREAL	EMPYREAN	EMULGENT
	ENABLERS	ENAMBERS	ENCODERS	ENDOWERS	ENFOREST	ENJOYERS	ENSHIELD	ENTICERS	ENTIRELY
	EPAULETS	EPITHEMA	EUROPEAN	EVANGELS	EVANGELY	EXACTERS	EXALTERS	EXCITERS	EXHALENT
	EXHUMERS	EXOSPERM	EXURGENT	FAITHFUL	FANCIFUL	FEASTFUL	FIENDFUL	FORCEFUL	FORGEFUL
	FREAKFUL	FRISKFUL	FROWNFUL	GAPINGLY	GASLIGHT	GAZINGLY	GLYCOGEN	GUIDAGES	GUNFIGHT
	GUNSIGHT	HARDSHIP	HAUNCHED	HAUNCHER	HAUNCHES	HEADSHIP	HEROSHIP	IDEALISM	IDEALIST
	IDEALITY	IDEATING	IDEATION	IDENTIFY	IDENTISM	IGNATIUS	IGNOMIES	IMBROILS	IMPALING
	IMPARITY	IMPAVING	IMPEDING	IMPERIAL	IMPERILS	IMPERISH	IMPETIGO	IMPLYING	IMPOLICY
	IMPOLITE	IMPOSING	IMPUNITY	IMPURIFY	IMPURING	IMPURITY	IMPUTING	INACTIVE	INDOCILE
	INDUCIVE	INDUVIAL	INEQUITY	INERTIAL	INERTIAS	INFAMIES	INFAMIZE	INFERIAL	INFUSIVE
	INHABITS	INHERITS	INJURIED	INJURIES	INRADIUS	INSCRIBE	INSCRIPT	INSOCIAL	INSOLITE
	INSULIZE	INTERIAL	INTERIMS	INVALIDS	INVARIED	INVERITY	IRONLIKE	ISLAMITE	ISLAMIZE
	ISOAMIDE	ISOCLINE	ISTHMIAL	ISTHMIAN	LANCELOT	LANDSLIP	LINGULAE	LINGULAR	MARCHMEN
	MARKSMEN	MARSHMEN	MAYTIMES	MISNAMED	MISNOMED	MISNOMER	MOSLEMIC	MYELOMAS	NAPKINED
	NECKINGS	NERVINGS	NERVONIC	NEURONAL	NEURONIC	NEURONYM	NEWTONIC	NORLANDS	NORMANDS
	NORMANDY	NORMANLY	NOTHINGS	NOUMENAL	NUISANCE	OBLATORY	OCEANOUS	OCHEROUS	OCTAPODY
	OILSTONE	OILSTOVE	OLATIONS	OMNIVORA	OMNIVORE	OMNIVORS	OPACIOUS	OPENWORK	OPTICONS
	ORATIONS	OUTBLOWN	OUTCROPS	OUTCROWN	OUTCROWS	OUTDROPS	OUTFLOWN	OUTFLOWS	OUTFROWN
	OUTGLOWS	OUTGROWN	OUTGROWS	OUTSCOLD	OUTSCORE	OUTSCORN	OUTSHONE	OUTSHOVE	OUTSHOWN
	OUTSNORE	OUTSPOKE	OVARIOLE	OVARIOUS	OVATIONS	OVERBODY	OVERBOIL	OVERBOLD	OVERBOWL
	OVERBOWS	OVERCOAT	OVERCOIL	OVERCOLD	OVERCOWS	OVERDOGS	OVERFOLD	OVERFOND	OVERFOUL
	OVERGOAD	OVERGODS	OVERGOWN	OVERHOLD	OVERHOLY	OVERJOYS	OVERLOAD	OVERLOCK	OVERLONG
	OVERLOUD	OVERMOST	OVERPOST	OVERPOTS	OVERSOAK	OVERSOCK	OVERSOFT	OVERSOLD	OVERSOUL

```
OVERSOWN OVERTOIL OVERTOLD OVERTOPS PACHYPOD PERIAPTS PLATYPOD PLATYPUS PROTYPES
PTEROPUS RAGWORKS RAGWORTS RAINDROP RAMPIRED RAMPIRES RANCORED RAPTORES RAPTURED
RAPTURES READORNS REBOARDS RECHURNS RECTORAL REGUARDS REJOURNS RESTORAL REWHIRLS
REYNARDS RHETORIC RIBWORKS RICHARDS RYECORNS SACRISTY SARCOSIN SAWDUSTY SPLITSAW
SUBCASTE SUBMISED SURBASED SURMISAL SURVISED SYMPOSIA SYNAPSED SYNAPSID TABLETOP
TAPESTRY TAPISTRY TARLETON THEMATIC THIBETAN THIRSTED THRIFTED THROATED THWARTED
THWARTLY THYMATES THYMETIC THYMOTIC TOILETRY TOLUATES TOWPATHS TRIBUTED TRIBUTES
TRIBUTYL TRUANTCY TRUANTED TRUANTLY TSINGTAO TURGITES TWELFTHS TYRANTED UNABRUPT
UNABSURD UNACQUIT UNADJUST UNAMBUSH UNARGUED UNCLOUDS UNCLOUDY UNCLOUTS UNDILUTE
UNIMBUED UNMATURE UNPIQUED UNPLOUGH UNRITUAL UNROBUST UNSEXUAL UNSTRUCK UNVALUED
UNVALUES UPCOLUMN URANIUMS WIDTHWAY WORLDWAY
```

ABCDEBAA LANDFALL SEAMLESS SEATLESS SELFNESS SEXINESS

ABCDEBAB ESPOUSES NEOPRENE READHERE RESPHERE

ABCDEBAC DISCOIDS NIGHTING RESAWERS RESCUERS RESIDERS RESINERS RESIZERS RESUMERS
SIMPLISM

ABCDEBAD DIKESIDE ERASURES NOSEBONE RECAMERA ROCKWORK SIDEWISE

ABCDEBAE REFUSERS REPOSERS REVISERS SEDATEST

ABCDEBAF AMISHMAN ANEMONAL ARBITRAL AUDITUAL DIOPSIDE DIPLOIDS DIPLOIDY EIGHTIES
```
EMBALMED EMBALMER EMPLUMED EMPLUMES ENJOINED ENJOINER ENLIMNED ENPLANED ENPLANES
ENRUINED ENSIGNED ENTWINED ENTWINES ESPOUSED ESPOUSER ESPRISED FISHWIFE FIXATIFS
GAMEBAGS GNAWINGS HANUKAHS INOGENIC INSOMNIA KINGLIKE LACTEALS LANDSALE LATERALS
LATRIALY LUNGFULS NAVIGANT NICOTINA NICOTINE NICOTINS NIMBLING RAILCARS REACHERS
REALTERS REBATERS REBUKERS RECITERS RECOVERS RECOVERY REDIVERT REDUCERS REFINERS
REFINERY REFUTERS REGALERS REGOVERN REIGNERS REINFERS REINSERT REINTERS REINVERT
RELATERS RELAXERS RELAYERS RELINERS RELIVERS RELOWERS REMAKERS REMOVERS REPLIERS
RETAKERS REVILERS REVIZERS REVOKERS REWAGERS REWATERS ROADWORK SEAMIEST SECUREST
SEDGIEST SIMPLIST SIXTYISH SUBCAUSE SUBCRUST SUBFLUSH SUBHOUSE TABULATE TAILGATE
TEARLETS TEMPLETS THOUGHTS TIMERITY TINSMITH TOPKNOTS TRIPARTS TURNOUTS
```

ABCDEBBA FOGPROOF FOREHOOF FOXPROOF LONGWOOL REINDEER SEDUCEES

ABCDEBBC BODYHOOD FLAGELLA FOREDOOR HOMEROOM JOKEBOOK POTSHOOT

ABCDEBBD CORDWOOD WORKBOOK

ABCDEBBE DEVISEES FORENOON REVISEES SCIROCCO STILETTE

ABCDEBBF BOATHOOK CLINALLY COATROOM COPYBOOK CORKWOOD DEVOTEES DOGPROOF DOMEBOOK
```
DOUBLOON DOVEFOOT FEDAYEEN FLORALLY FLOTILLA FOREBOOT FOREDOOM FOREHOOD FOREHOOK
FORELOOK FORELOOP FORETOOK GLOBALLY HELPMEET KOHINOOR LEGATEES MONKHOOD NEWSREEL
NOTEBOOK PERIGEES PLENALLY PLURALLY POETHOOD POLTROON POSTBOOK PREMARRY REFUGEED
REFUGEES RENOMEES RESUMEED ROADBOOK ROSEWOOD SOAPROOT SOAPWOOD SOFTWOOD SONGBOOK
STILETTO TOWNHOOD WORDBOOK
```

ABCDEBCA MORIFORM SERVIERS TENDMENT   **ABCDEBCB** MENTHENE NATURATA

ABCDEBCC BESTNESS JESTRESS PREAGREE RESTLESS VESTLESS WESTNESS

ABCDEBCD BACKPACK BACKTACK CATENATE DINGEING DINGLING DINGYING DOWNTOWN JINGLING
JINGOING MAINTAIN MINGLING OUTSHUTS PACKSACK PICKWICK PIKELIKE PLANULAN POTSHOTS
RESTIEST RINGLING SENTIENT SINGEING TINGEING TINGLING WINGDING WINGLING

ABCDEBCE PENITENT PERUSERS

ABCDEBCF ANCIENCY ANEMONES ANGLINGS BARNYARD BEAKHEAD BOATLOAD BOLTHOLE BOURNOUS
BRAVURAS BRETHREN CARTWARE CATBOATS CLAMFLAT CONFRONT CORESORT COUNTOUR CRATERAL
CRITERIA CURATURE DENIZENS DERATERS DERIVERS DERNIERS DISGUISE DOUBTOUS ENDHANDS
ENTRANTS FARMYARD FATIGATE FILTHILY FIREBIRD FISTWISE FLECKLED FOREWORD FOREWORN
FORSWORE FORSWORN GAINSAID HAIRTAIL HANDBANK HARDWARE HEADGEAR HEADWEAR HINDWING
HORNWORK HORNWORM HORNWORT HUMDRUMS HYPOTYPE IMPROMPT INTRANTS ITERATED ITERATES
JAILBAIT KANTIANS KINDLING KINGPINS LARBOARD LATINATE LICORICE LOWBROWS MAINSAIL
MANTUANS MATURATE MEATHEAD MERITERS MESHIEST MILFOILS MINORING MINUTING MISGUISE
MISPOISE MISPRISE MISRAISE MISTYISH MONAXONS MORATORY PARKWARD PARTIARY PERCHERS
PERIDERM PERUKERS PESKIEST PINCHING PINGUINS PLAGULAE PLANULAE PLANULAR POLYFOLD
PRECURED PRECURES PRETIRED PRETIRES PREWIRED PREWIRES RELABELS SANDBANK SATURATE
SHANGHAI SHEATHED SHEATHER SINEWING SMELTMEN STOCKTON TARBOARD TINKLING TREMORED
TRICERIA TRIMERIC UNCHANCE UNCHANCY UNCLENCH UNCLINCH UNEARNED UNTAINTS VICTRICE
VITALITY WASHFAST WINCHING WINKLING WIREBIRD XYLENYLS

ABCDEBDA ENSCONCE SCIENCES SURNOUNS TEASIEST   **ABCDEBDB** AESTHETE ASPERSES

ABCDEBDC FOREGOER INSTANTS MISERIES THRESHER UNDEANED VESTLETS

ABCDEBDD INTERNEE NEWSLESS   **ABCDEBDE** ASPERSER KIWANIAN THRESHES

ABCDEBDF ASPERSED BIASWISE BIFACIAL BIRACIAL BIRADIAL CASTRATI CASTRATO CESAREAN
COALHOLE COPYBOYS DECRIERS DILUVIUM DIOECIES DISKLIKE DOGTROTS DOWNGONE FINERIES
FOREGOES GIPSYISH GIPSYISM HANDMADE HANGTAGS HINDSIDE HOMEGOER HOMINOID INTERNED
INTERNES LANGRAGE LANGUAGE LEARNERS LIVERIED LIVERIES MAINLAND MANYWAYS NEWSIEST
NICETIES NODULOUS OILERIES OUTGAUGE PEARLERS RAINBAND REINTEND REINVENT SCIENCED
SCIENCER SINKLIKE THRESHED TIMELIER TRUEBRED UNREINED UNVEINED UNWEANED UPLEAPED
UPTEMPER VICARIAL VICARIAN VINERIES WEARIERS WIFELIER WINERIES WISELIER YEARNERS

ABCDEBEA SECURERS   **ABCDEBEB** RETINENE   **ABCDEBEC** DESIRERS

ABCDEBED PLATELET

ABCDEBEF ANEMONOL ATHLETES BLADELET BROKERED CAPITATE CAVITATE CENTRERS COJURORS
CRATERED FEMALELY FLAGELET FLAKELET FLAMELET GLOBELET GRUYERES HABITATE HABITATS
HEBRAEAN KINDLILY KINGLILY LIKENING LIVENING MORTUOUS PROFERED REMANENT RIPENING
SANITATE SENILELY SIRENING SLAVELET STOMATAL STRIATAL STYLETED STYLITIC UNOMENED
UNOPENED VAGINANT VAPORARY WIDENING WINDPIPE WISENING

ABCDEBFA DARESAID DECKHEAD DOMINOED DOWNFOLD DOWNHOLD DUMFOUND EASTLAKE ENSUANCE
ENTRANCE FERNLEAF GIRDLING GIRTHING NICOTIAN NIGERIAN SACKBAGS SALTPANS SAMOVARS
SANDBAGS SANDBARS SAPHEADS SAURIANS SEAGOERS SEAMLETS SEDUCERS SELTZERS SEMILENS
SEMIPEDS SETOVERS SICKLIES SIGMOIDS SILPHIDS SILURIDS SIRLOINS SIXFOILS SNAKINGS

SOUPCONS STEALTHS STOMATES STRIATES SULPHURS TEARIEST TEGUMENT

ABCDEBFB ARBITRER ARMOURER CAMERATA CETYLENE DECOHERE DECYLENE GENOVESE HEMOCELE
ISOBASES ISOLYSES KEROSENE LEBANESE LEGPIECE MEUNIERE NEPALESE PANORAMA PEKINESE
PROCURER SAYONARA SEAPIECE SEPTIEME

ABCDEBFC BEDSTEAD BESIRENS BESTREWS BIGHTING BISCUITS CAKEWALK DISHEIRS DISJOINS
DISMAILS DISMAINS DISPAIRS DISTAINS ENSAINTS FIGHTING FIGURING GASBOATS GASTHAUS
HIDEBIND KESTRELS LIGATING LIGHTING LONGHORN MISCOINS MISEDITS MISJOINS MISTRIES
NESTLERS OBEYABLE ONSTANDS OUTSPURT PIERLIKE POLYFOIL POSITONS POSITORS POSTBOYS
PRECURSE PREMORSE RADICAND RESOJETS RETICENT RIGHTING SATURANT SELFHEAL SEMIBEAM
SIGHTING STRICTER THRASHER THRUSHER TIERLIKE TIGERING UNDAMNED UNDARNED UNDAWNED
UNDOWNED UNSAINTS UNSCENTS UNSLINGS UNSTINGS UNSTONES UNSWINGS UPSLOPES URETHRAE
VIGORING VITALIST WASHDAYS WASHRAGS ZOETROPE

ABCDEBFD AIRSHIPS BAKEWARE BAREFACE BOREHOLE BORESOME BOWSHOTS CANEWARE CASEMATE
DISTRICT DOVECOTE FEASTERS FELTIEST FIBERIZE FIRELIKE FIRESIDE FOREBODE FORECOME
FOREDONE FOREGONE FORENOTE FOREPOLE FORSLOWS FRISURES FUNICULI GENTLEST GONESOME
GYNETYPE HANDMAID HEFTIEST HEISTERS JOKESOME KEISTERS KINSHIPS LACERATE LANDWARD
LANDYARD LAYERAGE LIFETIME LIGHTISH LIKEWISE LINESIDE LOCKWORK LONESOME LOVESOME
MACERATE MARSHALS MEATIEST MIDSHIPS NAMESAKE NIGHTISH NOSEHOLE OILSKINS OUTSLUGS
OUTSPUES PALEFACE PEATIEST PIGSKINS PIGSTIES POLYGONY POLYTOMY POLYTONY QUIETUDE
RACEMATE RIBSKINS RIDGLING RIPELIKE SALEWARE SIDELINE SIDEWIPE SINEWIZE SIRENIZE
SUBDRUID TIDELIKE TIGERINE TOYSHOPS UNSCENIC VESTMENT VICELIKE VINELIKE VINEWISE
VIPERINE VISELIKE WARDMAID WATERAGE WEBSTERS WELSHERS WIFELIKE WINELIKE WIRELIKE
WISELIKE WOBEGONE WORKFOLK YARDLAND

ABCDEBFE ABSORBER ASPERSOR BACKSAWS BIOPSIES DARESAYS DEBASERS DECISERS DEVISERS
DISUNION FLORALIA GAINSAYS GEARSETS HABITANT HACKSAWS HANDSAWS HEADSETS JACKSAWS
KINESICS LAUREATE MIRAGING NAUSEATE PLANTLET PRELARVA REMOTEST REPATENT RIGHTIST
SEMIDEAD SIDEKICK SILAGING SIRENIAN SUBFAUNA THRASHES THRUSHES TRAVERSE UNCORNER
VISAGING WAYLEAVE WINTRIER

ABCDEBFF BACKFALL BACKWALL BEAMLESS BUNGFULL DEAFNESS DEARNESS DEBTLESS DEFTNESS
DEMONESS DEVILESS DEWINESS FASTBALL FEARLESS FEATNESS FECKLESS FELONESS FELTNESS
FERNLESS GAMEBALL GEARLESS GERMLESS HANDBALL HEADLESS HEATLESS HEIRLESS HERBLESS
LANDMASS LECTRESS LEFTNESS LEWDNESS MARSHALL MATGRASS MEANLESS MEATLESS NECKLESS
NUMSKULL OUTBLUFF PACKWALL PEAKLESS PERTNESS RAINFALL REALNESS RECKLESS REINLESS
RENTLESS RINGBILL ROUNDOFF SEMICELL SIDEHILL TEAMLESS TEARLESS TERMLESS TOPCROSS
VAUXHALL VEINLESS VENTLESS VERBLESS WEAKNESS WEIRLESS WINDMILL

ABCDEBFG ABSORBED AEROGELS AIRFOILS ALVEOLUS AMISHMEN ANCIENTS ANCIENTY ANEMONIC
ANODYNES ANODYNIC ANOGENIC APOTYPES APOTYPIC ARBOURED ARMOIRES ARMOURED ASCENSOR
ATHLETIC BACKDATE BACKGAME BACKHAND BACKLAND BACKHAUL BACKLASH BACKSAWN BACKWARD
BACKWASH BACKYARD BADINAGE BALDPATE BANDCASE BANDEAUX BANDTAIL BANGTAIL BARONAGE
BASILARY BEADIEST BEAKIEST BEAMIEST BEANIEST BECIVETS BEFRIEND BEHOVELY BELOVEDS
BESTREWN BETOKENS BEWATERS BIFOLIUM BIGAMIES BIGAMIST BIGAMIZE BIGOTISH BIMARINE
BINARIUM BINOXIDE BIPEDISM BIRCHING BIRDLIFE BIRDLIKE BIRDLING BIRDWISE BIRTHING
BISERIAL BITHEISM BLACKLEG BODYWORK BOILDOWN BONEWORK BOREDOMS BOVIFORM BOWFRONT
BOWKNOTS BROCARDS BROKERLY BUCKJUMP BUGHOUSE BURNOUTS CABSTAND CALTRAPS CAMPWARD
CAMSHAFT CAPITALS CATENARY CATERANS CATHEADS CAVITARY CERULEAN CIDERISH CIDERIST

```
CLOAKLET  CLOUDLET  COALPORT  COENJOYS  COLATORY  COLIFORM  COMATOSE  COMATOUS  COMEDOWN
COMETOID  CONFLOWS  CONGLOBE  CONGROID  CONIFORM  CONTROLE  CONTROLS  COPILOTS  COPYHOLD
CORAZONS  CORNEOUS  CORNLOFT  COTSWOLD  COUNTORS  COVENOUS  COVETOUS  COVINOUS  DATEMARK
DEBATERS  DEBOWELS  DEBRIEFS  DECAYERS  DECIBELS  DECOYERS  DEFACERS  DEFAMERS  DEFIBERS
DEFILERS  DEFINERS  DEFLUENT  DEFOREST  DELATERS  DELAYERS  DELIBERS  DELIMERS  DELIVERS
DELIVERY  DEMIBELT  DEMIREPS  DEMURELY  DEMUREST  DEPHLEGM  DEPTHENS  DEVILERS  DEVOTERS
DEWATERS  DIATRIBE  DIHELIOS  DIHELIUM  DILATING  DILATION  DILATIVE  DILUTING  DILUTION
DILUTIVE  DILUVIAN  DILUVION  DIMPLIER  DIMPLING  DINGHIES  DIOECIAN  DIPSTICK  DIRTYING
DISALIGN  DISALIKE  DISCLIKE  DISFAITH  DISHLIKE  DISHLING  DISJOINT  DISPAINT  DISPOINT
DISPRIZE  DISQUIET  DISUNIFY  DISUNITE  DISUNITY  DISVOICE  DITCHING  DITHEISM  DOMINOES
DONATORS  DONATORY  DOVECOTS  DOWNCOME  DOWNMOST  DOWNPOUR  DOWNSOME  EARFLAPS  EASTLAND
ENCHANTS  ENCRINAL  ENROUNDS  ENSIGNCY  ENSIGNRY  EPITAPHS  ERYTHRIC  ERYTHRIN  ESPOUSAL
FABULATE  FACEMARK  FAIRWAYS  FAREWAYS  FARMHAND  FARMLAND  FASCIATE  FATHEADS  FEATHERS
FEATHERY  FEIGNERS  FEINTERS  FERNIEST  FETCHERS  FIBROIDS  FICKLING  FIDELITY  FIDUCIAE
FIDUCIAL  FIELDING  FIELDISH  FIENDISH  FIENDISM  FIGURIAL  FIGURINE  FIGURISM  FIGURIST
FIGURIZE  FILCHING  FILTHIER  FINALISM  FINALIST  FINALITY  FINALIZE  FIRELING  FIRSTING
FISHLIKE  FISHLINE  FISHLING  FISTLIKE  FISTLING  FITCHING  FIVEPINS  FIXATING  FIXATION
FIXATIVE  FLYBELTS  FOAMBOWS  FOLDBOAT  FORCLOSE  FOREBODY  FOREHOLD  FORELOCK  FOREMOST
FOREPOST  FORETOLD  FORETOPS  FOULSOME  FOURSOME  FOXGLOVE  FULCRUMS  FULGOURS  FUMEDUCT
FUMIDUCT  FUNICULE  FURLOUGH  GAINWARD  GATEWARD  GATEWAYS  GEOTHERM  GERATELY  GERMIEST
GIANTISH  GIANTISM  GIANTIZE  GLOBULAR  GLOBULES  GLOBULET  GLOBULIN  GLYCOLID  GOALPOST
GOITROUS  GOLDWORK  GOLFDOMS  GONAPODS  GRAVURES  GROCERLY  GUNHOUSE  HABITANS  HABUTAES
HAIRBAND  HAIRCAPS  HAIRLACE  HALFPACE  HANDBAGS  HANDCARS  HANDCART  HANDFAST  HANDRAIL
HANDSALE  HARDBACK  HARDBAKE  HARDCASE  HARDPANS  HARDSALT  HARDTACK  HARDTAIL  HARDWAYS
HAULBACK  HAULYARD  HAVILAND  HAYSTACK  HEADIEST  HEADREST  HEARKENS  HEARTENS  HEAVIEST
HECKLERS  HEDGIEST  HERBIEST  HERBLETS  HILARITY  HINDUISM  HINDUIZE  HIRELING  HOMEBODY
HOMEBORN  HOMETOWN  HOMEWORK  HOPELOST  HORIZONS  IMBALMED  IMPALMED  IMPLUMED  IMPLUMES
INBOUNDS  INCARNED  INCHANTS  INFERNAL  INFERNOS  INSTANCE  INSTANCY  INTERNAL  INTRANCE
INTRENCH  INTURNED  JACKDAWS  JACQUARD  JACULATE  JAILMATE  JAILWARD  JAILYARD  JERKIEST
JINGLIER  JINGOISH  JINGOISM  JINGOIST  JUNCTURE  JUNEBUDS  KEMPIEST  KINDLIER  KINETICS
KINGFISH  KNOWINGS  LABORANT  LACEBARK  LACERANT  LAKEWARD  LAMINARY  LAMINATE  LANDFAST
LANDGATE  LANDMARK  LANDRACE  LANDWASH  LANDWAYS  LANEWAYS  LAOTIANS  LAPBOARD  LAPIDARY
LAPIDATE  LATEWARD  LATVIANS  LAUDIANS  LEACHERS  LEADIEST  LEAFIEST  LEAGUERS  LEAKIEST
LEATHERN  LEATHERS  LEATHERY  LEAVIEST  LEDGIEST  LEDGMENT  LEGUMENS  LIBATING  LIBATION
LIBERIAN  LIGATION  LIGATIVE  LIMERICK  LIMPKINS  LINGUIST  LIPSTICK  LISZTIAN  LITANIES
LITHOING  LIVERING  LIVERISH  LOADSOME  LOBIFORM  LOCATORS  LOCUTORS  LOCUTORY  LONGBOAT
LONGBOWS  LONGFORD  LOTHSOME  MAHICANS  MAHOGANY  MAILBAGS  MAINWARD  MAJORATE  MAKEFAST
MANDRAKE  MANTEAUS  MANTRAPS  MANUFACT  MARCHAND  MARCHANT  MARINADE  MARINALS  MARINATE
MARTIANS  MARXIANS  MARYLAND  MATBOARD  MAYORALS  MEAGRELY  MEALIEST  MEANDERS  MENACERS
MENSWEAR  METALERS  MIAOWING  MICALIKE  MICASIZE  MICATING  MICATION  MIDPOINT  MIDVEINS
MIGHTIER  MIGHTIES  MIGHTILY  MIGRAINE  MILADIES  MILCHING  MILKFISH  MINACITY  MINORIST
MINORITE  MINORITY  MINUTIAE  MINUTIAL  MIRTHING  MISBUILD  MISBUILT  MISCHIEF  MISCUING
MISDOING  MISDRIVE  MISERING  MISFAITH  MISFEIGN  MISGUIDE  MISPAINT  MISPOINT  MISPRINT
MISPRIZE  MISTHINK  MISTRIAL  MISWRITE  MITERING  MONITORS  MONITORY  MONTJOYS  MOREFOLD
MORPHONS  MORPHOUS  MORPIONS  MOUFLONS  NARWHALE  NARWHALS  NATURALE  NATURALS  NAVIGATE
NEATHERD  NECKLETS  NECKWEAR  NEGATERS  NEIGHERS  NERVIEST  NEWSBEAT  NICETISH  NICOTISM
NICOTIZE  NIGHTIES  NODULOSE  NOVATORS  NOVATORY  OATMEALS  OBVIABLE  OEDIPEAN  ORCHARDS
OUTBLUSH  OUTDRUNK  OUTFLUES  OUTFLUNG  OUTFLUSH  OUTHAULS  OUTLAUGH  OUTSLUNG  OUTSPUED
OUTSPURN  OUTSWUNG  OUTWRUNG  PACKWARE  PACKWAYS  PAGINARY  PAGINATE  PALEWAYS  PALISADE
PALMWARD  PANHEADS  PANORAMS  PARDHANS  PARKLAND  PARKWAYS  PARTIALS  PASTRAMI  PATHWAYS
PATINAED  PAYLOADS  PEACHERS  PEACHERY  PEAKIEST  PEARLETS  PECKIEST  PEDALERS  PEDATELY
```

PEDIMENT PERINEAL PERINEUM PERKIEST PHAETHON PHINEHAS PICKLING PIERCING PIGSTICK
PIGTAILS PILCHING PILGRIMS PILOTING PILOTISM PINKFISH PINRAILS PINTAILS PIRACIES
PIRACING PIRATING PIRATISM PIRATIZE PISTLING PITCHIER PITCHING PIVOTING POETDOMS
POLAROID POLIGONS POLIMORF POLYCOTS POLYGONS POLYNOID POLYNOME POLYTONE POLYZOAN
POLYZOIC POMEROYS PONCHOED PORTEOUS PORTHOLE PORTIONS POSTHOLE PREBURNS PREFORMS
PREMORAL PRETARDY PREWARNS PREWORTH PROCURAL PROCURED PROCURES PROGERIA PROMERCY
PROMERIT PROVERBS PROVIRUS PUNCTUAL PUNCTURE RACEWAYS RACKWAYS RADICALS RADICANT
RADICATE RAILFANS RAILWAYS RAINWASH RAMHEADS REABSENT READIEST READVENT REASCEND
REASCENT REDIGEST REDOLENT REDUCENT REFLUENT REFOMENT REGIMENS REGIMENT REIMPELS
REINFECT REINFEST REINJECT REINVEST RELAMENT RELUCENT REMODELS REMOTELY RENOVELS
REOBJECT REPANELS REQUIEMS RESIDENT RESQUEAK REWAKENS REWIDENS RIESLING RINGLIKE
RINGSIDE RINGTIME RINGWISE RIVALING RIVALISM RIVALITY RIVALIZE RIVETING RUBICUND
SABOTAGE SALEYARD SALIVANT SALIVARY SALIVATE SALUTARY SANDRAKE SANITARY SANTIAGO
SCENICAL SCRUNCHY SECATEUR SECURELY SEDATELY SEDIMENT SEIGNEUR SEMIDEAF SERAJEVO
SERAPEUM SERVIENT SHEIKHLY SIBARITE SIBERIAN SICKLIED SICKLIER SICKLING SIDELING
SIGHLIKE SIGNLIKE SILURIAN SIMONIAC SIMONIAL SIMONIER SIMONITE SIMONIZE SIMPLIFY
SIMPLING SIMULIZE SIRLOINY SMELTMAN SOAPROCK SOAPWORT SOLATORY SOLENOID SOLIFORM
SOLUTORY SOMEBODY SOUPBONE STEALTHY STENOTIC STOMATIC STRAITED STRAITEN STRAITLY
STRIATED STRIATUM STRICTLY SUBACUTE SUBADULT SUBEQUAL SUBROUND SUBTRUDE SUBTRUNK
SULPHURY SURMOUNT TABLEAUS TABLEAUX TABULARE TABULARS TABULARY TAILBACK TAILBAND
TAILRACE TAILWARD TAXICABS TAXIWAYS TEACHERS TEACHERY TEINDERS TENDRELS THRASHED
THRESHAL TIBERIAN TIBERIUS TICKLIER TICKLING TICKLISH TIGERISH TIMBRING TINFOILS
TINGLISH TIPSYING TIRADING TOILSOME TOILWORN TOWNFOLK TRICORNE TRICORNS TUBEFULS
UNAMENDS UNATONED UNBLINDS UNBRANDS UNBRINED UNCHANGE UNCLINGS UNCOINED UNCOINER
UNDAINTY UNDERNAM UNDERNIM UNDOINGS UNFIENDS UNFLANKS UNFRANKS UNFRINGE UNGAINED
UNGAINLY UNGIANTS UNGOWNED UNHORNED UNHYMNED UNIRONED UNISONAL UNJOINED UNJOINTS
UNKILNED UNLIMNED UNLOANED UNMOANED UNOPENLY UNOPINED UNPAINED UNPAINTS UNPAWNED
UNPAWNER UNPLANED UNPLANKS UNPLANTS UNPRINCE UNPRINTS UNSCANTY UNSIGNED UNSPONGY
UNSTONED UNTHANKS UNTHINKS UNTOWNED UNTOWNER UNTRANCE UNTRENDS UNTWINDS UNTWINED
UNTWINER UNTWINES UNWARNED UNWRENCH UPSLOPED UPWARPED URETHRAL URETHRAS VAGINATE
VALEWARD VALIDATE VANGUARD VAPORATE VAULTAGE VAUNTAGE VEALIEST VEINLETS VENOMERS
VICARIES VICARIUS VIGORISH VIGORIST VINOSITY VIPERIAN VIPERISH VIRTUING VISERING
VISORING VITALISM VITALIZE VITAMINE VITAMINS VIXENISH VOLUTOID VOMITORY VOMITOUS
VORAGOES WARHEADS WARPLANE WASHLAND WASHMAID WASHRACK WASHTAIL WASTLAND WAVEMARK
WAYBEAMS WEARIEST WEATHERS WEATHERY WEDGIEST WEIGHERS WEIRDEST WELCHERS WENCHERS
WIELDING WIGTAILS WILDFIRE WIMPLING WINDFISH WINDLIFT WINDLIKE WINGFISH WINGLIKE
WINTRIFY WINTRILY WINTRISH WISPLIKE WITCHIER WITCHING WONDROUS WORKBOAT WORKSOME
WORMHOLE YIELDING YORKTOWN

ABCDECAA SKEWNESS SOURPUSS STEMLESS STEPLESS   **ABCDECAB** ESTUATES STERNEST

ABCDECAC TRAUMATA   **ABCDECAD** GINSENGS NEIGHING

ABCDECAE EXTORTER SVELTEST

ABCDECAF AEROGRAM AFTERTAN CANDENCY CONJUNCT CONVINCE ENDIADEM ENGORGED ENGORGES
ESTUATED EXTORTED GRAFTAGE GRAINAGE GUARDAGE IROQUOIS ISOPLOID LATENTLY RAILBIRD
RAINBIRD REALGARS SAILFISH SAINTISH SEACOAST SKIRMISH SLAPDASH SMIRKISH SPEWIEST
TANGENTS TENDANTS TRIALITY TRIPLITE TRIUNITY UNODIOUS UXORIOUS

ABCDECBA DESPISED DESPOSED DEVOLVED DRAWCARD EVINCIVE MARJORAM RENOWNER REVOLVER

SCIATICS STEMLETS

ABCDECBB GERMFREE NEGLIGEE PLAYBALL RENOWNEE USEDNESS

ABCDECBC CESTUSES DESPISES PERJURER PREMIERE VERDURER

ABCDECBD BEDSIDES BIVALVIA FRESHERS PLASMALS SCIATICA VERDURED WRESTERS

ABCDECBE BELADLED CREASERS GREASERS REHASHES RETASTES

ABCDECBF ADIPOIDS AIRSTRIP ARTISTRY BEGINGER BEKICKED BELADLES BEMAIMED BLOWHOLE
BREAKERS CAMELMAN CANTONAL CARBURAN CENTONES CLAVIALS CLODPOLE CONVENOR CORDEROY
CORDUROY CREAKERS CREAMERS CREAMERY DEGORGES DESPISER DEVOLVES DRAGBARS DRAWBARS
DREAMERS DREAMERY FEISTIER FLIMSILY FLINTILY FOREIRON FREAKERY GAMESMAN GLACIALS
GRAYWARE GRENIERS HENBANES IRONWORK NEWLYWED PENTANES PENTINES PERDURES PERJURED
PERJURES POLIGLOT POLYGLOT PREMIERS PROCTORS PUDENDUM RAMPSMAN RECANCEL REGAUGED
REGAUGES REHASHED REKICKED RENOWNED REPUMPED RETASTED REVOLVED REVOLVES SCARFACE
SENTINEL SINFONIA SINFONIE SKINLIKE SLINKILY STAGNATE TRAMCARS TRAMYARD TREADERS
UNIFYING UROCHORD WREAKERS WRECKERS

ABCDECCA ABSCISSA   **ABCDECCD** KNOTROOT OVERLEER OVERPEER OVERSEER SPONTOON

ABCDECCE AUTOETTE OVERSEES

ABCDECCF ABERDEEN ALOEROOT ALOEWOOD CARBERRY CHEATEES COBWEBBY COLVILLE CROWFOOT
HOLDALLS IRONWOOD KNOBWOOD OVERDEEP OVERFEED OVERKEEN OVERKEEP OVERSEED OVERSEEN
PLEDGEES PRESTEEL SHOPBOOK SHOWROOM

ABCDECDA DISEASED GLINTING GRINDING SHUTOUTS SOULFULS STERNERS SWERVERS

ABCDECDB FRIEZIER SEATMATE   **ABCDECDC** DISEASES MISEASES

ABCDECDD CAREFREE LICENCEE PATENTEE

ABCDECDE BRINGING CHANTANT CLINGING CRINGING FLINGING HYPERPER SLINGING STINGING
SWINGING THINGING TWINGING WRINGING

ABCDECDF ACIDOIDS AMNIONIC AMOUROUS ARTISTIC AUTISTIC AVERTERS BLINDING BLINKING
BLOWDOWN BRISKISH CAMELMEN CHINKING CLERKERY CLINKING CONTENTS DEINKING DIASTASE
DISTASTE DRINKING EVINCING FAINTING FEINTING FLINTING FRESHEST GAIETIES GAMESMEN
GHANIANS GUILTILY HANGINGS HERITRIX INTERTEX INTEXTED JOINTING LICENCED LICENCER
LICENCES LONGINGS MAINLINE MAINPINS MISEASED MISTASTE MOISTISH MUTISTIC OCTANTAL
PAINTING PATENTED PIERCERS PLAYDAYS POINTING PRECHECK PRINCING PRINTING PUREBRED
QUERIERS RANGINGS REINKING SAINTING SHERBERT SHOWDOWN SLINKING SLOWDOWN SNOWFOWL
SPATIATE STARWARD STINKING STOWDOWN SVELTELY THINKING THISWISE TRIAXIAL UGANDANS
UNIAXIAL UNREARED UNTESTED UPREARED URANIANS WHEATEAR

ABCDECEA DIPLOPOD DORMERED EXALTATE SHEARERS SMEARERS SPEARERS SWEARERS TRAINANT

ABCDECEB OSTEITIS REIMBIBE STAGNANT

ABCDECEC BARTERER BORDERER CORNERER FORGERER GRANDADA LARDERER MONTANAN MURDERER SORCERER WARDERER

ABCDECED ALIGNING BORDERED DEIGNING FEIGNING LARDERED MURDERED REIGNING

ABCDECEE CONVENEE MURDEREE

ABCDECEF ALIENING BARTERED CATHETER CHORIOID CLEARERS COAPTATE CONGENER CONVENED CONVENER CONVENES CORNERED CRAWDADS CURIARAS DISBOSOM GARNERED GARTERED GRANDADS MONTANAS ORTHITIC PINKENED PORTERED REINSIST SORCERED STOPCOCK TAILPIPE UNDERDRY VINTENER WORSERED

ABCDECFA DISBASED DISCASED DISNOSED DISPOSED DRAWBAND EFOLIOSE EMACIATE EMPURPLE ENCIRCLE ERADIATE ETIOLIZE EVACUATE EVALUATE EXACUATE EXCIRCLE EXOSPORE EXOSTOME GRIEVING GRISTING GUILDING GUILTING HEIMLICH KNAPSACK RECONCUR SAILFINS SANDINGS SCANDALS SCENTERS SCEPTERS SEAFOAMS SENDINGS SHELTERS SHELVERS SHERBETS SHINDIES SHINDIGS SHOEBOYS SHOPBOYS SHOWDOMS SITUATES SKEINERS SKELTERS SLAVIANS SLEDGERS SMELTERS SMIDGINS SMITHIES SNAPBAGS SNEAKERS SOLUBLES SPARTANS SPEAKERS SPECKERS SPECTERS SPENCERS SPENDERS STADIALS STEALERS STEAMERS STICKIES STINGIES SWEATERS SWELTERS TRANSACT TRIADIST TRIALIST

ABCDECFB BEPIMPLE BEPURPLE BRICKIER BRISKIER CHIEFISH CHILDISH CRIMPIER CRISPIER DEIONIZE DENOUNCE DRIFTIER DRINKIER FASCISTA FLAXTAIL FRINGIER FRISKIER GRISLIER ISOTRONS LEACHATE PERFORCE PRICKIER REIGNITE REINCITE REINVITE RENOUNCE SEAPLANE SEAQUAKE SEPTUPLE STALWART TENDANCE THICKISH THIEVISH THINGISH TRICKIER UNSEASON VEINLIKE VEINWISE

ABCDECFC BRINDISI DAIQUIRI DISBASES DISCUSES DISGUSTS DISMASKS DISMASTS DISNESTS DISPOSES DISPOSTS DISRESTS ECSTASIS FASCISMS FASCISTS GEOPHOTO HARBORER MARTYRER MISCASTS MISLESTS MOSAISTS PRESCENE TOEPIECE UPROARER VISCOSES

ABCDECFD ALIENIZE BRUSHUPS BRUSQUES CHESTERS CONSENTS CRISPINS CRISTIES CURSORES DIESTERS DYESTERS EROSIONS FLESHERS FLIRTIER FRESHENS FRESHETS GRADUAND GUESTERS HEADBAND HEADLAND HEADWARD IMPEOPLE IMPROPER MERCURIC NITRATOR OUTDATED OVERBEAR OVERDEAR OVERFEAR OVERGEAR OVERHEAR OVERNEAR OVERWEAR OVERYEAR QUESTERS QUIETIVE QUIRKIER RETHATCH SHIRKIER SHIRTIER SMIRKIER SPENCEAN SWIRLIER TWIRLIER UNPEOPLE UNPROPER UNTHATCH VEIGLING WEIGHING WHIRLIER WHISKIES

ABCDECFE BRIDGING CHORDOID CLOISONS COEXTENT CONDENSE DRAGSAWS FLIMSIES FLOTSONS FRIDGING GREATEST HEADSAWS HEARSAYS HERBARIA JOINTIST MARTYRLY OVERSEAS OVERSETS OVERSEWS OVERTEST PLEASERS PUNGENCE QUIETIST REACTANT STANDARD TRIUNION UNLADLED UNTASTES WHIMSIES

ABCDECFF AGEDNESS AGENTESS AWEDNESS BRIMFILL CLERGESS CLERKESS CRANDALL CREWLESS DREGLESS FRETLESS GRAYWALL GREYNESS HEADWALL IDEALESS MEATBALL OVERFELL OVERSELL OVERTELL OVERWELL PIEDNESS PIERLESS POETLESS POETRESS PRATFALL PREBLESS PREDWELL PREGUESS QUEDNESS SPATFALL TRAPBALL TRIPSILL VIEWLESS WHEYNESS

ABCDECFG AIRBORNE AIRBURST AIRPORTS AIRSCREW ALIENISM ALIENIST ALIQUIDS AMENDERS AMOEBOID AMOEBOUS AMPHIPOD AQUEDUCT AQUIFUGE AREOLETS ATELIERS AVENGERS AVERMENT AVERSELY AVIONICS AXIOLITE BAITFISH BANKINGS BENIGNLY BETROTHS BIOCHORE BIOPHORE

```
BIOPHORS BIOSCOPE BIOSCOPY BIVALVED BIVALVES BLACKARM BLANKARD BLEAREST BLENDERS
BLENHEIM BLETHERS BLIMPISH BLINDISH BLINKIER BLINKIES BLITHING BLITZING BLOCKOUT
BLUECUPS BOATWARD BOATYARD BONDINGS BRAHMANI BRAHMANS BRAHMANY BRICKING BRICKISH
BRIDLING BRIEFING BRISKING BRISLING BRITAINS BROWNOUT BROWPOST BRUSQUED BUILDING
BUNTINGS CANIONED CANTONED CANYONED CARBURET CARPORTS CHAINAGE CHAPEAUS CHAPEAUX
CHAPLAIN CHAPRASI CHARLADY CHATEAUS CHATEAUX CHEAPENS CHEAPEST CHEATERS CHEATERY
CHEQUERS CHEWIEST CHILDING CHINKIER CHIPLING CHIRPILY CHIRPING CHITLING CHITLINS
CHORIONS CINZANOS CITRATED CITRATES CLAIMANT CLAMBAKE CLAYBANK CLAYPANS CLAYWARE
CLEANERS CLEANEST CLEAREST CLEATERS CLEAVERS CLIMBING CLINGIER CLIQUIER CLIQUISH
CLIQUISM CLOYSOME COALBAGS COALRAKE COALYARD COELDERS COENDEAR COEXTEND COLDSLAW
COLESLAW CONFINED CONFINER CONFINES CONSANED CONTENDS CONTINUA CONTINUE CONVENTS
CRANIATE CRAWDABS CRIMPING CRISPILY CRISPING CROUTONS CROYDONS CURATRIX CURSORIA
CUTWATER DAINTIER DAINTIFY DAINTILY DAIRYING DEIFYING DESPISAL DETRITAL DETRITUS
DIAGRAMS DIAGRAPH DIAPHANE DIAPHANY DIETHERS DIPROPYL DISPOSAL DISPOSER DOGFIGHT
DRAFTAGE DRAINAGE DRAWBACK DRIFTING DUNKINGS EDGINGLY EDIFYING ELUVIUMS EMOTIONS
ENORMOUS ENTOPTIC EUCTICAL EVACUANT EVICTING EVICTION EXIGUITY EXISTING FAINTISH
FAIRLIKE FAIRYISH FAIRYISM FANIONED FARMERLY FASCISMO FAUTEUIL FENLANDS FIELDENS
FIELDERS FIERCELY FIERCENS FIERCEST FIREARMS FIRETRAP FLAGRANT FLAGRATE FLAMBANT
FLANKARD FLAPJACK FLATCAPS FLATCARS FLATWARE FLATWAYS FLECKENS FLECKERS FLEXIEST
FLICKIER FLICKING FLIMSIER FLINGIER FLINTIER FLIRTING FLIRTISH FOISTIED FOISTING
FONTANGE FOREARMS FOREGRIP FORMERLY FORWARDS FORWARNS FREQUENT FRICTION FRIEZING
FRISKILY FRISKING FROGNOSE GAINLIER GEOSCOPY GEOTROPY GLACIATE GLADIATE GLEANERS
GLORIOSA GLORIOUS GRADUATE GRAYBACK GRAYPATE GREATENS GUARDANT GUILTIER GUNHANDS
HAIRLIKE HAIRLINE HAIRPINS HARBORED HEADCAPS HEADMARK HEADRAIL HEADSAIL HEADWARK
HEADWAYS HECTICAL HECTICLY HEISTING HOISTING HUNTINGS HYDRIDES ICTUATED ICTUATES
IDAHOANS IDEOGENY IMPURPLE INAURATE INEXPERT INOSCOPY INTACTLY INTORTED INTRATES
INVOLVED INVOLVER INVOLVES ISODROME ISOPHONE ISOPHOTE ISOTROPE ISOTROPY JAILBIRD
JOISTING KNEADERS KNOTHOLE LAITHING LANDINGS LEADBACK LEADWAYS MAIDLIKE MAIDLING
MANHUNTS MANSONRY MARTYRED MENDINGS MERCURID MINUENDS MISWASTE MOIREING MOISTIER
MOISTIFY MOISTING MORPHREY MORTARED MUNDANES MUNTINGS MYOPHORE MYOSCOPE NITRATED
NITRATES NORWARDS OBADIAHS OBEDIENT OPENHEAD OPIATING OPUSCULE ORESTEAN OUTACTED
OUTDATES OUTGATES OUTMATCH OUTPATHS OUTPITCH OUTWATCH OUTWATER OUTWITHS OVERBEAT
OVERBEND OVERBENT OVERBETS OVERDEAL OVERDECK OVERDENS OVERFELT OVERGETS OVERHEAD
OVERHEAP OVERHEAT OVERHELD OVERHELP OVERJETS OVERKEPT OVERLEAD OVERLEAF OVERLEAN
OVERLEAP OVERLEWD OVERMELT OVERNEAT OVERNETS OVERSEAL OVERSEAM OVERSEND OVERSENT
OVERSEWN OVERWEBS OVERWELT OVERWEND OVERWENT OVERWEPT OVERWETS OVERZEAL PAINTIER
PAIRWISE PANTINGS PATENTLY PATENTOR PATHETIC PEACOATS PEARMAIN PENDANTS PERFORMS
PERIORAL PERTURBS PHANTASM PHANTASY PHARMACY PHIALINE PHIALING PIERHEAD PINBONES
PLAGIARY PLANKAGE PLANTAGE PLANTARY PLATEAUS PLATEAUX PLAYBACK PLAYFAIR PLAYMATE
PLAYWARD PLEADERS PLEATERS PLEDGERS PLOWBOYS POINTIER POLYCLAD PORTERLY PORTURED
PORTURES POTENTIA POTENTLY POTLATCH PRECLEAN PREDIETS PREDWELT PRESTEAM PRETZELS
PREVIEWS PRICKING PRICKISH PRISTINE PUDENDAL PUNGENCY QUADRAIN QUADRANS QUADRANT
QUADRATE QUADRATS QUANDARY QUARTANO QUARTANS QUATRAIN QUATRALS QUICKIES QUICKING
QUIETING QUIETISM QUILTING QUIRKILY QUIRKING QUIRKISH QUIRTING QUISLING RAGINGLY
RAILSIDE RAMPSMEN RANKINGS RATBITES RECHUCKS REIFYING REINDICT REPULPIT RHIZOIDS
RHOMBOID RISPOSTE ROADWAYS ROISTING ROUNDUPS RUINLIKE SEABOARD SEACRAFT SEATRAIN
SHAGTAIL SHELTERY SHIFTIER SHIFTILY SHIFTING SHIRKING SHIRTING SHOPFOLK SHOPWORK
SHOPWORN SHOWBOAT SHOWGOER SITUATED SKIMPIER SKIMPILY SKIMPING SKIRLING SKIRTING
SLACKAGE SLAMBANG SLAPJACK SLICKING SLINKIER SLOWPOKE SMELTERY SMIRKING SMITHIAN
SMITHIED SMITHIER SMITHING SNAPBACK SNAPJACK SPANIARD SPIELING SPIRTING SPITFIRE
STACKAGE STANZAED STANZAIC STAYLACE STEMHEAD STICKIED STICKIER STICKILY STICKING
```

STIFLING STINGIED STINGIER STINGILY STINKIER STIRLING STOPWORK SUITLIKE SWANMARK
SWAYBACK SWIFTIAN SWIFTING SWINGIER SWIRLING SYNGENIC TAILPINS TAILWISE TAILZIED
TANGENCY TARWORKS TEABOARD TEAMLAND THAILAND THEOREMS THERMELS THIAMIDE THIAMIDS
THIAMINE THIAMINS THICKING THIEVING THIRDING TIERCELS TRACKAGE TRAINAGE TRAMPAGE
TRAMWAYS TRIACIDS TRIADISM TRIALISM TRIAMIDE TRIAMIDS TRIAMINE TRIAMINO TRIAMINS
TRICKILY TRICKING TRICKISH TRIDAILY TRIFLING TRIGLIDS TRILBIES TRIMLINE TRIOXIDE
TRIOXIDS TROMBONE TROMBONY TURMERIC TWEAKERS TWELVERS TWIFOILS TWIGLIKE TWINLIKE
TWIRLING TWOSCORE UNAFRAID UNAGHAST UNBARBED UNBRIBED UNCHECKS UNCLICKS UNDEADLY
UNDERDIG UNDERDIP UNDERDOG UNDERDOT UNEXPECT UNEXPERT UNGORGED UNGORGES UNHASHED
UNKICKED UNKIRKED UNMAIMED UNPALPED UNTASTED UNTILTED UNTROTHS UPCHECKS UPROARED
UPTILTED URGINGLY UROSCOPY VENDINGS VERACRUZ VIAGRAPH WAISTING WANTONED WANTONER
WANTONLY WARBIRDS WARLORDS WEIGHINS WEIRDING WEIRDISH WHARFAGE WHIMSIED WHIPBIRD
WHIPLIKE WHIRLING WHISKIED WHISKING WHISPING WHISTING WHITLING WHITRICK WIELDERS
WITHSTAY WRISTING WRITHING YIELDERS

ABCDEDAA SAFENESS SAGENESS SAMENESS SHOELESS SIDELESS SIDENESS SIRELESS SOLENESS
SORENESS SURENESS

ABCDEDAC AUTOBOAT ENSTATES SATIRIST SEMITISM   **ABCDEDAE** TYPESETS

ABCDEDAF ACRIDIAN ACTINIAE ACTINIAS AEROBOAT ALPINIAS AMOEBEAN APHIDIAN APODIDAE
AUXILIAN AUXILIAR ENDPAPER ENMITIES ENSTATED ENTIFIED ENTIFIES EPAGOGES EQUITIES
EXPIRIES EXTRARED FELICIFY FLUIDIFY GEMOLOGY ISAGOGIC LAUDEDLY LOADEDLY MARITIME
MITOSOME MYOEDEMA MYXEDEMA NEVADANS NOTICING OBLIVION OVERBROW OVERCROP OVERCROW
OVERDROP OVERGROW OVERTROD POLYTYPE PREADAPT RAVELERS RAVENERS RECOLORS REHAZARD
REHONORS RIPENERS RIVETERS SATIRISM SCRIBISM SEMIDISK SEMINIST SENILISM SNAILISH
SOBEREST SOLIDISH SPRITISH SQUIRISH SQUIRISM STOICISM SWAINISH TEPIDITY TOXICITY
TUBELETS TUMIDITY UNJOYOUS UNPOROUS VOLITIVE VOMITIVE

ABCDEDBA DENTATED   **ABCDEDBB** USHERESS

ABCDEDBC GESTATES RESTATES STEARATE UNGIVING VERIFIER

ABCDEDBD CENSUSES PERSISES UNSERENE

ABCDEDBE DOMINION EMBOSOMS FAMILIAL IMBOSOMS LATINIAN SABINIAN

ABCDEDBF AERIFIED AERIFIES AGROLOGY ALCOHOLS ANTISINE ANVILING AUXILIUM BAKEMEAT
BAREHEAD BASIDIAL BASILIAN BEAMSMEN BEPITIED BEPITIES CENSUSED CLUBABLE DIALKLIC
DISAVAIL ENFILING ENFIRING ENLIFING ENLIVING ENRIVING ENTICING FAMILIAE FAMILIAR
FANCICAL FARCICAL FRIEZERS GALICIAN GESTATED GRIEVERS GRUELERS HAMIDIAN HELMSMEN
HEPTITES HUMOROUS INDECENT INFERENT INHALANT INHERENT JAMESEAN JUDICIUM LAKEHEAD
LEONINES LEVITIES MAGICIAN NAPHTHAS PARISIAN PECTATES PENTITES POSITION PREALARM
PROAWARD RESTATED SAGELEAF SATIRIAL SEMIFIED SEPTATED SNAILING STOICITY TAMILIAN
TEAMSMEN TUMOROUS UNAIDING UNAILING UNAIMING UNCEMENT UNCITING UNDECENT UNDIVINE
UNFILING UNFIRING UNFIXING UNHIDING UNHIVING UNLIKING UNLIMING UNLIVING UNMIXING
UNOILING UNPILING UNRECENT UNREPENT UNRISING UNSIDING UNTIEING UNTILING UNTIRING
UNVACANT UNWIRING VERIFIED VERIFIES VERITIES VOLITION

ABCDEDCA SCREWERS STREWERS   **ABCDEDCB** DYSPEPSY METALATE REDIVIDE RETINITE

ABCDEDCC BASELESS BASENESS HOSELESS MUSELESS NOSELESS OVERFREE ROSELESS WISENESS

ABCDEDCF ACTIVITY ADENINES ADVISIVE AMITOTIC BASILISK BEAMSMAN BLACKCAP DENIZING
ENDOPODS ERGOLOGY FETIDITY FINEMENT FLYAWAYS FOLDEDLY FOREVERS FRAMEMAN FUTILITY
HASIDISM KILOVOLT KITAMATS MANIKINS MOLDEDLY MOTILITY MOTIVITY MUNITING MUTINITY
MUTIVITY NATIVITY NOTELETS OPTICITY OPTIMITY OVERBRED OVERDREW OVERFRET OVERGREW
PACIFICS PHENINES PREGAGED PREGAGES QUINONIC STAMPMAN TEAMSMAN ULTIMITY UNLEVELS
WHITETIP

ABCDEDDA DANEWEED DOVEWEED   **ABCDEDDC** FORESEER

ABCDEDDE FORESEES GODMAMMA

ABCDEDDF ALIENEES FIREWEED FOREKEEL FORESEEN FOREWEEP MULETEER PINEWEED POKEWEED
RAPESEED TIMEKEEP TINEWEED

ABCDEDEA CYSTITIC GRAINING GROINING SOBERERS   **ABCDEDEB** FEMININE USHERERS

ABCDEDEC CYSTITIS MASTITIS

ABCDEDEF ADHERERS ALTERERS ARGININE AUGERERS BASINING BEDINING BLAINING BRAINING
CABINING CATERERS CHAINING COHERERS COVERERS DEFINING DELINING DILATATE DOMINING
DRAINING ERMINING FAMINING FEMININS FRAMEMEN GODPAPAS HOMININE HOVERERS LATINING
LIVERERS LOWERERS LUMINING MASTITIC MITERERS MUTINING NAPERERS PLAINING RAPINING
REFINING RELINING REPINING RESINING SATINING SHRINING SKEINING SLIMEMEN SPLINING
STAINING STOWAWAY TAPERERS TRAINING TWAINING UKALELES UNDERERS UNWILILY WAFERERS
WAGERERS WATERERS WAVERERS

ABCDEDFA CELOZOIC CENOZOIC CHOLELIC CYTOZOIC DICTATED DISGAGED DISPOPED DOPEHEAD
ECTOSOME ENDAMAGE ENDOSOME EPICYCLE EQUITIME ESCALATE ESCAPADE ESCAPAGE ETHICIZE
EXCAVATE EXCITIVE EXHALATE GRAILING HIERARCH NUMIDIAN RATIFIER RECOLOUR REHONOUR
SANIFIES SANITIES SATIRICS SAVOROUS SCHEMERS SEMITICS SOLICITS SPIELERS SURVIVES
SYNODOUS THROWOUT TIMEKEPT TIREDEST TULIPIST

ABCDEDFB ADHEREND AMOEBEUM ASPIRINS ASPOROUS BASILICA BRAINIER CYTOLOGY DECISIVE
DEFINITE DELAWARE DELAYAGE DERISIVE DESITIVE DEVILIZE ECSTATIC ECTOZOIC EGOIZING
EMPIRISM ENTOZOAN ENVISION ETHICIST FEMINIZE FRUITIER GENITIVE GENOSOME GRAINIER
LEGITIME MEDICINE MYCOLOGY OTHEREST PANETELA PETALAGE POLITICO PYROLOGY RECIDIVE
REDAMAGE RELAXATE REMANAGE RETINIZE REVACATE SEMIFINE SEMILIVE SEMITIZE SEPARATE
THEOSOPH TYPOLOGY TYROLOGY UMPIRISM UNVISION

ABCDEDFC ACTIVIST AGNITION ANTEVERT BASIFIES BASILICS BATEMENT BREAKAGE CLEARAGE
CLEAVAGE CODIFIED COMITIUM CREOSOTE CRYOLOGY DISGAGES DISPOPES DOMINIUM DREAMAGE
FAMILISM FEMINISM FLEABANE FOREBEAR FOREHEAR FOREYEAR GASIFIES GASPIPES HOMINISM
INSTATES INTEREAT INTEREST LADIFIED LATINIST LUMINISM MODIFIED MUNITION NATIVIST
OBLIVIAL OFTENEST OPTIMIST OUTEREST OVERTRUE OVERURGE POLICIAL PURIFIER REGIVING
ROSELETS SIDEHEAD STRIPIER SURVIVER SURVIVOR THEODORE TIDEHEAD TUNISIAN UNSTATES
UPGIVING UPSTATES

ABCDEDFD AFTEREYE ANTECEDE CONSISTS HIMALAYA NOVELESE PERSISTS RUTABAGA TIGEREYE
UMBILICI UNDEREYE UNSEVERE

ABCDEDFE AEROSOLS BONESETS COVISITS CREOSOLS DEMIHIGH DEMITINT DILATANT EQUITIST
FIRESETS FORESETS FRUITIST HYMENEAN MONILIAL OBLIGING OPTIMISM POLITIST PYRENEAN
QUIETEST RESILIAL REVISITS SEMIHIGH UNBOSOMS UNFILIAL UNTIDIED

ABCDEDFF ABLENESS BAKERESS BARENESS BLUENESS BONELESS BOWELESS CAGELESS CARELESS
CATERESS CHIEFESS CODELESS CORELESS CURELESS CUTENESS DATELESS DIRENESS DOWERESS
DURELESS FACELESS FADELESS FAMELESS FAREWELL FINELESS FIRELESS FORETELL FUMELESS
GAMELESS GAMENESS GATELESS GAZELESS HALENESS HAREBELL HATELESS HAVELESS HAZELESS
HIDELESS HIRELESS HIVELESS HOMELESS HOPELESS HOPEWELL HUGENESS IDLENESS INTERESS
JOKELESS LAMENESS LATENESS LIKENESS LIVENESS MAKELESS MALENESS MANELESS MATELESS
MEGAWATT MODELESS MORENESS MOVELESS MUTENESS NAMELESS NOTELESS PAGELESS PALENESS
PANELESS PURENESS RAGELESS RATELESS RIFENESS RIMELESS RIPENESS RITELESS ROBELESS
RUDENESS TAMELESS TAMENESS TAPELESS THROWOFF TIDELESS TIMELESS TIRELESS TONELESS
TRUENESS TUBELESS TUNELESS VANELESS VICELESS VILENESS VINELESS VIPERESS VOTELESS
WAGELESS WAKELESS WAKENESS WANELESS WARELESS WARENESS WAVELESS WIDENESS WIFELESS
WINELESS WIRELESS YOKELESS ZONELESS

ABCDEDFG ACRIDITY ACROLOGY ACTIFIED ACTIFIER ACTIFIES ACTINIUM ACTIVISM ACTIVIZE
ACUITIES ADHERENT ADHIBITS ADMIRING ADMIXING ADVISING AEROFOIL AEROLOGY AFTEREND
AGRONOMY ALBINISM ALGICIDE ALGIDITY ALIENERS ALPINISM ALPINIST AMBITION ANTICIZE
ANTIVICE APHIDIUS APIOLOGY AQUILINE AQUINIST ARTIFICE ASPIRING ATHENEUM ATROPOUS
AUDITING AUDITION AUDITIVE AUDIVISE AURIFIED AURIFIES AUTOLOGY AUTONOMY AUTOSOME
AVOIDING AXIOLOGY BAGPIPER BANDIDOS BASEMENT BASIFIED BASIFIER BATIKING BECOLORS
BECOLOUR BEFIRING BELIMING BELIVING BEMIRING BEMIXING BERIDING BETIDING BETIRING
BICOLORS BICOLOUR BIDCOCKS BIFOROUS BILCOCKS BIMOTORS BIOCYCLE BIPOROSE BIPOROUS
BLUEHEAD BOLIVIAN BOLIVIAS BOLIXING BONEHEAD BOVICIDE BOVINITY BRAIDING BRAIDIST
BRAILING BRAINISH BRAISING BRAIZING BRIEFEST BROADAXE BROILING BRUISING BRUITING
BUCKSKIN BULIMIAC BULIMIAS BULIMIES BURNINGS CANDIDLY CASEMENT CAVITIED CAVITIES
CHAIRING CHAISING CHIEFERY CHIEFEST CHOIRING CHROMONE CHROMOUS CLAIMING CLOAKAGE
CODIFIER CODIFIES COGENERS COHERENT COHIBITS COMITIAL COMITIES COMITIVA CONEHEAD
CONIDIAL CONIDIUM CONVIVAL CONVIVED CONVIVES COREBELS COREGENT CORNINGS COSTATED
COTISING COURTRIE COVETERS CROATANS CRUELEST CRUISING CUBELETS CUPIDITY CURATAGE
CURBABLE CUTAWAYS CYANINES CYTOSOME DARKSKIN DARNINGS DAVITING DAWCOCKS DAWNINGS
DAZEMENT DEBILITY DEBITING DECANALS DECISING DECISION DECOLORS DECOLOUR DECOROUS
DEFICITS DEFILING DEFINISH DELIMING DELIMITS DELIRIUM DEMISING DEMOLOGY DERISION
DERIVING DESIRING DESIZING DEVILING DEVILISH DEVILISM DEVISING DIACYCLE DICTATES
DICTATOR DIGERENT DOCILITY DOMICILE DOMIFIES DOMINICA DOMINICK DOMINIES DOMITIAN
DORICISM DORICIZE DOVEKEYS DOVELETS DOWELERS DOZENERS EARNINGS EIGHTHLY EMPIRICS
EMPIRING ENCOLORS ENCOLOUR ENDOZOIC ENHAZARD ENTOMOID ENTOZOAL EPAGOGIC EQUINIAS
EQUINITY EQUIRIAS ETHANALS ETHICIAN ETHICISM ETHOLOGY ETHYNYLS ETIOLOGY EUROPOID
EUSTATIC EXCIDING EXCISING EXCISION EXCITING EXHALANT EXHIBITS EXPIRING FACETELY
FACILITY FACTOTUM FAKIRISM FAMILIES FAMILIST FELICITY FELONOUS FEMINIST FEMINITY
FERNANDO FIREBEDS FLAIRING FLEABAGS FLOATAGE FLUIDISM FLUIDIST FLUIDITY FLUIDIZE
FLUOROID FLYPAPER FOREDECK FOREDESK FOREHEAD FORELEGS FORELEND FOREMEAN FOREMELT
FORENEWS FOREPEAK FORESEAT FORESEND FOREWENT FRAILING FRAILISH FRUITING FRUITION
FRUITIVE FUGITIVE FUMIDITY FUNEREAL FUSILIER FUSINITE GASIFIED GASIFIER GAVELERS
GAZEMENT GELIDITY GELIDIUM

ABCDEEAA ENROLLEE   **ABCDEEAB** ANDORRAN UNDERRUN

ABCDEEAC DISWOODS ENDULLED ENROLLER ENTURRET MISDEEMS

ABCDEEAE EMBOSSES ENBUSSES ENMASSES ENMOSSES

ABCDEEAF AMPULLAE AMPULLAR ANCILLAE ANCILLAS ARIETTAS EMBARREL EMBITTER EMBOGGED EMBOSSED EMBOSSER EMBUSSED EMPALLED ENCUPPED ENHATTED ENMASSED ENMOSSED ENRIBBED ENROLLED EQUALLED EQUIPPED EQUIPPER ESCOTTED ESTALLED ESTOPPED EXCUSSED EXTOLLED EXTOLLER REFLOORS TAPROOTS

ABCDEEBA DEBAGGED DEBARRED DEBUGGED DEBURRED DEBUSSED DECAPPED DEFATTED DEGASSED DEGUMMED DEHULLED DEMOBBED DEMURRED DERATTED DETINNED DEVILLED HANUKKAH PUYALLUP REBUTTER RECAPPER RECOPPER REDIPPER REDUBBER REHAMMER REJIGGER RELAPPER REMITTER REPASSER RESUFFER RETANNER

ABCDEEBB REMITTEE

ABCDEEBC BEDIMMED BEDIPPED BEDULLED MEDALLED PEDALLED REDIGGED REDIPPED REDUBBED UPSWEEPS

ABCDEEBE BEMUDDED DEBUSSES DEGASSES DEMURRER DEPASSES PELISSES REBUDDED REKISSES REMASSES REMISSES REPASSES RESODDED RETOSSES

ABCDEEBF BACILLAR BECAPPED BECUFFED BEFALLEN BEFANNED BEFITTED BEFOGGED BEFURRED BEGALLED BEGOTTEN BEGUMMED BEGUTTED BEHAMMER BEHAPPEN BEHATTED BEJAZZED BEJAZZES BEJIGGED BEKISSED BELITTER BEMANNED BEMARRED BEMATTED BEPATTED BEPILLED BEPUFFED BEROLLED BERUFFED BESODDEN BESOTTED BETAGGED BETASSEL BETOSSED BEWALLED BEWIGGED BOUILLON CAMILLAE COLESSOR COTILLON DEBITTER DECAPPER DEGASSER DEGUMMER DETASSEL DEVILLER EMBLOOMS MADONNAS MAGELLAN MANILLAS MAXILLAE MAXILLAR METALLER OUTISSUE PEDALLER PETALLED REBAGGED REBIDDEN REBILLED REBILLET REBITTEN REBUFFED REBUFFET REBUTTED RECALLED RECAPPED RECOLLET RECONNED REFALLED REFANNED REFILLED REFITTED REGILLED REGINNED REHAPPEN REHIDDEN REHOBBED REJAGGED REKILLED REKISSED RELAPPED RELOTTED REMANNED REMAPPED REMASSED REMILLED REMISSED REMITTED REMOPPED REPASSED REPINNED REPOLLED REPOTTED REPUFFED RESUNNED RESUPPED RETAGGED RETANNED RETILLED RETINNED RETIPPED RETOSSED REWALLED SAGITTAL SEPALLED SIBYLLIC UNGREENS VANILLAS

ABCDEECB BELITTLE PREOFFER   **ABCDEECE** GRANDDAD

ABCDEECF CANTEENS DISROOST DOLITTLE GRANDDAM PREANNEX RANGOONS REDWOODS TRIASSIC UNLITTLE

ABCDEEDA CYRILLIC DOWELLED DURESSED RAVELLER RIVETTER ROSETTER SIROCCOS

ABCDEEDB CRUELLER GRUELLER INCOMMON UNCOMMON

ABCDEEDC HOSANNAS MISDEEDS MODELLED MOSELLES MUSETTES RISOTTOS ROSELLES ROSETTES SHREDDER VANILLIN YODELLED

ABCDEEDE CARESSES COVESSES DURESSES ENHORROR FINESSES IMBEDDED INFERRER INTERRER OGRESSES SHREDDED UNBEDDED UNLESSES UNTEDDED UNWEDDED UPNESSES VOWESSES

ABCDEEDF BIGTOOTH BIOASSAY BOWELLED CAPETTES CARESSED CAYENNES CURETTED CURETTES DINETTES DISARRAY DOGTEETH DOYENNES DUXELLES ENSORROW FACETTED FINESSED FINESSER GAVELLED GAVELLER GAZELLED GAZELLES GAZETTED GAZETTER GAZETTES GNEISSIC GRUELLED

HOTELLED HOVELLED HOVELLER HOWELLED IMPALLAS IMPELLED IMPELLER IMPENNED INFERRED
INHELLED INSETTED INSETTER INTERRED LAYETTES MISARRAY MODELLER MORELLES MOYENNES
NOVELLER ONSETTER OUTPEEPS PALETTES PANELLED RAVELLED REGATTAS REHOLLOW RIVELLED
RIVETTED ROSETTED SAWTEETH SAWTOOTH TOWELLED UNBEGGED UNBELLED UNBOTTOM UNFELLED
UNFETTER UNHEMMED UNHOLLOW UNITOOTH UNJELLED UNLETTED UNPEGGED UNTERRED UNVESSEL
UNWEBBED UNWETTED UPSETTED UPSETTER UPWELLED VOWELLED YODELLER

ABCDEEFA EMBATTLE EMBOTTLE ENDAZZLE ENGROOVE ENMUFFLE REMITTOR SEABOOTS SEAFOODS
SIXTEENS SOTWEEDS SUBCOOLS SUBPOOLS SUBROOTS SUBTEENS SUNROOMS SUNWEEDS

ABCDEEFB ADMITTED BEDAZZLE BEFUDDLE BEJUGGLE BEMUDDLE BEMUFFLE BEMUZZLE BEPUDDLE
BEPUZZLE BERATTLE BETIPPLE BRAILLER CAMELLIA INTERRAN INTERRUN PREOCCUR REBOTTLE
RECHOOSE REPUDDLE RESADDLE UNBARREN UNBATTEN UNBIDDEN UNBITTEN UNCOFFIN UNDERRAN
UNFALLEN UNFATTEN UNFITTEN UNGOTTEN UNHAPPEN UNHIDDEN UNLITTEN UNRIDDEN UNROTTEN
UNSADDEN UNSODDEN UNWARREN

ABCDEEFC CAROLLER DISROOFS DISROOTS ENSTOOLS ENWALLOW FESTOONS INSHOOTS INSTEEPS
MISCOOKS MISKEEPS MORALLER ONSWEEPS PREISSUE RESHOOTS REWALLOW ROSELLAS SCRAPPER
SCRUBBER SHRILLER SPRIGGER STRAPPER STRIPPER STROLLER STROPPER STRUMMER THRILLER
THROBBER UNDAMMED UNDIMMED UNDIPPED UNDOFFED UNDOGGED UNDOLLED UNDOTTED UNROLLER
UNSHEETS UNSPEEDS UNSTEELS UNSTEEPS UPSHOOTS

ABCDEEFD ANISEEDS FORSEEKS HAYSEEDS IMBEZZLE LINSEEDS NUTSEEDS OATSEEDS OILSEEDS
SHELFFUL SKIDOOED UNMEDDLE UNMETTLE UNSETTLE

ABCDEEFE ABHORRER BYPASSES FOCUSSES IMBOSSES IMPASSES MELISSAS MISADDED MOLASSES
MORASSES SQUADDED UNCODDED UNFLEECE UNFREEZE UNKISSES UNLIDDED UNMADDED UNPADDED
UNPASSES UNPODDED UNRODDED UNSLEEVE UNWADDED

ABCDEEFF ADMITTEE

ABCDEEFG ABHORRED ADMITTER AFLUTTER AGLIMMER AGLITTER ANVILLED ARMHOOPS ARPEGGIO
ASHIMMER ASNIFFLE AWFULLER BACILLUS BEDROOMS BEHALLOW BESMOOTH BETALLOW BIGROOTS
BRAILLED BUGWEEDS BULREEDY BURNOOSE BYPASSER CARILLON CAROLLED CARTOONS CATHOODS
CAVILLED CAVILLER CHAUFFER CHEROOTS CHINOOKS CIMARRON CORALLED COSUFFER CUBHOODS
CULOTTES CUTWEEDS CYRILLAS DAMFOOLS DAYBOOKS DAYROOMS DEBLOOMS DEBUTTON DEMURRAL
DILEMMAS DISALLOW DISANNEX DISANNUL DRAGOONS DUBONNET ELFHOODS ELKWOODS ENCOLLAR
ENFURROW ENHALLOW ESCALLOP ESTOPPAL FELUCCAS FESTOONY FOCUSSED GADZOOKS GAVOTTED
GAVOTTES GIRAFFES GOMBEENS GORILLAS GRAILLES GRIEFFUL GUMWEEDS GUNWOODS HARPOONS
HAYWEEDS HENROOST HOCUSSED HOGWEEDS ICEROOTS IMBOSSED IMPALLED IMPELLOR INBREEDS
INCREEPS INCURRED INCUSSED INFLOODS INGROOVE INKWEEDS INKWOODS INROLLED INRUBBED
INWALLED IVYWEEDS IVYWOODS JOHANNES JOYWEEDS JURASSIC KAMLOOPS KILDEERS LAMPOONS
LAWBOOKS LEGROOMS MANGOOSE MANHOODS MANROOTS MAYWEEDS MEDALLIC MEDULLAR MEDULLAS
MELASSIC METALLIC MIDWEEKS MISAPPLY MOLASSED MOLUCCAN MORALLED MORASSIC MUNGOOSE
MYNHEERS NOBILLED NUTHOOKS OBMISSED OUTHEELS OUTPEERS OUTWEEDS OUTWEEPS PARCOOKS
PAROLLES PAVILLON PAYBOOKS PHIALLED PIGFOOTS PIGWEEDS PINHOOKS PINWEEDS PIONEERS
PIONEERY PLATOONS PLYWOODS POTASSIC PRALEENS PREALLOT PREALLOW PRECOOKS PRECOOLS
PREDOOMS PREFOOLS PROCEEDS RAGWEEDS REBALLOT REBLOOMS REBUTTAL REBUTTON RECOMMIT
REFALLOW REFLOODS REGALLOP REHALLOW REMISSLY REMITTAL RESMOOTH RESUMMON RESUPPLY
RICOTTAS RIVALLED ROUGHHEW RUBELLAS SCRABBLE SCRABBLY SCRAGGED SCRAGGLY SCRAMMED
SCRAPPED SCRAPPLE SCRIBBLE SCRIBBLY SCROLLED SCRUBBED SCRUBBLY SCRUFFED SCRUFFLE

SHRILLED SHRUBBED SHRUGGED SPLATTED SPLATTER SPLITTED SPLITTEN SPLITTER SPLUTTER
SPRADDLE SPRAGGED SPRAGGLY SPRATTED SPRATTLE SPRIGGED SPRITTED SPROTTLE SQUABBED
SQUABBER SQUABBLE SQUABBLY SQUADDER SQUALLED SQUALLER SQUATTED SQUATTER SQUIBBED
SQUIBBER SQUIDDER SQUIGGLE SQUIGGLY SQUIRREL STRADDLE STRAGGLE STRAGGLY STRAPPED
STRIPPED STROLLED STROPPED STRUGGLE STRUMMED TAPROOMS TARIFFED TARWOODS TEAROOMS
TEAROOMY THRALLED THRILLED THROBBED TYPHOONS TYRANNIC TYRANNIS TYRANNUS UMBELLIC
UMPTEENS UNBAGGED UNBARRED UNBARREL UNBATTED UNBEGGAR UNBIGGED UNBILLED UNBITTED
UNBITTER UNBLOODY UNBLOOMS UNBOGGED UNBOLLED UNBOSSED UNBOTTLE UNBREECH UNBREEZY
UNBROOCH UNCALLED UNCALLOW UNCAPPED UNCAPPER UNCELLAR UNCHEERY UNCOFFER UNCOFFLE
UNCOGGED UNCOLLAR UNCROOKS UNDAZZLE UNFAGGED UNFATTED UNFELLOW UNFIBBED UNFILLED
UNFITTED UNFLOORS UNFREELY UNGASSED UNGIBBET UNGILLED UNGLOOMS UNGLOOMY UNGREEDY
UNHALLOW UNHATTED UNHIPPED UNHISSED UNHOBBLE UNHOGGED UNHOPPED UNJAGGED UNJAMMED
UNJARRED UNJOGGED UNKILLED UNKISSED UNLAPPED UNLOGGED UNLOPPED UNLOTTED UNMALLED
UNMAPPED UNMARRED UNMASSED UNMATTED UNMELLOW UNMILLED UNMISSED UNMOBBED UNMOPPED
UNMOSSED UNPALLED UNPARREL UNPASSED UNPATTED UNPILLED UNPITTED UNPOLLED UNPOTTED
UNRAMMED UNRIBBED UNRIDDLE UNRIGGED UNRIPPED UNROBBED UNROLLED UNROTTED UNSADDLE
UNSAPPED UNSIPPED UNSLEEPY UNSMOOTH UNSOTTED UNSPEEDY UNTAGGED UNTAPPED UNTARRED
UNTILLED UNTIPPED UNTOGGLE UNTOLLED UNTOPPED UNTORRID UNTOSSED UNVATTED UNWAGGED
UNWALLED UNWALLET UNWARRED UNWHEELS UNWIGGED UNWILLED UNWILLES UNWITTED UNZIPPER
UPBARRED UPCHEERS UPFILLED UPFITTER UPLADDER UPROLLED UPSADDLE UPSETTAL UPSITTEN
UPVALLEY VOCALLER WATERRUG WAYBOOKS WITLOOFS

ABCDEFAA EDUCATEE EMPLOYEE ENDORSEE ENLISTEE ESCORTEE ESCROWEE EXAMINEE LANDFILL
LONGBILL SACKLESS SAINTESS SALTNESS SANDLESS SATYRESS SCARLESS SCUMLESS SHIPLESS
SHOTLESS SHOWLESS SHUNLESS SHUTNESS SICKLESS SICKNESS SIGHLESS SIGNLESS SILKNESS
SINKLESS SKINLESS SLABNESS SLIMNESS SLOWNESS SMUGNESS SNAPLESS SNOWLESS SOAPLESS
SOCKLESS SODALESS SOFTNESS SONGLESS SOUPLESS SOURNESS SPANLESS SPOTLESS SPRYNESS
SPURLESS SPYGLASS SQUIRESS STARLESS STAYLESS STIRLESS STOPLESS SUBCLASS SUBPRESS
SUCHNESS SUCKLESS SUNDRESS SUNGLASS SWAYLESS

ABCDEFAB ALOGICAL ANGLICAN ANTIGUAN ANTILEAN ARCHLIAR ASTERIAS DEMINUDE EDUCATED
ENDARKEN ENFASTEN ENGRAVEN ENHARDEN ENRICHEN ENTRYMEN ESCRIBES ESQUIRES ESTABLES
ISRAELIS LENDABLE LENTICLE LEVIABLE MEALTIME MEANTIME MYECTOMY NECKLINE NEPHRONE
ORIENTOR READMIRE REASPIRE REFIGURE REIGNORE REINJURE REINSURE REMANURE RENATURE
REPOSURE RESQUARE SECTWISE SEMIBASE SEMINASE SEMINOSE SHARKISH SHARPISH SHORTISH
SHREWISH SMARTISM STABLEST STAGIEST STARDUST STARIEST STARKEST STEDFAST STOCKIST
STONEIST STONIEST SYNCRASY TEMPLATE

ABCDEFAC AMRITSAR ASTIGMAT AUTOCRAT DESPONDS DISBANDS DISBENDS DISCARDS DISCORDS
DISLOADS DISPANDS DISPENDS DISTENDS EARTHIER ENDORSED ENRICHER ENSHADES ENSLAVES
ENSTORES ENSTYLES ERSATZES EXSURGES GOSLINGS INTERLIT INTERMIT ISCHEMIC LIENABLE
MISFORMS MISTERMS NEGATING NUTRIENT ORNATION ORNITHON OVERSHOE PRESHAPE RUSTLERS
STEPWISE THERMATE TOEPLATE UNDERBUD UNLAWFUL WILDFOWL

ABCDEFAD CAUSTICS CONTRACT DOGSLEDS EMBRACER ENGRAVER EPISODES EPISTLES EXTRUDER
EXUDATED FIRESAFE INTARSIA INTERLIE LAWYERLY LIKEABLE LINEABLE LIVEABLE LOSEABLE
LOVEABLE LUGSAILS MELANOMA OPERATOR PARSNIPS PENSHIPS PIESHOPS PRAECIPE PRESHIPS
RACKWORK REABSORB ROASTERS RODSTERS ROISTERS ROUSTERS SAGEROSE SALTIEST SCLEROSE
SLATIEST SOMEWISE SUBTLEST SUBTLIST TOLERATE TRISALTS TRISECTS

ABCDEFAE AFTERWAR AFTONIAN AMNESIAS ARMENIAN ATHENIAN ATRESIAS CLARENCE COALESCE

COMPESCE EMBODIED EMBORDER EMBUSHES EMBUSIES ENDORSER ENFORCER ENLARGER ENLODGED
ENRIDGED EXHORTER EXPORTER EXTASIES PINESAPS REVISORS SCANTEST SHORTEST SMARTEST
SPERMISM SUBLEASE SUBMERSE SUBTENSE SUBVERSE SURCEASE SWIFTEST SYLPHISH TRANSITS
UNDERFUR UNWILFUL UPAVENUE WHIPSAWS

ABCDEFAF AEROSTAT ARIZONAN CODPIECE ECLIPSES EMBOLDED EMBRASES EMBURSES EMPHASES
ENCLOSES ENDORSES ENFOLDED ENGILDED ENGIRDED ENHOUSES ENQUIRER ENSHADED ENTHUSES
ETHNOSES EXCLUDED EXODUSES EXPANDED EXPANSES EXPLODED EXPLORER EXPLOSES EXPULSES
EXTRUDED MARXISMS METONYMY MONKISMS MORPHEME SUDANESE TOPCASTS TOPMASTS TOURISTS
TOWMASTS TOWNISTS TRAVESTS TZARISTS

ABCDEFAG ABNERVAL ABNORMAL ACEROLAS ACHENIAL ACHORDAL ACHROMAS ACHROMAT ACTIONAL
ADENOMAS ADLERIAN ADNERVAL ADNEURAL ADOPTIAN ADUMBRAL ADVERBAL AENIGMAS AESOPIAN
AFTERBAY AFTERDAY AFTERGAS AGENTIAL AIRWOMAN AISLEWAY ALBERTAN ALBUMEAN ALDERMAN
ALEUTIAN ALGEBRAS ALGERIAN ALGOMIAN AMERICAN AMERICAS AMNESIAC AMOEBIAN AMPHORAE
AMPHORAL AMPHORAS ANHEDRAL ANICULAR ANTHERAL ANTIDRAG ANTIFOAM ANTIPHAL APHORIAS
APICULAR APTERIAL ARCHDEAN ARCHIVAL ARGENTAL ARTESIAN ASTERIAL ASTERNAL ASTURIAN
ATOMICAL ATYPICAL AURELIAN AUSTRIAN AUTOGRAM CALORICS CELIBACY CENTRICS CERAMICS
CHRONICA CHRONICS COADVICE COAGENCY COMEBACK COMPLICE CONFLICT CORNETCY CORNSACK
DAPHNIDS DEFRAUDS DELTOIDS DEMIGODS DERMOIDS DIAMONDS DICHORDS DIEHARDS DIPHEADS
DISGRADE DOCKSIDE DOGHEADS DOWNSIDE DUNKARDS EARHOLES EARLOBES EARTHMEN EBONITES
EBONIZED EBONIZES ECHOIZED ECHOIZES ECLIPSED ECOTYPES ECTOPIES EDUCATES EGALITES
EGOTIZED EGOTIZES ELATIVES ELIXATED ELIXATES ELOCUTED ELOCUTES EMBANKED EMBARGED
EMBARGES EMBARKED EMBATHED EMBATHES EMBLAZED EMBLAZER EMBLAZES EMBODIER EMBODIES
EMBOGUED EMBOGUES EMBOILED EMBOLDEN EMBOWLED EMBRACED EMBRACES EMBRAKED EMBRAKES
EMBURSED EMBUSHED EMIRATES EMPLACED EMPLACES EMPLANED EMPLANES EMPLOYED EMPLOYER
EMPLOYES EMPRISED EMPRIZED EMPRIZES EMULATED EMULATES ENAMORED ENARCHED ENARCHES
ENBRAVED ENBRAVES ENCALMED ENCAMPED ENCASHED ENCHAFED ENCHAFES ENCHASED ENCHASER
ENCIPHER ENCISTED ENCLAVED ENCLAVES ENCLOSED ENCLOSER ENCOILED ENCOWLED ENCUMBER
ENCURLED ENCYSTED ENDGATES ENDIAPER ENFIRMED ENFLAMED ENFLAMES ENFLOWER ENFOILED
ENFOLDER ENFORCED ENFORCES ENFOULED ENFRAMED ENFRAMES ENGLOBED ENGLOBES ENGRACED
ENGRACES ENGRATED ENGRATES ENGRAVED ENGRAVES ENGULFED ENHALOED ENHALOES ENHOUSED
ENJAILED ENLARGED ENLARGES ENLISTED ENLISTER ENLOCKED ENLODGES ENMASKED ENMISTED
ENOLIZED ENOLIZES ENQUATER ENQUIRED ENQUIRES ENRAILED ENRICHED ENRICHES ENRIDGES
ENSILVER ENSLAVED ENSLAVER ENSOULED ENSTORED ENSTYLED ENTAILED ENTAILER ENTHUSED
ENTOILED ENTOMBED ENTYPIES ENWOMBED EPICURES EPICYTES EPIDOTES EPIGONES EPILATED
EPILATES EPILOBES EPISTLED EPISTLER EPITOMES EPOXIDES EPURATES EROGATED EROGATES
EROTIZED EROTIZES ERUDITES ESCALIER ESCARPED ESCORTED ESCRIBED ESCROWED ESPALIER
ESQUIRED ESTROGEN ETAMINES ETHNIZED ETHNIZES EULOGIES EUPHONES EVILDOER EVOCATED
EVOCATES EVOLUTED EVOLUTES EXAMINED EXAMINER EXAMINES EXAMPLED EXAMPLES EXCLUDER
EXCLUDES EXCURVED EXHANCED EXHANCES EXHORTED EXITURES EXORATED EXORATES EXPANDER
EXPANSED EXPIATED EXPIATES EXPLODER EXPLODES EXPLORED EXPLORES EXPLOSED EXPORTED
EXPUGNED EXPUGNER EXPULSED EXPULSER EXPUNGED EXPUNGER EXPUNGES EXPURGED EXPURGES
EXTRUDES EXUDATES GEARINGS GELDINGS GLAZINGS GLOVINGS GOLDBUGS GRADINGS GRATINGS
GRAVINGS GRAZINGS GROUPAGE HEXARCHY IDEASTIC IDLESHIP IMPUTRID INTAGLIO INTARSIO
INTERMIX INTREPID ISCHEMIA ISLANDIC ISOGENIC ISOMERIC ISONYMIC KENTUCKY KEYLOCKS
KINFOLKS KLONDIKE KNOBLIKE LANDFOLK LAVISHLY LEAFMOLD LIBERALS LIFTABLE LIMBERLY
LINEARLY LINKABLE LIQUABLE LISTABLE LITERALS LOBTAILS LOCKABLE LOCKABLY LOCKFULS
LOSINGLY LOVINGLY LOWISHLY LUCENTLY LUMBERLY LUMINALS LUMINOLS LURINGLY MALFORMS
MICROHMS MIDTERMS MISFRAME MISRHYME MODICUMS MORNTIME MURKSOME MYOGRAMS NASTYING
NATCHING NATURING NEBULONS NECKBAND NECKLAND NEGATONS NEPHRONS NESTLING NEUTRONS

NEWBORNS NOCTURNE NOCTURNS NORTHING NOSEBAND NOSEYING NOTCHING NOVATING NUCLEINS
NUCLEONS NUMERANT NURSLING OBJECTOR OBLATION OBTUSION OBVIATOR OESTRIOL OLFACTOR
OREGANOS ORVIETOS OUTLABOR OVERBLOW OVERCLOY OVERFLOW OVERPLOT OVERPLOW OVERSHOT
OVERSLOP OVERSLOW OVERSNOW OXIDATOR PREADOPT PRECOMPS PREWHIPS RACKETRY RAMBLERS
RANCHERO RANCHERS RANCOURS RANGLERS RAPINERS RATCHERS REACTORS REALTORS REDSHIRT
REFAVORS REFLAIRS REGISTRY REGULARS REIMBARK REIMPARK REIMPART REIMPORT REINCURS
REINFORM RELATORS RESTWARD RETIFORM REVIGORS REVISORY RIBALDRY RIBANDRY RIGHTERS
RINGBARK RINGWORM ROCKBIRD ROCKETRY ROCKWARD ROMEWARD ROSEMARY ROTIFERA ROTIFERS
ROUGHDRY ROUGHERS ROUNDERS ROUTIERS RUMBLERS RUNBOARD RUNIFORM RUNOVERS RUSHWORK
SAGEBUSH SALTBUSH SANDFISH SANDIEST SANDYISH SATYRISM SAUCIEST SAWHORSE SAXONISH
SAXONISM SAXONIST SCALIEST SCAMPISH SCARIEST SCHEMIST SCOUTISH SCREWISH SCURVISH
SEMIFAST SEPARIST SERAPIST SHADIEST SHAKIEST SHALIEST SHAPIEST SHARPEST SHIPMAST
SHOULDST SHOWCASE SHOWIEST SIDEWASH SIGNPOST SIMPLEST SLACKEST SLAKIEST SLANGISH
SLANGISM SLICKEST SLIPCASE SLOPIEST SLOTWISE SLUGFEST SLUMWISE SMARTISH SMOKIEST
SMOLENSK SNAKIEST SNARLISH SNEAKISH SNOUTISH SNOWIEST SOAPBUSH SOAPFISH SOAPIEST
SOLARISM SOLECISM SOLECIST SOLIDEST SOUNDEST SOUPIEST SPACIEST SPARKISH SPERMIST
SPRUCEST SPUMIEST SQUAMISH SQUAREST SQUARISH STABLISH STANDISH STOCKISH STORKISH
STORMISH STRAWISH STUMPISH SUBCREST SUCHWISE SUITCASE SULKIEST SURFIEST SURGIEST
SURLIEST SWAMPISH SYBARISM SYBARIST SYNODIST SYRACUSE TABORETS TAMWORTH TENACITY
THICKETS THICKETY TINMOUTH TINPLATE TIPCARTS TOADLETS TONALITY TONIGHTS TORMENTS
TOURISTY TOWNGATE TOWNSITE TOXICATE TRADUCTS TRAJECTS TRAPUNTO TRAVESTY TRIDENTS
TRINKETS TRINKETY TRIOLETS TRIPLETS TRUMPETS TRUMPETY TRUNCATE TRYPIATE TUGBOATS
TUNICATE TURNGATE TWIGLETS TYROLITE ULCEROUS UNARTFUL UNCASQUE UNCTIOUS UNDERBUY
UNDERCUP UNDERCUT UNDERHUM UNDERPUT UNDERTUB UNFAMOUS UNJOYFUL UNOPAQUE UNSHROUD
UNVIRTUE UNWOEFUL VOCATIVE WASHBOWL WASHDOWN WINDROWS

ABCDEFBA DEACONED DEATHBED DEBARKED DEBUNKED DEBURSED DECAMPED DECANTED DECARTED
DECASTED DECLARED DECLINED DECOATED DECUPLED DECURVED DEFANGED DEFLATED DEFOILED
DEFORCED DEFORMED DEFOULED DEFRAYED DEGLAZED DEGUSTED DEHAIRED DEHORNED DEHUSKED
DELAWNED DELINTED DELISTED DELOUSED DEMARKED DEMASTED DENSATED DEPAIRED DEPARKED
DEPARTED DEPHASED DEPICTED DEPLANED DEPLORED DEPLOYED DEPLUMED DEPORTED DEPRAVED
DEPRIVED DEPULSED DEPURGED DEPURSED DEPUTIED DERAILED DERANGED DESALTED DESCALED
DESCRIED DESIGNED DESILTED DESLIMED DESOILED DESORBED DESPITED DESPUMED DESTINED
DETACHED DETAILED DETAINED DETOURED DETRAYED DETURNED DEVALUED DEVASTED DEVIATED
DEVOICED DEVOURED DEWORMED DEZINCED DIHYBRID DISULFID DOWNTROD DRAWCORD DRUNKARD
ELUDIBLE ENFAMINE ENLUMINE ENSHRINE ENTHRONE EPISCOPE ETHYLATE ETIOLATE GNARLING
GNASHING LACRIMAL LACRYMAL LARYNGAL LENTICEL LUNGSFUL MISCLAIM MOVIEDOM NEUROGEN
NITRAMIN NOVATION RAINWEAR REACHIER REALINER REALIZER REANSWER REASONER REBOILER
REBUNKER RECANTER RECASTER RECIPHER RECKONER RECLINER RECLOSER RECOILER RECOINER
RECONFER RECONTER RECOUPER REFILTER REFINGER REFLOWER REFOLDER REFUNDER REGAINER
REGATHER REGISTER REJOICER RELAPSER RELASTER RELISHER RELOADER REMAINER REMINDER
REMUSTER RENTALER RENUMBER REPACKER REPASTER REPLACER REPONDER REPOWDER REPUGNER
REPULSER REQUITER RESAWYER RESHAPER RESHOWER RESIGNER RESILVER RESOLDER RESOLVER
RETAILER RETAINER RETIMBER RETINKER REUNITER REVAMPER REVOLTER REWINDER SAMBUCAS
SARCOMAS SCEPTICS SEALINES SEARCHES SECLUDES SEIZURES SELVAGES SEMIAPES SEMIAXES
SENTRIES SEPTANES SEPTILES SEPTIMES SERIATES SERINGES SERVAGES SERVICES SERVILES
SETLINES SEXTILES SKYLARKS SLEDFULS SOPRANOS STARLETS STEWPOTS STIGMATS STUDENTS
SUBGENUS SUBGYRUS SUBITOUS TAILCOAT

ABCDEFBB ASHINESS BENGALEE BLUEGILL DEPORTEE DESIGNEE DETAINEE LECTUREE PEDIGREE
PLAYBILL PLIMSOLL RESIGNEE SELVAGEE

ABCDEFBC ANGELING ANGERING ANTIRENT ARMYWORM AVERSIVE BALMORAL BANDSMAN BANDYMAN
BANKSIAN BANKSMAN BEDAMNED BEDAMPED BEDARKED BEDASHED BEDAWNED BEDIRTED BEDOLTED
BEDOUSED BEDRAPED BEDUCKED BEDUNCED BEDUNGED BEDUSKED BEDUSTED BENCHMEN BERLINER
BESAUCES BESHAKES BESHAMES BESLAVES BESLIMES BESMILES BESMOKES BESNARES BESPICES
BESTARES BESTORES BESTOVES BLASTULA CAESURAE CALENDAL CESTODES CHANGSHA CLAVIOLA
CREATURE DERAILER DERANGER DERINGER DESCALES DESCRIES DESLIMES DESMINES DESPITES
DESPOTES DESPUMES DICHOTIC DONATION DOWNFLOW FLEXIBLE FLYINGLY FOLDEROL FORMATOR
GANDHIAN GESTURES GLADIOLA GLANDULA GREYWARE HANDSPAN HANDYMAN HAUSFRAU LANCEMAN
LANDSMAN LENGTHEN LICHENIC LINCHPIN LUSCIOUS LUSTROUS MEDIATED MICROBIC NESTAGES
OVERGAVE OVERGIVE OVERLIVE OVERSAVE OVERWAVE PANHUMAN PASTORAS PERFUMER PERISHER
PERMUTER PERVADER PICTORIC PLYINGLY PRESCORE PRESHARE PRESTORE RANCHMAN RANGEMAN
RANKSMAN REDAUBED REDAWNED REDLINED REDOCKED REDUCTED RESCALES RESHAKES RESHAPES
RESHAVES RESHINES RESIDUES RESLATES RESLIDES RESMILES RESOLVES RESPACES RESPADES
RESPITES RESPOKES RESTAGES RESTAKES RESTYLES RESWAGES RETICKET SCEPTICE SEDUCTED
SERMONER TOREADOR TREASURE UNGAZING UNSATINS UNSTAINS VARIOLAR VERMINER VESICLES
VESTIGES VESTRIES VESTURES WANDSMAN WINESKIN WIREHAIR

ABCDEFBD ANGELINE ANGEVINE BALDHEAD BEGRIMER BRUSHERS CAESURAS CENSURES CRISPERS
CRUSHERS CRUSTERS DECRATER DEFRAYER DENSATES DEPRAVER DEPRIVER DIACETIC FORESHOE
FRISKERS FROSTERS GRASPERS GRISTERS GUILEFUL GUILTFUL HANDLOAD HEARTIER LEISURES
MAIDHEAD MALTREAT MEADOWED MEASURES METAZOEA MIOCENIC PEARLIER PLAYERLY REINSMEN
SEARCHER SWANDOWN TENSILES TENSURES UNDEFINE UNFELINE UNREFINE VERSATES WRISTERS
ZIRCONIC

ABCDEFBE AROUSERS BACONIAN BEDASHES BEGASHES BELADIED BELASHES BEWASHES BROWSERS
BRUISERS CRUISERS DEFORCER DEFORMER DEHORNER DEPARTER DESCRIER DESTRIER DIARCHIC
ENCAGING ENRAGING FETISHES GLADIOLI GOVERNOR GROUSERS HEARTLET HISPANIA INEXTANT
JEWISHES LACONIAN LINGERIE MELODIED NEWARKER PERISHES PLIMSOLS PRAISERS REBUSHES
REBUSIES RECASHES REGUSHES REINDUED REJUDGED RELISHES RELODGED REPASTES RESUNKEN
REWASHES REWISHES SAXONIAN SNUDGING TROUSERS TROWSERS UNCAGING UNEDGING UNPATENT
WAGONMAN WISTARIA

ABCDEFBF ATHEISTS ATOMISTS BECURSES BEDOUSES BEGILDED BEGIRDED BEGLIDED BELARDED
BELAUDED BEPRIDED BIOLYSIS CENSURER CITRONIN CONJUROR DECLARER DEHAIRER DELAPSES
DELOUSES DEPHASES DEPLORER DEPULSES DEPURSES DERMISES DEVOURER DIALYSIS FIBROSIS
GENIUSES GESTURER HELIOSES HEPTOSES HERALDED LECTURER LICHENIN MEASURER NEUROSES
PELVISES PERFUSES PERIODED PERMISES PERVADED REABUSES REALISES REAMUSES REBIASES
REBLADED RECHASES RECLOSES RECLUDED RECLUSES REFOLDED REFUNDED REGILDED REGUIDED
REHOUSES RELANDED RELAPSES RELOADED REMANDED REMINDED REMOLDED REPHASES REPULSES
RESPADED SECLUDED SECONDED STIGMATA UTOPISTS VELOURER VENTURER

ABCDEFBG ACRYLICS ADENOIDS ALPINELY ANDIRONS ANTIGENS ANTIMONY ANYTHING ARBITERS
ARCHFORM ASPINOSE ASTERISK ASTERISM ASTONISH ATROCITY AURELIUS AUREOLUS BACKFLAP
BACKSEAT BACKSLAP BACKSTAY BACTRIAN BADGEMAN BAILSMAN BARGEMAN BARONIAL BEACHIER
BEACHMEN BEACONED BEADSMEN BEAMSTER BEASTMEN BEAUTIED BEAUTIES BECALMED BECARPET
BECARVED BECARVES BECHASED BECKONED BECKONER BECLAWED BECOSTED BECRIMED BECRIMES
BECUDGEL BECURLED BECURSED BEDARKEN BEDIAPER BEDLAMER BEDMAKER BEDRAPES BEDTIMES
BEFILMED BEFINGER BEFISTED BEFLOWER BEFOAMED BEFOULED BEFOULER BEGASHED BEGIFTED
BEGLIDES BEGNAWED BEGOWNED BEGRAVED BEGRAVES BEGRIMED BEGUILED BEGUILER BEGULFED
BEHANGED BEHOLDEN BEHOLDER BEHYMNED BEKNIVED BELASHED BELAUDER BELFRIED BELFRIES
BELICKED BELOAMED BELOCKED BELONGED BELONGER BEMAILED BEMASKED BEMASTER BEMAULED

```
BEMITRED  BEMOANED  BEMOANER  BEMOATED  BEMOCKED  BEPARTED  BEPLUMED  BEPOWDER  BEPRAYED
BEPRIDES  BEQUOTED  BEQUOTES  BERHYMED  BERINGED  BEROGUED  BEROGUES  BEROUGED  BERUSTED
BESAUCED  BESHAMED  BESHAMEL  BESHIVER  BESHOWER  BESHRIEK  BESIGHED  BESILVER  BESLAVED
BESLAVER  BESLIMED  BESLIMER  BESLOWED  BESMILED  BESMOKED  BESNARED  BESNIVEL  BESOILED
BESOULED  BESOURED  BESPICED  BESPOKEN  BESTAYED  BESTORED  BESTOVED  BESTOWED  BESTOWER
BESUITED  BETAILED  BETAINES  BETALKED  BETASKED  BETINGED  BETINGES  BETOILED  BETRACED
BETRACES  BETRAVEL  BETUSKED  BETWINED  BETWINES  BEVOILED  BEWAILED  BEWAILER  BEWASHED
BEWASTED  BEWHITED  BEWHITEN  BEWHITES  BEWILDER  BEWINGED  BEWINTER  BEWONDER  BEWORKED
BEWORMED  BEWRITES  BEZIQUES  BIATOMIC  BICUSPID  BIETHNIC  BIMASTIC  BIOCYTIN  BIOGENIC
BIOLYTIC  BIOTYPIC  BIPHASIC  BLASTULE  BLEARILY  BLITHELY  BLOCKILY  BLOWSILY  BLOWZILY
BOATSHOP  BRAIDERS  BRAILERS  BRAINERS  BRANDERS  BRAWLERS  BRAWNERS  BRAZIERS  BRAZIERY
BREVIARY  BRIDGERS  BRIDLERS  BRIGATRY  BRINGERS  BROCHURE  BROGUERY  BROIDERY  BROILERS
BROILERY  BRONZERS  BROTHERS  CABLEMAN  CABLEWAY  CADENZAS  CADREMAN  CALDERAS  CALENDAR
CAMBRIAN  CAMELIAS  CANTORAL  CAPSHEAF  CAPSITAN  CAPSIZAL  CAPSULAR  CARDIGAN  CARDINAL
CARELIAN  CARLSBAD  CARNIVAL  CAROLEAN  CAROUSAL  CARTLOAD  CATHODAL  CAUSEWAY  CAVERNAL
CENSORED  CENSURED  CENTAGES  CENTIMES  CENTRIES  CENTURES  CERVIXES  CLAVIOLE  CLAVIOLS
CLOSABLE  CLOUDILY  CLUMSILY  COAUTHOR  COBISHOP  CODEBTOR  COEDITOR  COEMPLOY  COENAMOR
COGNIZOR  COHESION  COLATION  COMPUTOR  COMRADOS  CONVEYOR  COPASTOR  COPATRON  COQUITOS
CORTISOL  COSUITOR  CRADLERS  CRAFTERS  CRAGWORK  CRAMPERS  CRANKERS  CRANKERY  CRAWLERS
CREATORS  CRIBWORK  CRIMPERS  CRINGERS  CROAKERS  CROFTERS  CROWBARS  CROWDERS  CROWNERS
CROZIERS  CRUMBERS  CRUMPERS  DAIRYMAN  DALESMAN  DARTSMAN  DAYBREAK  DEBACLES  DEBUNKER
DECANTER  DECIPHER  DECLARES  DECLINER  DECLINES  DECOYMEN  DECUPLES  DECURVES  DEFAMIES
DEFLATES  DEFLOWER  DEFLUXES  DEFOAMER  DEFORCES  DEGLAZES  DELINTER  DELUSTER  DEMPSTER
DENTURES  DENUMBER  DEPICTER  DEPLANES  DEPLORES  DEPLUMES  DEPORTES  DEPRAVES  DEPRIVES
DEPURGES  DEPUTIES  DERANGES  DESALTER  DESIGNER  DESILVER  DESTONER  DETACHER  DETACHES
DETAILER  DETAINER  DETINUES  DEVALUES  DEVIATES  DEVILMEN  DEVOICES  DIABETIC  DIABOLIC
DIAGONIC  DIALOGIC  DIALURIC  DIALYTIC  DIATOMIC  DIATOMIN  DIATONIC  DIATORIC  DIAXONIC
DIAZOTIC  DIETOXIC  DIMETRIA  DIMETRIC  DIOGENIC  DIOLEFIN  DIONYSIA  DIONYSIC  DIOPTRIC
DIORAMIC  DIPHASIC  DIPHENIC  DIPLASIC  DIPLEGIA  DIPOLEIA  DIPSETIC  DISBRAIN  DISCLAIM
DISGENIC  DISHABIT  DISHERIT  DISMERIT  DISTRAIN  DIURANIC  DIURETIC  DOUGHBOY  DRAFTERS
DRAINERS  DRAWLERS  DRIFTERS  DRINKERS  DRINKERY  DRUMFIRE  DRUNKERS  DRUNKERY  DRUTHERS
EARTHIAN  EARTHMAN  EDUCANDS  ELFISHLY  ELVISHLY  ENACTING  ENAPTING  ENARMING  ENCAKING
ENCASING  ENCAVING  ENCHAINS  ENCODING  ENCORING  ENCROWNS  ENDORING  ENDOWING  ENDURANT
ENDURING  ENFACING  ENFAMING  ENFUMING  ENGRAINS  ENJOYING  ENLACING  ENLURING  ENMOVING
ENRACING  ENROBING  ENSURING  ENTHRONG  ENTRAINS  ENVIRONS  ENVOYING  EPISCOPY  ESCAPISM
ESCAPIST  FAIRHEAD  FAIRLEAD  FALERIAN  FAUSTIAN  FEALTIES  FEATLIER  FEATURED  FEATURES
FELONIES  FENAGLER  FETISHED  FETISHER  FIBROTIC  FIRETAIL  FISHTAIL  FISHWEIR  FLAGPOLE
FLASHILY  FLEXIBLY  FLORIDLY  FLOWABLE  FLOWABLY  FLUENTLY  FLUXIBLE  FLUXIBLY  FLYTAILS
FOREGLOW  FOREKNOW  FOREPLOT  FORESHOP  FORESHOT  FORESHOW  FORESLOW  FOURSPOT  FRACTURE
FRANKERS  FRAUDERS  FRETWORK  FRINGERS  FRONTERS  FROTHERS  FROWNERS  FRUITERS  FRUITERY
FRUMPERY  FUSARIUM  FUSEPLUG  GARTHMAN  GASTREAL  GAVELMAN  GENTILES  GENTRIES  GEORDIES
GERMANES  GESTURED  GLADIOLE  GLANDULE  GLEAMILY  GRAFTERS  GRAILERS  GRAINERS  GRAINERY
GRANTERS  GRANTORS  GRAZIERS  GRAZIERY  GRIFTERS  GRINDERS  GRINDERY  GRINTERS  GROANERS
GROINERY  GROUPERS  GROUTERS  GROWLERS  GROWLERY  GRUBWORN  GRUNTERS  GUARDFUL  HABITUAL
HANDCLAP  HANDFLAG  HANDGRAB  HANDICAP  HANDPLAY  HANDTRAP  HANDWEAR  HAWSEMAN  HEADSMEN
HEARTIES  HEATSMEN  HEAVYSET  HECTARES  HECTORED  HELMAGES  HEMLINES  HENWIVES  HEPTANES
HEPTODES  HERACLES  HERAKLES  HERBAGED  HERBAGES  HERDSMEN  HEROINES  HEROIZED  HEROIZES
HIBERNIA  HIBERNIC  HISPANIC  HISTAMIN  HISTORIC  HONEYPOT  HORSEBOY  HOTELDOM  HOUSEBOY
HOUSETOP  HUMORFUL  HYDROXYL  INCOGENT  INCRUENT  INDOGENS  INDOLENT  INFECUND  INFLUENT
INGRUENT  INHALENT  INHUMANE  INJURANT  INKHORNS  INKSTAND  INKSTONE  INSOLENT  INSULANT
INSURANT  INTHRONE  INTHRONG  INURBANE  INVOCANT  IRONBARK  IRONHARD  IRONWARE  JACKHEAD
```

```
JACKSHAY  JACKSTAY  JACOBEAN  JACOBIAN  JAMESIAN  JARGONAL  JESUITED  JETSONED  JETWARES
JUICEFUL  KEMPSTER  KERCHIEF  KEYHOLED  KEYHOLES  KEYMOVES  KEYNOTED  KEYNOTER  KEYNOTES
KINDSHIP  KINGSHIP  KNEADING  KNOBLING  LATCHMAN  LATHEMAN  LAYWOMAN  LEACHIER  LEACHMEN
LEADSMEN  LECTURED  LECTURES  LEFTOVER  LEGACIED  LEGACIES  LEGIONED  LEGIONER  LEGISTER
LEISURED  LENGTHED  LENIATED  LENIATES  LEPROSED  LEVANTED  LEVANTER  LICKSPIT  LISTERIA
LITURGIC  LOBATION  LOCARNOS  LOCATION  LOCATIOS  LOCUTION  LUMINOUS  LUPINOUS  LUTECIUM
MACHINAL  MACKINAW  MADEIRAN  MADEIRAS  MADREGAL  MADRIGAL  MADRONAS  MAESTRAL  MAGENTAS
MAINSTAY  MAJORCAN  MALDIVAN  MANDOLAS  MANDORAS  MANORIAL  MARGINAL  MARZIPAN  MASTHEAD
MATERIAL  MATERNAL  MATILDAS  MATRICAL  MATRONAL  MAZURKAS  MEADOWER  MEASLIER  MEASURED
MEDFLIES  MEDIATES  MELANGED  MELANGER  MELANGES  MELODIES  MELTAGES  METHANES  METHONES
MICROBIA  MIDBRAIN  MILTONIC  MINERVIC  MISBEGIN  MISTRAIN  MORATION  MUCINOUS  MUTINOUS
NAILHEAD  NAUTICAL  NECKTIES  NECTARED  NEOCYTES  NEOFIBER  NEOLATER  NEOTYPES  NEPHITES
NERVATED  NERVATES  NERVULES  NERVULET  NETLAYER  NETMAKER  NEURITES  NEWCOMER  NEWCOMES
NEWTAKES  NIMRODIC  NITROLIC  NITROLIM  NUBILOUS  NUMBROUS  NUMEROUS  OMENTUMS  ONLAYING
ORACLERS  ORANGERY  ORBITARY  ORBITERS  ORDINARY  ORGANERS  ORNATURE  OUTARGUE  OUTVALUE
PADRONAS  PAKISTAN  PALESMAN  PALMYRAS  PANCREAS  PANDORAS  PARENTAL  PARMESAN  PARODIAL
PARSEVAL  PARTISAN  PASTORAL  PASTURAL  PATERNAL  PATRONAL  PEACHIER  PEACHLET  PEARLIES
PEBRINES  PECKAGES  PECTINES  PECTIZED  PECTIZER  PECTIZES  PEDALFER  PEDALIER  PEDICLES
PEGBOXES  PELFRIES  PELTRIES  PENCILED  PENCILER  PENDULES  PENLITES  PENMAKER  PENSIVED
PENTACES  PENTAMER  PENTICES  PENTODES  PENURIES  PEONAGES  PEONIZED  PEONIZES  PERCALES
PERFIXED  PERFIXES  PERFUMED  PERFUMES  PERFUSED  PERISHED  PERLITES  PERMISED  PERMIXED
PERMIXES  PERMUTED  PERMUTES  PEROGUES  PERSONED  PERVADES  PETROLED  PEWMATES  PIGNOLIA
PIGNOLIS  PISTACIO  PLACIDLY  PLAGUILY  PLANTULE  PLAYFOLK  PLIANTLY  PLICABLE  PLIMSOLE
PLOWABLE  PLUCKILY  PLUGHOLE  PLUSHILY  PLUVIALS  PNEUMONY  POLYAXON  PORTICOS  POSEIDON
POSITRON  PRAETORS  PRAETORY  PRANCERS  PRANKERS  PRAWNERS  PREADORN  PREBOARD  PRECHART
PREGUARD  PRELATRY  PREMOURN  PRICKERS  PRIMEURS  PRINKERS  PRINTERS  PRINTERY  PRONGERS
PROWLERS  PSALMIST  PSYCHIST  PURLIEUS  PURSEFUL  QUAKEFUL  QUESTFUL  RADIOMAN  RAFTSMAN
RAILHEAD  RAINCOAT  RAISEMAN  RAMSTEAD  RANSTEAD  RATIONAL  REABUSED  REALINED  REALINES
REALISED  REALIZED  REALIZES  REALTIES  REAMUSED  REASONED  REAVOWED  REBACKED  REBAITED
REBATHED  REBATHES  REBAWLED  REBIASED  REBLADES  REBLAMED  REBLAMES  REBLOWED  REBOILED
REBOLTED  REBUDGET  REBULKED  REBUOYED  REBUSHED  REBUSIED  RECABLED  RECABLES  RECALKED
RECANTED  RECASHED  RECASKET  RECHAFED  RECHASED  RECHAWED  RECHISEL  RECHOSEN  RECKONED
RECLINED  RECLINES  RECLOSED  RECLUSED  RECOALED  RECOATED  RECOILED  RECOINED  RECOMBED
RECOMPEL  RECONVEY  RECOPIED  RECOPIES  RECOUPED  RECUMBED  REDBONES  REDISPEL  REDLINES
REDOCKET  REDPOLES  REFASTEN  REFILMED  REFLAMED  REFLAMES  REFLATED  REFLATES  REFLOWED
REFLUXED  REFLUXES  REFUGIES  REFULGED  REFULGES  REGAINED  REGALIES  REGIONED  REGLAZED
REGLAZES  REGLOVED  REGLOVES  REGLOWED  REGUIDES  REGUSHED  REHANGED  REHAULED  REHINGED
REHINGES  REHOUSED  REIMAGED  REIMAGES  REINDUES  REJAILED  REJOICED  REJOICES  REJOINED
REJOLTED  REJUDGES  REKINGED  RELACHES  RELAMPED  RELAPSED  RELASTED  RELICKED  RELICTED
RELIFTED  RELINKED  RELISHED  RELISTED  RELISTEN  RELOANED  RELOCKED  RELODGES  RELONGED
RELUCTED  REMAILED  REMAINED  REMANIES  REMASKED  REMASTED  REMINTED  REMOCKED  RENAILED
RENICKEL  RENOBLED  RENOBLES  RENTALED  REPACKED  REPASTED  REPAWNED  REPHASED  REPICKED
REPIQUED  REPIQUES  REPLACED  REPLACES  REPLANED  REPLANES  REPLATED  REPLATES  REPLAYED
REPLOWED  REPLUMED  REPLUMES  REPOCKET  REPOSTED  REPTILES  REPUDIES  REPUGNED  REPULSED
REQUITED  REQUITES  REQUOTED  REQUOTES  RESACKED  RESAILED  RESALTED  RESCALED  RESHAKEN
RESHAPED  RESHAVED  RESHINED  RESHOVEL  RESHOWED  RESIGNED  RESLATED  RESMILED  RESOAKED
RESOAPED  RESOFTEN  RESOILED  RESOLVED  RESPACED  RESPITED  RESPOKED  RESPOKEN  RESTAGED
RESTAKED  RESTOLEN  RESTOWED  RESTYLED  RESUCKED  RESUITED  RESULTED  RETABLED  RETABLES
RETACKED  RETAILED  RETAINED  RETALKED  RETHAWED  RETINUED  RETINUES  RETOMBED  RETUCKED
RETWINED  RETWINES  REUNITED  REUNITES  REVALUED  REVALUES  REVAMPED  REVINCED  REVINCES
REVOICED  REVOICES  REVOLTED  REVULSED  REWASHED  REWHITEN  REWISHED  RINGSAIL  RINGTAIL
```

ROGUEDOM ROTUNDOS ROUNDTOP RUCTIOUS RUNABOUT SAILBOAT SARCINAE SATURDAY SATURNAL
SAUCEMAN SAUCEPAN SEARCHED SECONDER SECTORED SEJOINED SELDOMER SELVAGED SEMIFLEX
SENTRIED SEQUINED SERIATED SERMONED SERMONET SERVICED SIGMATIC SIGNORIA SIPHONIC
SLANGILY SLEAZILY SLIDABLE SLIDABLY SLIGHTLY SLOVENLY SNACKING SNAFUING SNAGLINE
SNARKING SNARLING SNATHING SNEAKING SNORKING SNORTING SNOUTING SNOWBANK SNOWLAND
SOLATION SOLUTION SORBITOL SORPTION SOUTHRON STARLITE STORIATE STRENGTH STRIGATE
SUPERGUN SURGEFUL TABLEMAN TACKSMAN TAILHEAD TAILSMAN TALISMAN TAMPICAN TAPIOCAS
TENACLES TENDRIES TENSILED TENSILER TERMINED TERMINES THROUGHS TORNADOS TOUCHBOX
TOWNSBOY TRACKERS TRAILERS TRAILERY TRAINERS TRAMPERS TRAWLERS TREASURY TRICHORD
TRICKERS TRICKERY TRIFLERS TRIPLERS TROUPERS TRUCKERS TRUDGERS TRUMPERS TRUMPERY
TUBEROUS UNABLING UNACHING UNACTING UNADORNS UNAPTING UNARKING UNARMING UNASKING
UNBALING UNBARING UNBATING UNBAYING UNBODING UNBORING UNBOWING UNBOXING UNBOYING
UNBROWNS UNCAKING UNCARING UNCASING UNCAVING UNCHAINS UNCOGENT UNCOPING UNCORING
UNCROWNS UNCTIONS UNDRYING UNDYEING UNEASING UNEATING UNFACING UNFADING UNFELONY
UNFLYING UNFRIEND UNGRAINS UNHALING UNHATING UNHAVING UNHEXING UNHOPING UNHOSING
UNICORNS UNJOKING UNKEYING UNLACING UNLADING UNLAWING UNLAXING UNLAYING UNLEARNS
UNLEARNT UNLIKENS UNLOVING UNMAKING UNMARINE UNMATING UNMAZING UNMEWING UNMOVING
UNPAVING UNPAYING UNPLIANT UNPOSING UNPRYING UNRACING UNRAKING UNRAVING UNRAYING
UNROBING UNROPING UNROVING UNROWING UNSALINE UNSAMING UNSAVING UNSAYING UNSEWING
UNSEXING UNSHRINE UNSHRINK UNSILENT UNSOLING UNSPRING UNSPYING UNSTRAND UNSTRING
UNSTRONG UNSTYING UNTAKING UNTAMING UNTAXING UNTHORNS UNTHORNY UNTHRONE UNTRAINS
UNTRYING UNVOTING UNWADING UNWAKING UNWAVING UNWAXING UNWRYING UNYOKING UREAFORM
URSIFORM USHERISM VALERIAN VARIETAL VARIETAS VARIOLAS VAROLIAN VASCULAR VAULTMAN
VAUNTLAY VECTORED VECTURES VEHICLED VEHICLES VEINAGES VENDAGES VENTAGES VENTURED
VENTURES VERBATED VERBATES VERBOTEN VERMINED VERTICEL VERTICES VESTURED VICTORIA
VIPEROID VOCATION VOLATION VOLCANOS VOLUTION VULCANUS WALKSMAN WARDSMAN WASHROAD
WASHTRAY WASTEMAN WATCHMAN WATERMAN WAUKEGAN WAXERMAN WAYBREAD WEAKLIER WEAPONED
WEAPONER WEBMAKER WEFTAGES WEIGHMEN WEIGHTED WEIGHTER WELCHMEN WELCOMED WELCOMER
WELCOMES WELFARED WELFARES WELSHMEN WILDSHIP WINDSAIL WINDSHIP WISTERIA WORKSHOP
WRACKERS WRINGERS WRITHERS WRONGERS YACHTMAN YARDSMAN YAWLSMAN YEASTIER YOKELDOM
ZAMINDAR ZEALOTER ZEOLITES ZEPHYRED ZIRCONIA

ABCDEFCA AGNOMINA CHIASMIC CHIASTIC CLIMATIC CLITORIC DARTFORD DRAWHEAD DRENCHED
ESTIMATE ESTRIATE ESTRUATE EXVOTIVE GENTLING GUNSLING LAUGHFUL NORTHERN SALICYLS
SANDBINS SCANDIAS SCAPULAS SCEPTRES SCORPIOS SCRAPERS SCRIBERS SCRIVERS SETBOLTS
SHELTIES SHRINERS SHRIVERS SHROVERS SIRUPERS SKETCHES SPATULAS SPEAKIES SPECKLES
SPECTRES SPRAYERS SPUMEOUS SPURIOUS STAMINAS STEADIES STENCHES STRAWERS STRAYERS
STRIDERS STRIKERS STRIPERS STRIVERS STROKERS STUDIOUS SUNDOWNS SYMPTOMS SYRUPERS
TUSKIEST

ABCDEFCB ACIDOTIC ACIDURIC ADEMPTED ASCETICS BECHANCE BEGRUDGE BESPOUSE BLUSHFUL
BREACHER BREASTER BREATHER BREWSTER CHANUKAH CREAKIER CREAMIER CREASIER DESPOUSE
DETONATE DRAWGEAR DREAMIER DRENCHER FREAKIER FRENCHER FRENZIER FRESCOER GELDABLE
GLYCERYL GRANULAR GREASIER GYRATORY HELPABLE JESTWISE KNEADMEN MELTABLE MENTHANE
MENTHONE METAXITE NECKLACE ORACULAR PENSIONE PLANETAL PREACHER PREALTER PRECOVER
PREFACER PREINFER PRELUDER PREMAKER PREMIXER PREMOVER PRESAGER PRESIDER PRESUMER
PROACTOR PROBATOR PROLABOR PROMISOR PROVISOR RELIABLE RESPONSE SCIENTIC SCIOPTIC
SEMIDOME SLIPRAIL STANDPAT STOCKPOT SYLVANLY TREACHER TREADLER TREMBLER TRENCHER
TRIUMVIR TSARINAS WELDABLE WREATHER WRENCHER WRESTLER

ABCDEFCC BUSHLESS BUSINESS BUSYNESS CHEROKEE COSINESS COSTLESS DISCLASS DISKLESS

DISTRESS DISTRUSS DUSKNESS DUSTLESS FASTNESS FISHLESS GUSTLESS HOSTLESS JUSTNESS
LASHNESS LASTNESS LOSTNESS LUSHNESS MASTLESS MISCLASS MISGUESS MISTLESS MISTRESS
MOLEHILL OPERATEE OVERKNEE POSTLESS RASHNESS RISKLESS ROSINESS RUSTLESS SKETCHEE
TASKLESS TUSKLESS UNSTRESS VASTNESS WISHLESS WISHNESS WISTLESS

ABCDEFCD ALDEHYDE ALUMINUM BANGLING BONDLAND BUNGLING BURSTERS BUSTIEST CLANSMAN
CLAPTRAP COKELIKE CONSIGNS CORSAIRS CRANEMAN CRANKMAN CREDITED DANGLING DISHWASH
DISTREST DISTRUST DUSTIEST EASTMOST ELDORADO ENCHURCH FLATBOAT FRESCOES FRESHIES
GUSTIEST GAMESOME GODSENDS GUSTIEST HASTIEST HEADLOAD HOLEABLE INCHURCH JANGLING
JUNGLING KLANSMAN LITERATE LOCKPICK LONGEING LUSTIEST MANGLING MANSIONS MISTRUST
MISTRYST MOLECULE MUSTIEST NASTIEST NAUSEOUS NOSEWISE OINTMENT OUTSERTS OUTSIFTS
OVENSMEN OVERLIER PASTIEST PENSIONS PICKBACK PICKLOCK PINECONE PREDATED PREDINED
PRELABEL PRESAGES PRESIDES PRESUMES QUADRIAD RANGLING ROADHEAD ROENTGEN ROSEWISE
RUCKSACK RULEABLE RUSTIEST SCANDIAN SNOWPLOW SOMETIME SUKIYAKI SUREFIRE TANGLING
TANGOING TENSIONS TOADHEAD UNDECIDE UNEDITED VASEWISE VASTIEST WANGLING WASHDISH
WASTIEST WESTMOST WRESTLES YARDBIRD

ABCDEFCE BRAINPAN CHAINMAN CONSTANT DISPENSE DISPERSE DRAINMAN GRAINMAN OVERDYED
PHRASERS PROUNION SHEARIER SMEARIER SPEARIER SPIRALIA STEADIED STERNMEN TRAINMAN
TREADLED UNEASIES UPRISERS VENISONS

ABCDEFCF ACIDOSIS ADIPOSIS ALTOISTS AMENUSES AMINOSIS AMITOSIS AUTOISTS BETRUSTS
CHEMISES CHORISOS CLEANSES DIECASES DIONYSOS ENTRUSTS ENTWISTS FOETUSES GRENADED
INTRUSTS METRISTS MYELOSES OBELISES OUTCASTS OUTFASTS OUTJESTS OUTLASTS OVERUSES
PATRISTS PLEXUSES PRECIDED PRELUDED PREMISES PRESIDED PREVIDED PREVISES PROVISOS
RETOASTS ULTIMATA UNELIDED UNERODED UNEVADED UNTWISTS VETOISTS WHIRLGIG

ABCDEFCG ABORTION ABSTRUSE ABUSEFUL ACETINES ACETIZED ACETIZES ACETONES ADOPTION
AGENCIES ALEWIVES AMENUSED AMIDSHIP ANDROIDS ANTIDOTE ARITHMIC ARSONIST AYRSHIRE
BANDYING BANJOING BANTLING BEACHMAN BEADSMAN BEASTIAL BEASTMAN BEDWARDS BENCHING
BETAINTS BEWIDOWS BIRDLORE BLACKMAN BLEACHED BLEACHER BLEACHES BOARDMAN BOATHEAD
BOATSMAN BONUSING BOUTIQUE BRACHIAL BRADSHAW BRAKEMAN BREACHED BREACHES BREADMEN
BREAKMEN BREASTED BREATHED BREATHES BREVITED BREWAGES BROMPTON BRONCHOS BROWNTOP
BRUSHFUL BRUSHOUT BUCOLICS BUNCHING BUNDLING BUNTLINE BURGHERS BURGLARS BURGLARY
BURNFIRE BUSHIEST BUTMENTS BUTYLATE BUTYRATE CANDLING CANDYING CANOEING CANTLINE
CANTLING CAREWORN CAUSEFUL CAUTIOUS CENTRING CHAIRMAN CHAIRWAY CHALDEAN CHAMBRAY
CHEAPIES CHELATED CHELATES CHESTIER CHIANTIS CHLORYLS CHOIRBOY CHORIZOS CHURNFUL
CLAUDIAN CLEANSED CLEANSER CLERGIES CLITORIA CLITORIS COASTMAN CODHEADS COEMPTED
COENURES COLUMELS CONDEMNS CONSIGNE CONTAINS CONTEMNS CORSETRY CRANEWAY CRATEMAN
CREMATED CREMATES CRENATED CRENATES CULPABLE CULPABLY CURATORS CURATORY CURDLERS
CUSHIEST CZARINAS DASHIEST DEACONAL DECLUTCH DECYLICS DENOTING DEPLUMPS DERISORY
DETRACTS DEWCLAWS DIAGONAL DIASTRAL DIEMAKER DILUTELY DISABUSE DISBURSE DISCLOSE
DISFLESH DISHORSE DISHOUSE DISPOUSE DISPURSE DOLEFULS DOLENTLY DONATING DOUBTFUL
DOUGHNUT DRACHMAE DRACHMAL DRACHMAS DRACULAS DRAFTMAN DRAGBOAT DRAGOMAN DRAGSMAN
DRAWBEAM DRAWSPAN DRENCHES DRIFTPIN DULCETLY DUNGEONS DUNKLING DUSKIEST DYARCHAL
DYEMAKER DYEWARES ENCROACH EPIDOTIC EPIGAMIC EPILOGIC EPISODIC EPITOMIC EPITONIC
EVOCATOR EXAMPLAR EXTINCTS EXTRACTS FAIRSHIP FANCYING FARCEURS FARTHERS FERVOURS
FIELDMEN FILMABLE FIREBURN FIREWARD FIREWORK FIREWORM FLAGBOAT FLAMBEAU FLASHPAN
FLATHEAD FLECKIER FLEDGIER FLESHIER FLETCHER FLETCHES FLEXURED FLEXURES FOLDABLE
FOLKSILY FOLKTALE FONDLING FORAGERS FORAYERS FORBEARS FOREHARD FOREMARK FOREPART
FORESTRY FORETURN FOREWARD FOREWARM FOREWARN FOREYARD FORWEARS FORWEARY FRECKLED

```
FRECKLES FRENATES FRENCHED FRENCHES FRENZIED FRENZIES FRESCOED FRESHMEN FUELIZER
FUNGIANS FURTHERS GARBLERS GASHIEST GASHOUSE GENTIANS GILDABLE GIRDLERS GLEAMIER
GODHEADS GODWARDS GOLDENLY GOURDFUL GRAECIAN GRANDMAS GRANDPAS GRATEMAN GRAYCOAT
GRAYHEAD GRENADES GUARDIAN GUERNSEY GUNFLINT GUNPOINT GUSHIEST GUSTOISH HANDGUNS
HANDLINE HANDLING HANGMENT HANKLING HARBOURS HARBOURY HARLOTRY HARPIERS HARTFORD
HEADSMAN HEATSMAN HELICALS HERALDRY HERITORS HERMITRY HERTFORD HOLDABLE HONEYING
HOUSEBUG HOUSEFUL HURDLERS HUSKIEST HUTMENTS HYDROIDA HYDROIDS ICEBOXES IGNORANT
INCROACH INCROUCH INTUBATE IRONSHOD IRONSHOT JETPORTS JONAHING JONTHANS JUNGIANS
KEATSIAN LACONICS LANGUENT LANTERNS LATCHETS LEACHMAN LEADSMAN LIEBCHEN LINTERNS
LIPOTYPE LITURATE LOADSMAN LOADSTAR LONGHAND LOTMENTS LUNCHING LURCHERS LUSHIEST
LYMPHOMA LYNCHING LYREBIRD LYRIFORM MALIGNLY MARBLERS MARCHERS MARINERS MASHIEST
MATURITY MENACING MENDIANT MENTHANS MENTIONS MERITORY MIDLANDS MOLDABLE MOLECULA
MOLTENLY MONEYING MORALERS MORNWARD MORTUARY MOTIVATE MOURNFUL MOUTHFUL MUDHEADS
MUENSTER MULISHLY MULTIPLE MULTIPLY MUNCHING MUSHIEST MUSKIEST MUTILATE MYELINES
NAUTILUS NEWSHAWK NORTHERS NOVATIVE NUTMEATS OATHLETS OBELISED OBELIZED OBELIZES
OBLATELY OBSTRUSE OBTURATE OBTUSITY OLEANDER OLEFINES ONERATED ONERATES OPERATED
OPERATES OPTIMATE ORIGAMIS ORNAMENT ORNATING OUTCANTS OUTCASTE OUTFEATS OUTPARTS
OUTWAITS OUTWASTE OUTWRITE OVERAGES OVERAWED OVERBLEW OVERDYES OVERFLEW OVERLIES
OVERSMEN OVERSPED OVERSTEP OVERUSED OVIGENIC OWLISHLY OXIDASIC OZARKIAN PALEGOLD
PALMFULS PALTERLY PALTRILY PANELING PARCHERS PARDNERS PARLOURS PARSONRY PARTNERS
PATIENTS PATRIOTS PAUSEFUL PEIGNOIR PENCHANT PENGUINS PHILONIC PIANOLAS PIERAGES
PIEWOMEN PINEBANK PINELAND PIRATERY PLACEMAN PLANETAS PLATEMAN PLATEWAY PLATINAS
PLEIADES PLENTIES PLOWSHOE PLUMEOUS PLUVIOUS POETIZED POETIZER POETIZES POETRIES
POLITELY POSTWISE POUCHFUL PRANDIAL PREACHED PREACHES PREACTED PREBAKED PREBAKES
PRECIDES PRECISED PRECITED PRECITES PREDATES PREDINES PREFACED PREFACES PREFINED
PREFINES PREFIXED PREFIXES PRELATED PRELATES PRELIVES PRELUDES PREMAKES PREMATED
PREMATES PREMISED PREMIXED PREMODEL PREMOVED PREMOVES PRENAMES PRENOTED PRENOTES
PRESAGED PRESUMED PRETONES PREVIDES PREVISED PREVOTED PREVOTES PRIMATIC PRISMOID
PROTAGON PSILOTIC PULINGLY PUNCHING PUNCTING PUSHIEST QUEASIER QUELCHED QUELCHES
QUENCHED QUENCHER QUENCHES QUESTMEN QUIXOTIC RANCHING RANDYING RANKLING RASPIEST
RATCHETS RATCHETY REINSTIL RELIABLY RENAMING RETAUNTS RHIZOMIC RHIZOTIC RINGBONE
ROADSMAN ROGUINGS RONTGENS ROSEBUSH ROSEDUST ROSEFISH RULINGLY RUNDOWNS RUSHIEST
RUSTYISH SANDLING SANGUINE SATURITY SCALEMAN SCALEPAN SCAPULAE SCAPULAR SCATULAE
SCEPTRED SCORPION SEAWOMAN SELDOMLY SEMICOMA SERIFORM SHAFTMAN SHAFTWAY SHEARMEN
SHELFIER SILENTLY SILKENLY SILVERLY SKETCHED SKETCHER SLEAZIER SLEIGHED SLEIGHER
SLEUTHED SMOKEBOX SNAPHEAD SNEAKIER SNOWDROP SOLEMNLY SOLVABLE SOLVABLY SOLVIBLE
SONGLAND SOUNDFUL SPACEMAN SPADEMAN SPATULAR SPEARMEN SPECIMEN SPECKIER SPECKLED
SPECTRED STACKMAN STAGEMAN STAGHEAD STAIRWAY STAKEMAN STAMINAL STEADIER STEADMEN
STEAMIER STENCHED STICKPIN STOCKBOW STONEBOW SUBTRIBE SULTRILY SUNBLIND SUNBLINK
SUNKLAND SWEATIER TAILSPIN TECHNICA TECHNICS TENDRONS TENORING THEORIES THOMPSON
THRIVERS THROWERS TIEMAKER TIERSMEN TINHORNS TORCHERS TRACHEAL TRACHEAN TRACKMAN
TRACKWAY TRAGICAL TRAILMAN TRAILWAY TRAINWAY TREACLED TREACLES TREADLES TREMBLED
TREMBLES TRENCHED TRENCHES TRIAZOIC TRIBASIC TRICHOID TRIGONIA TRIGONIC TRIGONID
TRILOGIC TRIMESIC TRIPLOID TRIPODIC TRIPOLIS TRISOMIC TRUCKFUL TRUNKFUL TUSKWISE
TWEAKIER TWINSHIP ULTIMATE UNAFLOAT UNASTRAY UNEAGLED UNEASIED UNEASIER UNECHOED
UNELATED UNELOPED UNEMPTED UNERASED UNESPIED UNETCHED UNEVOKED UNEXILED UNIAMBIC
UNIMPAIR UNLIABLE UNLIABLY UNLIKELY UNLIVELY UNLORDLY UNLOTHLY UNLOVELY UNREGARD
UNSAFEST UNSPARSE URANICAL VARIFORM VAUNTFUL VENOMING VINELAND VIOLATOR VOCALICS
VOLANTLY VOLATILE VOLUBILE VULGARLY WARBLERS WASHIEST WASPIEST WENCHING WHALEMAN
WHARFMAN WHIPTAIL WHOREDOM WINELAND WIREBARS WITHOUTS WORKGIRL WORKYARD WREATHED
WREATHEN WREATHES WRENCHED WRENCHES WRESTLED WRETCHED WRETCHES XYLENOLS XYLITOLS
```

YEATSIAN YOUTHFUL

ABCDEFDA ASTIGMIA CUBISTIC DIGESTED DIRECTED DISEMBED DIVERGED DIVERSED DIVERTED
DIVESTED DOWNBEND DOWNHAND DOWNLAND EMULABLE GAUNTING GLANCING GRANTING GRUNTING
NAPOLEON NEVADIAN NOMADIAN NOVATIAN RACEGOER SAFETIES SATURNUS SCALPELS SCARFERS
SCORNERS SEDULOUS SEMIAXIS SERGINGS SHARKERS SHARPERS SHIPLAPS SHIRKERS SHORTERS
SIDEAGES SILENCES SKIRTERS SMIRKERS SNARLERS SNORTERS SPARKERS SPORTERS SPURNERS
SPURTERS STAGINGS STARVERS STOPGAPS STORIERS STORMERS SUBAREAS SUBFIEFS SUBTEXTS
SUMATRAS SURETIES SURGINGS SWARMERS SWIRLERS SWORDERS

ABCDEFDB ADJECTED ADVERSED ADVERTED BAPTISTA BESTIATE CLOUDFUL DESKLIKE GHOSTISH
INHEAVEN KNEADMAN NECKLIKE ONTARIAN ORIENTER PEAKLIKE PREALTAR PSYCHICS REINSANE
STRAWHAT SYNCRACY UNBEATEN UNDERMEN UNDERPEN UNHEAVEN UNPOISON UNVIRGIN UNWEAKEN
WEIGHAGE

ABCDEFDC ABSENCES APERTURE BESTRUTS BIDENTED BOSNIANS DIRECTER DISPULPS DISTENTS
DISTORTS FORESTER GESTALTS INDEARED INDEBTED INTERMET INTERSET JONATHAN LECITHIC
LINESMEN MONAGHAN NUTSIEST OBSERVES OVERCARE OVERDARE OVERDURE OVERFIRE OVERSURE
OVERTARE OVERTIRE OVERTURE PRETASTE SCREAMER SCREWIER SHREWDER SPREADER STREAKER
STREAMER THREADER UNDECKED UNDEFIED UNDELVED UNDERBED UNDERFED UNSEIZES UNSELVES
UPRENDER UPSTARTS

ABCDEFDD ABSENTEE BARTLETT BIASNESS DIRECTEE FOREKNEE HONEYBEE LICENSEE OBJECTEE
POTENCEE SUPERFEE THISNESS THUSNESS TRESPASS UNDECREE UNDERSEE

ABCDEFDE AVENGING BAKSHISH CHANGING CHANSONS CHASTEST CLANGING COURSERS DANSEUSE
DIVERTER EDMONTON ELONGING FLANGING FRESHISH HEMICTIC INMESHES INSERTER INVERTER
INWEDGED LOUNGING MODERNER MOISTEST MOUNTANT OBSERVER OCEANIAN OVERTART PLUNGING
QUIESCES REOUTPUT ROMANIAN RUMANIAN SLANGING SPHERIER SPONGING SUDANIAN SUPERBER
SYRINGIN TAVERNER THONGING TOWERIER UNHEDGED UNIALGAL UNMESHES UNWEDGED WATERIER
WAVERIER WHATSITS WRONGING

ABCDEFDF ADVERSES ASCENDED BAPTISTS BIOTESTS CARTISTS CELTISTS CHUTISTS CONTESTS
CULTISTS DENTISTS DIVERSES ECLIPSIS EGOTISTS FLUTISTS FRIENDED IMPENDED INVERSES
KANTISTS LEFTISTS LICENSES OBVERSES OSTENDED PROTESTS PUNTISTS SHIELDED SPREADED
THREADED UNBEADED UNGELDED UNHEADED UNHERDED UNLEADED UNWELDED UPBEARER

ABCDEFDG ABJECTED ABSCONCE ABSENTED ABSENTER ACHORION ACTINOID ADORNERS ALDERMEN
ALPINOID AMENDING AMNIOTIC ANTISKID ANTISLIP ASCENDER ASPECTED ASPERGED ATHEIZED
ATHEIZER ATHEIZES BAKERIES BEASTISH BIMANUAL BIMESTER BINAURAL BISECTED BIVENTER
BLANKING BLENDING BLONDINE BLUESTEM BLUNTING BOARDERS BOUNCING BOUNDING BOWERIES
BOWLFULS BRANDING BRASHEST BREADMAN BREAKMAN BRISKEST BROADWAY BRONZINE BRONZING
BRUNTING BYLAWMAN CABERNET CALENDER CARLISLE CAVERNED CESARIAN CHANTING CHARGERS
CHARMERS CHARTERS CHASTISE CHINBONE CHIRPERS CHLORION CHUNKING CHURNERS CLANKING
CLIENTED CLONKING CLUNKING COBELIEF CODEINES COHELPER COKERIES COLEADER COLIBRIS
COLUMBUS COMEDIEN COMEDIES COMELIER CONAXIAL CONTEXTS CONTRITE COPESMEN CORNBINS
CORNLAND CORUNDUM COSEATED COTERIES COUNTING COURIERS COURTERS COVERLET COVERSED
CRANKING CRISPEST CROATIAN CRONYING CULTRATE CUNEATED CURLEDLY CUTANEAL DALESMEN
DAUNTING DEARBORN DELUVIUM DEMISUIT DEMOTION DETAINAL DEVOTION DIALKYLS DIGESTER
DISCOACH DISGORGE DIVERGES DOLESMEN DOMAINAL DOMANIAL DOWERIES DOWNBENT DOWNLINE
DRUNKENS DUNKIRKS DUPERIES EGOISTIC ENARBORS ESKIMOID ETHIOPIA ETHIOPIC ETONIANS

EURASIAN EURISTIC FABULOUS FAIENCES FAKERIES FAULTILY FEBRUARY FERNLAND FETISHIC
FIGEATER FILMDOMS FILTRATE FLANKING FLENSING FLIRTERS FLOATMAN FLOATSAM FLUENCES
FLUNKING FLUSHEST FLYEATER FOGEATER FOILABLE FOMENTED FOMENTER FOREDGES FOREKNEW
FORELIES FORESHEW FORESTED FORESTEM FORESTEP FOREVIEW FORGINGS FORKLIKE FORTIETH
FORTLETS FORTUITY FOUNDING FRANKING FRINGENT FRISKEST FROGLEGS FROLICLY FRONDENT
FRONTING FURLABLE FUSARIAL GALERIES GAMESTER GASCHECK GASELIER GAVELMEN GAYETIES
GAZEBOES GIMCRACK GLAUCOUS GONADIAL GORSIEST GOVERNED GRATUITY GRUNIONS GUARDERS
HAIRWORK HALIOTIS HANGDOGS HAUNTING HAWKLIKE HELICOID HEMIOPIC HEMIZOIC HESIODIC
HEXAGRAM HOARDERS HOLISTIC HOLYDAYS HOMEBRED HOMELIER HONEYDEW HORSIEST HOTELIER
HOTELMEN HOUNDING HUMECTED HUNDREDS HYGIENIC IMPOSTOR INCEPTED INCUBOUS INFECTED
INFECTER INFESTED INFESTER INGESTED INGESTER INJECTED INLEAKED INMESHED INORDERS
INSEAMER INSECTED INSERTED INTERBED INTERPEL INTERSEX INTERWED INVECTED INVERSED
INVERTED INVESTED INWEAVED INWEAVES ISOCRACY ISOLABLE JAUNTING JIMCRACK JOINHAND
JOKESTER JOUNCING JUDAICAL JUDAICAS JURISTIC KINDREDS LABEFIED LABEFIES LABURNUM
LAMENTED LAMENTER LANDSIDE LATENCES LAVENDER LAYERMEN LECITHIN LEDGINGS LICENSED
LICENSER LIMEADES LINEAGED LINEAGES LINEATED LINEATES LINEBRED LOCANDAS LODGINGS
LOGISTIC LOUSIEST LOZENGED LOZENGER LOZENGES LUCERNES LUSTRATE MACKLIKE MALISTIC
MANEUVER MANTLETS MARTLETS MARTNETS MASKLIKE MERGINGS METAZOAL METAZOAN MILEAGES
MISGAUGE MOLESTED MOLESTER MONAURAL MONAXIAL MONISTIC MONKLIKE MONTEITH MORAINAL
MORAVIAN MOSAICAL MOUNDING MOUNTING MOURNERS MUCKRAKE MURIATIC MUSKLIKE NAPERIES
NEBULOUS NEOCRACY NEWSCAST NOTARIAL NOVEMBER NUMERIES NUTCRACK OBJECTED OBSERVED
OBTAINAL OCTAVIAN OCULARLY OPENBAND ORCADIAN ORGANZAS ORIENTED ORNITHIC OUTBRIBE
OUTCRACK OUTEDGES OUTGANGS OUTKICKS OVERBARK OVERBARS OVERBURN OVERCARD OVERCURL
OVERHARD OVERHURL OVERLARD OVERMARK OVERPART OVERTURN OVERWARD OWLERIES OXYETHER
OZARKERS PAILFULS PALESMEN PANDOWDY PARENTED PARKLIKE PARTLETS PAYCHECK PERIODIC
PHONYING PIGEONED PIGEONER PINCHECK PIRANHAS PLAINTIF PLANGENT PLANKING PLANTING
PLAYBOYS PLUNKING POLEAXED POLEAXER POLEAXES POLESMEN PORTENTS PORTLETS POSTDATE
POSTNATE POTENCES POUNCING POUNDING POWERMEN PRACTICE PRACTICO PRACTICS PRANCING
PRANKING PREAXIAL PRECINCT PREMIUMS PRIESTED PROATLAS PROAVIAN PROCINCT PROLIXLY
PROSAISM PROSAIST PROSIEST PROTECTS PROTEXTS PROUDFUL PUBLICLY PUCKLIKE PURGINGS
PURISTIC PURSIEST QUANTONG QUARTERS QUIESCED QUOTIETY REANOINT RECANVAS REINFUND
RELAYMAN REMOTION REPLIALS REPTANTS RESINOID RETAINAL RETINOID REUNIONS ROADBEDS
ROADSIDE ROCKLIKE ROMANZAS ROSACEAN ROSEATED ROUGHAGE ROUNDING RUBAIYAT SACKLIKE
SAFETIED SAILORLY SALEGOER SCANTING SCENTING SCHIZOID SCIENTER SCRAPMAN SCREAMED
SCREWMEN SCRIVEIN SEMIOTIC SEQUITUR SHANKING SHANTUNG SHEARMAN SHIELDER SHINBONE
SHUNTING SIGNMENT SILENCED SILENCER SILENTER SKYCOACH SLANTING SOCKLIKE SOLEMNED
SOLEMNER SOMALIAN SOUNDING SPANKING SPEARMAN SPENDING SPERMARY SPLENDER SPREADEN
SQUEAKED SQUEAKER SQUEALED SQUEALER SQUEAMED STALKILY STANCING STANDING STEADMAN
STEAMCAR STOLENLY STOLIDLY STONYING STOUPFUL STREAKED STREAMED SUBTILTY SUBTLETY
SUMATRAN SUPERMEN SURETIED SWANKING SYRIANIC SYRINGIC TAILORLY TALESMEN TANKLIKE
TAPERIES TASKLIKE TAVERNED TAWNYING TENUIOUS TERNIONS THANKING THREADEN THUSWISE
TIDESMEN TOURNERY TOWERMEN TOWNLAND TRANCING TREADWAY TRENDING TRIAPSAL TRIVALVE
TRUNKING TURKLIKE TURNPINS TUSKLIKE TUXEDOES TWIRLERS UMPTIETH UNBELIED UNBELIEF
UNBELTED UNCEASED UNCEILED UNDELVES UNDERLET UNDERSEA UNDERSET UNDOCTOR UNFEARED
UNFELTED UNFESTER UNFORGOT UNGEARED UNGLADLY UNHEADER UNHEALED UNHEAPED UNHEATED
UNHEAVED UNHEDGES UNHEFTED UNHEIRED UNHELMED UNHELMET UNHELPED UNHEROED UNHEROES
UNIVALVE UNLEAFED UNLEARED UNLEASED UNLEAVED UNLEAVES UNLEVIED UNMEATED UNMELTED
UNMERGED UNMERGES UNMESHED UNMETRED UNORDERS UNPEACED UNPEACES UNPECKED UNPELTED
UNREAPED UNREAVED UNREAVES UNRESTED UNSCARCE UNSCOTCH UNSEALED UNSEALER UNSEAMED
UNSEARED UNSEATED UNSECRET UNSEIZED UNSERVED UNTEAMED UNTEASED UNTEMPER UNTERMED
UNVEILED UNVEILER UNVERSED UNVESTED UNVETOED UNWEAVED UNWEAVES UNWEDGES UNWELTED

```
UPENDING UPHEAVED UPHEAVEN UPHEAVER UPHEAVES UPHELMED UPRAISAL URGENCES VALENCES
VALUROUS VAUNTING VERANDAH VERANDAS VIALFULS VIBURNUM VIOLABLE VIOLABLY WATERIES
WATERMEN WAXERMEN WEDGINGS WELSHISM WHATNOTS WHIRLERS WHIRLERY WOUNDING YOKEAGES
YPSILOID
```

ABCDEFEA AMPHIBIA CHOLINIC CRENITIC CRETINIC CYANITIC DAMPENED DANGERED DARKENED
DIAPERED DICKERED DIPLEXED DITHERED DOCKETED DRIVELED DUPLEXED DUSKENED ECOSTATE
ELUCTATE EXCITATE GLEANING GROANING NEOPAGAN NOBLEMEN NORSEMEN RACKETER ROCKETER
SAPONINS SAVORERS SCOURERS SOCKEYES SPIREMES SQUARERS STIMULUS STYRENES SUBNEXES
SUBVENES SUGARERS SULTANAS SUPREMES SURVENES SWAHILIS SYNAGOGS SYPHILIS TRIBELET

ABCDEFEB ASPIRERS CLIMATAL DENOTATE DRIVELER GROVELER HEMATITE HEPATITE HESITATE
ISOMERES KNIFEMEN LEVITATE MEDITATE PRECOLOR PREDONOR SEMIRARE SOMBRERO TRAVELER
TRICOLOR TROWELER

ABCDEFEC BADGERED BRASILIA BUDGETED BURDENER CANOEMEN COENGAGE COESTATE CUDGELED
DARKENER FIDGETED FISHEYES GARDENER HARDENER HARKENER INSURERS LACTIFIC LANCEMEN
LARCENER MARKETER NUCLIDIC OBTUSEST ORDINAND ORGANING PARLEYER PRESTATE RANGEMEN
SACRIFIC SHRIEKER SPECTATE UNDIETED UNSIEGES VISCUOUS WAGONING

ABCDEFED BALDENED BIPLANAL BOLDENED BRINEMEN BURDENED BURSITIS CHINAMAN CINDERED
CRANEMEN CYANIDIN GANDERED GARDENED GLUCINIC GLYCIDIC GLYCINIC GOLDENED HARDENED
HINDERED HOSEPIPE HOYDENED LEUCITIC LOADENED LOUDENED MAIDENED MANTELET MILDENED
MILDEWED MISREFER MYOSITIS OKINAWAN PANDERED PONDERED POWDERED PROCIVIC REOSTATS
SCAREDER SOLDERED SPECIFIC SPIDERED STONEMEN SUBLEVEL SUNDERED SWINEMEN TANDEMED
TINDERED WANDERED WARDENED WILDERED WINDERED WONDERED

ABCDEFEE CONFEREE PROTEGEE

ABCDEFEF ANSWERER ANTHESES ANURESES BADGERER BANTERER BICKERER BOTHERER BROUHAHA
BUCHANAN CANTERER CIPHERER CONFRERE COSHERER CUMBERER CURIOSOS DIOCESES FALTERER
FAUTERER FILTERER FINGERER FLOWERER FOSTERER GATHERER GLOWERER GLUTININ HAMPERER
HANKERER HINDERER HUNGERER IMPRESES LATHERER LIMBERER LINGERER LOITERER LUMBERER
LUSTERER MASTERER MISBEDED MOTHERER MUCKERER MUSTERER NUMBERER OYSTERER PALTERER
PANDERER PANTERER PILFERER PLATERER PONDERER POWDERER PUCKERER QUAVERER QUIVERER
SHIVERER SILVERER SIMPERER SINCERER SLAVERER SLIVERER SOLDERER SUNDERER TAMPERER
TIMBERER TINKERER WANDERER WINTERER WITHERER WONDERER

ABCDEFEG ABJURERS ABORIGIN ACHIEVED ACHIEVER ACHIEVES ADJURERS ADJURORS ADMIRERS
ADORNING ADVENING ALMONING ALUMINIC AMORITIC AMORNING ANSWERED ANTHEMED ANTIPOPE
ANTLERED APERITIF APOSITIC APRONING ASTROLOG AXOMETER BACKENED BADGEMEN BANTERED
BARGEMEN BASKETED BATHERED BATONING BEATIFIC BETONING BICKERED BIOMETER BIPLANAR
BIRDEYES BISCAYAN BISONANT BISTERED BLOWPIPE BOILERED BOTHERED BOURNING BRACELET
BRAKEMEN BRAMINIC BRASILIN BRAWNING BRAZENED BRAZILIN BRIDEMEN BROMIDIC BROWNING
BUCKETED BUCKETER BUDGETER BUMPERED BUNKERED BUSHELED BUSHELER CABLEMEN CADREMEN
CAMBERED CANKERED CANTERED CANTILIE CARNEYED CARPETED CASTERED CAUSEYED CHAIRERS
CHAPELED CHAPELET CHASTITY CHIGNONS CHISELED CHISELER CHOKERED CHOREMEN CHURNING
CIENAGAS CIPHERED CLAVERED CLEANING CLOSENED CLOSETED CLOVERED CLOWNING CLOYNING
COAGULUM COARSEST COARSISH COBLEMEN COENURUS COGITATE COMITATS COMPERED COMPERES
COMPETED COMPETES CONSTATE CONTEXED CONTEXES CONTRARY CONVEXED CONVEXES CONVEYED
CONVEYER COPHASAL COPLANAR CORBELED CORDELES CORNPIPE CORSELET CORSETED CORTEGES

CORTEXES COSENING COSHERED COUPELET COVENANT COWARDRY COZENING CRATEMEN CRAVENED
CRIPSEST CROWNING CRUSTATE CUDGELER CUMBERED CURFEWED CURVETED DAMPENER DAPHNINS
DAVENING DEBONING DEFRAYAL DELICACY DEMAGOGS DEMAGOGY DERMITIS DETUNING DIABETES
DIAMETER DIORAMAS DIPLANAR DIPLEXER DIPLEXES DIPMETER DISCOLOR DISHEVEL DISHONOR
DOCILELY DOMINANT DOWNPIPE DOZENING DROWNING DUKHOBOR DUPLEXER DUPLEXES EJACULUM
ENSPIRIT EXPLICIT FACILELY FALSENED FALTERED FASTENED FASTENER FATHERED FAVORERS
FIDGETER FIGURERS FILTERED FINGERED FLATUOUS FLEXUOUS FLORETED FLOWERED FLOWERET
FOLDAWAY FORCELET FORGEMEN FORGETEL FOSTERED FOTHERED FROGEYES FROWNING FULMINIC
FUNERARY FUTILELY GAMECOCK GASKETED GATHERED GENTILIC GEORAMAS GEYSIRIC GIMLETED
GIVEAWAY GLOVEMEN GLOWERED GLOXINIA GOBLETED GOITERED GOLDENER GOLDEYES GOPHERED
GOSPELED GOSPELER GRANITIC GRAPELET GRATEMEN GRAVELED GROVELED HACKERED HALFCOCK
HALTERED HAMLETED HAMPERED HANKERED HASTENED HASTENER HAWKEYES HEPTANAL HERMITIC
HIDEAWAY HOARSEST HOGMANAY HORNPIPE HORSEMEN HOSTELED HOSTELER HOUSEMEN HUNGERED
HUNKERED HUSKENED HYDROSOL HYGIENES IGNORERS IMPLETED IMPLETES IMPLEXED IMPONENT
INDOLYLS INDRAWAL INFLEXED INJURERS JACKETED JASPERED JESUITIC JINGODOM JOCKEYED
JOINERED JUMPERED JUNKETED JUNKETER JUSTENED KASHERED KATYDIDS KOSHERED KUWAITIS
LABORERS LACKEYED LADENING LAMPERED LANCETED LARGENED LATENING LATHEMEN LATHERED
LAWYERED LEARNING LEMONING LICHENED LICHENES LIMBERED LINGERED LISTENED LISTENER
LITERARY LODGEMEN LOITERED LOUVERED LUMBERED LUMINANT LUMPERED LUSTERED MACHETES
MACKEREL MAGNETED MAGNIFIC MANURERS MARKETED MARTINIS MARVELED MASKERED MASONING
MASTERED MASTODON MATURERS MECHANAL METHANAL MICROZOA MINUETED MIOCENES MISBEGET
MISCOLOR MISFERED MISTERED MONKEYED MONTEREY MORAINIC MORBIFIC MORSELED MORTGAGE
MORTIFIC MOTHERED MOTLEYED MOTLEYER MOURNING MOYENING MUCKERED MUSTERED MYELITIC
MYELITIS MYSTIFIC NAIVETES NEGRITIC NEGRODOM NEPHILIM NEURITIC NEURITIS NEUROPOD
NICKELED NICKERED NOWHERES NUMBERED OBSCENER OBTUSISH OLDENING OLEFINIC ORDINANT
OUTENING OUTVIGIL OVICULUM OVIPARAE OVIPARAL OXANILIC OXANILID OXIMETER OYSTERED
PACKETED PALMERED PALMITIC PALMITIN PALTERED PARCELED PARLEYED PARTENED PASTELED
PEDAGOGS PEDAGOGY PENDULUM PESHAWAR PETRIFIC PHONEMES PHONEYED PICKAWAY PICKEREL
PICKETED PICKETER PICKEYES PILFERED PILNESER PILSENER PINCERED PINKERED PINKEYES
PLACEMEN PLANETED PLATEMEN PLOTINIC POCKETED POCKETER POIGNANT PONTIFIC PORTLILY
POSTANAL POSTERED POTHERED POUTERED PRAWNING PREBASAL PRECAVAL PREGNANT PRELIMIT
PRENASAL PRENATAL PRENAVAL PRESIDIA PRESIDIO PREVISIT PRIMATAL PRIZEMEN PROCANAL
PROHIBIT PROLIFIC PRONAVAL PROSEMEN PROSTATE PROTEGES PROVENED PROVENES PUCKERED
PULSIFIC PULVINIC PUNCTATE PURSEWEB PURVEYED PYELITIC PYELITIS PYGMAEAN PYRENINS
PYRONINE PYRONINS QUAKERED QUANTITY QUARTETS QUAVERED QUINTETS QUIVERED RACKETED
RAVENING REBONING REOWNING REQUISIT RESONANT RETUNING REZONING RIBALDLY RICHENED
RIDGELET RIFLEMEN RINGEYES ROCHETED ROCKAWAY ROCKETED ROUTEMEN RUMINANT SAFENING
SALVIFIC SANCTITY SAUCEMEN SAUCERED SAUTERED SCALEMEN SCANTITY SCORNING SCRIEVED
SHALEMEN SHAREMEN SHIREMEN SHIVERED SHOREMEN SHOVELED SHOVELER SHOWERED SHRIEKED
SICKENED SICKENER SICKERED SIGNETED SILKENED SILVERED SIMPERED SLAKENED SLATEMEN
SLAVEPEN SLAVERED SLIDEMEN SLIVERED SLOPEMEN SLOVENED SNIVELED SNIVELER SOAKENED
SOCKETED SOFTENED SOFTENER SOMBERED SOMNIFIC SPADEMEN SPAWNING SPECULUM SPICULUM
SPIKELET SPIKEMEN SPINELET SPINERET SPIRELET SPURNING STAGEMEN STAKEMEN STAMENED
STERNING STILEMEN STOREMEN STOREYED STOVEMEN STOWERED SUBMETER SUBRIGID SUBTLELY
SUBVENED SUCKERED SULFIDIC SULFINIC SULFITIC SURVEYED SWIVELED TABLEMEN TABORERS
TAMPERED TAVERNRY THISAWAY THORNING THRONING TICKLELY TIMBERED TINKERED TINSELED
TOADPIPE TOKENING TOLUENES TORPEXES TRAPEZED TRAPEZES TRAVELED TREMOLOS TRICOLON
TROWELED TUCKAWAY TUCKERED TURKENED TURNAWAY TURNCOCK TYMPANAL UDOMETER ULSTERED
UMPIRERS UNBOLDLY UNBREWED UNCALMLY UNCHEWED UNCLEVER UNCLEWED UNDERARM UNDERCRY
UNDERORB UNDERPRY UNFLEXED UNFRIGID UNHOLILY UNIBASAL UNICOLOR UNIREMES UNISEXED
UNOBEYED UNPIECED UNPIECES UNSIEGED UNSKEWED UNSPEWED UNSPIRIT UNSTEWED UNVIEWED

UPHEAVAL URALITIC URANITIC UROCELES VAMPIRIC VAPORERS VASCULUM VERTICIL VESTIGIA
VIAMETER VIRTUOUS VOLITATE VOLUTATE VORTEXES WAKENING WALTERED WASHERED WASTEMEN
WASTERED WHALEMEN WHATEVER WHITENED WHITENER WHOMEVER WHOSEVER WICKEDER WICKERED
WILTERED WINKERED WINTERED WISTENED WISTERED WITHERED WIZARDRY WOMANING WORKADAY
WORSENED WOUNDEDS YEARNING ZEOLITIC ZITHERED ZODIACAL

ABCDEFFA DOWNFEED DROPSEED DUCKWEED FLYPROOF MAYBLOOM MUSHROOM SAWBILLS SAWMILLS
SCHNAPPS SETWALLS SHAMPOOS SHAWNEES SHERIFFS SHUTOFFS SKYFULLS SMACKEES SOAPLEES
STAMPEES STANDEES SUBCELLS SUBHALLS SUBTILLS SUNFALLS

ABCDEFFB BORDELLO CANBERRA CORNETTO DECLASSE ESCROLLS FLYWHEEL MANTISSA MARCELLA
TRAPDOOR UNSCREEN

ABCDEFFC AMORETTO BESNUFFS BESPILLS BOSWELLS CHENILLE CRETONNE CREVASSE DARTMOOR
DESKILLS DISTAFFS ENSTALLS GODSPEED INSHELLS INSTALLS INSWELLS ISABELLA JOYFULLY
LADYHOOD MASTIFFS MAYBERRY MISCALLS MISFALLS MISTELLS RESTAFFS RESTUFFS RESWILLS
UNSHELLS UNSKILLS UNSPELLS UNSWELLS UPSWELLS

ABCDEFFD BANSHEES BEAMROOM BIRDSEED BYSTREET CARTBOOT CLASHEES HARDWOOD MAIDHOOD
MAIDWEED OUTSELLS UPSTREET

ABCDEFFE ADVISEES ANISETTE BRUNETTE COMTESSE COQUETTE CORNETTE CORVETTE DUCHESSE
JULIENNE JULIETTE LARGESSE LIONESSE MASKETTE NARCISSI NOBLESSE NOISETTE NOUVELLE
ROCHELLE ROULETTE VIGNETTE VIOLETTE

ABCDEFFG ADOPTEES ADVOWEES AIMFULLY AIRSPEED ALUMROOT AMPUTEES ANTEROOM ANTHILLS
ANTIPOOL ANTPROOF ARCHFOOL ARTFULLY AUNTHOOD BACKDOOR BACKHEEL BACKROOM BACKWOOD
BAILWOOD BANDHOOK BAREFOOT BARGELLO BARKPEEL BARSTOOL BASTILLE BATHROOM BATONEER
BEARFOOT BENTWOOD BOUCHEES BOXTREES BRIDALLY BRIGETTY BROCHEED BRUTALLY BUGPROOF
BUSHWOOD CABINEER CALFHOOD CAMEROON CASEBOOK CASEWOOD CATPROOF CHAPBOOK CHARGEES
CHATWOOD CHISELLY CHORALLY CHORDEES CLAYWEED CLUBFEET CLUBFOOT CLUBROOM CLUBROOT
CLUBWEED CLUBWOOD COGWHEEL CONFETTI CONGREED CONGREES CONGREET CONTESSA COSTALLY
COWBELLS COWBERRY CRABWEED CRAWFOOT CREVALLY CROWFEET DATEBOOK DENTALLY DEWFALLS
DEWLAPPY DILUTEES DISBLOOM DISCREET DISMALLY DISPROOF DISTALLY DOMINEER DONATEES
DORSALLY DRAFTEES DRAWOFFS DUCKFEET DUCKFOOT EARMUFFS EARWIGGY ENDBALLS ENODALLY
EPICALLY FALSETTO FESTALLY FEUDALLY FIANCEES FIREBOOT FIREWOOD FISCALLY FISHPOOL
FISHWEED FLAMBEED FLATWOOD FLAXSEED FLAXWEED FONTALLY FORGETTS FORMALLY FOURTEEN
FRUGALLY FUSILEER GASPROOF GENIALLY GIFTBOOK GIRLHOOD GOATWEED GOSPELLY GRABHOOK
GRANDEES GRANTEES GRAVELLY GUARDEES GULFWEED HANDBOOK HANDLOOM HARDBOOT HAREFOOT
HEADROOM HEIRLOOM HIPBERRY HORNWEED HYMNBOOK HYPOGEES ICEFALLS INCUBEES INDWELLS
INKBERRY INKWELLS IREFULLY IRONWEED ITCHWEED IVYBELLS JACKBOOT JACKWEED JESTBOOK
JOVIALLY JUBILEES KINGHOOD KNAPWEED KNITWEED KNOBWEED KNOPWEED KNOTWEED LACEWOOD
LACROSSE LAMBHOOD LANDBOOK LAUGHEES LAWPROOF LEADOFFS LIBRETTO LIEPROOF LIFEHOOD
LINTSEED LORIKEET MANFULLY MARKOFFS MARQUEES MATEHOOD MATINEES MAXWELLS MEATHOOK
MEDIALLY MENIALLY MENTALLY MESIALLY MILKWEED MILKWOOD MINTWEED MINUETTO MISCARRY
MISCREED MIXBLOOD MONTILLA MORDELLA MORTALLY MOUNTEES MUDPROOF MULBERRY MUSKEGGY
MUTINEER NETBALLS NEURALLY NEWSBOOK NEWSROOM NORMALLY NUTMEGGY OAKBERRY OBLIGEES
ORDINEES OUTBLEED OUTBREED OUTCARRY OUTFALLS OUTGREEN OUTKILLS OUTMARRY OUTSALLY
OUTSLEEP OUTSPEED OUTSWEEP OUTWALLS OUTWELLS OUTYELLS OVERALLS OVICELLS PALMETTO
PALTROON PAROLEES PASTILLE PAYROLLS PEARWOOD PILOTEES PINBALLS PINFALLS PINKWEED
PINKWOOD PINWHEEL PITFALLS PLAYBOOK PLAYROOM PLUMETTY PONTIFFS POSTALLY POTBELLY

PREBILLS PREBLOOM PREFLOOD PRUNELLA PUGAREES PUNTILLA QUADROON QUATROON QUINELLA
RAINPOOL REBLUFFS RECTALLY REDBILLS REDWALLS RIDEOFFS RIGADOON RITUALLY ROCKWEED
SAGEWOOD SALEROOM SALTWEED SAWBELLY SEAFLOOD SELFHOOD SEMIPOOR SERFHOOD SERIALLY
SEXUALLY SHERWOOD SICKROOM SIGNALLY SILKWEED SILKWOOD SINFULLY SINGALLY SINKROOM
SITUALLY SIXPENNY SLUTHOOD SNAPWEED SNIVELLY SOAPWEED SOCIALLY SOURWEED SOWBELLY
SPIGOTTY SPINALLY SPIRALLY SUBCREEK SUBFLOOR SUNBERRY SUNPROOF SWANHOOD TANKROOM
TANPROOF TEAKWOOD TEASPOON TEQUILLA TICKSEED TICKWEED TINSELLY TONSILLA TOURNEES
TRAINEES TRIBALLY TRIPENNY TROCHEES TURNOFFS TWINHOOD TWOPENNY UMBRALLY UMBRELLA
UNAGREED UNASLEEP UNDREGGY UNDROSSY UNEGALLY UNFLOSSY UNFRILLS UNFRIZZY UNGLOSSY
UNGRASSY UNICELLS UNPRETTY UNREALLY UNSCHOOL UNTRILLS UPTRILLS VENIALLY VERBALLY
VERNALLY VESTALLY VISUALLY VOUCHEES WASHROOM WAXBERRY WAXBILLS WAYBILLS WETPROOF
WIFEHOOD WOEFULLY WRYBILLS YEARBOOK

ABCDEFGA ACTINULA ALOPECIA ALYMPHIA AMBROSIA AMORPHIA ANECDOTA ANGELICA ANOREXIA
ANOXEMIA ANTHEMIA APOCRITA APTERYLA ASPHYXIA ATROPHIA CAESURIC CARBOLIC CARBONIC
CATHODIC CATHOLIC CEPHALIC CHERUBIC CHOLERIC COSMETIC CUNEATIC CYANOTIC CYANURIC
DACOITED DAPHNIOD DAPHNOID DECKHAND DECKLOAD DIALYZED DISABLED DISARMED DISBOARD
DISCAGED DISCLOUD DISCUTED DISFAMED DISHOARD DISMAYED DISORBED DISOWNED DISPACED
DISPONED DISPREAD DISPUTED DISRATED DISRAYED DISROBED DISTUNED DISYOKED DIVORCED
DIVULGED DIVULSED DOCKHEAD DOCKIZED DOCKLAND DOCKYARD DOLTHEAD DRAGONED DROPHEAD
DROPSIED DRUMHEAD DUALIZED DUCKPOND DUMBHEAD DUNGYARD DUSTBAND EARPHONE EASYLIKE
ECHOWISE EDUCABLE EDUCIBLE EDUCTIVE EGYPTIZE ELONGATE ELUVIATE EMBOLITE EMBOLIZE
EMBRONZE EMIGRATE EMULSIVE ENACTIVE ENCHARGE ENCLOTHE ENCRADLE ENFIGURE ENMARBLE
ENSAMPLE ENSILAGE ENSUABLE ENVIABLE ENVISAGE EPILOGUE EQUALIZE EQUATIVE EQUINATE
EQUIPACE EQUIPAGE EQUIVALE EQUIVOKE ERGAMINE ERGATIVE ERGOTINE ERGOTISE ERGOTIZE
ERODABLE ERODIBLE EROSIBLE ERUPTIVE ESCALOPE ESCAROLE ESTRANGE EUCHROME EULOGISE
EULOGIZE EURYDICE EVADIBLE EVANGILE EVASIBLE EVITABLE EVOCABLE EXACTIVE EXCHANGE
EXCOURSE EXCUSIVE EXFIGURE EXHUMATE EXOCLINE EXOCRINE EXORABLE EXORCISE EXORCIZE
EXPILATE EXPIRATE EXPOSURE EXSCRIBE EXUNDATE EXUVIATE FOREHALF GALOPING GAMBLING
GARBLING GAUDYING GELATING GHOSTING GLACEING GLEAMING GLOAMING GLOATING GLORYING
GOURDING GRAFTING GRAPHING GRASPING GRAYLING GREASING GREAVING GROUPING GROUSING
GROUTING GROWLING GRUELING GRUMPING GUARDING GUESTING GULCHING GYRATING HEMPBUSH
HOUNDISH HUMANISH HYACINTH KINSFOLK KNITBACK LESIONAL LIGHTFUL LOATHFUL LODGEFUL
LONGTAIL LUBRICAL MAGICDOM MAJORISM MANIFORM MATURISM MEALWORM MEGACOSM MELODIUM
MELODRAM METALISM MORALISM MYCELIUM MYCODERM MYOPLASM NARCOTIN NEGATION NEGATRON
NEOMYCIN NEURAXON NIGHTMAN NIGHTMEN NITROGEN NOBLEMAN NORSEMAN NORTHMAN NORTHMEN
NYMPHEAN OBLIGATO PAWNSHOP POETSHIP PRESTAMP RAGOUTER RAGTIMER RANSOMER RATIONER
RAVISHER RAWHIDER REANCHOR RECAPTOR REDACTOR REDUCTOR REFAVOUR RETAILOR REVIGOUR
RINGSTER ROADSTER ROBUSTER ROMANCER ROUTINER RUGMAKER RUINATOR SACKFULS SACKINGS
SALIENTS SALINOUS SALIVOUS SALTINES SALTINGS SALUTERS SAMPLERS SANCTUMS SANDBOYS
SANDHOGS SANDKEYS SANDLOTS SANDPITS SAPIENTS SAPLINGS SARDINES SATCHELS SAUCIERS
SAUNDERS SAUNTERS SAVIOURS SAVORIES SAWBONES SAWBUCKS SAWFLIES SAXONIES SCABINUS
SCABIOUS SCABROUS SCALDERS SCALINGS SCALPERS SCAMPERS SCANTIES SCARIOUS SCHERZOS
SCHOLARS SCLEROUS SCOLDERS SCORINGS SCOURGES SCOUTERS SCOWLERS SCRIVENS SCROTUMS
SCROUGES SCRUPLES SCURVIES SEABIRDS SEAFOLKS SEAFOWLS SEALINGS SEAMINGS SEAPORTS
SEARINGS SEATINGS SECTIONS SECULARS SEMIARCS SEMIBAYS SEMICUPS SEMIGODS SEMINALS
SEMINARS SEMIPROS SENATORS SENDOUTS SEQUOIAS SERAPHOS SERBIANS SERFDOMS SERINGAS
SERVANTS SERVINGS SERVITUS SETBACKS SETDOWNS SETLINGS SETWORKS SHACKLES SHACKUPS
SHADINGS SHAFTERS SHAKINGS SHAMBLES SHANDIES SHANKERS SHANTIES SHAPINGS SHARINGS
SHARPENS SHARPIES SHAVINGS SHEBANGS SHIFTERS SHINDLES SHINGLES SHIPBOYS SHIPFULS
SHIPWAYS SHOALERS SHOCKERS SHOEINGS SHOPFULS SHOPLETS SHORINGS SHORTENS SHORTIES

```
SHOTGUNS  SHOUTERS  SHOWINGS  SHRIVELS  SHUCKERS  SHUNTERS  SHYLOCKS  SICKBEDS  SICKLERS
SIDEBARS  SIDECARS  SIDEWAYS  SIGHTENS  SIGHTERS  SIGNORAS  SILTAGES  SILVANUS  SIMPLERS
SIMULARS  SIMULERS  SINGLERS  SINGLETS  SINKAGES  SINUATES  SKATINGS  SKEPTICS  SKEWINGS
SKIDWAYS  SKINFULS  SKYLINES  SKYPORTS  SKYWARDS  SLACKENS  SLACKERS  SLAKINGS  SLANDERS
SLANTERS  SLATHERS  SLATINGS  SLAVINGS  SLAVIZES  SLAYINGS  SLEIGHTS  SLEWINGS  SLICKENS
SLICKERS  SLINGERS  SLINKERS  SLIPWAYS  SLITHERS  SLOUCHES  SLUDGERS  SLUICERS  SLUMBERS
SMACKERS  SMALTERS  SMALTZES  SMARTENS  SMARTIES  SMIDGENS  SMIRCHES  SMITHERS  SMOCKERS
SMOLDERS  SMOTHERS  SMUDGERS  SNAILERS  SNATCHES  SNICHERS  SNICKERS  SNIFTERS  SNITCHES
SNORKELS  SNORTLES  SNOUTERS  SOAKINGS  SOARINGS  SOCIALES  SOCIATES  SOCIETAS  SOFTNERS
SOILAGES  SOLACERS  SOLDIERS  SOLVENTS  SOMATICS  SOMEWAYS  SORBATES  SORGHUMS  SOUNDERS
SOURINGS  SOUTANES  SOUTHERS  SOUWARDS  SOWBACKS  SOWBANES  SOYBEANS  SPACINGS  SPACIOUS
SPACKLES  SPANGLES  SPANIELS  SPANKERS  SPARKIES  SPARKLES  SPATULES  SPATURES  SPAWLERS
SPAWNERS  SPAYINGS  SPECIALS  SPECIOUS  SPELUNKS  SPERMOUS  SPEWINGS  SPHERICS  SPHINXES
SPINDLES  SPINODES  SPINULES  SPIRALES  SPIRANTS  SPIRULAS  SPITFULS  SPITZERS  SPLAYERS
SPLICERS  SPLUNGES  SPLURGES  SPOILERS  SPOKANES  SPONGERS  SPORADES  SPOUTERS  SPRITZES
SPUMONES  SPUMONIS  SPUNKIES  SPUTNIKS  SQUADERS  SQUALIDS  SQUALORS  STABLERS  STACKERS
STADIUMS  STAINERS  STALKERS  STAMPERS  STANDBYS  STANDERS  STAPLERS  STARCHES  STARDOMS
STARINGS  STARKENS  STAVINGS  STENCILS  STEPWAYS  STERNALS  STERNUMS  STEROIDS  STEWARDS
STEWBUMS  STEWPANS  STICKERS  STICKLES  STICKUMS  STICKUPS  STIFLERS  STINGERS  STINKERS
STIPENDS  STIPULES  STOCKERS  STOMACHS  STOMPERS  STOPINGS  STORAGES  STORKENS  STOWAGES
STOWINGS  STROMBUS  STRUDELS  STUDIERS  STUMBLES  STUMPERS  STURDIES  STYLINGS  STYLIZES
SUBATOMS  SUBCLANS  SUBCOATS  SUBDATES  SUBDEANS  SUBEDITS  SUBFACES  SUBFIXES  SUBFORMS
SUBGYRES  SUBHEADS  SUBHERDS  SUBHEROS  SUBITEMS  SUBJACKS  SUBJECTS  SUBJOINS  SUBLIMES
SUBLINES  SUBMAINS  SUBMINDS  SUBNOTES  SUBPARTS  SUBPLATS  SUBPLOTS  SUBPLOWS  SUBPORTS
SUBRACES  SUBRENTS  SUBTACKS  SUBTENDS  SUBTILES  SUBTONES  SUBTRAYS  SUBTYPES  SUBVEINS
SUBVERTS  SUBZONES  SUCKLERS  SUCRATES  SUCTIONS  SUGARIES  SULFATES  SULFIDES  SULFITES
SULPHIDS  SULTANES  SULTRIES  SUMPAGES  SUNBATHS  SUNBEAMS  SUNBIRDS  SUNDIALS  SUNDRIES
SUNDROPS  SUNFOILS  SUNGLOWS  SUNWARDS  SURCOATS  SURFACES  SURFEITS  SURGEONS  SURNAMES
SURTAXES  SURVIEWS  SWAMPERS  SWANKERS  SWANKEYS  SWANKIES  SWATCHES  SWATHERS  SWAYINGS
SWIFTENS  SWIFTERS  SWINDLES  SWINGERS  SWINGLES  SWITCHES  SYLPHIDS  SYMBIONS  SYNCHROS
SYNODALS  SYNODIES  SYNOVIAS  SYNTAXES  SYRINGAS  SYRINGES  TACKIEST  TALKFEST  TALKIEST
TANGIEST  TARDIEST  TASHKENT  TAWNIEST  TENORIST  TENURIST  THAWIEST  THEOCRAT  THEORIST
THICKEST  THICKSET  THYMIEST  TIDEFLAT  TOADIEST  TOLERANT  TONALIST  TORCHLIT  TOUGHEST
TOWNIEST  TOXICANT  TRANSECT  TRANSEPT  TRANSMIT  TRAPNEST  TRAWLNET  TRIBOLET  TURBOJET
TURFIEST  TURNCOAT  TURNSPIT  TYPECAST  WASHBREW  WITHDRAW  WITHDREW  YEASTILY  YEOMANLY
YEOMANRY  YOUTHILY
```

ABCDEFGB
```
           ACENTRIC  ACETONIC  ACETURIC  ACETYLIC  ACHROMIC  ACOUSTIC  ACROSTIC  ADJOINED
ADJUSTED  ADONIZED  ADSORBED  AERODYNE  AEROLITE  ANDROGEN  ANHEDRON  ANTIPHON  ARGUFIER
ASCRIVES  ASEPTICS  ASPEROUS  ASTOUNDS  ASTROIDS  ASUNDERS  BACTERIA  BEADLIKE  BEAMLIKE
BEARHIDE  BEARLIKE  BECLOTHE  BEDFRAME  BEFAMINE  BEFRINGE  BEGIRDLE  BELGRADE  BELTWISE
BEMANTLE  BEMINGLE  BENDSOME  BENDWISE  BEPLAGUE  BEPRAISE  BERTHAGE  BESMUDGE  BESTARVE
BESTRIDE  BESTRIPE  BESTRODE  BETANGLE  BLAMEFUL  BLAREFUL  BLASTFUL  BRANCHER  BRASHIER
BRAWLIER  BRAWNIER  BRIDALER  BRIGHTER  BRISTLER  BROACHER  BROMIZER  BRONZIER  BROWNIER
BROWSTER  BRUSHIER  CAMBODIA  CAROLINA  CATHEDRA  CEINTURE  CELIBATE  CENOBITE  CENTRALE
CENTRODE  CENTUPLE  CHURLISH  CLANGFUL  CLERGIAL  CLIENTAL  CLITORAL  CRAFTIER  CRAMPIER
CRANKIER  CREDITOR  CREMATOR  CROAKIER  CROUPIER  CRUMBIER  CRUMPLER  CRUSADER  CRUSTIER
DEBRUISE  DECIMATE  DECORATE  DEFIABLE  DEFIANCE  DEFIGURE  DELATIVE  DELIBATE  DELICATE
DELPHINE  DELUSIVE  DEMIROBE  DEMITONE  DEMITUBE  DEMIURGE  DEMONIZE  DENATURE  DENIABLE
DENOTIVE  DENTICLE  DEPILATE  DEPUTIZE  DERIVATE  DEROGATE  DESCRIBE  DESOLATE  DETHRONE
DETONIZE  DEVIABLE  DEVIANCE  DEVOCATE  DEVOLUTE  DEVONITE  DEXTRANE  DEXTRINE  DEXTROSE
```

```
DRAFTIER DRAGSTER DRAWLIER DROWSIER DRUGSTER DRUMLIER EMBOLISM EMBOLIUM EMPORIUM
ENACTION ENCOLUMN ENDBRAIN ENDOCRIN ENTRYMAN ESCRIPTS ESPINALS ESTAMINS ESTRIOLS
FEARSOME FEASIBLE FEMINATE FENCIBLE FENDABLE FERNLIKE FLEXURAL FRONTIER FROSTIER
FROTHIER FRUMPIER GARDENIA GELATINE GEMINATE GEMSTONE GENDARME GENOTYPE GEOPHYTE
GERMLIKE GHOULISH GLOBICAL GLORYFUL GLYCEROL GRANDEUR GRIMACER GROUNDER GROUTIER
GROWLIER GRUMBLER GRUMPIER HACIENDA HARMONIA HEADLIKE HEADLINE HEADNOTE HEADROPE
HEATLIKE HEBRAIZE HELPMATE HELPSOME HEMATINE HEMATOSE HEMIPODE HEMITONE HEMITYPE
HEMOCYTE HEMOLYZE HEMPLIKE HEPATIZE HERBLIKE HERITAGE HERNIATE HEROLIKE INGOTMAN
INGOTMEN INKERMAN ISHMAELS ISOBATHS ISOCRATS ISOLANTS ISOLATES ISOPACHS ISOTYPES
JAPONICA JEALOUSE JERKSOME KATCHINA KELPWARE KERATODE KERATOME KERATOSE KEROSINE
KETONIZE KEYSTONE KNIFEMAN LACHRYMA LEGATINE LEGATIVE LEMONADE LOTHARIO MAGNESIA
MAGNOLIA MAJOLICA MANITOBA MARCHESA MARIPOSA MARSUPIA MAUSOLEA MEDALIZE MEDICATE
MEDIOCRE MEGATYPE MELODIZE MENARCHE MENDABLE MERINGUE MESALIKE MESOLITE MESOTYPE
MESQUITE METALINE METALIZE METCALFE MODERATO MOSQUITO MYOPATHY MYSTICLY NEARSIDE
NEBULITE NEBULIZE NEBULOSE NECKHOLE NEGATIVE NEMATODE NEOPHYTE NEPHRITE NESTABLE
NESTLIKE NEVADITE ORALIZER ORANGIER ORDAINER ORPHANER OSTERIAS PACHEMIA PALESTRA
PEARLITE PEDICULE PEDICURE PEMBROKE PENALIZE PENDICLE PENTACLE PENUCHLE PENUCKLE
PENWRITE PERFLATE PERIDOTE PERIGONE PERIOGUE PEROXIDE PERSONAE PERSUADE PESTHOLE
PIROSHKI PLACEFUL PLAINFUL PLATEFUL PLAYGIRL PLYMETAL PRANCIER PRANKIER PRANKLER
PREDATOR PREFAVOR PREHUMOR PRELABOR PREMOLAR PRESOLAR PREVISOR PRICKLER PRISONER
PRIVATER PRODUCER PROFANER PROFILER PROFITER PROFUSER PROMISER PROVIDER PROVINER
PYRAMIDY REACTIVE READVISE REBOUNCE REBUCKLE REBUNDLE RECHANGE RECLOTHE RECOUPLE
REDOUBLE REFUSIVE REGALIZE REGULATE REGULIZE REHANDLE REHUMBLE REIMPOSE REINDUCE
REINFUSE REINVADE REJUMBLE REKINDLE RELATIVE RELIANCE RELIGATE RELOCATE REMANTLE
REMINGLE REMOLADE REMOTIVE RENDIBLE RENOTICE RENOVATE RENTABLE REOBLIGE REPLIQUE
RESALUTE RESAMPLE RESINATE RESOLUTE RESONATE RESPLICE RESTABLE RESTIFLE RETACKLE
RETICULE RETINULE RETUMBLE REUSABLE REVOCATE REVOLUTE RIGATONI SALONICA SAMBOUKA
SATURNIA SEABORNE SEADROME SEAMLIKE SEDATIVE SEDUCIVE SEIZABLE SEMICONE SEMINATE
SEMINOLE SEMINUDE SEMITONE SEMITUNE SEMPLICE SENDABLE SERFLIKE SEROTYPE SERVABLE
SEXTUPLE SKEWBACK SKIMBACK SKIPJACK SLATEFUL SLOTHFUL STAGHUNT STAKEOUT STANDOUT
STEPAUNT STINKPOT STONECAT STONEPUT STRAIGHT STRAUGHT STREIGHT STRIDENT STRIOLET
STRIPLET STRUMPET SYLVANRY SYMPATHY SYMPHILY SYMPHONY SYNARCHY TEAHOUSE TEAMWISE
TEARLIKE TEMPLIZE TENDABLE TENSIBLE TRADUCER TRAMPLER TRANSFER TRASHIER TRIBUNER
TRICKLER TRIMBLER TROUBLER TROUGHER TROUNCER TRUCKLER TRUMPHER TRUNCHER TRUNDLER
TSUNAMIS UNACTION UNARISEN UNBOLDEN UNBROKEN UNCHOSEN UNCRAVEN UNDARKEN UNDERMAN
UNDERPAN UNDERPIN UNDESIGN UNDRIVEN UNFASTEN UNFOLDEN UNFROZEN UNGOLDEN UNGRAVEN
UNHARDEN UNLOADEN UNMAIDEN UNMODERN UNMOLTEN UNORDAIN UNPARDON UNPRISON UNPROVEN
UNREASON UNRECKON UNSHAKEN UNSHAPEN UNSHAVEN UNSIPHON UNSOLEMN UNSPOKEN UNSTOLEN
UNSTRAIN UNSTREWN UNTHROWN UNWASHEN UNWEAPON URINATOR URNMAKER UTOPIAST VALENCIA
VALKYRIA VENALIZE VENDABLE VENDIBLE VENGIBLE VENIABLE VENOMIZE VENTHOLE VERBIAGE
VERNACLE VERNICLE VERSABLE VERSICLE VERTIBLE VESICATE VESICULE VESTIBLE VESTLIKE
WRANGLER WRINKLER
```

```
ABCDEFGC ABDUCTED ABRIDGER ABSCINDS ABSCONDS ABSINTHS ABSOLVES AFEBRILE AGENTIVE
ALCHEMIC ALEHOUSE ALTRUIST ANECDOTE ARSENICS ARSENOUS ASCORBIC ATHROUGH AUGERING
AUSPICES BACTERIC BAEKLITE BANDSMEN BANDYMEN BANKSMEN BASHINGS BASINETS BASTILES
BASTINGS BASTIONS BATONIST BEDSTAND BEGAZING BEGLUING BENCHMAN BENJAMIN BESCORNS
BESCOURS BESPLITS BESPRAYS BESPURTS BESTAINS BESTAMPS BESTIALS BESTINGS BESUGARS
BESWARMS BETAUGHT BIDSTAND BISMUTHS BISPORES BIYEARLY BLASTOMA BOGEYING BONDSMAN
BONDSMEN BOSQUETS BOTANIST BOYISHLY BRANCHIA BREVIATE BUSHINGS BUSLOADS BUSTARDS
CAGELING CAROUSER CARTONER CASEFULS CATFIGHT CISTERNS CLERKAGE CODSHEAD COENDURE
```

```
COENZYME COEQUATE COEXPIRE COLUMNAL CORDINER CORPSIER COSTINGS COSTUMES CREASOTE
CREDIBLE CRENULAE CRYINGLY CULMINAL CUSHIONS CUSPIDES CUSPINGS CUSTARDS CUTHBERT
CYANEMIA CYMBALOM CYSTIDES CYSTINES CYSTOIDS CYSTOMAS CYTOLIST DACTYLIC DARKLIER
DELAYFUL DELUVIAL DESCANTS DESIROUS DESPAIRS DESPOILS DESTAINS DESTROYS DESUGARS
DIASPORA DIRECTOR DISABLES DISAVOWS DISBARKS DISCAGES DISCANTS DISCEPTS DISCERNS
DISCERPS DISCUMBS DISCUTES DISFAMES DISFORMS DISGOWNS DISGULFS DISHELMS DISHFULS
DISHMOPS DISHOMES DISHORNS DISHPANS DISHRAGS DISJECTS DISLEAFS DISLOCKS DISMARKS
DISOBEYS DISPARKS DISPARTS DISPLAYS DISPORTS DISPUTES DISRANKS DISRATES DISROBES
DISROUTS DISRUPTS DISTUNES DISTURBS DISTURNS DISTYLES DISYOKES DUSTBINS DUSTINGS
DUSTPANS DUSTRAGS DYEHOUSE EASTINGS ELASTICA ENCHORIC ENCRATIC ENDBOARD ENSTAMPS
ENTOCYST EPSILONS ETHNARCH FAGOTING FASHIONS FASHIOUS FASTINGS FESTIALS FINESPUN
FISHBEDS FISHLETS FISHNETS FISHPOTS FISHWAYS FISTULAS FLEABITE FORGIVER FORSAKER
FORSWEAR FUNCTION FURNACER GASLOCKS GASTRINS GASWORKS GATEPOST GESTAPOS GESTIONS
GLAUCOMA GODCHILD GOLDTAIL GOSCHENS GOSHAWKS GRIMALDI GUESTIVE HANDIRON HANDYMEN
HASTINGS HASTLERS HIDELAND HONDURAN HONEYBUN HORSECAR HOSPICES HOSTAGES HOSTILES
HOSTINGS HOSTLERS HUMANISM HUMORISM HUNTSMAN HUNTSMEN HUSBANDS HUSKINGS HUSTINGS
HUSTLERS HYDERBAD HYDRACID HYDRATED HYDRAZID HYDROXID HYMENIUM ICEHOUSE ICEQUAKE
IDEOTYPE INCABLOC INDARTED INDORSED INDRAPED INDUCTED INDULGED INSCAPES INSHAVES
INSHORES INSPECTS INSTEAMS INSTORES INSTYLES INSULARS INSUREDS INSURGES INSWAMPS
INTERACT INTERCUT INTERLOT INTERMAT INTHRUST ITERABLE ITERANCE JARGONER JASMINES
JESTINGS JOSTLERS JUMBOISM JUNCTION JUSTICES KALISPEL KELOIDAL KIDNAPED KINGSMAN
KINGSMEN LACTONIC LADYBIRD LADYFIED LADYKIND LANDIRON LANDSMEN LARKSPUR LASHINGS
LASTINGS LATEMOST LATHIEST LEGATING LESBIANS LINESMAN LINKSMAN LINKSMEN LUNCHEON
LUSHINGS LUTANIST LUTENIST LYNCHPIN MANDOLIN MARBLIER MARSHIER MASHINGS MASKINGS
MASONERS MASQUERS MASTINGS MASTOIDS MATUREST MECHANIC MELODIAL MERCATOR MESOBARS
MESQUITS MESTIZAS MESTIZOS MIDSTEAD MINERVAN MISBEARS MISCROPS MISDATES MISDEALS
MISDOERS MISFARES MISFATES MISHAVES MISHEARS MISKNOWS MISLEADS MISOBEYS MISPENDS
MISPLAYS MISREADS MISRULES MISTRALS MISTUNES MISTURNS MISWENDS MISWORDS MISWORKS
MORTICER MORTISER MOSLINGS MOTLIEST MUSICALS MUSKRATS MUSTANGS MUSTARDS MYTHIEST
NATURIST NESTFULS NOMADISM NOSEGAYS NOSTRILS NOSTRUMS OBEYANCE OBSCURES OCTUPLET
OESTRINS ONSIGHTS OPENABLE OPENSIDE OPERABLE OPERANCE ORDAINED OUTCHEAT OUTDRAFT
OUTDWELT OUTFEAST OUTFIGHT OUTNIGHT OUTPAINT OUTPLANT OUTRIGHT OUTSCENT OUTSIGHT
OUTSKIRT OUTSLEPT OUTSMART OUTSPENT OUTSWEPT OUTWREST OVENLIKE OVENWARE OVENWISE
OVERABLE OVERBADE OVERBAKE OVERBASE OVERBITE OVERCAME OVERDATE OVERFACE OVERFILE
OVERFINE OVERGAZE OVERHALE OVERJADE OVERLACE OVERLADE OVERLINE OVERMATE OVERNAME
OVERNICE OVERSIDE OVERSIZE OVERTAKE OVERTAME OVERTIDE OVERTIME OVERTYPE OVERWADE
OVERWAKE OVERWIDE OVERWISE PALMSFUL PANCHEON PANCHION PANTHEON PARDONER PASTEURS
PASTILES PASTIMES PASTINGS PASTRIES PASTURES PENTAGON PENWOMAN PETULANT PHYSICKY
PIEHOUSE PISTLERS PISTOLES PITCHOUT PLACENTA PLANURIA PLEASURE PLESANCE POETLIKE
POETWISE PORTLIER POSTAGES POSTBAGS POSTERNS POSTINGS POSTURES PREACUTE PREAMBLE
PRECLOSE PRECLUDE PREGNATE PREGUIDE PREIMAGE PREIMBUE PREJUDGE PRENTICE PREQUOTE
PRESOLVE PRESTIGE PREUNITE PREVALUE PREVOGUE PRYINGLY PULMONAL PUNCTION PUNTSMAN
PUNTSMEN PURVEYOR PUSHRODS RADIUSED RANCHMEN RANKSMEN RASHINGS RASPINGS REGALING
REGLUING RESCINDS RESHUNTS RESINOLS RESINOUS RESLANTS RESOUNDS RESPLITS RESPONDS
RESTACKS RESTAINS RESTAMPS RESTINGS RESTOCKS RESUINGS RETAUGHT ROGUEING ROMANISM
ROSEBUDS ROSEWAYS RUSHINGS SANCTION SCRAPIER SCRAWLER SCRIPTER SCROUGER SCRUNGER
SCRUPLER SEMIFORM SERVITOR SHEDABLE SHEDLIKE SHRIMPER SHRINKER SIDEHOLD SIDEWARD
SOCRATIC SONARMEN SPECIATE SPLENIAL SPRAWLER SPRINGER SPRINTER SPRITZER SPROUTER
SPRUCIER STEARINE STEARONE STEMLIKE STEMWARE STEPHANE STEPLIKE STERNAGE STEWABLE
STRAINER STRANDER STRANGER STRAWIER STRINGER STRONGER SUGARING SULFAMYL SULFENYL
SURFACER SURNAMER SURVEYOR SYNODIAN THEORIZE TIDELAND TIDEWARD TIERABLE TINWOMAN
```

TINWOMEN TONGSMAN TONGSMEN TORCHIER TOYISHLY TRACHOMA TRYINGLY TURBINER TURBOCAR
TURNOVER TYMPANUM UNDAMPED UNDARKED UNDASHED UNDERAID UNDERBID UNDERHID UNDERLID
UNDIALED UNDISHED UNDOCKED UNDRAPED UNHEALTH UNRASHER UNREPAIR UNSAVORS UNSCALES
UNSCREWS UNSHADES UNSHALES UNSHAPES UNSHAWLS UNSHEAFS UNSHORES UNSIGHTS UNSLATES
UNSLAVES UNSOBERS UNSOLVES UNSPEAKS UNSPIKES UNSPOILS UNSTACKS UNSTICKS UNSTOCKS
UNSTORES UNSTRAPS UNSTRIPS UNSWEARS UNSWEATS UNTHRIFT UPRAISER UPSHIFTS UPSTAGES
UPSTAIRS UPSTANDS UPSTARES UPSWARMS UPSWINGS URETHANE UTENSILE VASEFULS VENUSIAN
VENUTIAN VESTINGS VIEWABLE VOTARIST WAGERING WANDSMEN WARBLIER WASHINGS WASHOUTS
WASHPOTS WASHTUBS WASTINGS WASTRELS WATCHOUT WATERPIT WATERPOT WESTINGS WHEYFACE
WHEYLIKE WINCHMAN WINCHMEN WINDBURN WINGSPAN WORDSTER WORTHIER WRECKAGE YESHIVAS

ABCDEFGD ABUSIONS ABUTMENT ACESHIPS ADHESIVE ADSTRICT AJUTMENT ALGERINE ALTHOUGH
AMBERITE AMETHYST AMINOGEN AMOSITES ANGELIZE ANGSTERS ANHELOSE ANISOLES ANODISED
ANODIZED ANTELOPE ANTELUDE ANTSHIPS APHETIZE APOSTLES ARMSIZES ARSENITE ASPERITE
ATREMBLE AUTOGIRO AUTOGYRO BAKELITE BAKELIZE BAKERITE BALEFIRE BANSHIES BANTUIST
BASELIKE BEAGLING BEDSOCKS BIRDLAND BLASTERS BLASTIDS BLASTIES BLISTERS BLITHEST
BLUENOSE BLUSHERS BLUSHETS BLUSTERS BOARDIER BOASTERS BOLSTERS BONDAGED BONDMAID
BONELIKE BORSCHES BORSCHTS BORSTALS BRAESIDE BRINEMAN BRISKENS BRISKETS BRISQUES
BRISTLES BRISTOLS BROGUING BUNTIEST BUOYANCY BURGLING CAGELIKE CAMELINE CANELIKE
CANEWISE CAPELINE CAPEWISE CAPSIZES CAPSULES CARSHOPS CARTIEST CATSKINS CAVELIKE
CELSIANS CENTRIST CHASINGS CHASTENS CHASTIES CHINAMEN CHORTLER CHORUSER CHURLIER
CITEABLE CLANSMEN CLASHERS CLASPERS CLODHEAD CLOSINGS CLOSURES CLUSTERS COASTERS
CODERIVE COHESIVE CONDITED CONSULTS CONSUMES CONTEMPT CONTRAST COPEMATE CORELATE
CORSAGES CORSITES CORSIVES CORSLETS COSHEATH COTENURE COUGHING COURAGER COURTIER
COUTHEST COVERAGE COVETISE COWSKINS COWSLIPS COZENAGE CRANKMEN CRANKPIN CRISPENS
CROSBIES CRUELIZE CRUSADES CRYSTALS CURSINGS CURSIVES CYANOGEN DAMSITES DATELINE
DECLINAL DESTRUCT DIASPERS DIASTEMS DIASTERS DIGLYCOL DISLOYAL DISROBER DOESKINS
DOGSHIPS DOGSKINS DOMELIKE DORSALES DORSIANS DOUGHING DOVELIKE DOWNSMAN DOWNSMEN
DOWNTURN DRACONIC DRASTICS DUCKWALK DUNELIKE DUSTCOAT DYASTERS DYSAPHIA EARSHOTS
ELASTICS ELASTINS ELFSHIPS ELUSIONS ELYSIUMS ENARBOUR ENDSHIPS ERASIONS ESTANCIA
EUONYMIN EURYTHMY EVASIONS FACEWISE FAIRGOER FARTHEST FATELIKE FAWNSKIN FELSPARS
FIASCOES FIBSTERS FINEABLE FIREABLE FIVESOME FLASHERS FLASKERS FLUSHERS FLUSKERS
FLUSTERS FLUTIEST FLYSWATS FOISTERS FOREDATE FOREGAME FOREGATE FORELINE FORELIVE
FOREMADE FORENAME FOREPALE FORESIDE FORETAKE FORSAKES FORTHCUT FORTHSET FOUNTAIN
FRANKLIN FRAYEDLY FRISCOES FRISKETS FROGLING FROSTEDS FUNERATE FURTHEST FUSELAGE
GAMELIKE GATELIKE GATEWISE GERONIMO GHOSTERS GIVEABLE GLISTENS GLISTERS GLUCONIC
GLUCOSIC GLYCEMIC GLYCERIC GLYCONIC GLYERIDE GLYSTERS GNARLIER GNOSTICS GOATIEST
GODSHIPS GOLDBIRD GOLDHEAD GOURDIER GOUTIEST GOWNSMAN GOWNSMEN GRANDSON GRECANIC
GRENADIN GRISTLES GRUESOME GUMSHOES GUNSHOPS GUNSHOTS GYPSEOUS GYPSITES GYPSTERS
HACKWORK HAMSTERS HANDSLED HARELIKE HEADMOLD HEADWORD HEPATICA HEPATOMA HEXAPODA
HIREABLE HOGSKINS HOGSTIES HOISTERS HOLSTERS HOMELIFE HOMELIKE HOMESITE HOPSACKS
HORNSMAN HORNSMEN HORSINGS HOSELIKE HOTELIZE HOTSPURS HOUNDMAN HOUNDMEN HOUSINGS
HYDRATOR IMPROVER INCERATE INKSHEDS INLEAGUE INSECURE INSHEATH INSTRUCT INTRUDER
INTRUSOR JAVELINE JIBSTAYS JOBSITES JOLTIEST JORDANED JOUSTERS JOYRIDER JUSTMENT
JUVENILE KERATOMA KEYSLOTS KIOSQUES KITSCHES KLANSMEN LAKESIDE LARCENIC LATESOME
LAUGHING LAWSHIPS LAWSUITS LAYSHIPS LEAGUING LEASINGS LEFTMOST LIBERATE LIFESOME
LIKESOME LOBSTERS LOFTIEST LOVEMATE LURESOME LUSTRANT MADELINE MAESTROS MAGNETON
MALEFICE MALTIEST MARTINET MEAGRING MERSIONS METABOLA MICROBAR MIDSOLES MIGRATOR
MINEABLE MINSTERS MISDATED MISDREAD MISLABEL MISRULER MISTREAT MOBSHIPS MOBSTERS
MODELIZE MODERATE MOISTENS MONETIZE MONSTERS MOUNTAIN MOUSINGS MOVEABLE MULTIJET
MUSELIKE NAGSTERS NAKEDIZE NARCOTIC NEMATODA NEWSBOYS NORTHEST NOSELIKE NOTECASE

```
NOTEWISE  NOVELIZE  NUMERATE  OBSTRUCT  OBTRUDER  OLDSTERS  OLYMPIUM  ORKNEYAN  OSTALGIA
OUTDARED  OUTRAGER  OUTSAILS  OUTSEAMS  OUTSENDS  OUTSIDES  OUTSIGHS  OUTSINGS  OUTSIZES
OUTSLIPS  OUTSPANS  OUTSPINS  OUTSWIMS  OVENSMAN  OVERHAIR  OVERSTIR  OXIDATED  OXYSALTS
PAGELIKE  PAILSFUL  PAISLEYS  PALOMINO  PANSIDES  PARDONED  PARSLEYS  PARTYIST  PECORINO
PERSIANS  PERSONAS  PHASMIDS  PHYSICKS  PIASTERS  PIASTRES  PICKFORK  PICKWORK  PILSNERS
PISTOLET  PITEABLE  PLAGUING  PLANKTON  PLASTERS  PLASTICS  PLASTIDS  PLASTINS  PLATIEST
PLUMBISM  PLUNGEON  POINTMAN  POINTMEN  POLEMIZE  POLYGAMY  POLYGENY  POLYMERY  PORELIKE
PORTMENT  POSTCART  POSTFACT  ROUGHING  POUNDMAN  POUNDMEN  PRESIFTS  PRESIGNS  PRISAGES
PRODUCED  PROSAICS  PROSECTS  PROSINGS  PULSATES  PULSIONS  PUNSTERS  PURSLETS  QUESTORS
QUIETAGE  QUOTIENT  RACELIKE  RACELINE  REDSKINS  REINSMAN  RETSINAS  RIDEABLE  RIKSHAWS
RIPSACKS  ROPEABLE  ROPELIKE  ROSELIKE  ROSETIME  ROUGHING  ROUNDMAN  ROUNDMEN  ROUSINGS
RUMSHOPS  RUNTIEST  SARCOTIC  SCALEFUL  SCHEDULE  SCREWAGE  SCURFIER  SCURVIER  SEAGOING
SEMOLINO  SHADOWED  SHARKIER  SHOELACE  SHOEMAKE  SIDEBONE  SIDENOTE  SIDERATE  SIDETONE
SILKWORK  SINECURE  SIZEABLE  SLINGMAN  SLINGMEN  SMARTIER  SMILEFUL  SMIRCHER  SNARLIER
SNORTIER  SOBERIZE  SOLECIZE  SOLENITE  SORTMENT  SPARKIER  SPARKLER  SPONGIAN  SPORTIER
SPRECKLE  STARCHER  STONEMAN  STORMIER  STURDIER  SUBCONIC  SUBDATED  SUBTRACT  SUNDAYED
SUPERATE  SUPERLIE  SWINEMAN  SWINGMAN  SWINGMEN  SYDNEIAN  SYNAPHEA  SYNCOPIC  SYNERIZE
TABLEFUL  TALEWISE  TAPELIKE  TAPELINE  TASKWORK  TEASHOPS  TERSIONS  THINGMAN  THINGMEN
THONGMAN  THONGMEN  THORNIER  THREADLE  TIMEABLE  TIRESOME  TOLEWARE  TONSURES  TOPSAILS
TOPSIDES  TOUGHING  TOWNSMAN  TOWNSMEN  TRADUCED  TRILOBAL  TRISOMES  TROCHAIC  TRUELIKE
TRUELOVE  TRYSAILS  TUBELIKE  TUBERCLE  TUBERIZE  TUBEROSE  TUESDAYS  TUNEABLE  TUNESOME
TURNDOWN  TURSIONS  TWINBORN  TYPEABLE  TYPECASE  TYPEFACE  ULCERATE  UNABSORB  UNADORED
UNBECOME  UNBETIDE  UNBEWARE  UNDERAGE  UNDERLIE  UNDERLYE  UNDERTIE  UNDESIRE  UNFEMALE
UNILOBAL  UNLEGATE  UNREMOTE  UNREPOSE  UNSEDATE  UPGRADER  UPSHEATH  VANDYKED  VANELIKE
VASELIKE  VASELINE  VERSANTS  VERSIONS  VIBRATOR  VOLCANIC  VOTEABLE  VOUSTERS  VOWELIZE
VULCANIC  WAISTERS  WAKETIME  WARSHIPS  WARTIEST  WAVELIKE  WAYGOING  WAYSIDES  WHISKERS
WHISKEYS  WHISPERS  WHISTERS  WHISTLES  WHITEOUT  WINSOMES  WISEACRE  WORKBANK  WORLDFUL
WORSHIPS  WORSTEDS  WRINGMAN  WRINGMEN  YESHIBAH  YESHIVAH  YOKEABLE  YOKEMATE  YOKEWISE
YORETIME  YULETIDE  ZONELIKE
```

```
ABCDEFGE  ABJUDGED  ABRIDGED  ABSURDER  ADEPTIST  ADOLESCE  ADVISERS  ADVISORS  AGITPROP
AMBIENCE  AMBUSHES  AMNESICS  ANHYDRID  ANTERIOR  ARGOSIES  AUDIENCE  BACKSETS  BANISHES
BLUNTEST  BOHEMIUM  BRANDIED  BRINDLED  BULGARIA  BYRONIAN  CARNEGIE  CAUSERIE  CERAMIUM
CETONIAN  CHAINMEN  CHARGING  CHARTIST  CHESTNUT  CHIASMUS  CHILDBED  CHOLEATE  CHOLEINE
CHRISTOS  CHROMISM  CHROMIUM  CHRYSALS  COARSENS  COGITANT  COMITANT  COMPENSE  CONSERVE
CONTAGIA  CONTRAIR  CONVERGE  CONVERSE  COUNSELS  COURTLET  CRIMSONS  CUNARDER  CURTSEYS
CURTSIES  CYSTEINE  CYTOSINS  DANISHES  DEBUTANT  DEMOTIST  DENTALIA  DENTARIA  DEPOSALS
DEPOSITS  DEVISALS  DEVISORS  DEVONIAN  DILUTANT  DILUTENT  DISARMER  DISLEAVE  DISPEACE
DIVERTOR  DIVORCER  DONATIST  DOWNSETS  DOWNSITS  DRAINMEN  DROPKICK  DROPSIES  DYARCHIC
DYNAMISM  DYNASTES  DYSTAXIA  EGOMANIA  EMBRYONY  EMULSINS  EMULSORS  ENTRYWAY  EQUITANT
ERGOTIST  ESTONIAN  EVULGING  EXCISORS  EXCITANT  EXCUSALS  EXPOSALS  EXPOSITS  EXULTANT
FAINTEST  FAMISHES  FLAUTIST  FLEDGING  FLORENCE  FLOTSAMS  FOCUSERS  FORAGING  FOREPUMP
FORLEAVE  FRETSAWS  FRONTLET  FROSTBIT  FRUITLET  FUCHSIAS  FULGENCE  GALOSHES  GAUNTEST
GAUNTLET  GRAINMEN  GROUNDEN  GYMNASIA  HANDSETS  HEBRAICA  HELSINKI  HESITANT  HOARSENS
HOMAGING  HORTENSE  HUNGARIA  HUNGRIER  HURONIAN  HYMNARIA  IBOUNDEN  IMBORDER  IMPARTER
IMPASTES  IMPLEDGE  IMPORTER  IMPOSERS  IMPOTENT  INCREASE  INCREATE  INDORSER  INFORMER
INFUSERS  INGUSHES  INPUSHES  INRUSHES  INTERCUR  INTERWAR  INVASORS  INVERTOR  KIBOSHES
LAVISHES  LEVITANT  LIGHTEST  LOCKSETS  LOQUENCE  MEDITANT  MEDUSANS  MENISCUS  MIDVERSE
MIGHTEST  MILKSOPS  MINUTEST  MISKNOWN  MISORDER  MISPENCE  MOUNTLET  MYCELIAL  MYCENIAN
MYCOSINS  NEARCTIC  NEBRASKA  NEPOTIST  NUCLEASE  NUCLEATE  NUCLEOME  NYMPHISH  ONRUSHES
OPALESCE  OPULENCE  OUTCRIER  OUTFENCE  OUTWEAVE  OVERGANG  OVERHIGH  OVERKICK  OVERTILT
```

```
OVERTINT OVERTIPT PALTRIER PARISHES PARODIED PARVENUE PATIENCE PERUSALS PEYOTIST
PHIALFUL PHYSALIA PHYSARIA PLEDGING PLOUGING PLOWGANG POINTLET POLESAWS POLISHES
POLITEST POTASHES POULTIST PRACTIST PREKNOWN PRENTIST PRESTANT PREUNION PROLABIA
PROTENSE PROVENCE PROVENUE PRUDENCE PUCKSIES PUNCTIST PUNISHES PURITANT PUTRESCE
QUESTANT RADISHES RAVISHES RECAGING REDUCTIC REFUSALS REMUTANT REOUTFIT REPAGING
REPOSALS REPOSITS REVISALS RICKSHAS RIGHTEST RIPOSTES ROUGHISH ROUMANIA SALIENCE
SAPIENCE SAUTERNE SAVORIER SCANTLET SCAVENGE SCOURGER SCOWLFUL SCRANTON SEMITACT
SEWAGING SHORTCUT SHRUNKEN SIXPENCE SLEDGING SLUDGING SMILEAGE SMUDGING SMYRNIAN
SPINDLED SPLODGED SPOILFUL SPURGING SQUARIER SQUIRTER STERNMAN STODGING STURDIED
SUBMANIA SUBMERGE SUBORDER SUBORNER SUBPRIOR SULTRIER SUPERIOR SWINDLED TRAINMEN
TRANSOMS TREASONS TRIALKYL TRUDGING TRUNDLED TRYPSINS TWINDLED TWOPENCE ULTERIOR
ULTONIAN UNBADGED UNBASTES UNBODIED UNBORDER UNCLEAVE UNCORKER UNCREATE UNDERAIR
UNFIERCE UNFLEDGE UNGARTER UNHARBOR UNHASTES UNIVERSE UNLASHES UNLODGED UNMARTYR
UNMASHES UNPASTES UNRIDGED UNSHELVE UNVISORS UNWASHES UNWISHES UNWORKER UPCANYON
UPHARBOR UPRISALS UPWASHES UTENSILS VANISHES VIOLENCE VOLITANT VOYAGING WAGONMEN
WHIMSEYS WHINDLED WHITSUNS WINDSORS WINESAPS WINESOPS WITHSAYS WORKYDAY WRISTLET
YACHTIST YARMELKE
```

```
ABCDEFGF ABOUNDED ACIDOSES ACQUIRER ADENOSIS ADIPOSES ADONISES ALOGISMS ALOPECIC
ALPHOSIS ALUMINON AMBROSES AMORISTS AMYLOSES ANCHORER ANGLISTS ANGOLESE ANTHESIS
ANURESIS ANYWHERE APOTHECE ARMPIECE ATHEISMS BALINESE BAPTISMS BATHOSES BECRUSTS
BEDPOSTS BIOLYSES BRIGADED BROCADED BRUTISMS BUNDISTS CALPYSOS CAMPUSES CAPTURER
CAROTENE CAROUSES CASHMIRI CELTISMS CHEKISTS CHEMISTS CHORUSES CHROMENE CITRUSES
CLAMORER CLONISMS CLONUSES COEXISTS COINHERE COITUSES COMBUSTS COMPARER COMPLETE
CONFIDED CONFUSES CONGESTS CONJURER CONTUSES COPYISMS COPYISTS CORAISES COSHARER
COWARDED COWHIDED CRETISMS CRUSADED CRYOSTAT CULTISMS CUTLASES CYANIDED CYANOSES
CYANOSIS CYPRUSES CYTOGENE CZARISMS CZARISTS DEFROSTS DIALYSES DIONYSES DIONYSUS
DISCRETE DIVULSES DUALISMS DUALISTS DUELISTS EBONISTS ECHOISTS EGOTISMS EMPHASIS
ENCLASPS ENCRISPS ENCRUSTS ENGRASPS ENIGMATA EROTISMS EXHAUSTS EXODISTS FATUISMS
FAUNISTS FAUVISMS FAUVISTS FAVOURER FIBROSES FLATUSES FLORISTS FLUORENE FLYPASTS
FORMISTS GABFESTS GANYMEDE GASOLENE GEODISTS GERMANIN GJEDOSTS GLIMPSES GLUCOSES
GLUTENIN GLUTOSES GLYCONIN GLYCOSES GNOMISTS GOTHISMS GROUNDED GYMKHANA GYMNASTS
GYROSTAT HARPISTS HARVESTS HEMOSTAT HEROISMS HIATUSES HORNISTS HYGEISTS HYMNISTS
HYPNOSES HYPNOSIS ICARUSES IMPLODED IMPLORER IMPRESTS IMPULSES INBURSTS INCLASPS
INCLOSES INCLUDED INCLUSES INCRESTS INCRUSTS INCURSES INDORSES INFOLDED INQUESTS
INROADED INSPHERE INTRUDED INTRUSES ISLANDED ISOPHENE ISOPLERE ISOPRENE ISOTHERE
JUDAISMS JUDAISTS KANTISMS KASHMIRI KIELBASA KLANISMS LABOURER LACTOSES LAMPISTS
LAPSIDED LAUDISTS LEFTISMS LEUCOSIS LEUKOSIS LEVYISTS LIQUORER LITMUSES LOBSIDED
MALTOSES MANTISES MARCHESE MARXISTS MIDWESTS MILANESE MISBODED MISOGYNY MISOXENE
MORGIANA MORTISES MYCOSTAT MYOTASIS MYRIADED NARCISMS NARCISTS NARCOSES NARCOSIS
NECROSIS NEURISMS NEUROSIS NIMBUSES OBELISKS OBLIGATA OBSCURER OBTRUDED OBTUNDED
OCTYLENE OCULISTS ODALISCS ODALISKS ODYLISMS ODYLISTS OILCASES ONWARDED ORALISMS
ORALISTS ORGIASTS ORPHISMS ORPHISTS OUTCASES OUTGASES OUTSIDED OVARISMS OVARISTS
OVICYSTS OVULISTS OXIDASES PALMISTS PANEGYRY PARCHISI PASTURER PATHOSES PECORINI
PEONISMS PERIGYNY PHONESIS PHONISMS PHORESIS PICTURER PINCASES PLIOCENE POLYGENE
POSTURER PRECASTS PRECYSTS PREDUSKS PREGUSTS PREVOSTS PRIMUSES PROMISES PROTASES
PROVIDED PROXYSMS PRUDISTS PYRACENE PYROSTAT PYROXENE RADIUSES RAWHIDED REALISMS
REALISTS REBOASTS RECLASPS RECOASTS REHOISTS RHEOSTAT RICTUSES RINGASES ROMANESE
ROTUNDED ROULADED SAMOYEDE SAVOURER SCHEMATA SEMIGALA SHROUDED SPERMATA SPLENDID
STAMPEDF STRANDED SUBATDED SULFIDED TABOURER THORACIC THYMUSES TIMORESE TIROLESE
TORYISMS TOURISMS TRAIPSES TRAVISES TRIBASES TRIPOSES TROPISMS TYMPANON TYPHOSIS
```

TYROLESE TZARISMS UNBLADED UNCARDED UNCHIDED UNCLASPS UNCLOSES UNCORDED UNCRESTS
UNCRISPS UNFOLDED UNFORDED UNFROSTS UNGILDED UNGIRDED UNGOADED UNGOLDED UNGRADED
UNGRASPS UNGRIEVE UNHAIRER UNHOISTS UNHORSES UNLARDED UNLOADED UNLORDED UNMAIDED
UNMOLDED UNPOISES UNRAIDED UNROADED UNSHADED UNSORDID UNSPADED UNSPHERE UNTRADED
UNVOIDED UNWARDED UNWILDED UNWORDED UNWRESTS UPBANDED UPBLASTS UPCLOSES UPFOLDED
UPGRADED UPRAISES URANISTS URATOSIS UROCYSTS UTOPISMS VACUISTS VAPOURER VAUDISMS
VETOISMS VICTORER VIRTUOSO VULGARER WALKISTS WALRUSES WATCHEYE WAYPOSTS WIZARDED
YORKISTS ZANYISMS ZEALISTS ZOLAISMS ZOLAISTS

ABCDEFGG ACIDNESS ACUPRESS ALBINESS ARCHNESS ARIDNESS ARTINESS BACKFILL BACKLESS
BALDNESS BANDLESS BANDROLL BANKFULL BANKROLL BAPTISEE BAPTIZEE BARKLESS BARONESS
BATHLESS BEADROLL BEDSTAFF BETHRALL BIRDCALL BIRDLESS BOATLESS BODILESS BODYLESS
BOLDNESS BONDLESS BOXINESS BRAGLESS BREAKOFF BRIMFULL BRIMLESS BROWLESS BUCKAROO
BUCKEROO CAGINESS CALMNESS CAPTRESS CATSKILL CHAPLESS CHINLESS CITYLESS CITYNESS
COATLESS COGNIZEE COGSWELL COLDNESS COMBLESS COMPRESS CONGRESS CORNBALL CORNBELL
CORNLESS CORNWALL COUNTESS COUNTREE COVERALL COWGRASS COZINESS CROMWELL CROWBELL
CROWBILL CURATESS CURBLESS CURTNESS DAFTNESS DAMPNESS DARKNESS DINGWALL DINTLESS
DISAGREE DIVORCEE DOCTRESS DOPINESS DOURNESS DOWINESS DOWNFALL DOWNHILL DOWNLESS
DOZINESS DRUGLESS DUCKBILL DUCTLESS DUMBNESS DUNGAREE DUNGHILL DUSTFALL DYESTUFF
ENSCROLL ENTHRALL ENTHRILL FAIRNESS FAKINESS FANGLESS FAVORESS FILAGREE FIREBALL
FIREHALL FIRMLESS FIRMNESS FLATNESS FLIPNESS FOAMLESS FORDLESS FOREHALL FOREPASS
FORKLESS FORMLESS FOULNESS FOXINESS FOZINESS FUMINESS FUNDLESS GAINLESS GAMINESS
GARBLESS GAUDLESS GIANTESS GIFTLESS GLADNESS GLIBNESS GLUINESS GLUMNESS GORINESS
GORMLESS GRAYMILL GRAYNESS GRIMNESS GRIPLESS GRITLESS GRUBLESS HACKTREE HAIRBELL
HAIRLESS HALFNESS HANDBELL HANDBILL HANDCUFF HANDFULL HANDLESS HARDNESS HARMLESS
HARPLESS HAWKBILL HAZINESS HEADSILL HOARNESS HOLINESS HOMINESS HORNBILL HORNLESS
HOURLESS HUMPLESS HUNTRESS HURTLESS HYMNLESS IMPORTEE INDORSEE INDUCTEE INSCROLL
INTHRALL IRONLESS ITCHLESS JACKEROO JACKROLL JAMBOREE JUMPNESS JURYLESS KIDNAPEE
KILOWATT KINDLESS KINGLESS KITHLESS KNOTLESS LABORESS LACINESS LAIRDESS LAZINESS
LIMPNESS LOGINESS LOUDNESS MARKLESS MARQUESS MATINESS MAYORESS MIDGRASS MILDNESS
MILKNESS MINDLESS MISAGREE MISTFALL MOANLESS MORNLESS MOTHBALL MOTHLESS MUCHNESS
MURKNESS MUSCOGEE MUSHBALL MUSKOGEE NEWSBILL NIMBLESS NORMLESS NOTIFYEE NUTSHELL
OPENBILL OUTBLESS OUTCLASS OUTDRESS OUTDWELL OUTSKILL OUTSMELL OUTSPELL OUTSPILL
OUTSWELL OVALNESS OVERCALL OVERCULL OVERFALL OVERFILL OVERFULL OVERHALL OVERHILL
OVERMILL OVERPASS OVERPUFF OVERTILL PACKLESS PACKNESS PAINLESS PANGLESS PARDONEE
PARTLESS PATHLESS PHARISEE PIRATESS PITHLESS POKINESS PORKLESS PORTLESS PORTUGEE
PRECHILL PRESCOTT PRIMNESS PRINCESS PROMISEE PUNJABEE PUSHBALL RACINESS RACKLESS
RAINLESS RANKLESS RAPTNESS RICHNESS RIFTLESS RINDLESS RINGLESS RINGTOSS RINGWALL
RIVALESS ROADLESS ROCKFALL ROCKLESS ROPINESS ROSEHILL ROWINESS RUMPLESS RUNGLESS
RUTHLESS SANDHILL SEMIBALL SEMIDULL SEMIROLL SHOEBILL SIDEHALL SIDEWALL SIGNALEE
SKINBALL SNOWBALL SNOWBELL SNOWFALL SOFTBALL SOURBALL SPITBALL STANDOFF STOWBALL
SUBDRILL SUBROGEE TACKLESS TANGLESS TANKLESS THAWLESS TICKLESS TINGWALL TOADLESS
TOMBLESS TOPDRESS TOWNLESS TRAMLESS TRAMPESS TRIMNESS TURFLESS TWIGLESS TYPINESS
UGLINESS UMPIRESS UNSHRILL UNTHRALL VICARESS VICTRESS VINTRESS VOIDLESS VOIDNESS
VOTARESS WAGONESS WAITRESS WANTLESS WARDLESS WARINESS WARMNESS WARTLESS WATERLOO
WAVINESS WAXINESS WHIPTREE WICKLESS WILDNESS WINDBALL WINDFALL WINDLASS WINDLESS
WINGLESS WITHNESS WONTLESS WORDLESS WORDNESS WORKLESS WORMLESS ZIONLESS